communication:
the study of
human interaction

C. David Mortensen

University of Wisconsin

communication: the study of human interaction

McGraw-Hill Book Company

New York	St. Louis	San Francisco
Düsseldorf	Johannesburg	Kuala Lumpur
London	Mexico	Montreal
New Delhi	Panama	Rio de Janeiro
Singapore	Sydney	Toronto

Library of Congress Catalog Card Number 76-172659

07-043395-X

1 2 3 4 5 6 7 8 9 0 K P K P 7 9 8 7 6 5 4 3 2

This book was set in Melior by John C. Meyer
& Son, and printed and bound by Kingsport
Press, Inc. The designer was Marsha Cohen; the
drawings were done by Hank Iken. The editors
were Robert Weber and James R. Belser.
Peter D. Guilmette supervised production.

FOR JUDY

contents

preface

Communication: The Study of Human Interaction is designed to provide a comprehensive and broadly based introduction to the study of human communication. The topics in the text borrow freely from the insights of numerous scientific disciplines and focus on the crossroads where psychology, sociology, and communication research share an overlapping interest in understanding the interplay of forces at work in various communicative situations. Of central concern are the diverse factors—verbal and nonverbal—that bear directly on the dynamics of communication in face-to-face encounters.

This book is the first attempt to base an integrated treatment of human communication on an in-depth survey of the vast outpouring of scientific literature. In examining the underpinnings of communicative behavior, no single field has a monopoly on insight. Relevant data spring from a range of social sciences—from the inclusive interests of anthropology and social psychology to the narrowly defined concerns of cybernetics—and cross the disciplinary lines of linguistics, speech communication, mass communication, and political science, among others. Not surprisingly, in any attempt to sift such an amorphous and sprawling body of literature one must be prepared for a task that is nothing less than staggering. To illustrate: The preparation of this volume required a systematic review of over one hundred scientific journals, a survey of some 100,000 titles, and a working bibliography of 6,000 articles. Yet even so extensive a coverage fails to exhaust a field that only recently has come to discover the problems associated with an embarrassment of riches. Since the subject lacks either fixed boundaries or universally recognized dimensions of inquiry, the search for fundamentals requires some arbitrary decisions about what to underscore and what to omit. Topics were selected here in accordance with a bias that is avowedly away from stimulus-response notions, learning theories, computer simulation, or other mechanistic analogues; instead, the book's framework is grounded in the assumptions of systems theory and transactional psychology. The effort to reduce our material to manageable proportions has resulted in chapters that provide in-depth coverage of a limited number of representative topics rather than a more inclusive and perhaps superficial treatment.

The framework advanced in this book is multidimensional; it presents the concept of communication not as isolated phenomena or a singular, purely idealized process, but as interrelated constituent processes that operate at varying levels of complexity and acquire significance only in the context of larger intrapersonal, interpersonal, or sociocultural systems of behavior. The text is intended for a broad audience. Its integrated treatment of topics and the interdisciplinary tenor of its content are designed for virtually any introductory course in the social sciences with an interest in surveying the scientific literature on communication, particularly courses in speech communication, social psychology, and related disciplines. Since the text is intended to be suitable both for the professional and for the general reader, the language and level of discussion are as nontechnical as possible, and leading concepts are detailed in the introductory chapters. Throughout the text suggested readings and liberal citations of relevant literature are intended not so much to document as to challenge the reader interested in further inquiry.

This undertaking required the collaboration of many people, and it is not possible to acknowledge all who contributed to its conception, its struggle, and its completion. I am indebted to several critics who were willing to go beyond the standards of scrutiny usually expected. Portions of the manuscript were read by John W. Bowers of the University of Iowa; Donald K. Darnell of the University of Colorado; John Hadwiger of Eastern Illinois University; Douglas H. Huenergardt of the University of Wisconsin; James C. McCroskey, Illinois State University at Normal; and Glen Mills, University of California at Santa Barbara. Marvin Shaw, University of Florida, read the entire manuscript and made numerous helpful suggestions. And to Gerald R. Miller, Michigan State University, I am deeply indebted for contributing so markedly to every stage of development from initial conception to final manuscript.

Limitations of space and language prevent sufficient acknowledgment to Mary Jahn, who for three years of collaborative effort served as critic of blemished prose and brought creativity and inspiration to the work. Every page bears the imprint of her gifted and sensitive judgments.

The staff at McGraw-Hill, principally editors Robert Fry and Robert Weber, created ideal conditions for unencumbered pursuit of a long-standing personal vision. For reasons known best to the three of us, they deserve much of the credit for the completed manuscript.

Gratitude is due also to the University of Wisconsin for granting a research leave to finish the manuscript and to Diane Huenergardt for her professional preparation of it.

Finally, I owe much to Judy, Deborah, and Lance for their understanding and willingness to extend the necessary rainchecks.

C. David Mortensen

communication: the study of human interaction

one
founda-
tions

one

a frame of

reference

Among living creatures only man has the creative capacity to live simultaneously in two realms of experience, the physical and the symbolic. The sound, sight, taste, smell, and touch of people, events, and objects comprise the raw data of our physical world; and the composite assumptions and hunches about the way things "really are" make up our sense of the symbolic. It is not man's nature to participate totally in either world to the exclusion of the other. In neither can he remain an aloof bystander. Physical facts, after all, do not speak for themselves. They carry no automatic or proper significance. We have no way to divorce our participation in the physical realm from the way we represent our experience in the abstract, for the two are inexorably intertwined. Similarly, symbolic meaning does not spring full-blown from the sheer course of events; it must be created. And in human affairs it is created only by placing the particulars into some larger frame of reference, an image or model through which the specifics can be interpreted in abstract form. Ordinarily, the more complex the event, the greater the number of physical sensations, and the more abstract the image becomes.

Because of our extraordinary gift of language, we have the capacity not only to create images of our every experience but also to talk about them. Out of the accumulation of social encounters, we form and share common images. Every moment of conversation adds to the assumptive biases each man has about himself and about the possibilities of entering another's thought world. Images are acquired so automatically, and with such pervasive regularity, that most people are only vaguely aware of their constancy and profound effects. Though formed for the most part in an unconscious way, these assumptive biases, taken together, dictate the meaning we attribute to events. Thus, as Barnlund (1968b) noted, "It is not events themselves, but how men construe events, that determines what they will see, how they will feel, what they will think, and how they will respond [p. 25]."

The images men share about communication—and about its possibilities—largely regulate what sort of encounters each person will seek or avoid. Consider the alternative interpretations of the following three social incidents. Each one approximates events experienced in the course of a single day. First, here is a description of a conversation between an operator at a telephone-answering service and a subscriber (Haber, 1969):

> "Hello . . . Hebert—ah, Harbart residence. Just a minute." (The voice goes off the phone for one minute, 55 seconds.) "Yeah?"
> "Hello, this is Miss Haber. I'm calling from Los Angeles. Are there. . . ."
> "Just a *moment*." (Off the phone 45 seconds.) "Uh-huh?"
> "Are there any. . . ."
> "*Just a moment*." (Off the phone two minutes, 25 seconds.) "Yes?"
> "*Messages!* For Pete's sake, I'm calling from *California!*"
> "One *moment*." (Off the phone another two minutes.) "No message."
> "I've been away for *three* weeks. Do you mean to tell me that *no one* has called?"
> "Well, they didn't leave any messages."
> "Well, would you mind checking again? For what this call's costing, I'd like to have at least one message to show for it."
> "Oh, wait a minute." (Forty seconds.)
> "Here's a couple. They were in the wrong box. Dolores musta' done that."
> "Please!"
> "Mr. Lackamoose called, Mr. Moorx and Dr. Fisher."
> "I've never heard of any of them. Did they leave their numbers?"
> "One *moment*."
> "*Wait!* Don't go off the line again. . . ."

The writer then commented:

> Unfortunately, that conversation between me and my answering service was not imaginary. (Except for the names of my callers. I found out later, much later, that they were Mr. Bartholomew, Mrs. Morse, and Mr. Viser— old friends whose real names had lost something in the translation.) It's a sample of the kind of dialogue that takes place not infrequently between Manhattan's 175 telephone-answering services and their 50,000 subscribers [p. 68].

The second incident is typical of the commentary about communication to be found in editorial pages of newspapers, journals, and books by social critics; it is taken from the editorial page of a Sunday newspaper (Elegant, 1970).

AMERICANS CAN'T COMMUNICATE

The past two weeks have not been the most comfortable time for a resident abroad to visit the United States, nor have they been the most illuminating. . . . Nonetheless, some shafts of light have pierced the clouds of rhetoric and the fog of emotion. They may be—indeed, they are probably—warped, for I have found that it is all but impossible for anyone to think clearly and dispassionately in the present atmosphere. Perhaps because of the confused background, first impressions do stand out clearly. . . .

The real issues appear to be: Discontent with the status quo, demands for instant gratification in instant solutions—and, *chiefly, failure of communication. The communication gap transcends the much-discussed generation gap. Americans obviously communicate with great difficulty, regardless of age; they're almost incapable of communicating with the outside world.*

Arriving in the United States is like climbing into a pressure-cooker, in part because of the tension stimulated by the President's decision [regarding Viet Nam] but, in greater part, because of the tension inherent in American life. It is, therefore, not remarkable that *dispassionate analysis and communication are rare,* while emotion and isolation appear to be primary characteristics of American society.

Those tendencies are, of course, greatly magnified by a minority's deliberate intent.

Young people who cry out that older people do not "relate" to them are basically correct. *Many of their mothers and fathers do not communicate with each other.* . . .

The basic fault is the elders', since their obvious power over their children did not breed complimentary responsibility.

Belatedly aware of responsibility, some elders are now attempting to communicate. *The effort is often not merely belated, but impossible.* The wall of willful mutual incomprehension is too high [italics added].

The third incident is taken from a full-page newspaper advertisement sponsored by the Avco Corporation; it concerns the power of the mass media to foster communication:

If
you have
something
important to tell
America,
we'll put you on
national television
to say it

You read it right.
You.
Not a movie star or a noted author or a celebrated activist or an official spokesman for some lobby or pressure group. America hears from them.

It's you we're after. You, the ungrouped, individual American *with something to say and no place to say it.* We think what you believe, what you feel, what you like about this country, what you don't like about it, and what you'd like to see done with it, are vital.

Yet it's harder and harder to be heard.

There is a tendency, as life in America becomes more complex and our population keeps growing, for the individual to feel his voice is too small, is lost, that his opinions no longer count.

Why are we at Avco concerned? Simple enough.

This country's greatness has been achieved by individuals and the quality of her future depends on them equally. . . .

We cannot arrange for millions of Americans to talk on TV, but we have committed ourselves to do just as much as we can. Here's the plan.

Our time is your time

Beginning in August this year we are turning over our television commercial time—time we'd ordinarily spend talking about our divisions, the products they make and the services they provide—turning it over to individual Americans like yourself.

Americans who strike us as having something fresh and original to say to their countrymen. . . .

The rest of America may not agree with you. We at Avco may not agree with you. *The important thing is: we will all have seen and heard you. One American speaking his mind* [italics added].

The three seemingly dissimilar incidents have two common themes. First, each reflects how difficult it is to conceive of or to describe communication in impersonal or neutral terms. In each case, the image of communication is bound to the personal evaluation and feelings that link attitudes toward self, the actions of others, and culturally defined patterns of behavior. The subscriber to the telephone-answering service suffered a sequence of minor indignities merely to get some personally satisfying information. The writer of the newspaper article found it impossible to separate his observations about the difficulties of communicating in the United States from the wider substrata of his political, social, and perhaps religious views. And the newspaper advertisement also ties the import of communication to feelings of personal worth and democratic values. The second common denominator of these three incidents is also striking: Each excerpt reflects an unquestioning faith in the power and significance of *attempting* to communicate, difficulties notwithstanding. Note again the parallels. The subscriber in the abortive telephone conversation refused to hang up the phone, even after the interminable delays, interruptions, distortions, misunderstandings, and preoccupations of a bungling operator at the other end of the line. To the end she pleaded with the operator not to go "off the line again," thereby expressing what is probably a universal need to have at least *something* to show for every communicative exchange, regardless of costs and frustrations. In a similar vein, the newspaper editor called on all sides "to listen to each other," even after proclaiming the climate in the United States too chaotic to achieve mutual understanding. The newspaper advertisement, if taken at face value, also affirms the principle of being heard, even when "it's harder and harder to be heard," under circumstances where "one voice is too small, is lost, . . . and no longer counts." The critical thing, the ad intones, is not the cost or the number of people who, by implication, will not be heard, but that "we will all have seen and heard you." What is revered here is the act of communication divorced from its reasoned worth or social consequences.

Despite these common elements, the excerpts suggest two rather distinct, and in some ways conflicting, assumptions about the essential nature of communication. The implications of these images are worth pursuing in detail, for they reveal the consequences of conceiving of communication in alternative ways.

MISCONCEPTIONS ABOUT COMMUNICATION

The prevailing image in the newspaper editorial is one of the most commonly heard—the notion of a *communication gap* or *breakdown.* At its heart is the tendency to think of social malfunctioning and disruption as an abnormality that must be repaired or replaced. Further, the terms *gap* and *breakdown* imply that "normal" communication is a matter of bridging individual differences in viewpoint and interpretation—purely a semantic problem. By definition, then, so long as two parties "work" at talking and listening intently to one another, at seeking to "really communicate" by resolving their differences, the malfunction or gap between them supposedly will ·be eliminated. Less obvious, perhaps, is the tendency—once the language of "communication breakdown" is accepted—to reduce the complexities of verbal interchange to mechanistic operations and to search for tangible "obstacles," "barriers," and "roadblocks" to effectual communication (Smith, 1970).

An additional consequence of such reasoning is the tendency to see more and more evidence of malfunctioning until all social disruption and conflict is explained as a gap in communication. Once this happens, it is not difficult to take the final step, to dismiss altogether the possibility of establishing meaningful communication. In many quarters, this deeply seated pessimism toward the possibilities of communication is already much in vogue. Current despair over human misunderstanding seems a result of a wider sense of alienation and disaffection. Adherents of social protest groups, in particular, are prone to say that our unquestioning faith in the power of the written and spoken word is misplaced—that the business of human talk between young and old, between black and white, between the haves and the have-nots is but an empty and meaningless enterprise. People in positions of authority and high station do not listen to the disenfranchised. In short, the argument goes, talk is cheap, and the hope for "relevant dialogue" is a cruel delusion, an appeal for an exercise in futility. The idea of talk without communication is well underscored in these lyrics from "The Sound of Silence" by Simon and Garfunkel:

> . . . and in the naked light I saw ten thousand people, maybe more, people talking without speaking, people hearing without listening, people writing songs that voices never shared . . . No one dared disturb the sound of silence . . . and, the people bowed and prayed to a neon god they made. . . .*

Rarely is the notion of communication breakdown more in evidence than in the attempts to explain discord within families. In many quarters talk of a "generation gap" or "credibility gap" is now replaced by references to a "communication gap." Typical of what many take to be a growing disaffection among members of families is the conclusion drawn from a study of family relations in a small community in upstate New York after the seventeen-year-old son of a Methodist minister died from an overdose of barbiturates (Associated Press news release, Oct. 12, 1970). One recurring theme described was the total absence of communication between the parents and their teen-age sons and daughters. A seventeen-year-old boy said, "I suppose I'd like them to understand me a little better, but there is a barrier on both sides. I don't listen to them, they don't listen to me." In similar context, a college student wrote the following in response to an essay "On Being an American Parent" (*Time*, Dec. 22, 1967):

> I could never tell my parents anything, it was always "I'm too busy . . . too tired . . . that's not important . . . that's stupid . . . can't you think of better things . . ." As a result, I stopped telling my parents anything. *All communication ceased.* I have only one important plea to parents. . . . *Listen, listen, and listen again.* Please, I know the consequences and I am in hell [p. 7, some italics added].

In angry tones parents retorted (Toole, 1970):

> Too many youngsters are eccentric boors. They will not listen, they will only shout down. They will not discuss, but, like 4 year olds, they throw rocks and shout.

It indeed would be difficult to find strata of American life that are devoid of attempts to explain events with the language of "communication gaps," "barriers," "breakdowns," and "obstacles."

* © 1964 Paul Simon. Used with permission of the publisher.

The Telephone Switchboard

In addition to the imagery of "communication breakdowns" is one that compares human interaction to the activities of a *telephone switchboard*. This notion identifies urban life with the activities of a vast and intricate switchboard where man is the communicator and the metropolis is a massive network of possibilities for communication. Not surprisingly, the switchboard image conceives of communication in technological terms—wires and switches, inputs and outputs, channels and transmitters, cross circuits and transmission lines. The idea of a switchboard gains credence from an almost universal faith in the power of technology to solve social ills and to promote public welfare. Most striking is the widespread acceptance of McLuhan's "global village," a vast electronic network that shrinks the space between West and East to that of a hamlet. McLuhan (1965) wrote:

> Today, after more than a century of electronic technology, we have extended our central nervous system itself in a global embrace, abolishing both space and time as far as our planet is concerned. Rapidly we approach the final phase of the extensions of man—the technological simulation of consciousness, where the creative process of knowing will be collectively and corporately extended to the whole of human society, much as we have already extended our senses and our nerves by the various media . . . as electronically contracted, the global is no more than a village. Electronic speed in bringing all social and political functions together in a sudden impulsion has heightened human awareness of responsibility to an intense degree [pp. 3–5].

McLuhan went on to argue convincingly that "any media has the power of imposing its own assumptions on the unwary." The same idea holds, it might be said, of all images—they impose assumptions that are far-reaching and not altogether obvious. For example, once we accept a switchboard image of communication, with all its technological overtones, we come to expect of human interaction what is tacitly expected of technological performance; unwittingly the astonishing advances of technology get superimposed on our ideas of efficiency in the fragile business of talking to each other. If a technological age compels, as McLuhan insisted, "commitment and participation," then it is not unreasonable to view involvement and relevance as the keys to any interpersonal encounter. If the electronic switchboard can be expected to create a vast and efficient network of extensions and connections, then McLuhan was right in insisting that "the aspirations of our time for wholeness, empathy and depth of awareness is the national adjunct of electronic technology [p. 5]."

The allusions to communication breakdowns and gaps or telephone switchboards certainly do not exhaust the possibilities. Communication can be represented in the abstract in any number of ways. Until recently the most popular conceptions have been mechanistic operations where communication is likened to the operations of telegraph and transportation systems, radio transmitters, conveyer belts, assembly lines, computer activity, and electrical gadgets. A more recent vogue is the psychologically oriented imagery of "turning on" and "rapping" or the states of "identification," "mystico," "I-Thou relationships," and "relevant dialogue."

The Dangers of Misconceptions

The above images of communication need to be brought into the open for a number of reasons. First, we must recognize that the business of creating analogies to represent experience is unavoidable and necessary. The very act of communicating with other people during the greatest part of our waking hours—some claim 80 percent of the time—inevitably creates idealized notions and assumptions about what is essential to communication and what is not. Obviously there is a tremendous difference between assumptions that bear out reality and those that give a grossly distorted impression of the requirements of effectual communication. Hence, much is to be gained by bringing the underlying assumptions into the open. We need to examine them in large measure because images constitute a set of ground rules for the way we handle ourselves and the way we interpret our communicative activities. Ordinarily, the ground rules are only vaguely understood; yet they are the determinants of communication and its adjudged significance.

For example, the notion of gaps and breakdowns automatically portrays communicative activity as a directional and linear sequence of events —much like electronic impulses traveling from beginning to end in a telephone system or digital computer. Once this linear, one-way analogy is accepted, it is almost impossible not to think of communicative difficulties as a result of some malfunctioning that occurs along the line. To correct a breakdown, one is tempted to search for the part or element that needs repair, much as a telephone repairman looks for a break in circuits along a row of telephone lines (Smith, 1970). Even worse, communication tends to be defined in all-or-nothing terms: Either the system works or it does not; the signals arrive at their destination, or they are blocked somewhere along the line. Running through the previous quotations about communication breakdown is an implicit and mistaken notion that "no" communication occurred. Supposedly, whenever people fail to arrive at an identical point of view, we can merely assume that they have—almost by definition—"failed to communicate." For example, the teen-agers all spoke of certain "barriers" or "obstacles" that prevented any communication, even though a good deal of verbal exchange took place. And the editor used absolute terms when he referred to people as being "incapable of communicating" and to the "failure of communication" as though it were some "rare" or "impossible" state to achieve. As a consequence, those with an interest in improving communication are lead to search for barriers, obstacles, gaps, and roadblocks that prevent communication from taking place. In Chapter 2 we will see why the breakdown image is such a dangerous misconception. At this point it will suffice to note that *communication does not necessarily stop simply because people stop talking or listening.* To the contrary. The teen-ager who complained about his parents still "got the message," which he interpreted to be his parents' indifference and lack of respect.

The switchboard image also has consequences that need to be examined. Again, the tendency is to regard aspects of interpersonal relationships in technological terms that are, we presume, amenable to mechanical repair. Thus, if people feel isolated and lost, the answer is clear: Give them the enormous resources of computers (for dating purposes), telephone-answering services (to ensure interpersonal contact), and the mass media (as an outlet for their views). If it is "harder and harder to be heard," let representatives of the silent majority speak out. Never mind the cost of 62,000 dollars for one minute of prime television time; allow the forgotten man to unburden himself before a waiting nation. Similar "remedies" abound in all aspects of human affairs. Theologians can turn to Madison Avenue to create proper commercials on behalf of the church. Even the tough problems of politicians—particularly those lacking a proper image—can be handled by media specialists who know that political commercials are most effective when placed in a nonpolitical setting, next to a newscast if possible. And if the public does not want to hear a particular candidate, there is always the "voice over" technique, where the screen shows only a political problem—a polluted river or a crowded ghetto—and the candidate's face is never seen nor his voice heard. There are techniques for creating "canned spontaneity" and, with the help of a good lighting man, an image of warmth and congeniality.

But a less obvious problem with the switchboard concept is that of getting man to accept the switchboard as an extension of his self-image. All too often we are prone to regard the switchboard not as an extension of our ears and voice, but as an intrusion, a mechanical beast of burden. It extends us, but not always at the moment of our choosing. It also tyrannizes. The clamoring of the telephone demands instant attention, fractionalizing and dividing other activities, switching out some events while it switches in others. The added irony is that the switchboard itself has caused communication failure. For despite the complexity of a national switchboard system that spans an incredible 700 million miles of wires, cables, microwave relays, switches, and some 500 million billion interconnections, the system can and often does break down. The following account describes the situation well (*Newsweek,* Sept. 29, 1969):

> Using the telephone right now is like plugging into a mystery. Strange sounds, voices and events greet the phone user each day, especially when he calls during a "peak" hour in any major American city. Dial Kansas City, for example, and you may get San Francisco. Talk several minutes to a

friend and you may find yourself suddenly in the middle of somebody else's two-way conversation as well. Instead of a dial tone, there are bongs or gongs. Or perhaps nothing, no sound at all, sometimes for hours. The phone company's official line for such complaints is that the product has gotten too popular for its own good. Thanks to affluence, gabby teenagers and the company's persuasive ad campaigns—which have convinced Americans, among other things, to long-distance dial rather than write a letter—circuits are overloaded, it says, beyond anybody's wildest forecasts [p. 70].

The breakdown and switchboard images deserve attention for still another, more significant reason. Despite their similarities, the two images presuppose conflicting views of communication. The notion of communication gaps, with its focus on disruption and malfunctioning, is essentially a negative one. On the other hand, the switchboard image is positive in outlook. It accentuates the marvels of technology and the ever-widening range of channels and connections made instantly available by electronic hardware. Taken together, the two images underscore what is a central dilemma, and perhaps irony, of contemporary times: In a period marked by unprecedented possibilities for communication, there is also an unprecedented expression of doubt about whether any "real communication" occurs. In an age of technological triumph and advanced communicative facilities, what Ellinghaus (1969) called "one of the great natural resources," the public has become increasingly conscious of "people talking without speaking, people hearing without listening. . . ." Note that the editor cited earlier viewed communicative failure as the central problem of our day. This view can be seen also in a host of plays, novels, and poems that deal with the dominant themes of the decade: alienation, separateness, isolation, lack of understanding, despair. The irony is that all the questioning is occurring at a time when the advances of technology permit instantaneous, breath-taking view of the moon and a satellite system makes global television possible by the flick of a dial.

Although the dilemma must be taken seriously, the conflict between the possibilities and limitations of communication may be more apparent than real. Perhaps the public today is generally more sensitive to the requirements of communication and takes them less for granted than in earlier times. Perhaps, too, this increased sensitivity is a direct by-product of our technological advances. On the other hand, some would insist that electronic hardware, switchboards, and relay systems have little to do with people's ability to engage in meaningful interaction on a one-to-one basis. In any case, the disparity between the possibilities and limitations of communication cannot be resolved so long as we attempt to account for it in idealized and abstract terms. Though images may be valuable in establishing the ground rules in our study, they are of little use in accounting for key problems in precise terms. The requirements and possibilities of communication can only be understood by examining what is fundamental to all communicative behavior and by gaining some understanding of the forces that determine the process and outcome of complex communicative events. The first requirement is to shift from a concern with general images of communication to more precise ways of approaching the assumptions underlying the complexities of communicative behavior. These key assumptions can best be understood in postulate form.

COMMUNICATION POSTULATES

Discovering the meaning of the term *communication* is not unlike the problem of defining any abstract concept. In conventional usage, abstract terms such as *education, motivation, behavior,* and *perception* seem clear enough, though their precise boundaries are not. Sometimes, however, conventional usage is inadequate. Until recently, for example, few would have thought to question the conventional use of the terms *life* and *death*. The distinction perhaps is all too clear. And yet with the advances in medical science, it is now possible to sustain life artificially, often for extended periods of time, in the hope of miraculous recovery. Furthermore, the possibility of transplanting vital organs heightens the difficulties of weighing matters of life and death. Since the time and circumstances in which life can be sustained are only vaguely known, each situation requires a medical authority to make a somewhat arbitrary decision in determining the final irrevocable moment when death occurs.

The need for greater precision is inherent in all scientific enterprises. In the case of the term *communication,* few would have qualms about saying that it occurs whenever people attempt to use the power of spoken or written words to influence others. And yet here is where the difficulties occur. Does our common-sense notion mean that communication is limited solely to human activity? Do machines communicate? Is all communication a matter of using spoken or written words? What is meant by the idea of *influence*? Must the influence be intentional? If so, what about overheard or accidental speech that nonetheless modifies the behavior of a bystander? Is all thinking to be regarded as communication?

These questions may appear to be a trivial exercise in pedantry. But the willingness to engage in such preliminary concerns is necessary to avoid terminological confusion and to gain insights that transcend intuition and common sense. Moreover, without some attention to definitional matters, the study of communication can all too easily proliferate to an ever-widening range of activities until it encompasses all human experience and goes even beyond to the realm of machines and lower animals in a regression line that eventually rules out nothing. Still, the business of finding a workable conception of communication is not without its hazards. The term can be conceived so broadly that it loses value as a scientific object of study. Conversely, if defined too narrowly, it can be reduced to a trivial and inconsequential concern. In short, we cannot escape the somewhat arbitrary risks inherent in definition. Furthermore, another type of risk occurs if we search for a highly compartmentalized definition, one that categorically and arbitrarily decides what communication is and what it is not. Little wonder that the attempts to evolve a universally acceptable definition of communication have resulted only in a proliferation of conflicting notions! Over ninety-five have appeared in print, according to one account (Dance, 1970). The most fruitful alternative to an exhaustive and exclusive definition is one that specifies the conditions deemed necessary for an act of communication to be said to occur. The concern, then, is with *fundamental attributes* rather than with an exhaustive and definitive description. These fundamental aspects or conditions can best be surveyed within the framework of a single broadly conceived postulate: *Communication occurs whenever persons attribute significance to message-related behavior.*

This broad conception implies a number of supporting assumptions and postulates. The concept of *transaction* calls attention to a way of looking at reality. It views events as dynamic, on-going, a process of interacting forces in a state of constant change. The forces are not static; they cannot be properly understood as unchanging or fixed elements in time and space. As Berlo (1960) insisted, happenings do not have "a beginning, an end, a fixed sequence of events [p. 24]." A communicative transaction changes, as Dance (1967) observed, in the very act of examining it. No single particular operates apart from the totality of forces at work in the event itself. Changes in any one aspect of the process invariably affect all other constituent aspects of behavior. This transactional orientation calls attention to several secondary postulates.

Communication Is Dynamic

There are any number of ways to conceive of a process of change. The simplest and least satisfactory is to think of change as synonymous with movement or activity, an unbroken sequence in which the operation of any one element, A, effects changes in B which in turn effect further changes in C and so on. Such a click-clack, mechanistic notion of change impoverishes the concept of communication by reducing it to the activity and chance we associate with conveyer belts, a falling line of dominoes, or the clatter of billiard balls on a pool table. In sharp contrast is the more complex notion of *dynamic change,* one in which an indefinitely large number of particulars interact in a reciprocal and continuous manner. Each successively smaller level of activity is itself a composite of interacting elements. An example is the activity of the nervous system. In reference to the complex interacting forces at work within the nervous system, Lashley (1954) wrote:

> Theories of neuron interaction must be couched, not in terms of the activity of individual cells, but in terms of mass relations among the cells. Even the

simplest bit of behavior requires the integrated action of millions of neurons; . . . I have come to believe that almost every nerve cell in the cerebral cortex may be excited in every activity. . . . Differential behavior is determined by the combination of cells acting together rather than by cells which participate only in particular bits of behavior [p. 116].

Another level of dynamic change takes place in perception, of which Platt (1968) commented:

Our perception-process goes over continuously into our larger manipulation of the world around us. We do not think of perception as manipulation, because the brain somehow organizes our ever-changing visual observation-fields into a continuous seen-and-remembered "stable world," and because simple passive observation, even with moving eyeballs, changes the objects and relations of this "stable world" very little, so that we think of it as unaffected by our observation; but manipulation it is, nevertheless, manipulation by the electrical signals in the out-going nerves, by the motion of the eyeballs, and finally by the hands [p. 96].

The difference between static and dynamic conceptions of change is like the difference between adjusting light in a room with a light switch and with a rheostat. The former permits only an all-or-nothing change, whereas a rheostat allows a gradation of change much like the dimming of house lights in a theater. Yet even the rheostat grossly oversimplifies. For the level at which change occurs in human interaction is not one of isolated particulars, or even of combinations of elements; rather, it occurs at the most inclusive level of consciousness—the sense each party has of the total event. Above all, we must resist the temptation to think of change in a tangible sense as we would a physical thing. Communication simply is not analogous to a process where something changes as it is "passed" or "transferred" from one person or setting to another. It is less misleading to think of communication as an occurrence, a happening, rather than something that exists in and of itself.

Finally, dynamic change implies a transaction that is not static, yet through all the fluctuations maintains its stability and identity. There is a certain evolving, elastic quality to the experience of communicating with another human being. The act is constantly taking new shape, but only in a state of equilibrium that changes along lines which are consistent with the immediate expectations and past experience of the respective parties. The sequence may change the participants in some discernible way, but never in ways that are completely foreign to what has already taken place. As Kelley (1963) stated, "If one is to understand the course of the stream of consciousness, he must do more than chart its head waters; he must know the terrain through which it runs and the volume of the flood which may cut out new channels or erode old ones [p. 83]." In subsequent chapters we will learn much about the mechanisms and strategies which a person uses to stabilize and maintain his sense of identity throughout events charted by forces of change. Somehow, in ways not well understood, man seeks change and novelty in ways that do not undermine his stability or feelings of identity and uniqueness.

Communication Is Irreversible

The concept of irreversibility has a direct heritage in the adage which insists that a man can't step in the same river twice: the very act changes the man and the river. The past influences one's sense of the present and what is anticipated about the future. And yet the past can never be reconstructed or reclaimed. It was the irreversible and irretrievable succession of events that Thomas Wolfe underscored in his classic novel *You Can't Go Home Again*. The transactional, flowlike qualities of communication may be taken literally as truth. Research on perception suggests that human beings do not perceive at any single time; in the stream of consciousness there is no literal sense of the instant, no sharp beginning or sharp ending, no lines of demarcation in what we perceive of the physical world. In operational terms, Platt (1968) insisted that there is no direct past or future, only the present instant; he likened this to a "rowboat anchoring in a flowing river, which may bear the gashes of the past logs that have floated by but which never experiences any part of the river except where it is. In such a system, the only moment of decision and change, the only time there is, is now [p. 84]." Whyte (1954) compared time to a line running "through each succeeding wakeful hour of the individual's past life. . . . Time's strip of film runs forward, never backward, even when resurrected from the past. It seems to proceed again at time's own unchanged pace [p. 117]." Human experience flows, in the words of Barnlund (1970), as a stream, in a "single direction leaving behind it a permanent record of man's communicative experience [p. 93]."

      Irreversibility assumes that people engaged in communication can only go forward from one state to the next. It also gives import to the spontaneity of the existing moment of experience and to the accumulative significance of what unfolds. As communication ebbs and flows, its content and meaning ever widen. Each phase of the on-going sequence helps to define the meaning assigned to each succeeding aspect of what is said and done. Seen in this light, no statement, however repetitious, can be regarded as pure redundancy. Somehow, repetition of even the same signal alters the larger significance of the exchange. Once the transaction begins, there can be no retreat, no fresh start, no way to begin all over again.

Communication Is Proactive

When a person engages in an act of communication, he does so totally; nothing less than his entire dynamic as a person and his total, immediate field of experience is involved. This recognition complicates matters. At once it contradicts images that reduce communication to an exercise in translation or to any action that ensures agreement between what is said and what is understood. The immediate implication is that communicative behavior cannot be understood properly apart from the psychological and social determinants of individual behavior generally—and we shall be concerned with perception, motives, emotions, beliefs, and feelings later on. But for now, let us emphasize that this link between the transaction of communication and the psychological processes does not imply that *any* behavior automatically qualifies as communication. Rather, *there are certain communicative aspects in all social situations, and these bear most directly on the interaction of the respective parties.*

It is somewhat fashionable today to explain human behavior in images that presuppose man to be a passive respondent to stimuli. This passive, or *reactive,* model is held in particularly high esteem by adherents of stimulus-response paradigms and certain learning theories, and by students of the mass media who are prone to think of society as an undifferentiated mass of inert respondents who wait to be altered in predetermined ways by all-powerful manipulators of advertising, brainwashing, and hidden persuasion. The following statement by Meerloo (1968) summarizes the reactive approach:

> Our technical means of communication, especially the press, radio, movies, and TV *have gradually exerted a peculiar weakening influence on people's critical capacities.* Too much sensational imagery, reading and hearing is offered to our senses. The feast is too rich for our stomachs. *We lose all sense of proportion.* Advertising continually insinuates dissatisfaction with the products we have at hand. We are living in the richest country in the world. Yet we are daily urged to feel most deprived. Television *hypnotizes* us in our own living rooms. *We feel trapped in a web of technical communications* with their confusing and conflicting persuasions and *we cannot escape.*
>
> Technical devices of advertising and propaganda—those new media with their paradoxical messages—*gradually break down our barriers of criticism.* Glued to the TV screen, *people become passive and apathetic,* and compulsively want to drink in the overabundance of communications like greedy babes with a bottle. We are all a little bit *slave* to the great television hypnosis. Instead of looking inward and reviewing our thoughts and meditations, *we are held in a vise* by a screen that dribbles away our time [p. 84, italics added].

What such a reactive image ignores is the tremendous capacity of the human organism to select, amplify, and manipulate the signals that assault his senses. It ignores the fact that people engaged in communication are *proactive* because they enter the transaction totally. In subsequent chapters we will discover abundant evidence that incoming sensory data are not so much arranged and stamped into categories as they are amplified, selected, and transferred into patterns that fit the expectations of the individual. The notion of man as a detached bystander, an objective and dispassionate reader of the environment, is nothing more than a convenient artifact. Among living creatures man is the most spectacular example of an agent who amplifies his every activity, first in the way he perceives it, and then in the way he modifies his environment. The man-made world is, in the words of Platt (1968), a world that is increasingly "what we have seen, studied and shaped ourselves." As a consequence, we construe the environment in ways that make it ever more docile and manageable. Later chapters will show that what we cannot easily manage, we conveniently ignore.

The intricate activity of the brain is further testimony to the proactive dimension of communication. The brain does not suddenly become inert simply because no immediate physical stimuli demand instantaneous and focused attention. Here are Langer's (1942) comments about the brain:

> If it were, indeed, a vast and intricate telephone exchange, then it should be quiescent when the rest of the organism sleeps. . . . Instead of that, it goes right on manufacturing ideas—streams and deluges of ideas, that the sleeper is not using to *think* with about anything. But the brain is following its own law; it is actively translating experience into symbols, in fulfillment of a basic need to do so. [p. 33].

Man, to be sure, reacts to his surroundings; and in doing so he, in turn, acts upon the environment—by constructing meaning, assigning significance, ruling out, distorting some items, adding others, and ordering the stream of conscious thought by rules and tactics largely unique to his own chemistry.

It is a rare social situation that does not extract from its participants a measure of active commitment, a sense of vested interest in what is said and done. Even when the psychological stakes seem trivial, the minimal needs to preserve identity and self-esteem are there. Furthermore, the very act of expressing one's views serves to heighten the stakes; when others react in approval or indifference, hostility or accord, the sense of personal involvement is intensified. And, we shall discover, once the interaction moves to topics that are highly ego-involving, there is no way to retreat from the lines of self-defense and personal influence. Indeed, in the marketplace of social contact, few can for long remain passive, inert spectators or detached bystanders.

Communication Is Interactive

The cycle from self to world and back again has no sharply defined boundaries, for the human organism does not live as a self-contained, set-off entity. The minimum condition for communication is a more or less constant monitoring of the two realms of experience, the physical and the symbolic. As we said earlier, no event in our physical world has any self-contained or proper significance; nor, for that matter, does activity within us. Meaning occurs, rather, when we interpret or assign significance to the objects of our experience. However, assignment of meaning cannot be properly understood apart from the constant succession of interacting forces that influence us, both internally and externally. As Kelley (1963) wrote:

> A person can be a witness to a tremendous parade of episodes, and yet, if he fails to keep making something out of them, or if he waits until they have occurred before he attempts to reconstrue them, he gains little in the way of experience from having been around when they happened. It is not what happens around him that makes a man experienced; it is the successive construing and reconstruing of what happens, as it happens, that enriches the experience of his life [p. 73].

The term *interaction* suggests a reciprocal influence. In matters of communication this mutual influence may take place on two fronts. One is an individual, or *intrapersonal*, level, where a person assigns significance to messages apart from the presence of another person. This we will consider as a part of information processing in Chapter 3. The second form of interaction is *interpersonal*; it takes place between two or more parties and consists of a complex process whereby each maintains a shared frame of reference, or coorientation, as we will discuss in Chapter 4. It is important not to think of either form of interaction—intrapersonal or interpersonal—as the discrete action of particulars working under separate power; nor even to think of them as balancing elements in causal connection. The notion of interaction entails the far more complex idea of *interdependence*—a mutual influencing process among countless factors, each functioning conjointly so that changes in any one set of forces affect the operations of all other constituent activity in a total field of experience (Sereno and Mortensen, 1970).

The concept of interaction has important implications for our ideas of what a message is. For instance, if there is no way to divorce events from their assigned significance, then clearly a message cannot be reduced to a static entity, words on a page or sounds that have their own built-in or proper sense, much like the fixed barter values of coins. Conversely, when viewed in a functional perspective, *a message consists of whatever unit of behavior serves to link the parties of communication.* This behavior may be *verbal* (as in the case of writing and conversation) or *nonverbal* (such as gestures, eye contact, and facial expression). To qualify as a verbal or nonverbal message cue, the behavior must fulfill two requirements. First, it must be available for inspection. Unnoticed or unattended aspects of joint behavior do not constitute a functioning message. Second, the behavior must be interpreted as significant by at least one of the parties. Consequently, that which constitutes a message cue for one person may not function as one for others. In a situation where only one person is present—where a person writes a letter, for example—the two criteria of availability of cues and assigned significance apply as they would in the situation where two or more communicants are present. Hence, behavior constitutes a message when it is verbal or nonverbal, personal or public, shared by all or only by some. We will explore the fascinating complexity of a vast range of message cues in Chapters 5 and 6, which deal with the verbal and nonverbal dimensions of interaction.

Communication Is Contextual

Communication never takes place in a vacuum; it is not a "pure" process, devoid of background or situational overtones; it always requires at least one's minimal sensitivity to immediate physical surroundings, an awareness of setting or place that in turn influences the ebb and flow of what is regarded as personally significant. To be sure, the context of communication comprises physical characteristics—seating arrangement, color and light, physical space, and the like—but it is much more than the sense of these physical things. It includes the less tangible matter of atmosphere and ambiance, of *sociocultural background.*

Situational factors, we will find, do much to define the emotional and expressive overtones of what is said and done. Context may engender a sense of psychological comfort and warmth, an inviting and congenial atmosphere, or one of threat, distance, and detachment. Often the exact meaning of what is said cannot be separated from the significance of the immediate context. Watzlawick (1967) illustrated the impact of context by citing the following incident described by Lorenz (1952, p. 43):

> In the garden of a country house, in plain view of passers-by on the sidewalk outside, a bearded man can be observed dragging himself, crouching, round the meadow, in figures of eight, glancing constantly over his shoulder and quacking without interruption. This is how the ethologist Konrad Lorenz describes his necessary behavior during one of imprinting experiments with ducklings, after he had substituted himself for their mother. "I was congratulating myself," he writes, "on the obedience and exactitude with which my ducklings came waddling after me, when I suddenly looked up and saw the garden fence framed by a row of dead-white faces: a group of tourists was standing at the fence and staring horrified in my direction." The ducklings were hidden in the tall grass, and all the tourists saw was totally unexplainable, indeed insane, behavior [p. 20].

Our concern with the context of communication will also include what Brockriede (1968) calls the "encompassing situation," an elaborate set of implicit conventions and rules imposed on an individual's behavior in given *types* of social situations. The distinction between *immediate* and *encompassing context* is largely one of inclusiveness. The impact of a particular social situation—of a neighborhood police station, record store, or tavern—constitutes immediate contexts for communication, whereas one's image of police stations, record stores, and taverns corresponds to the influence of an encompassing context.

The impact of context, therefore, is never exhausted by one's immediate surroundings alone. Context is a fascinating and elusive concept that will be examined in Chapters 8 and 9, where we will discover that it can be extended to apply to ever-widening levels of inclusiveness which eventually embrace all social and cultural milieux.

THE STUDY OF COMMUNICATION

Scientific research on human communication is expanding at a spectacular rate. Investigators from diverse fields have declared their vested interest in studying communication's place in the conduct of individuals, groups, complex organizations, institutions, and even cultures. Where the term *communication* once suggested only telephone lines and TV signals, it now is identified with the full gamut of human behavior. One review of developments in the field lists more than twenty academic disciples currently doing research on some phase of human interaction (Knower, 1966). The physical sciences contribute to the study of communication largely by way of technical subfields bearing the headings "cybernetics," "information theory," and "general systems theory." The vigorous activity in the social sciences spans the interests of anthropologists, psychologists, sociologists, educators, and specialists in mass media and speech communication. At times *communication* appears to be a catch-all word. Anthropologists view culture as communication. Social psychologists explain the interface between individuals and groups as communication. Linguists identify their work on language as communicative in emphasis; and journalists trace the flow of information from the mass media to society in terms of a "multistep-flow" process of communication. Still other approaches cross a host of disciplinary lines from political science to business administration, ecology, and phonetics. Finally, in the humanities, rhetoricians and philosophers provide a rich legacy of tradition and doctrine on human interaction. Since the so-called science of human communication cuts through so many fields, it cannot, in a strict sense, claim to be a single discipline at all. It is rather, as Schramm (1963) indicated, an extraordinarily active crossroads of research and theory, a focal point of the social sciences that Lasswell (1965) called the "very center of contemporary intellectual concern."

With the outpouring of scientific research coming from so many new quarters, the field of communication is decidedly unsettled and amorphous. It has yet to establish its boundaries and accepted first principles. Adding to this untidy state of affairs is a lack of theoretical integration in the field, a problem initially noted by Hovland (1948) and Fearing (1953) and, more recently, by Stephenson (1969) and Krippendorff (1969), among others. Twenty-five different conceptions of the term *communication* can be found in current research literature, and the definitions of communication seem almost as numerous as the number of articles on the subject (Dance, 1970; Minter, 1968). In the absence of established first principles, it is hardly surprising that the field of communication should so often be criticized as a "teeming wilderness of facts and notions, instances and generalizations, proofs and surmises [Smith, 1966]" and as "a jungle of unrelated concepts . . . and a mass of undigested, often sterile, empirical data [Westley and MacLean, 1957]."

But the lack of theoretical order should not be overstated, as it is not an automatic obstacle to study. After all, few fields spring forth full-blown with an a priori set of clearly defined, neatly arranged theoretical foundations. The most compelling justification for an applied field of knowledge is not *order* but *excitement*; namely, that a sufficiently large number of investigators stake a claim to an important, previously unrecognized or undervalued problem or object of inquiry, and they subsequently find their labors productive and rewarding. Moreover, the topics and content of established formal disciplines typically derive, as Brown (1965) noted, from the accumulation of research into persistent problems, usually combined with heavy borrowing, camp following, and a shuffling of theoretical speculations from other fields. The topics of new fields evolve in comparative independence of those same topics encountered in related subfields. It would be difficult, for example, to isolate the single principle that separates biophysics from biochemistry, neurology from physiology, or social psychology from experimental psychology. The reward of the early stages of any multidisciplinary scientific enterprise is the extent to which the camp following and borrowing generates new insights and new means of contributing to our general knowledge of human conduct. Therefore, the field of human communication can be approached most fruitfully as a relatively new and exciting historical development, not as a fixed set of theoretical constructs.

The central concern of the field of communication, and in a primitive way the goal of this book, is *to understand what is fundamental to all acts of communication.* While few would contest the underlying assumption that a core of fundamental knowledge does exist, there is less agreement about what the underlying structure of knowledge is exactly, or even how best to understand it. The problem is clear: The more we focus on what is unique to any particular communicative situation, the less apt we are to keep in focus what is common to large classes of interaction. Still, if we become too general and study communication in the most idealized and abstract terms, we may also lose sight of factors that operate in a large class of communicative situations but do not function *uniformly* across all social situations. An alternative strategy is needed, therefore, which at the outset abandons the pretense that a "pure" interaction process can be superimposed uniformly on all matter of social conduct. As Cassirer (1953) convincingly demonstrated, the number of common elements or uniform aspects of behavior decreases rapidly (approaching zero) as the scope or size of a class of objects or events becomes larger.

A MULTIDIMENSIONAL APPROACH

Fortunately, there are alternatives to choosing between grossly oversimplified and confounding images of communication, on one hand, and equally false, idiosyncratic aspects of isolated or narrow-range situations, on the other. One clue is that a subject as complex as communication is best approached through a "probing action," that is, through in-depth, comprehensive observation from different angles and varying perspectives. It is hoped that the results of careful and selective probing will permit a more realistic and balanced perspective than that which could be attained by static or compartmentalized frameworks of study. Admittedly, selectivity can overlap and be arbitrary, but this danger is inherent to any mode of thought and need not be regarded as an obstacle to our study.

Probably the least troublesome and most straightforward probing action is that which seeks to explain the dynamics of communication from within a *multidimensional framework of differing yet closely interrelated levels of activity*. The concept of *level* pertains to the degree of complexity, and it has a twofold aspect: the *size* of the unit of measurement and the *range*, or inclusiveness, of events under observation. The biologist, for example, may examine the intricate organization of leaves through a microscope adjusted to a predetermined series of focal points, a gradation from small to large. He may also vary the number and types of leaves he compares. The results of each level of study can then be fitted into a larger framework.

Three major ranges serve to study the fundamental and complex aspects of communication, and each has its own hierarchy of constituent processes. First is the *intrapersonal system* of communication, which focuses on the dynamics of the experience for each respective party. Second is the more inclusive range of the *interpersonal system,* which considers the dynamics of the experience for A in relation to B. And third is the most inclusive range, the *sociocultural system*; this examines the dynamics of communication as they are influenced by situational, social, institutional, and culturally defined patterns of behavior. In Chapter 2 we will examine some implications of viewing communication as a system of behavior; for now, it is necessary only to note that the three classes of behavior differ primarily in complexity. They are no more separate than the act of changing the power of the microscope "separates" the subject matter of the biologist. Each system has both distinctive and common attributes. Their relationship can be readily understood by studying the framework shown in Figure 1.1.

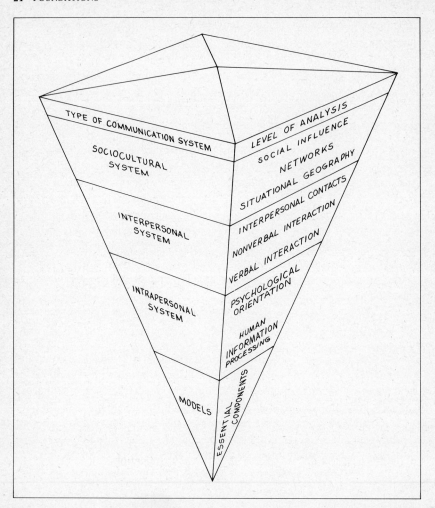

Figure 1.1 *The systems of human communication. The intrapersonal, interpersonal, and sociocultural systems of communication share certain essential components, or common denominators. Each of the higher and successively more complex dimensions of behavior depends on the accumulative influence of the other systems and on their respective dimensions of activity.*

The multidimensional orientation advanced in this book departs from traditional approaches to the field of communication. At once it rejects the fruitfulness of dividing a tremendous range of communicative behavior on the basis of *any single attribute or characteristic.* An example of such a singular division is the tendency to divide all communicative events by the number of persons involved in the interaction. Another example is the attempt to classify communicative behavior on the basis of functional considerations, such as whether the message is designed to persuade or to inform or whether it takes place in the context of mass communication or a face-to-face encounter. While all these factors may influence the tenor of communication, their importance often has been grossly overstated. In addition, such singular distinctions also can have a dangerous and unnecessarily fractionalizing impact on the field, for they invariably ignore the *multiplicity* of factors needed to differentiate large classes of communicative behavior. They tend to make highly arbitrary distinctions in either-or terminology, thus confusing the *attributes* and characteristics of the systems with the underlying nature or *essence* of the behavior itself. For example, sometimes a distinction is made between the subfields of interpersonal communication (two or three interactants), group communication (four to twelve persons), and mass communication. Yet this distinction presupposes that a *single* attribute—namely, the number of participants—can provide a sufficient theoretical basis on which to examine *classes* of verbal behavior; in fact, the number of participants is often among the least important of all possible considerations. In what sense, it might be asked, is the face-to-face conversation of seven people different from the interpersonal communication that takes place in a conversation conducted under identical circumstances except that only two people happen to be present? Along similar lines, are not all situations in which people assign meaning to cues from the mass media also inextricably tied to the nature of their contacts in face-to-face situations? These questions do not presuppose that the varying number of interactants is of incidental importance. Obviously, a communicative exchange between two people is apt to differ in some respects from one that takes place among seven or eight people; but the number of people present does not, in itself, constitute a sufficient basis upon which to define the larger parameters of a field as diverse and heterogeneous as communication.

A multidimensional theoretical framework offers additional advantages to the study of communication. The most striking is simply that at present no single theory of communication exists, and too little is known about the subject to classify a vast proliferation of data under any single attribute of the entire process. A multidimensional framework eliminates the difficulties of trying to force all the complexities of communicative behavior into a single, all-encompassing criterion that invariably ignores both the differences in constituent processes and the interactions among various clusters of factors. Also, a multidimensional framework does not force us to choose among competing theories (learning, cognitive balance, social exchange) or even theoretical orientations (functional versus structural, psychological versus anthropological). There are positive reasons, too, for maintaining a flexible, noninvariant structure that cuts through the insights of a multiplicity of approaches. While the multidimensional orientation may lack the order of a more monastic view, it is

far more consistent and in keeping with the state of knowledge in a field composed mainly of a proliferation of concepts, assumptions, and loosely knit
research findings.

In short, with a multidimensional framework we are better able to
give free range to Burk's notion of "using all there is to use," from whatever
intellectual persuasion, so long as the particulars contribute to our understanding of what is fundamental to communication. Since there is no single
synthetic theory of communication, either in print or in promise, the existing
state of knowledge requires a modest means of establishing the underpinnings
of the field.

The Plan of the Book

The chapters of this book should be approached with several working principles
in mind. One, the notion of *nonelementalism,* which insists that no single element in a complex process has meaning in isolation; insofar as the current
state of knowledge permits, each level of analysis and each communicative
system is related to the need for a holistic view of communication. Another
important principle is *selectivity.* In each chapter, some aspects of communication are omitted in order to focus more intensely upon the operations of other
aspects. It is also important to remember that the more concrete the level of
analysis, the more detailed and precise the information gained—but the less
clear the relationship of the particulars under study to the larger context in
which communication occurs. For example, when the discussion concerns some
aspect of a human being's sensory activity, one may lose sight of the pressures
in a given social situation and how they may influence what sensory data is
ignored and what is selected for future interpretation. Conversely, the more
inclusive the level of analysis, the more apt one is to lose sight of the particulars. Therefore, the relationship of part to whole must always be considered
within the integrative framework of the chapters. The following chapter,
"Communication Models," contains an introduction to various communication systems, depicted through a variety of models, analogues, and descriptive
classificatory schemas.

Part Two, "The Intrapersonal System," focuses on the psychological
dynamics of the individual participants in any communicative act. But the unit
of interest in the intrapersonal system is not limited to situations where only
one person is present; rather, the focal point is the dynamic interplay of forces
at work on individual participants, regardless of how many are present.
Throughout the book, the content of chapters will progress from small to large
units of measurement. Chapter 3, "Human Information Processing," deals with
our struggle to assign meaning or significance and then to respond to the deluge
of signals that ceaselessly assault the senses. Chapter 4 builds upon the founda-

tional aspects of information processing and describes the subjective experience of "Psychological Orientation," the attitude or psychological frame of reference which we maintain toward ourselves and our interaction with others.

Part Three, "The Interpersonal System," deals with three closely related aspects of interaction. Verbal message cues are discussed in Chapter 5, "Verbal Interaction"; then they are coupled with nonverbal cues, discussed in Chapter 6, "Nonverbal Interaction." These two, in turn, influence the meaning people assign to the contacts they establish and maintain with others, explored in Chapter 7, "Interpersonal Contacts."

Finally, Part Four, "The Sociocultural System," enlarges the scope and range of the subject still further to include the characteristic influences at work, first, in our immediate physical surroundings, discussed in "Situational Geography," Chapter 8. Chapter 9, "Communication Networks," deals with the next and more inclusive concern—the influence one situation has on another. At last, the inner workings of all constituent processes are integrated in a description of the major patterns of communication in "Communication and Social Influence," Chapter 10.

SUGGESTED READINGS

Barnlund, D. C. "Communication: The Context of Change," in C. E. Larson and F. E. Dance (eds.), *Perspectives on Communication.* Milwaukee: Speech Communication Center, 1968, pp. 24–40.

Dance, F. E. "The 'Concept' of Communication," *The Journal of Communication,* 20:201–210, 1970.

Lasswell, H. D. "The Role of Communication Arts and Sciences in University Life," *Audio-Visual Communication Review,* 13:361–373, 1965.

Minter, R. L. "A Denotative and Connotative Study in Communication," *The Journal of Communication,* 18:26–36, 1968.

Schramm, W. "Communication Research in the United States," in *The Science of Human Communication.* New York: Basic Books, 1963, pp. 1–16.

Sereno, K. K., and **Mortensen, C. D.** (eds.). *Foundations of Communication Theory.* New York: Harper & Row, 1970.

Watzlawick, P., Beavin, J., and **Jackson, D. D.** *Pragmatics of Human Communication.* New York: Norton, 1967.

two

---

communication models

Man's need to create images of his experiences is ineradicable; and, after
defining them in personal terms, he wants to share them with others. Images,
we discovered in Chapter 1, are idealized and abstract forms of thought. The
act of forming images requires some mode of representation to make them
explicit: charts, diagrams, comparisons, mathematical equations, classification
systems, analogues, and so forth. Some images are, in actuality, idealized
models designed to make abstract experience concrete and meaningful to others.

In the broadest sense, *a model is a systematic representation of an
object or event in idealized and abstract form.* Models are somewhat arbitrary
by their nature. The act of abstracting eliminates certain details to focus on
essential factors. For example, an engineer may wish to build one type of model,
namely a replica, of a prototype airplane. His aim is to test the effect of wind on
a radical concept of wing design. Therefore, he must decide what factors bear
most directly on the question at hand and then incorporate them into the model.
He must at the same time ignore those items he considers extraneous. He thus

finds it unnecessary to replicate all details of an actual airplane. The number of seats and the arrangement of the wheel housing units are less important than obtaining a precise model of such key factors as weight distribution, speed, and heat resistance.

In human affairs, however, scientists rarely design miniature physical models to replicate their objects of study, mainly because their interest is not something tangible or physical. In designing models of communication, the general objective is to construct a model that most accurately and usefully shows what is fundamental to all acts of communication, or to all instances of large classes of communicative behavior, such as small-group interaction and persuasion. The models may assume any number of forms. Some may be *visual*, as in the case of a mechanical analogy between computers and human thought, *pictorial* as in maps and diagrams, or simply *verbal*, as in generalized findings from case studies. Sometimes the form may be *mathematical* or *statistical*, to gain maximum precision and rigor. The key to the usefulness of a model is the degree to which it conforms—in point-by-point correspondence—to the underlying determinants of communicative behavior. While a model may combine both replicative and symbolic features, most models of communication are mainly symbolic and intangible in the sense that they rely on abstract ideas and concepts to represent the unit of behavior under study. In most cases, the closer the correspondence between the attributes of the model and the object of inquiry, the greater the potential payoff to the designer. But before examining several models of communication, we should gain perspective on the potential usefulness and drawbacks associated with what is rapidly becoming a most fashionable scientific enterprise.

THE ADVANTAGES OF MODELS

One major function of a model is to provide a coherent frame of reference for scientific inquiry. Models are to the scientist what road signs and guardrails on a freeway are to the motorist. They are needed to formalize a discipline, to give it distinctive or characteristic province, and to save it from "aimless proliferation of empirical facts in all directions" (Sherif, 1966, p. 51). A good model is useful, then, in providing both general perspective and particular vantage points from which to ask questions and to interpret the raw stuff of observation. The more complex the subject matter—the more amorphous and elusive the natural boundaries—the greater are the potential rewards of model building.

Few crossroads of the social sciences have less formalized or less obvious boundaries than communication does. The study of communication in interpersonal behavior must at once be linguistic, psychological, sociological, and anthropological. Yet it cannot be conceived merely as a composite of those related disciplines in a simple additive or accumulative way. Therefore, the model designer has the formidable task of accounting for the underpinnings of communication in all their divergence and far-reaching implications. At the same time he is able to relate points of interest from among a host of related disciplines to prevent his own frame of reference from becoming an aimless conceptual sprawl that equates communication with human behavior in all its manifest forms. But while the task of establishing boundaries may be arbitrary, it need not be capricious. And the absence of undisputed parameters of investigation need not be regarded as an obstacle to study. Indeed, there is much to relish in the fact that the question "What does communication entail?" can never be answered in total or in a categorical way that rules out the perplexities which make communication a fascinating study.

Models also clarify the structure of complex events. They do this, as Chapanis (1961) noted, by reducing complexity to simpler, more familiar terms. This is particularly important when dealing with an activity comprising a vast, seemingly countless number of influences. Without the guidelines of what to look for and how to interpret what we see, the study of communication could become a dreary trudge through a morass of separate items, each understandable only within the particular situation in which it occurs. Models can reveal what to look for, how to identify levels of analysis, how to separate the idiosyncratic from the common, and how to focus on the major contingencies of what is said and done.

Thus, *the aim of a model is not to ignore complexity or to explain it away, but rather to give it order and coherence.* By looking for the underlying structure of an event, we minimize the danger of becoming sidetracked by particulars whose influence no one can predict. With the aid of a high-powered model, the isolated pieces of information can assume meaningful patterns. What once seemed a result of forces that are unique to a particular time and place suddenly has meaning as part of larger patterns. Only when these patterns are discovered can one hope to move from the confines of isolated description to a low-order level of explanation and then, in turn, to increasingly accurate levels of prediction. In short, a useful model is a touchstone for moving from description (the "what" of communication) to explanation and prediction (the "why" of communication).

At another level models have heuristic value; that is, they provide new ways to conceive of hypothetical ideas and relationships. This may well be their most important function. With the aid of a good model, suddenly we are jarred from conventional modes of thought. As the particular attributes of events are shifted to more idealized modes of representation, the initial context is transferred to a new perspective on the same event. What happens, then, is that the model designer studies an event by transcending its immediate confines. Often the novel conception of old problems reveals misguided assumptions, exposes gaps in knowledge, and eventually leads to new attacks on unknown territory (Bridgman, 1959; Lachman, 1960). A spectacular illustration is the enormous amount of time that men wasted trying to build a flying machine that flapped its wings like a bird. Though the mechanical model could not explain how birds fly, it did lead to an understanding of the law of aerodynamic lift and eventually paved the way to airfoils that could be used in flights. Less dramatic is the attempt of model designers to conceive of communication in terms of a fixed source of information and a final destination—as in the transmission of radio receiver and transmitter. Only with the use of a new model, one incorporating the concept of feedback (borrowed, incidentally, from another mechanical analogy—the computer), did communication models begin to account for some of the reciprocal, or two-way, influences which operate in interpersonal affairs. Ideally, any model, even when studied casually, should offer new insights and culminate in what can only be described as an "Aha!" experience.

THE LIMITATIONS OF MODELS

The criticism most often leveled against models is that they invite oversimplified ways of conceiving of problems. The tendency is to read more into a model than what is there and to tacitly associate the *form* of representation with the *totality* of the event being modeled. Say we decide to model communication in face-to-face situations after the mechanical activity of a radio transmitting system. Once we admit the comparison, the temptation is to reduce the myriad factors associated with speech production to a "transmission phase," and the equally complex forces at work with the listeners to a "reception phase." Next we lapse into calling—and perhaps considering—human beings "transmitters" and receptors of information. Obviously, what began as a rather innocent and straightforward comparison soon gets out of hand. Before long some critic charges that those model builders see human beings as nothing more than mechanical gadgetry. While the fault may reside in part with the handling of the comparison, there is no denying that much of the work in designing communication models illustrates the oft-repeated charge that anything in human affairs which can be modeled is by definition too superficial to be given serious consideration. Worse yet, such work can provide ammunition for Duhem's (1954) belief that model construction is superfluous and a refuge for weak minds.

We can guard against the risks of oversimplification by recognizing the fundamental distinction between simplification and oversimplification. By definition, and of necessity, models simplify. So do all comparisons. As Kaplan (1964) noted, "Science always simplifies; its aim is not to reproduce the reality in all its complexity, but only to formulate what is essential for understanding, prediction, or control. That a model is simpler than the subject-matter being inquired into is as much a virtue as a fault, and is, in any case, inevitable [p. 280]." So the real question is *what* gets simplified. Insofar as a model ignores crucial variables and recurrent relationships, it is open to the charge of over-simplification. If the essential attributes or particulars of the event are included, the model is to be credited with the virtue of parsimony, which insists—where everything is equal—that the simplest of two interpretations is superior. Simplification, after all, is inherent in the act of abstracting. For example, an ordinary orange has a vast number of potential attributes; it is necessary to consider only a few when one decides to eat an orange, but many more must be taken into account when one wants to capture the essence of an orange in a prize-winning photograph.

Another caution stems from the recognition that models are sophisticated versions of scientific analogies. An analogy compares two things *in principle only*. Note that the comparison is only partial. Hence, a model must allow one to cut through the noncomparable and potentially distracting aspects to the essence of the behavior under study. The scientist who uses an electronic computer as an analogue for the human brain does not necessarily reduce man to a machine. He need not equate the brain and machine in appearance, speed, power, or final end-products to make fruitful comparisons of the way each groups and organizes incoming signals. Furthermore, the fact that he uses the language of a mechanical system does not in the slightest reduce the legitimacy of the comparison to human affairs. It is important to remember that a model simply posits that in specifiable ways, *not in total*, the thing being modeled acts "like this." In the words of Chapanis (1961), "A model can tolerate a considerable amount of slop [p. 118]." Clearly, oversimplification may be a shortcoming in designing models, but this risk is inherent to thought itself and does not disappear when one vows to avoid making scientific parallels (Barnlund, 1968).

Model-Behavior Confusion

Critics also charge that models are readily confused with reality. The problem typically begins with an initial exploration of some unknown territory. To reduce uncertainty, one investigates an uncharted domain or sketches a map which consists of a patchwork of hunches and guesses. Then, instead of filling in the details of the map and correcting its internal detail when the territory is explored, the map maker becomes more attached to the simplicity of the map than to the labyrinth of his object of study. Then the model begins to function as a substitute for the event: in short, the map is taken literally. And what is worse, another form of ambiguity is substituted for the uncertainty the map was designed to minimize. What has happened is a sophisticated version of the general semanticist's admonition that "the map is not the territory." Spain is not pink because it appears that way on the map, and Minnesota is not up because it is located near the top of a United States map. The model *represents* a process of communication, but it does not *constitute* the process. Nor is it a literal description of reality. A principal of a school may become intrigued with a model that describes classroom interaction in terms of "inputs" and "outputs," "response repertoires," and "feedback cycles," but his technical lexicon should not be confused with what the children *actually experience* as they talk and listen to each other.

Undoubtedly, the model-reality problem is due in large measure to faulty interpretation and not to any inherent liabilities of models as such. The proper antidote lies in acquiring skill in the art of map reading.

Premature Closure

The model designer may escape the risks of oversimplification and map reading and still fall prey to dangers inherent in abstraction. To press for closure is to strive for a sense of completion in a system. The very nature of a model imposes closure because of the way it includes some factors while ruling out others as extraneous. So while the process of abstraction may bring a complex event into manageable proportions, that may be a liability. The less that is known about the subject, the greater becomes the danger of premature closure. As Kaplan (1964) elaborated,

> The danger is that the model limits our awareness of unexplored possibilities of conceptualization. We tinker with the model when we might be better occupied with the subject-matter itself. In many areas of human behavior, our knowledge is on the level of folk wisdom . . . incorporating it in a model does not automatically give such knowledge scientific status. The majority of our ideas is usually a matter of slow growth, which cannot be forced. . . . Closure is premature if it lays down the lines for our thinking to follow when we do not know enough to say even whether one direction or another is the more promising. Building a model, in short, may crystallize our thoughts at a stage when they are better left in solution, to allow new compounds to precipitate [p. 279].

Since the danger of premature closure is not due to the fallibilities of thought generally, there are no hard-and-fast rules for minimizing the problem. One can reduce the hazards only by recognizing that physical reality can be represented in any number of ways.

THE USE OF ALTERNATIVE MODELS

If a given model does not represent the underpinnings of communication with reasonable fidelity, it can be altered or abandoned, or the useful features can be incorporated into another model. An example from early research on human attention will illustrate. In 1957 Broadbent designed an elegantly simple model of human attention, which he likened to a Y-shaped tube (Figure 2.1). The tube was so designed that when two balls were placed in the two branches at the top, only one ball at a time could pass downward through the main passageway. If the two reached the juncture at exactly the same time, they would jam, and neither would pass through. Broadbent likened the jamming process to what happened when two bits of information reached the human sensory system simultaneously. The model was easy to visualize and still made it possible to conceive of human attention in the abstract. For years

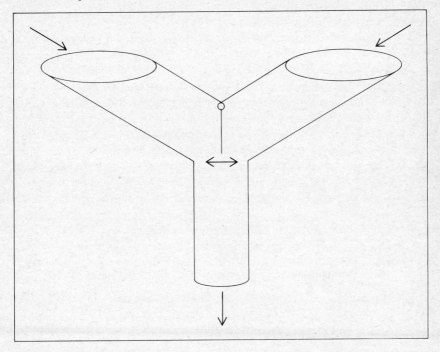

Figure 2.1 *Broadbent's model of human attention. (After Broadbent, 1957.)*

it was the most frequently cited approximation of what the human organism does in multichannel listening. Soon subsequent investigations uncovered evidence that under certain circumstances people seemed to recognize ignored items *even when they were not directly attending to them.* The notion of jamming was an inadequate explanation for this new development. Clearly the model could not stand unaltered in the face of so much new evidence. Therefore, each investigator had to make a decision. Some chose to work on modifications of the filter model, while others adopted new models based on a hierarchy of listening tests. The details of the ensuing controversy need not concern us at this point, for we will return to them in Chapter 3. The point of relevance here is that there is nothing immutable about the approximations posited by a particular model; it is always subject to modification or abandonment.

In the remainder of this chapter we will examine several communication models. There are strong logical grounds for examining alternative designs. One is the immediate need to guard against the risks of oversimplification, confusion of models with reality, and premature closure. Only by examining alternative models do we lessen the odds of forming a prematurely fixed conception of communication. So little is known about our subject that it is not possible to identify flatly what communication is and what it is not. Also, the use of numerous models provides a conceptual tool for cross-checking the assumptions of any particular model.

There are many other fringe benefits of tracing the major efforts in model building, not the least of which is heuristic. Communication models can be most profitably examined in a playful intellectual spirit. Modeling, after all, is a form of intellectual play, a "grown-up sophisticated version of a child's game," as Chapanis (1961) said, but a game nonetheless. Much of the potential fun is missed if models are approached as one would a five-page math formula. Modeling is one way of gaining general perspective and specific insight, much of which comes from the willingness to speculate, to spin out implications (as well as postulates), to check one analogy against another, to identify gaps in knowledge. Models provide an opportunity to make practical application, to serve as a tooling-up exercise for more advanced topics, to grasp the complexity of forces at work in even the simplest act of communication, and to gain an appreciation for the theoretical orientation which governs the conduct of communication research. Finally, through a review of model building we can gain fresh appreciation for the advances in knowledge that have been made as models were refined through criticism and subsequent modification.

A MATHEMATICAL MODEL

Claude Shannon, an engineer for the Bell Telephone Company, designed the most influential of all early communication models. His goal was to formulate a theory to guide the efforts of engineers in finding the most efficient way of transmitting electrical signals from one location to another (Shannon and Weaver, 1949). The model (Figure 2.2) conceived of a communication system made up of five necessary functions for the transmission of information: (1) A *source* generated one signal from a number of alternative possibilities. The signal was then traced from a (2) *transmitter* through a (3) *channel* to some (4) *receiver,* where the transmitted signal was reconverted into its original form for its (5) *destination.* The concept of *message* is designated as any input into the transmitter, while distracting disturbances which occur at any point in the channel fall under the heading of *noise.* In the case of a telephone conversation, the spoken word of one person is *encoded* (transformed into an electrical impulse by the transmitter) and then is sent through telephone lines (the channel) to a receiver, where it is *decoded* into spoken words for the listener. Later Shannon introduced a mechanism in the receiver which corrected for differences between the transmitted and received signal; this monitoring or correcting mechanism was the forerunner of the now widely used concept of *feedback* (information which a communicator gains from others in response to his own verbal behavior; we will examine the concept of feedback in detail in Chapter 7). The concepts of decoding and encoding are central to problems considered in detail in Chapter 2.

As a solution to a technical problem, Shannon's model was a spectacular success. Within a decade a host of other disciplines—many in the

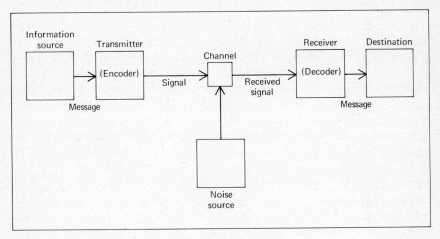

Figure 2.2 *A mathematical model of communication. (Reprinted with permission from Shannon and Weaver, 1949.)*

behavioral sciences—adapted it to countless interpersonal situations, often distorting it or making exaggerated claims for its use. Not surprisingly, the model was also taken as an approximation of the process of human communication. But the mathematical model proved to be a mixed blessing as a paradigm for human activity. On the plus side, few would contest the enormous heuristic value of Shannon's work both in stimulating research and in serving as a prototype of more refined models yet to come. Even more important, many of the concepts advanced by Shannon and Weaver served as remarkably useful analogies in the lexicon of research on communication in social situations. Among the most important of these concepts are the following:

Entropy. This is a way of measuring the amount of information a source conveys to a destination. The exact amount of transmitted information depends both on how much the destination knows beforehand and on the number of choices the source has in deciding what message to select from a number of alternatives. Stated somewhat more technically, entropy depends on the freedom of choice the source has in reducing the destination's uncertainty over the particular item or bit of information in the message that will occur next. Uncertainty or entropy, then, increases in exact proportion to the number of messages from which the source has to choose. In the simple matter of flipping a coin, entropy is low because the destination knows the probability of a coin's turning up either heads or tails. In the case of a two-headed coin, there can be neither any freedom of choice nor any reduction in uncertainty so long as the destination knows exactly what the outcome must be. In other words, the value of a specific bit of information depends on the probability that it will occur. In general, the informative value of an item in a message decreases in exact proportion to the likelihood of its occurrence.

Redundancy. Those items in a message that add no new information are redundant. Perfect redundancy is equal to total repetition and is found in pure form only in machines. In human beings, the very act of repetition changes, in some minute way, the meaning or the message and the larger social significance of the event. Zero redundancy creates sheer unpredictability, for there is no way of knowing what items in a sequence will come next. As a rule, no message can reach maximum efficiency unless it contains a balance between the unexpected and the predictable, between what the receiver must have underscored to acquire understanding and what can be deleted as extraneous.

Noise. Any additional signal that interferes with the reception of information is noise. In a technical system, noise consists of any discrepancy between the transmitted message and the one received. Noise is the ultimate limiter of communication; it functions, in however minute a way, in every type of communication system, human or mechanical. In electrical apparatus noise comes only from within the system, whereas in human activity it may occur quite apart from the act of transmission and reception. Interference may result, for example, from background noise in the immediate surroundings, from noisy channels (a crackling microphone), from the organization and semantic aspects of the message (syntactical and semantical noise), or from psychological interference with encoding and decoding. Noise need not be considered a detriment unless it produces a *significant* interference with the reception of the message. Even when the disturbance is substantial, the strength of the signal or the rate of redundancy may be increased to restore efficiency.

Channel Capacity. The upper limit of information that any communication system can handle at a given time is its channel capacity. To determine how much useful information a technical system can transmit at any one time, it is first necessary to know how much uncertainty or entropy a given signal will eliminate. The battle against uncertainty depends upon the number of alternative possibilities the message eliminates. Obviously, this is information in a very special and technical sense, but it does parallel countless everyday situations. Suppose you wanted to know where a given checker was located on a checkerboard. If you start by asking if it is located in the first black square at the extreme left of the second row from the top and find the answer to be no, sixty-three possibilities remain—a high level of uncertainty. On the other hand, if you first ask whether it falls on any square at the top half of the board, the alternative will be reduced by half regardless of the answer. By following the first strategy it could be necessary to ask up to sixty-three questions (inefficient indeed!); but by consistently halving the remaining possibilities, you will obtain the right answer in no more than six tries.

Not all or even most information in human encounters conforms to the discrete, yes-no type of signals processed by electrical apparatus. Rarely does the ebb and flow of everyday conversation resemble the firing of yes-no questions back and forth. Nonetheless, there is abundant evidence, much of which we shall detail in Chapter 3, that human beings are severely limited in the amount of information—of whatever type—they can interpret at any one time; moreover, the boundaries of the human channel capacity are so uniform that they can be specified with mathematical precision and at a high level of probability. In subsequent chapters we will return again and again to a range of communicative difficulties that people encounter when information comes too much and too fast.

Although few would contest the predictive power and heuristic value of the Shannon-Weaver model, its usefulness as an analogue to human affairs is open to question. Again, it is necessary to sift through abstraction and pin down exactly what it can be taken to represent and what it cannot. It is certainly analogous to the minimum components of face-to-face interchange and their relationships—namely, source, encoding, transmitted signal, channel, received and decoded signal, receiver, destination, monitoring, and the potential for noise throughout. With only slight changes in terminology, a number of nonmathematical schemas have elaborated on the major theme. For example, Harold Lasswell (1948) conceived of analyzing the mass media in five stages: "Who?" "Says what?" "In which channel?" "To whom?" "With what effect?" In apparent elaboration on Lasswell and/or Shannon and Weaver, George Gerbner (1956) extended the components to include the notions of perception, reactions to a situation, and message context.

Nonetheless, the engineering prototype model, for all its ingenious implications, is analogous in only a very secondary way to the world of human talk. Only a fraction of the information conveyed in interpersonal encounters can be taken as remotely corresponding to the teletype action of statistically rare or redundant signals. When two people share a matter of personal importance, neither can know in full the range of alternatives open to him, and those that are known can never be defined in discrete terms, let alone be divided in half. Though Shannon's technical concept of information is fascinating in many respects, it ranks among the *least* important ways of conceiving of what we recognize as "information." In Chapter 3 we will discover that human beings decode and encode information in ways that do not resemble, even slightly, the impulses of electronic hardware. Also, Shannon and Weaver were concerned only with technical problems associated with the selection and arrangement of discrete units of information—in short, with purely *formal* matters, not *content.* Hence, their model does not apply to semantic or pragmatic dimensions of language. Finally, the most serious shortcoming of the Shannon-Weaver communication system is that it is relatively static and linear. It conceives of a linear and literal transmission of information from one location to another. The notion of linearity leads to misleading ideas when transferred to human conduct; some of the problems can best be underscored by studying several alternative models of communication.

IN SEARCH OF NONLINEAR MODELS

The notion of communication as a linear, one-way event conflicts with the idea of a complex activity in which the respective parties are mutually dependent and where the degrees of freedom of choice are not fully known. In even the simplest communicative act, the participants send and receive information simultaneously. In the ebb and flow of conversation, the distinction between sender and receiver is useful only as a way of referring to the origin or destination of a particular item of information. Communication entails active participation; even the so-called indifferent listener gives signals about his reaction to what others say and do; and even total passivity constitutes a reaction of sorts. Moreover, since in human affairs the notions of sender and receiver must designate particular communicative *functions* and not static *entities,* our models must account for the reciprocal aspects of communication in something other than conveyor-belt terms. The dualistic aspects of communication are best represented by various nonlinear designs.

Wilbur Schramm (1954) was one of the first to alter the mathematical model of Shannon and Weaver. He conceived of decoding and encoding as activities maintained simultaneously by sender and receiver; he also made provisions for a two-way interchange of messages (Figure 2.3). Notice also the inclusion of an "interpreter" as an abstract representation of the problem of meaning. Schramm provided the additional notion of a "field of experience," or the psychological frame of reference; this refers to the type of orientation or attitudes which interactants maintain toward each other, a complex problem we will examine in detail in Chapter 3. Other model designers abstracted the

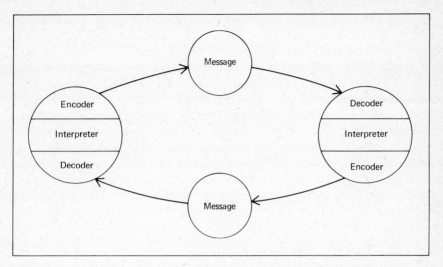

Figure 2.3 *Schramm's model of communication. (Reprinted with permission from Schramm, 1955.)*

dualistic aspects of communication as a series of "loops," (Mysak, 1970), "speech cycles" (Johnson, 1953), "co-orientation" (Newcomb, 1953), and overlapping "psychological fields" (Fearing, 1953).

The Helical Spiral

As a further alternative to linear models, Dance (1967) advanced the notion of a helix to depict communication as a dynamic process (Figure 2.4). The helix represents the way communication evolves in an individual from his birth to the existing moment. As Dance elaborated:

> At any and all times, the helix gives geometrical testimony to the concept that communication while moving forward is at the same moment coming back upon itself and being affected by its past behavior, for the coming curve of the helix is fundamentally affected by the curve from which it emerges. Yet, even though slowly, the helix can gradually free itself from its lower-level distortions. The communication process, like the helix, is constantly moving forward and yet is always to some degree dependent upon the past, which informs the present and the future. The helical communication model offers a flexible communication process [p. 296].

As a heuristic device, the helix is interesting not so much for what it says as for what it permits to be said. Hence, it exemplifies a point made earlier: It is important to approach models in a spirit of speculation and intellectual play. If judged against conventional scientific standards, the helix does not fare well as a model. Indeed, some would claim that it does not meet the requirements of a model at all. More specifically, it is not a systematic or formalized mode of representation. Neither does it formalize relationships or isolate key variables. It describes in the abstract but does not explicitly explain or make particular hypotheses testable. Given such serious limitations, some might then ask what good it is. The answer depends on our inclination to speculate—to engage in what Chapanis (1961) called "sophisticated play." The following two paragraphs illustrate the possibilities of approaching models in a sportive manner:

The helix implies that communication is continuous, unrepeatable, additive, and accumulative; that is, each phase of activity depends upon present

Figure 2.4   *The helical spiral as a representation of human communication. (Reprinted with permission from Dance, 1967.)*

forces at work as they are defined by all that has occurred before. All experience contributes to the shape of the unfolding moment; there is no break in the action, no fixed beginning, no pure redundancy, no closure. All communicative experience is the product of learned, nonrepeatable events which are defined in ways the organism develops to be self-consistent and socially meaningful (two ideas we will pursue in Chapter 4). In short, the helix underscores the integrated aspects of all human communication as an evolving process that is always turned inward in ways that permit learning, growth, and discovery.

Interesting features notwithstanding, there is reason to question some implications that stem from likening communication to a helix. For example, does not the helix imply a false degree of continuity from one communicative situation to another? Do we necessarily perceive all encounters as actually occurring in an undifferentiated, unbroken sequence of events? Does an unbroken line not conflict with the human experience of discontinuity, intermittent periods, false starts, and so forth? Is all communication a matter of growth, upward and onward, in an ever-broadening range of encounters? If the helix represents continuous learning and growth, how can the same form also account for deterioration and decay? What about the forces of entropy, inertia, decay, and pathology? And does not the unbroken line of a helix tacitly ignore the *qualitative* distinctions that inevitably characterize different communicative events? Also, what about movements which we define as utterly wasted, forced, or contrived? Along similar lines, how can the idea of continuous, unbroken growth include events we consider meaningless, artificial, or unproductive? Countless other questions could be raised. And that is the point. The model brings problems of abstraction into the open. It suggests certain possibilities and rules out others. It also may trigger an awareness of assumptions we often take for granted. In particular, the helix illustrates the possibility of conceiving of communication in unusual and creative ways.

A Conceptual Model

Recognizing the dangers inherent in borrowing models from unrelated fields, Westley and MacLean (1957) designed a model to represent all communicative acts—from the simplest face-to-face situation to the most complex social organization and the mass media. Westley and MacLean realized that communication does not begin when one person starts to talk, but rather when a person responds selectively to his immediate physical surroundings. In Figure 2.5a, each interactant responds to his sensory experience (X_1 . . .) by abstracting out certain objects of orientation (X_1 . . . $_{3_m}$). Some items are selected for further interpretation or coding (X') and then are transmitted to another person, who may or may not be responding to the same objects of orientation (X_{1b}), as represented in Figure 2.5b.

The Westley-MacLean model incorporated many factors that went unnoticed in earlier classification schemas. One is the important idea of a *sensory field* or, in Newcomb's (1953) words, "objects of co-orientation." Another is the significance given to *feedback*, conceived both as deliberate responses of one person to another and also as pervasive reactions expressed largely in unintentional and fortuitous ways. Another important component is the abstraction of C in Figure 2.5c, which represents the role of an intermediary, a person who gives some items of information to B about A. Examples include the neighborhood gossip who picks up information and passes it on—usually with embellishment—to a housewife, B, who does not have the time to visit directly with all her neighbors (Figure 2.5d). Since the person who gossips can transmit her juicy items about A to B in the total absence of A, the model applies to situations where not all communicators are present at one time.

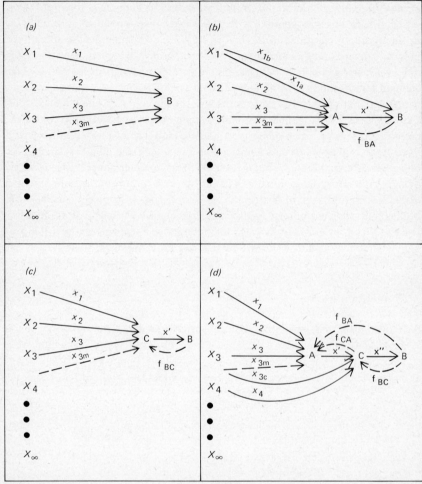

Figure 2.5 *A conceptual model of communication. (Reprinted with permission from Westley and MacLean, Jr., 1957.)*
(a) *Objects of orientation ($X_1 \ldots X$) in the sensory field of the receiver (B) are transmitted directly to him in abstracted form ($X_1 \ldots X_3$) after a process of selection from among all Xs, such selection being based at least in part on the needs and problems of B. Some or all messages are transmitted in more than one sense (X_{3m}, for example).*
(b) *The same Xs are selected and abstracted by communicator A and transmitted as a message (x') to B, who may or may not have part or all of the Xs in his own sensory field (X_{1b}). Whether on purpose or not, B transmits feedback (f_{BA}) to A.*
(c) *The Xs that B receives may result from selected abstractions which are transmitted without purpose by encoder C, who acts for B and thus extends B's environment. C's selections are necessarily based in part on feedback (f_{BC}) from B.*
(d) *The messages which C transmits to B (x'') represent C's selections both from the messages he gets from A (x') and from the abstractions in his own sensory field (X_{3c}, X_4), which may or may not be in A's field. Feedback moves not only from B to A (f_{BA}) and from B to C (f_{BC}) but also from C to A (f_{CA}). Clearly, in mass communication, a large number of Cs receive from a very large number of As and transmit to a vastly larger number of Bs, who simultaneously receive messages from other Cs.*

Another example of C is the editor of a college newspaper who reads student reactions to an issue and then decides which ones will appear in print. Finally, the agents of communication, A, B, and indirectly C, need not be conceived solely as persons. They may, for example, represent the flow of information from one organization to another, from the mass media to groups, or from one culture to another.

Though the model attempts to account for all communicative acts in an idealized way, it differentiates between mass communication and face-to-face situations on two grounds. One is that mass media typically involve fewer senses than do face-to-face situations. For instance, radio entails the sense of sound, while TV adds sight; but most interpersonal encounters involve *all* the senses. Second, the mass media typically permit only indirect and delayed feedback, whereas interpersonal situations center on instantaneous and direct feedback. Also, the model accounts for the flow of information in ways ignored by depictions of communication as simply a one-way ($\longrightarrow$) or two-way ($\rightleftharpoons$) interchange. Note that A and B are influenced by sensory information from all sides simultaneously, not just from a straight line that links the two in isolation from others or their surroundings.

A Mosaic Model

All the models examined so far, with the exception of the helix, described a process whereby a single message is transmitted from one person to receivers. The problem is that few communicative acts end with the interpretation of a single message. Clearly, a model is needed to account for composite *sets* of messages as they interact over time and across situations. One fascinating analogy is the "communication mosaic" advanced by Becker (1968), who assumes that most communicative acts link message elements from more than one social situation. In the tracing of various elements of a message, it is clear that the items may result in part from a talk with an associate, from an obscure quotation read years before, from a recent TV commercial, and from numerous other dissimilar situations—moments of introspection, public debate, coffeeshop banter, daydreaming, and so on. In short, the elements that make up a message ordinarily occur in bits and pieces. Some items are separated by gaps in time, others by gaps in modes of presentation, in social situations, or in the number of persons present.

To illustrate how the bits and pieces fit together, Becker offered a series of personal incidents and showed how they serve to link a number of otherwise disperse details:

> An informal test of the validity of this type of "mosaic" as an analogue of the communication process may be carried out if you consider the way in which your image of the murder of Martin Luther King and of the aftermath

of that murder was formed and recall that this was the image that affected the probability of your wiring your Congressman to vote for the open-housing law and may well affect some of your votes in the next election. I first heard of the assassination from a Chicago cab driver as we were coming in to the LaSalle Hotel for the Central States Speech convention. He wondered (aloud of course) whether President Johnson was going on television that night. My query about whether something new had occurred regarding the Viet Nam peace feelers brought the information about King. In rather quick but scattered succession over the next two days I heard snatches of conversation about these events in the hallways and lobby and meeting rooms of the hotel, I heard an assortment of newscasters and interviews with Negro and white leaders, I saw film footage of the burning and looting, I heard Whitney Young of the Urban League declaring that it was time for us self-styled white liberals to stop talking and start doing, I read stories in the Chicago papers about the events, I saw the store windows across from the hotel broken by one of a group of Negro youngsters who marched by, I heard an impassioned speech in a hotel room by a close friend justifying the burning and looting being done by Negroes in many parts of the country, I saw the hotel employees locking all of the entrances to the hotel but one, and I engaged in discussion with my friends and colleagues about whether it was safe to go out of the hotel for dinner. And these were only a small portion of the relevant messages to which I was exposed during that two-day period. Not only was I exposed to messages, I was forced to respond to many—to create my own messages and, in the process, to develop points of view about the events. Many of these communication transactions were redundant. I even heard myself responding to various individuals with the same phrases. In other words, there were two kinds of processes at work: there was an ever-increasing number and variety of pieces and sources of information and, at the same time, there was a certain amount of repetitiveness, of going through the same or similar transactions again and again [1968, p. 16].

Becker likens complex communicative events to the activity of a receiver who moves through a constantly changing cube or mosaic of information (Figure 2.6). The layers of the cube correspond to layers of information. Each section of the cube represents a potential source of information; note that some are blocked out in recognition that at any given point some bits of information are not available for use. Other layers correspond to potentially relevant sets of information.

The imagery of a mosaic calls attention to ideas ignored in other models. First, it depicts the incredible complexity of communication as influenced by a constantly changing milieu. More specifically, it also accounts for variations in exposure to messages. In some circumstances receivers may be flooded by relevant information; in others they may encounter only a few isolated items. Individual differences also influence level of exposure; some people seem to be attuned to a large range of information, while others miss or dismiss much as extraneous.

Different kinds of relationships between people and messages cut through the many levels of exposure. Some relationships are confined to isolated situations, others to recurrent events. Moreover, some relationships center on a particular message, while others focus on more diffuse units; that is, they entail a complex set of relationships between a given message and the larger backdrop of information against which it is interpreted.

There is also a range of relationships which are not explicit in the mosaic but which could readily be incorporated into Figure 2.6. It may be useful

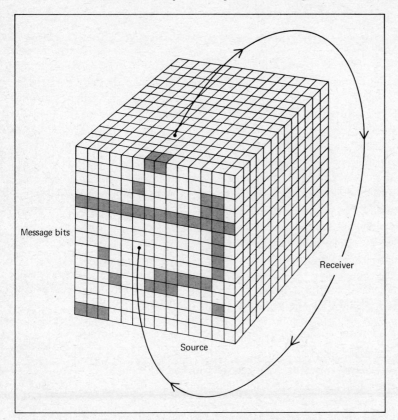

Figure 2.6 *A mosaic model of communication. (Reprinted with permission from Becker, 1968.)*

to conceive of an interaction between *two* mosaics. One comprises the information in a given social milieu, as depicted in the model; the other includes the private mosaic of information that is internal to the receiver. The internal mosaic is every bit as complex as the one shown in the model, but a person constructs it for himself. It consists of countless bits of sensory data that are constructed and reconstructed either independently or in connection with information originating in the physical world. Just as we have a vested interest in defining the mosaic of our physical surroundings, so we are committed to actively expanding and protecting our subjective and private world of thought. In both spheres of experience, we determine which message bits are relevant and which items give the greatest sense of order and continuity to a sequence of otherwise unrelated events. Admittedly, the idea of a dynamic interplay between two mosaics complicates the picture, but it more accurately represents the state of interpersonal conduct.

IN SEARCH OF FUNCTIONAL MODELS

One risk of regarding communication in abstract and idealized terms is that we somehow come to think of it as a singular or "pure" process, a "thing" devoid of particular context and background. Though much is to be gained by scrupulous use of abstractions, we must always relate the tools of the abstracting process—symbols, arrows, cubes, and the like—to particular types of social situations and to concrete classes of behavior. Face-to-face interaction does not occur in a social vacuum. It evolves between particular strangers, lovers, business competitors, students, faculty. The setting is always concrete: a threatening, dimly lit street; an intimate setting in a favorite café; the sweeping space in an office building; or a stuffy lecture hall. Furthermore, a communicative act functions always in the particular and the concrete.

A number of models underscore various functional aspects of communication. One of the earliest was designed by Ruesch and Bateson (1951), whose approach was to view communication from outside the context in which it functioned (Figure 2.7). They conceived of communication as functioning simultaneously at four levels of analysis. One is the basic *intrapersonal* process (level 1). The next (level 2) is *interpersonal* and focuses on the overlapping fields of experience of two interactants. *Group* interaction (level 3) comprises many people. And finally a *cultural* level (level 4) links large groups of people. Moreover, each level of activity consists of four communicative functions: *evaluating, sending, receiving,* and *channeling.* Notice how the model focuses less on the structural attributes of communication—source, message, receiver, etc.—and more upon the actual determinants of the process. A similar concern with communicative functions can be traced through the models of Carroll (1955), Fearing (1953), Mysak (1970), Osgood (1954), and Peterson (1958). Peterson's model is one of the few to integrate the physiological and psychological functions at work in all interpersonal events.

A Transactional Model

By far the most systematic of the functional models is the transactional approach taken by Barnlund (1970, pp. 83–102), one of the few investigators

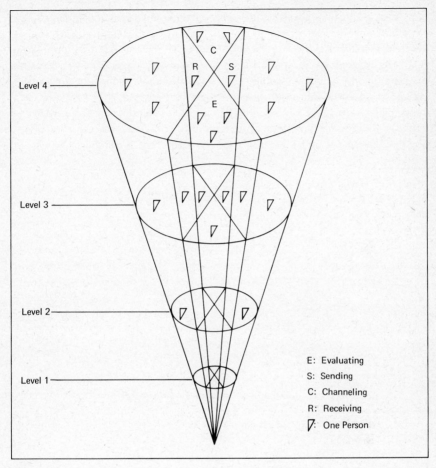

Figure 2.7 *The functional model of communication advanced by Ruesch and Bateson. (Reprinted with permission from Ruesch and Bateson, 1951.)*

who made explicit the key assumptions on which his model was based. Briefly, the assumptions posit a view of communication as *transactions in which communicators attribute meaning to events in ways that are dynamic, continuous, circular, unrepeatable, irreversible, and complex.* Barnlund translated the assumptions into diagrammatic form in two pilot models. The first deals with communication as it occurs at an intrapersonal level (Figure 2.8). Its most striking feature is the absence of any simple or linear directionality in the interplay between self and the physical world. The spiral lines connect the functions of encoding and decoding and give graphic representation to the continuous, unrepeatable, and irreversible assumptions mentioned earlier. Moreover, the directionality of the arrows seems deliberately to suggest that meaning is actively assigned or attributed rather than simply passively received.

Any one of three signs or cues may elicit a sense of meaning. Public cues (C_{pu}) derive from the environment. They are either *natural,* that is, part of the physical world, or *artificial* and man-made. Private objects of orientation (C_{pr}) are a second set of cues. They go beyond public inspection or awareness. Examples include the cues gained from sunglasses, earphones, or the sensory cues of taste and touch. Both public and private cues may be verbal or nonverbal in nature. What is critical is that they are outside the direct and deliberate control of the interactants. The third set of cues are deliberate; they are the behavioral and nonverbal ($C_{beh_{nv}}$) cues that a person initiates and

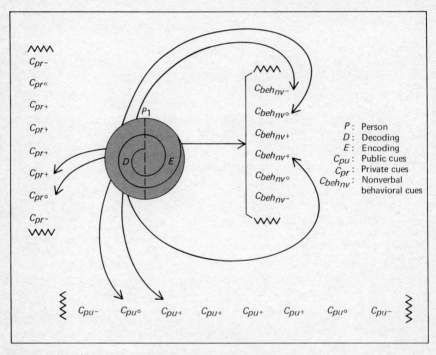

Figure 2.8 *A pilot model of intrapersonal communication. (Reprinted with permission from Barnlund, 1970.)*

controls himself. Again, the process involving deliberate message cues is reciprocal. Thus, the arrows connecting behavioral cues stand both for the act of producing them—technically a form of encoding—and for the interpretation that is given to an act of others (decoding). The jagged lines (〰〰) at each end of these sets of cues illustrate the fact that the number of available cues is probably without limit. Note also the valence signs (+, 0, or −) that have been attached to public, private, and behavioral cues. They indicate the potency or degree of attractiveness associated with the cues. Presumably, each cue can differ in degree of strength as well as in kind. The recognition of differing strength of cues has far-reaching significance for topics discussed in subsequent chapters, particularly the discussion of perception (Chapter 3), the importance of personal involvement (Chapter 4), and the effects of feedback (Chapter 7).

To illustrate how the three sets of cues influence the communication process, Barnlund described an incident concerning a patient waiting in his doctor's office:

> At the moment he is faintly aware of an antiseptic odor in the room, which reinforces his confidence in the doctor's ability to diagnose his illness ($C_{pu}+$). As he glances through a magazine ($C_{pr}0$) he is conscious of how comfortable his chair feels after a long day on his feet ($C_{pr}+$). Looking up, he glances at the Miro reproduction on the wall, but is unable to decipher it ($C_{pu}0$). He decides to call the nurse. As he rises he clumsily drops his magazine ($C_{beh_{nv}}-$) and stoops to pick it up, crosses the room ($C_{beh_{nv}}0$), and rings the call bell firmly and with dignity ($C_{beh_{nv}}+$) [p. 98].

Barnlund's second pilot model (Figure 2.9) focuses on dynamics underlying interpersonal levels of communication. Before any verbal interchange takes place between respective parties, a certain shift occurs in the interactants' psychological frame of reference. What each experiences is a heightened self-consciousness and a need to bring personal actions under closer surveillance and control. The acute sensitivity to personal actions corresponds with further changes in each person's perceptual field. The changes result in greater consciousness of those public cues that are available for visual inspection by others. At some time before anything is said, the actions of each person become sufficiently recognizable to constitute a message (M). At this point the sequence of events can be best followed by returning to the incident between the patient and the doctor:

> Dr. B, crossing the room, may initiate the conversation. Extending his hand, he says, "Mr. A! So glad to see you. How are you?" At this point, despite the seeming simplicity of the setting and prosaic content of the message, Mr. A must solve a riddle in meaning of considerable complexity. In a nonclinical environment where the public cues would be different, perhaps on a street corner (C_{pu}), Mr. A would regard this message (C_{beh_v}) as no more than a social gesture, and he would respond in kind. This, on the other hand, is a clinic (C_{pu}). Is this remark, therefore, to be given the usual interpretation? Even here, the nonverbal cues ($C_{beh_{nv}}$) of Dr. B, the friendly facial expression and extended hand, may reinforce its usual meaning in spite of the special setting. On the other hand, those words (C_{beh_v}) may be interpreted only as showing the sympathetic interest of

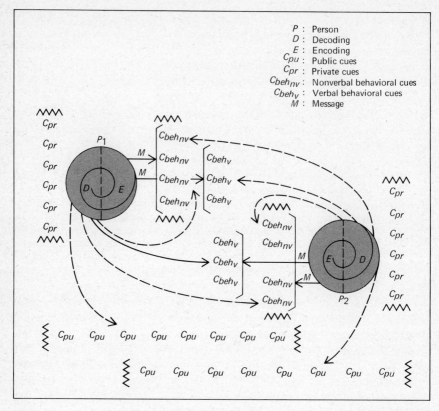

Figure 2.9 *A transactional model of interpersonal communication. (Reprinted with permission from Barnlund, 1970.)*

> Dr. B in Mr. A. In this case, the message requires no answer at all but is a signal for Mr. A to come into the office. In spite of the clinical setting (C_{pu}) and the gracious gesture ($C_{beh_{nv}}$), however, the last phrase (C_{beh_v}), because of a momentary hesitation just before it ($C_{beh_{nv}}$), might be an invitation for Mr. A to begin an account of his symptoms. In deciphering the meaning, Mr. A will have to assign and reassign valences so that a coherent interpretation emerges [p. 100].

During the same moments when Mr. A makes a decision about how to respond, Dr. B is going through a similar process. The incident continues:

> Dr. B is involved in weaving some interpretations of his own out of the cues he detects and the valences he assigns to them. Mr. A smiles back and says, "Nice to see you again, too. I wish the circumstances were different." At this moment Dr. B turns his attention from the carpet which needs repairing

(C_{pu}) to Mr. A. How should he interpret this message? Since they are in a clinic (C_{pu}) it is not surprising that Mr. A should speak of the "circumstances" of his visit. Yet, could this be a warning that the visit concerns a serious medical problem rather than a trivial one? Mr. A's relaxed posture $(C_{beh_{nv}})$ does not reinforce the former meaning, but his flushed face does $(C_{beh_{nv}})$. Or could this remark be no more than a semi-humorous reference to a past episode on the golf links (C_{pr})? In any case, Dr. B, like Mr. A, must reduce the ambiguity in the situation by experimentally assigning meanings to public, private, nonverbal and verbal cues, relating them to the surrounding conditions of time and place, and determining the extent of congruence or incongruence in the meanings given in them [pp. 100–101].

The incident is a microcosm of larger forces at work in any communicative situation. The transactional model is one of the best descriptive analogues of communication. It is distinguished by the number of factors it incorporates into a single schema, the number of levels of analysis it posits, and the avoidance of pitfalls common to other models.

Moreover, with one exception the model corresponds with the assumptions upon which it is based. The exception is the assumption that communication describes the evolution of meaning. In effect, the model presupposes that the terms *communication* and *meaning* are synonymous and interchangeable. Yet nowhere does the model deal in even a rudimentary way with the difficult problem of meaning. The inclusion of decoding and encoding may be taken as only a rough approximation of the "evolution of meaning," but such dualistic categories are not particularly useful in explaining the contingencies of meaning. About all that can be maintained is that communication —as the evolution of meaning—is a state that "begins at birth or before and continues without interruption until death." Hence, by making communication synonymous with the evolution of meaning, one of the two key terms becomes superfluous. If communication can be reduced to the evolution of meaning, then the proper pilot model would not bypass the problem of meaning but rather would deal with it explicitly as a preliminary to a model that would depict how meaning *functions* in communicative situations. The point is not to discount the enormous significance of the concept of meaning but rather to show a lack of correspondence between a model and its most fundamental assumption. Incidentally, much confusion can be eliminated by regarding meaning as a *necessary* but not *sufficient* condition for behavior to be communicative. If meaning is regarded as a sufficient condition for communication, its very constancy makes communication synonymous with human existence and thereby empties the concept of communication of any particular scientific value. In short, then, the alternative is to view communicative behavior as a social event that entails a particular type of meaning, namely that which evolves between interactants and the message cues they create and interpret.

IN SEARCH OF A SYSTEMS MODEL

It is necessary to take liberties with the concept of a model to deal with communication as part of a social system. In a broad sense a systems orientation is not a theory or model but rather a general orientation that seeks to understand man as an integrated whole rather than as a product of isolated components or a conglomeration of isolated functions. The systems orientation is also a reaction against attempts to view man in a fractional or simple additive way, that is, as psychological man, physiological man, social man. Concern is with the general, the aggregate, the organized backdrop in which events occur. The key assumption is that every part of the system is so related to every other part that any change in one aspect results in dynamic changes in all other parts of the total system (Hall and Fagen, 1956). It is necessary, then, to think of communication not so much as individuals functioning under their own autonomous power but rather as persons interacting through messages. Hence, the minimum unit of measurement is that which ties the respective parties and their surroundings into a coherent and indivisible whole.

Another corollary is the idea of an *open system*. A system is open if some exchange of matter, energy, or information takes place between the organism and the environment. The important point, however, is that the exchange or flow process occurs without disrupting what the organism experiences as coherence. In other words, the organism interacts with and is influenced by the environment but not in ways which destroy self-identity or psychological stability. On the other hand, a closed system is self-contained and uninfluenced by the environment; no energy or information penetrates from the outside. Examples of closed systems include the chemical reaction of sealed, insulated containers and the ticking of hand-wound clocks. In essence, then, the idea of communication as an open system denies the possibility that man can act in an automatic and self-contained manner, cut off from the constraints of his surroundings.

The ideas of general systems theory may seem rather abstract, but they nonetheless have far-reaching and specific implications for understanding the dynamics of interpersonal communication. Some of the most insightful were suggested in the form of axioms by Watzlawick and his associates (1967). The most innovative are described below.

The Impossibility of Not Communicating

Interpersonal behavior has no opposites. It is not possible to conceive of nonbehavior. If all behavior in an interactional situation can be taken as having potential message value, it follows that no matter what is said and done, "one cannot not communicate." Silence and inactivity are no exceptions. Even when one person tries to ignore the overtures of another, he nonetheless communicates a disinclination to talk. Ordinarily, when a person looks straight ahead or buries his head in a newspaper, there is no difficulty in "getting the message" that he wants only to be left alone. Nor is unintentional activity an exception. Most of what we communicate at a nonverbal level is accomplished with only minimal awareness and often with no conscious or intentional effort. Even the most calculating efforts of self-concealment and denial have potential significance. The fact that the cues are accidental or unintentionally given off only enhances their perceived importance.

The notion that "one cannot not communicate" requires only a single condition: that the behavior is actually interpreted or decoded by the other person. Two people can, after all, interact in marginal ways and still not communicate. When another person and you pass through a revolving door without actually recognizing each other's actions, you are interacting in the sense that your behavior is dependent on his—yet no assigned meaning takes place. The axiom that one cannot not communicate still holds, however, for any interactive situation where there is some *minimal interpretation* given to the behavior of the respective parties. This does not require that mutual interpretation or shared understanding occur. As we will discover, only in the rarest of social situations does the intended message approximate the assigned message.

Content and Relationship in Communication

All face-to-face encounters require some sort of personal recognition and commitment which in turn create and define the relationship between the respective parties. "Communication," wrote Watzlawick (1967), "not only conveys information, but . . . at the same time . . . imposes behavior [p. 51]." Any activity that communicates information can be taken as synonymous with the *content* of the message, regardless of whether it is true or false, valid or invalid. The aspect of relationship in communication invariably and automatically imposes on the meaning of content, for in the act of exchanging message content the communicants reveal something of themselves and the nature of their awareness of the other person. Each spoken word, every movement of the body, and all the eye glances furnish a running commentary on how each person sees himself, the other person, and the other person's reactions. From a content standpoint, it makes little difference whether one says "It is important to release the clutch gradually and smoothly" or "Just let the clutch go, it'll ruin the transmission in no time." The difference is in how two statements with approximately equivalent content define entirely different relationships.

The Punctuation of the Sequence of Events

There is a universal human tendency to organize a given interactional sequence and to do so along characteristic and predictable lines. To an outside observer, a given sequence of statements seems to unfold in an uninterrupted ebb and flow. One person notices another. They exchange greetings. One speaks, followed in turn by an interruption, further elaboration, another comment, a moment of silence, another statement, laughter, and so forth. However, the principals punctuate differently both from each other and from an outside observer. Each sees the interchanges from a particular beginning point, one that defines all that follows. The arbitrary way in which each punctuates the sequence of exchange is well illustrated in the following commentary by Bateson and Jackson (1964) on stimulus-response learning experiments:

> The sequence of trials is so punctuated that it is always the experimenter who seems to provide the "stimuli" and the "reinforcements" while the subject provides the "responses." These words are here deliberately put in quotation marks because the role definitions are in fact only created by the willingness of the organisms to accept the system of punctuation. The "reality" of the definition is only of the same order as the reality of a bat on a Rorschach card—a more or less over-determined creation of the perceptive process. The rat who said "I have my experimenter trained. Each time I press the lever he gives me food" was declining to accept the punctuation of the sequence which the experimenter was seeking to impose.
>
> It is still true, however, that in a long sequence of interchange, the organisms concerned—especially if these be people—will in fact punctuate the sequence so that it will appear that one or the other has initiative, dominance, dependence, dependency or the like. That is, they will set up between them patterns of interchange (about which they may or may not be in agreement) and these patterns will in fact be rules of contingency regarding the exchange of reinforcement [pp. 273–274].

Disagreements over punctuation points may cause damage to the definitions each party attaches to the relationship. Watzlawick diagrammed a marriage struggle in which the husband contributed his 50 percent in the form of passive withdrawal, while the wife relied on nagging criticism for her half. The husband always punctuated so that his withdrawal was a natural defense against his wife's nagging. The wife countered by explaining that she was forced into a critical state *because* of his passivity. Each saw the other as acting, rather than vice versa. Their difference in punctuation barely went beyond the pastime of children known as "you started it." The sequence can be represented in the series of contradictory triadic exchanges shown in Figure 2.10. Following what an independent observer would take as an arbitrary beginning point, the husband perceived only triads 2-3-4, 4-5-6, etc., as instances where his behavior (solid arrows) was merely a "response" to his wife's (broken arrows). The

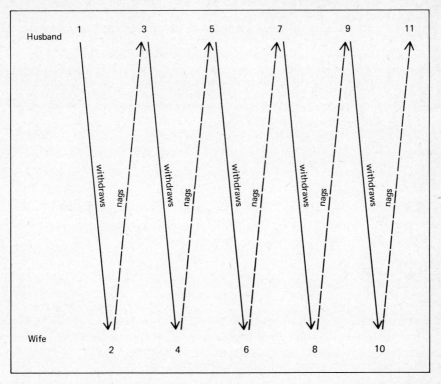

Figure 2.10 *Disagreement over the punctuation of a sequence of interaction. Each party views his own actions as mere responses to the other's provoking actions. (Reprinted with permission from Watzlawick et al., 1967.)*

wife punctuated oppositely; she perceived the exchange as falling into the triadic sequences organized as 1-2-3, 3-4-5, etc., in which she was *forced to react*—not to determine—her husband's behavior. Watzlawick offered the following example from a family counseling situation to illustrate the pattern:

Husband: (to therapist): From long experience I know that if I want peace at home I must not interfere with the way she wants things done.

Wife: That is *not* true—I wish you showed a little more initiative and did decide at least something every once in a while, because. . . .

Husband: (interrupting): You'd never let me do this!

Wife: I'd gladly let you—only if I do, nothing ever happens, and then I have to do everything at the last moment.

Husband: (to therapist): Can you see? Things can't be taken care of if and when they come up—they have to be planned and organized a week ahead.

Wife: (angrily): Give me *one* example in the last few years when you did do something.

Husband:	I guess I can't—because it is better for everybody, including the children, if I let you have your own way. I found this out very early in our marriage.
Wife:	You have never behaved differently, right from the start you didn't—you have always left everything up to me!
Husband:	For heaven's sake, now listen to this (pause, then to therapist)—I guess what she is talking about now is that I would always ask her what *she* wanted—like, "where would you like to go tonight?" or "what would you like to do over the weekend?" and instead of seeing that I wanted to be nice to her, she would get mad at me. . . .
Wife:	(to therapist): Yeah, what he still doesn't understand is that if you get this "anything-you-want-dear-is-all-right-with-me" stuff month after month, you begin to feel that *nothing* you want matters to him . . . [1967, pp. 97–98].

Since the conflict over punctuation is due to purely arbitrary convention, the yes-no-yes-no-yes quality of the exchange can go on ad infinitum. Formally stated, the axiom is: *The nature of a relationship is contingent upon the punctuation of the communicational sequence between the communicants.*

Symmetrical and Complementary Interaction

Relationships are never static. They change over time, either in the direction of maximizing similarities between people or in accentuating individual differences. A symmetrical relationship evolves in the direction of heightening similarities; a complementary relationship hinges increasingly on individual differences. The word *symmetrical* suggests a relationship in which the respective parties mirror the behavior of the other. Whatever one does, the other tends to respond in kind. Thus, an initial act of trust fosters a trusting response; suspicion elicits suspicion; warmth and congeniality encourage more of the same, and so on. In sharp contrast is a complementary relationship, where individual differences complement or dovetail into a sequence of change. Whether the complementary actions are good or bad, productive or injurious, is not relevant to the concept. Though the actions of each party are dissimilar from the other, they nonetheless complement or fit into an interlocking relationship where the uniqueness of one facilitates the natural inclinations of the other. For example, one person may prefer to hear himself talk, while the other is more inclined to listen. One may gravitate to a position of dominance, the other to one of submission. Such a relationship is complementary not because one tolerates the actions of the other, but rather because each behaves in a manner which presupposes and underscores the behavior of the other. In short, each definition of the relationship fits together in a complementary way. Note the marked differences in the tenor of these two excerpts taken from a structured family interview. (In the transcripts, the following abbreviations are used: H = husband; W = wife; Int = interviewer.)

Transcript	Comments by Watzlawick
Int: How, of all the millions of people in the world, did the two of you get together?	
H: We . . . both worked in the same place. My wife ran a comptometer, and I repaired comptometers, and . . .	H speaks first, offering a unilateral summary of the whole story, thereby defining his right to do so.
W: We worked in the same building.	W restates the same information in her own words, *not* simply agreeing with him, but instead establishing symmetry in regard to their discussion of this topic.
H: She worked for a firm which had a large installation, and I worked there most of the time because it was a large installation. And so this is where we met.	H adds no new information, but simply rephrases the same tautological sentence with which he began. Thus, he symmetrically matches her behavior of insisting on his right to give this information; on the relationship level they are sparring for the "last word." H attempts to achieve this by the finality of his second sentence.
W: We were introduced by some of the other girls up there. (Pause)	W does not let it drop; she modifies his statement, reasserting her right to participate equally in this discussion. Though this new twist is just as passive an interpretation as their "working in the same building" (in that neither is defined as having taken initiative), she establishes herself as "a little more equal" by referring to "the other girls," a group in which she was obviously the insider, not H. This pause ends the first cycle of symmetrical exchange with no closure.
H: Actually, we met at a party, I mean we first started going together at a party that one of the employees had. But we'd seen each other before, at work.	Though somewhat softened and compromising, this is a restatement which does not let her definition stand.
W: We never met till that night. (Slight laugh) (Pause)	This is a direct negation, not merely a rephrasing, of his statement, indicating perhaps that the dispute is beginning to escalate. (Notice however that "met" is quite an ambiguous term in this context—it could mean several things from "laid eyes

on each other" to "were formally introduced"—so that her contradiction of him is disqualified; that is, she could not, if queried, be pinned down to it. Her laugh also enables her to "say something without really saying it.")

H: (very softly): Mhm.

    (Long pause)

H puts himself one-down by agreeing with her—overtly; but "mhm" has a variety of possible meanings and is here uttered almost inaudibly, without any conviction or emphasis, so the result is quite vague. Even more, the previous statement is so vague that it is not clear what an agreement with it might mean. In any case, he does not go further, nor does he assert still another version of his own. So they reach the end of another round, again marked by a pause which seems to signal that they have reached the danger point (of open contradiction and conflict) and are prepared to end the discussion even without closure of the content aspect.

Int: But still, I have an image of dozens of people, or maybe more floating around; so how was it that the two of you, of all these people, got together?

Interviewer intervenes to keep the discussion going.

H: She was one of the prettier ones up there. (Slight laugh)

    (Pause)

W: (faster): I don't know, the main reason I started going with him is because the girls—he had talked to some of the other girls before he talked to me, and told them he was interested in me, and they more or less planned this party, and that's where we met.

H makes a strong "one-up" move; this dubious compliment places her in comparison with the others, with him as the judge.

She matches his condescension with her own version: she was only interested in him because he was initially interested in her. (The subject around which their symmetry is defined has shifted from whose version of their meeting will be told and allowed to stand to who got the trophy, so to speak, in their courtship.)

H: Actually, the party wasn't planned for that purpose—

A straightforward rejection of her definition.

W:	(interrupting): No, but it was planned for us to meet at the party. Meet formally, you might say. In person. (Slight laugh). We'd worked together, but I didn't make a habit of . . . well, I was around sixty women there, and ten or twelve men, and I didn't make it a habit of—	After agreeing with his correction, W repeats what she has just said. Her nonpersonal formulation has been weakened, and she now relies on a straight self-definition ("I am this kind of person . . ."), an unassailable way to establish equality.
H:	(overlapping): She was certainly backward—bashful type of worker as far as associating with uh, uh strange men on the place, yeah but the women knew it. (Pause) And I was flirtin' with lots of 'em up there (slight laugh). Nothing meant by it I guess, but just . . . (sigh) just my nature I guess.	H gives a symmetrical answer based on *his* "nature," and another round ends [pp. 111–113].

In analying the two excerpts, Watzlawick observed that content fades in relative importance as relationships evolve over time. Inevitably, the relational aspects assume critical importance. Each party gradually acquires a feeling for the rules and tactics required to maintain stability in their relationship over time. When the rules of a symmetrical or complementary encounter are broken, or suddenly changed, the situation is apt to become increasingly uneven or oscillating. In complementary relationships the risk is one of inflexibility, and in symmetrical relations the inattention to prevailing rules leads to an escalating process where the moves toward one-upsmanship soon get out of hand. A fascinating example of escalation occurs in Watzlawick's insightful analysis of the exchange between George and Martha in Edward Albee's play *Who's Afraid of Virginia Woolf?* Watzlawick begins with the following comments (1967, pp. 161–163):

> This struggle is established at the very beginning when George and Martha run through several quick symmetrical escalations, almost as if practicing, "merely . . . exercising," as George claims [p. 33]. The content is entirely different in each case, but their structure is virtually identical and momentary stability is reached by joint laughter. For instance, at one point Martha tells her husband, "You make me puke!" George considers this with facetious detachment:

> That wasn't a very nice thing to say, Martha.

> Martha: That wasn't *what*?
> George: . . . a very nice thing to say [p. 13].

> Martha persists less elegantly:

> I like your anger. I think that's what I like about you most . . . your anger. You're such a . . . such a simp! You don't even have the . . . the what? . . .

George:	. . . guts? . . .
Martha:	Phrasemaker! (Pause) [pp. 13–14]

Then they both laugh—at their teamwork, perhaps—and closure has been reached. Laughter seems to signal acceptance and so has a homeostatic, stabilizing effect. But it is by now apparent how pervasive is their symmetry, for even the slightest directive by one precipitates further struggle, with the other immediately retaliating in such a way as to define his equality. Thus Martha tells George to put more ice in her drink, and George, while complying, likens her to a cocker spaniel always chewing ice cubes with her "big teeth," and they are off again:

Martha:	THEY'RE MY BIG TEETH!
George:	Some of them . . . some of them.
Martha:	I've got more teeth than you've got.
George:	Two more.
Martha:	Well, two more's a lot more [p. 14].

And George, quickly switching to a known vulnerability:

I suppose it is. I suppose it's pretty remarkable . . . considering how old you are.

Martha:	YOU CUT THAT OUT! (Pause) You're not so young yourself.
George:	(With boyish pleasure . . . a chant): I'm six years younger than you are. . . . I always have been and I always will be.
Martha:	(Glumly): Well . . . you're going bald.
George:	So are you. (Pause . . . they both laugh) Hello, honey.
Martha:	Hello. C'mon over here and give your Mommy a big sloppy kiss [pp. 14–15].

And another escalation starts. George sarcastically refuses to kiss her:

Well, dear, if I kissed you I'd get all excited . . . I'd get beside myself, and I'd take you, by force, right here on the living room rug. . . .

Martha:	You pig!
George:	(Haughtily): Oink! Oink!
Martha:	Ha, ha, ha HA! Make me another drink . . . lover [pp. 15–16].

The subject now switches to her drinking, the escalation becomes bitter and leads into a power struggle over who is to open the door for the guests who have meanwhile arrived and keep ringing the bell.

Note here that just as neither will take an initiative or command from the other, so neither does anything *but* command or control. Martha does not say, "You can give me some more ice," much less "May I please have . . . ?" but "Hey, put some more ice in my drink, will you?" [p. 14]; similarly she orders him to kiss her and to open the door. Nor is she simply rude and ill-mannered, for not to act so is to put herself at a considerable disadvantage, as George shows later in the play with a well-executed maneuver before their guests, after Martha has openly ridiculed him:

George:	(With a great effort controls himself . . . then, as if she had said nothing more than "George, dear." . . .): Yes, Martha? Can I get you something?

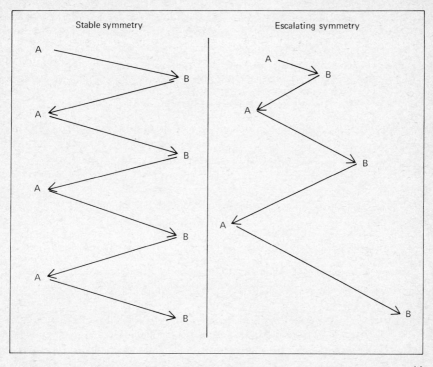

Figure 2.11 *Two symmetrical relationships. The relationship on the left remains stable over time, while that on the right escalates.*

Martha: (Amused at his game): Well . . . uh . . . sure, you can light my cigarette, if you're of a mind to.

George: (Considers, then moves off): No . . . there are limits, I mean, man can put up with only so much without he descends a rung or two on the old evolutionary ladder . . . (Now a quick aside to Nick) . . . which is up your line . . . (Then back to Martha) . . . sinks, Martha, and it's a funny ladder . . . you can't reverse yourself . . . start back up once you're descending. (Martha blows him an arrogant kiss.) Now . . . I'll hold your hand when it's dark and you're afraid of the bogey man, and I'll tote your gin bottles out after midnight, so no one'll see . . . but I will not light your cigarette. And that, as they say, is that. (Brief silence)

Martha: (Under her breath): Jesus! [pp. 50–1]

The dialog between Martha and George illustrates how easily the back-and-forth, tic-for-tac nature of a symmetrical relationship can escalate and get out of hand. The difference can be visualized along lines suggested in Figure 2.11. A stable, symmetrical relationship depends on the willingness of each party to respond in line with the moves of the other person. The situation remains stable only insofar as each person is content to mirror the behavior of the other person. Should one of the participants go beyond the evolving rules of their relationship, the other is also apt to overrespond. Soon the succession of overreactions becomes so severe that it disrupts the stability necessary for the maintenance of a symmetrical relationship.

The insights of general systems theory underscore the advances of some two decades of interest in designing models of communication. Several warrant mention. Most striking is the movement from static classification systems to forms of representation that more fully account for the exceedingly complex makeup of communication. In retrospect, the assumptions associated with linear ($\longrightarrow$) and simple two-way ($\rightleftharpoons$) exchange appear most naïve when compared with multidimensional forms of abstraction. Also, the early preoccupation with structural aspects of communication—source, message, channel, and receiver—is now eclipsed by the concern with communicative *functions* and the search for constituent processes. Note also the fundamental shift away from purely psychological and individual units of behavior to more dynamic properties of persons acting in interdependence with others. The concepts of feedback, punctuation, mosaic, reciprocity, escalation, complementary exchange, and multiple-message sets all reflect a subtle but significant shift in general theoretical orientation. Needless to say, the most sophisticated of models still manifests all the limitations and gaps in knowledge of the subject it models only in embryonic form. Therefore, it is best to think of models as aids in perspective on territory still largely uncharted. Yet uncharted territory is exactly the situation where an interest in map making is the most necessary and potentially rewarding of preliminary activities.

SUGGESTED READINGS

Barnlund, D. C. *Interpersonal Communication: Survey and Studies.* Boston: Houghton Mifflin, 1968.

Chapanis, A. "Men, Machines, and Models," *American Psychologist,* 16:113–131, 1961.

Deutsch, K. "On Communication Models in the Social Sciences," *Public Opinion Quarterly,* 16:356–380, 1952.

Gerbner, G. "Toward a General Model of Communication," *Audio-Visual Communication Review,* 4:171–199, 1956.

Kaplan, A. *The Conduct of Inquiry: Methodology for Behavioral Science.* San Francisco: Chandler, 1964.

Lackman, R. "The Model in Theory Construction," *Psychological Review*, 67:113–129, 1960.

Sereno, K. K., and **Mortensen, C. D.** *Foundations of Communication Theory.* New York: Harper & Row, 1970.

Watzlawick, P., Beavin, J., and **Jackson, D.** *Pragmatics of Human Communication.* New York: Norton, 1967.

two

---

the

intra-

personal

system

three
human
information
processing

Man is adrift in a sea of energy, a torrent of activity that constantly fashions his every habit and thought. The bombardment of the senses by what Meerloo (1967) called the "tiny seductions, the microconditionings" and "noxious pin-pricks" of daily experience surely contradicts any view we may have of man as a self-contained, autonomous entity operating within a well-boundaried self. He is rather to be viewed as the center of an uninterrupted flood of physical and social influences. The impingement of energy on the senses is, like the air we breathe, an atmosphere so pervasive that few are aware of its constancy or effects. From the most exhilarating human experience to the most listless, the brain continues its life-sustaining work; through periods of reflection to moments of deepest sleep, the nervous system strives to fulfill the conditions necessary for man to make sense of his unfolding experience.

The problem of how man translates raw sensory data into meaningful experience is the concern of *information processing*. Originating in the study of cybernetics, the concept of information processing tries to explain human behavior by drawing parallels with electronic processing machines. From the standpoint of communication, the proposition that "the brain is a machine" stirs heated controversy among scientists and philosophers alike. Many in the humanities consider "values," "sentiments," "conscience," "feelings," and "creativity" to be sanctuaries of human experience that are beyond comparison with electrical apparatus. Competent social scientists also insist that the brain is not electric, not wholly digital, and therefore not really a machine at all. But much of this controversy stems from the way the "brain-machine" issue is typically stated. Obviously the brain is not a machine. Nor does the activity of the brain—even a part of it—parallel the operations of *any* machine. What must be recognized is that not all activity inside the head need be interpreted in mechanistic terms to draw fruitful parallels between essential functions. So the question in practical terms is whether the construction and activity of the nervous system is sufficiently close to man-made operations so that knowledge of one is pertinent to an understanding of the other. Of further relevance is the potential *usefulness* of the processing approach to forms of human activity whose complexity exceeds the power of any single explanatory system. Despite the enormous limitations attendant to the study of the human organism as a processing system, one thing seems certain: The older mind/body dualism has steadily given ground to mounting evidence that the established natural laws apply to regularities underlying human as well as mechanical activity, particularly to those of the nervous system. As a result, the efforts of allied fields versed in cybernetic techniques are exploring new vistas in the realm of man's inner thought world.

The aim of information processing is to provide a consistent perspective in tracing what happens when raw sensory data are translated into conscious experience. This is the key assumption: The human organism is an integrated system of complex and interdependent functions designed to interpret events in ways that are consistent with its past experience and existing physical and psychological state. Note that the assumption does not advance hard-and-fast rules for determining the correspondence between events and their interpretation. In attempting to specify the range of correspondence between physical events and interpreted events, we must avoid two extremes. In asking. "Why do things appear as they do?" one extreme—known as naive realism—answers, "Because they are what they are." The opposite view, subjective realism, answers, "Because we see them that way." Both extremes are equally faulty. Naive realism assumes a uniform and exacting correspondence between appearance and reality, and subjective realism dismisses the problem as a private invention of each individual nervous system. The accumulative evidence indicates that any explanation of why communicative events appear as they do must account for an interaction between what physical events are and what human beings are. The approach of information processing assumes that a communicative act results from nothing less than a complex transaction between forces residing inside and outside the nervous system of respective parties. The transaction can no more be reduced to a concept of purely private experience than it can be to paradigms that reduce man to the level of passive respondent to external forces.

Man reacts, to be sure; but in so doing, he invariably creates. And in the act of creating or attributing meaning, all human transactions—however simple or automatic in appearance—far outstrip the complexity and the type of activity that characterizes man-made machines. Even the most complex computers have a fixed number of ways to process information. No present computer, however elaborate, can adjust to an infinite number of changes in its external environment unless modified by a programmer. A computer can correct itself, of course, but only in ways that follow basic rules or logic that can be determined beforehand. This is not to deny the staggering accomplishments of the computer age. We think of the talk concerning the possible installation of huge memory banks in Washington, programmed to carry a complete personal file on every citizen. Moreover, with moon shots and global satellite systems now a reality, many wonder about the feasibility of designing future machines patterned after the computer HAL in the space fantasy *2001*. HAL speaks, sings, makes decisions, and responds in ways that bear striking resemblance to the actions of his designers. Is HAL a possibility? If so, when? Many wonder openly. Others find the question too conjectural or merely amusing.

In any case, whether one is prone to see the gap between man and machine diminishing or growing, one thing is clear. Much can be gained by exploring the man-machine parallel insofar as we keep in mind the limitations and risks inherent in studying images and models generally (see pp. 32–34). By remaining sensitive to these risks, we are in a better position to press the man-machine parallel to the limits and then to go beyond it where it seems useful to do so. Remember also that we need not be trapped by the notion either that man is necessarily demeaned by the act of drawing mechanistic comparisons or, on the other hand, that to be consistent we are obligated to define the nervous system as nothing more than a complex of wires and integrated circuits. Eventually, we should understand more clearly how man differs from what he has designed. Particularly important is the need to recognize man's incredible capacity to interpret information in an infinite number of ways. Man is like the computer in that he has a self-imposed logic, but his is one that is dynamic, not static or predetermined. Moreover, rules of human thought are unique in that they change in the very act of using them. And further unlike mechanistic activity, man not only reacts to his environment, he also acts upon it; or more precisely, he *interacts* with it in unique ways which we will discuss in greater detail in Chapter 4.

Theoretically, human information processing includes the transfer of sensory data into any psychological state that affects some change in uncertainty. Since the potential sources of perceived change in uncertainty include virtually all variations in the physical world and all changes in one's physiological or psychological state, the range of possibilities is unlimited. Thus, both the nature of the rules and the range of signals represent a level of complexity that is magnitudes beyond our most sophisticated machinery.

A THEORY OF HUMAN INFORMATION PROCESSING

Most characteristic of man—and separating him from machines— is his tremendous capacity to *generate* and then to *control* the use of certain rules or strategies in handling information. The existence of these rules and strategies is necessary to explain the complexity, flexibility, and uniqueness of each individual. Therefore, in accounting for the distinctive aspects of human experience, it is as important to know about the impact of the rules and strategies of information processing as it is to pinpoint exactly what happens to a signal once it is in transit within the nervous system. To ignore these rule-centered considerations would be like trying to study the behavior of two football teams without the slightest acquaintance with the rules of their game. Moreover, an understanding of the interplay of processing strategies is necessary to account for the obvious but critical fact that humans process information in quite dissimilar ways and at different levels of thought. Often, similar events evoke quite dissimilar types of information processing. Take, for example, the simple act of going through a revolving door. Most of us do this quite automatically, attending only minimally to the sign on the door while passing through. In one instance a person reacts to the word *push* on the door as he begins his maneuver. In an otherwise identical situation, the same person encounters another four-letter word—this one an unprintable item— scratched over the original message. What makes these two instances dissimilar is not simply the meanings of two four-letter words, but rather the two distinct types of thinking activity that they trigger in identical contexts.

The question, then, is how best to account for obvious differences in types of thinking activity. One explanation, advanced by Schroder, Driver, and Streufert (1967), begins with the assumption that the level of processing varies widely from person to person and even within the same person in changing circumstances. When attending to a particular message cue, a person may respond at many different levels of thought. He may attack a relatively simple meaning or a composite of meanings; he may see few interrelationships or many. In addition, his response may be immediate or delayed. Hence, what is distinctive about human information processing is not so much the ability to learn or the capacity to handle complex blocks of sensory data as it is the ability to learn and generate different levels of meaning and to recognize possible alternatives in viewing the interrelationships within particular sets of meanings.

Countless aspects of everyday experience attest to man's capacity to attach alternative meanings to the same message cues. Consider a student who drives past a certain stop sign on a fixed route to the university each morning: The man, the event, the message cues, and the circumstance remain highly stable over time, and yet the meaning does not. Even after years of following the identical route, the level of his processing activity may change dramatically. Typically, the student may react at a low level of thought; it is largely uncritical and automatic. On most mornings he may be barely aware of the sign. At times he may not attend to it for even a fraction of a second. Yet one morning, while glancing absentmindedly at the sign, he suddenly becomes aware that the paint is fading and badly chipped. On subsequent mornings he may examine the sign more critically. Later he focuses on the letter S and immediately thinks of a letter he owes his parents 1,000 miles away. On still other mornings the sign may trigger responses that range from a check of his seat belt to the recall of a faint but painful memory of an accident involving failure to halt at another stop sign.

Integration Levels

From a technical standpoint, changing reactions to simple cues such as a stop sign represent what Schroder (et al., 1967) termed differences in the *integration level* of information processing. The concept of integration provides a useful way of referring to the organizational structure and complexity of various thought levels. At the simplest level of integration, a given number of message cues are processed uniformly, in accordance with a single rule or a few organizing principles, as indicated in Figure 3.1. Generally, low-level integration limits the ability of an individual to think in terms of complex inter-relations. The tendency is to avoid complex or alternate meanings. Each cue fits into a particular thought category in an either-or, black-white form of organization, usually with a minimum of conflict involved in the process of decision making. At low levels of information processing, persons ignore dis-

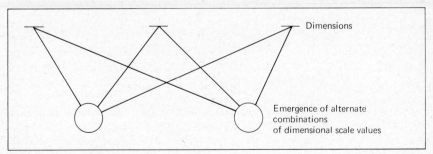

Figure 3.1 *A moderately low integration index. (Reprinted with permission from Schroder et al., 1967.)*

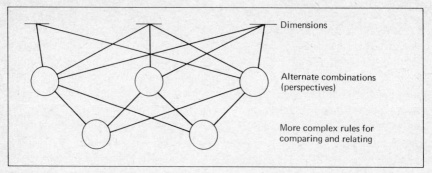

Figure 3.2 *A moderately high integration index. (Reprinted with permission from Schroder et al., 1967.)*

criminations and subtle distinctions in favor of highly personalized, compartmentalized rules of thought. For instance, if a person holds an extremely concrete attitude toward hippies and categorizes them in a simple way, all hippies will be integrated by a single rule of a judgmental nature: "bad," "dirty," "lazy," "immoral" or "good," "happy," "loving," "peaceful."

As information processing moves to higher, more complex levels of integration, important changes take place. Most obvious is the movement away from rigid, either-or patterns of thought. Simple judgments of "good" versus "bad" and "right" versus "wrong" give way to finer discriminations. Ambivalence and noncommitment also become part of decision making. A person is apt to say "I'm not sure" or "I don't know for certain." Moreover, a given situation tends to be perceived in alternate ways, with multiple perspectives and meanings (Figure 3.2). The number of rules and interconnections formed among thought patterns also increases. Higher-level integration permits not only more perspectives but also more ways of employing the rules that guide the transfer of the word to meaningful thought. Good-bad gives ground to degrees of goodness, not only in a general way, but also in larger dimensions of thought. For instance, the "goodness" rule for responding to hippies may be processed on the *dimensions* of social value, social change, health considerations, interpersonal contact, standards of affluence, effects of social protest, and so forth. With higher levels of integration come even greater flexibility and a demand for more information before decisions are made. Once acted upon, judgments remain less fixed, and the system is more open to alternative strategies of processing. By combining various rules of interpretation, an individual develops the ability to "track," or monitor, the environment in more ways than one. The higher the level of integration, the more tracking options are available. For instance, at moderately high levels of integration, a person has the capacity to

> view a social situation in terms of two points of view, see one in relationship to the other, perceive the effects of one upon the other. He is able to generate strategic adjustment processes, in which the effects of behavior

from one standpoint are seen as influencing the situation viewed from another vantage point. This implies, for example, that a person can observe the effects of his own behavior from several points of view; he can simultaneously weigh the effects of taking different views [Schroder et al., 1967, p. 21].

Finally, high integration levels maximize the chance for the use of alternative rules and strategies, and they generally enrich the possibilities for abstract thinking (Figure 3.3).

    The differences in integration levels must not be interpreted as mutually exclusive; rather they are interrelated and functional aspects of human thought. The various rules and strategies are, in one sense, analogous to the planning of a residential building: At the most concrete level of activity are the alternative rules followed by carpenters, electricians, and plumbers in placing window casements, electrical outlets, and water mains. These specific rules, like Schroder's schema, are relatively fixed aspects of the design hierarchy. At a more general level are the rules governing the layout of rooms and zones of the house, which in turn depend on the highest levels of rule and strategy for the very conception of the house. The analogy is also an approximation of alternative ways of discussing the larger interrelationships of house design. Similarly, a person's response to the word *hippie* may deal almost exclusively with factors governing the immediate connotations of the word, or it may require that some larger framework or underlying patterns of thought be understood.

Impact of the Environment

The incredible range of human processing activity cannot be adequately explained apart from the constant interplay between external stimuli and

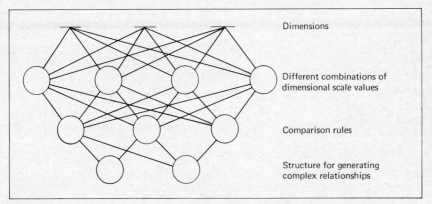

Figure 3.3 *A high integration index. (Reprinted with permission from Schroder et al., 1967.)*

corresponding internal activity of the individual. The impact of external events depends largely on their complexity. Simple environments—those which do not present diverse, ever-changing units of sensory data—stimulate only the lowest levels of processing. Up to a certain optimum level, increased complexity of environment triggers ever-higher levels of mental activity. Beyond the optimum point, the receiver must sharply reduce his intake of data. According to the theory advanced by Schroder and his associates, three factors play a primary role in determining environmental complexity: (1) *information load,* the number of informational units to which a person is exposed; (2) the degree of *diversity* in the information; and (3) the *rate* at which environmental information registers on the sense organs.

Information Load. The nervous system can handle only so much information at a time. Regardless of circumstances, a certain minimal amount of information is necessary to prevent a living organism from lapsing into an inert psychological state. Thereafter, further increases in information load stimulate more complex processing activity until a level is reached where the circuits literally become overloaded. Even single-celled organisms are known to become increasingly active as an electrical shock is increased in rate—but only up to a point where further increases in shock rate lead to a *decreased* rate of reaction (Granit and Phillips, 1956). And when human beings are deprived of complex and varied surroundings for prolonged lengths of time, they tend to become mentally sluggish. For example, people who are removed from any personal contact with the outside world experience marked changes in their psychological make-up. (We will examine some adverse effects associated with social isolation in Chapter 7.) From a processing standpoint, isolated persons shift first to more concrete and inflexible thinking patterns, then show increasing difficulty in making decisions in concert with others (Suedfeld, 1964b). Too much information, on the other hand, creates confused thinking and inefficiency in attempts to exchange information with others (Anderson and Fitts, 1958; Quastler and Wulff, 1967). However, the matters of past experience and expectation greatly complicate the question of information overload. For example, by laboratory standards, a rock concert constitutes a clear case of information overload. Powerful amplifiers keep the level of music well beyond the "safe" range of 80 to 85 decibels. Moreover, the very presence of hundreds of people in closed quarters further magnifies the amount of overtone and competing noise. And to the high audible levels must be added all the competing visual information: strobe lights, backdrop lights, and related gadgetry. All things considered, the information load should be well in excess of what the same people would find comfortable in other social circumstances. Yet through the hours of exposure to the din, most adherents of rock concerts profess to take great satisfaction in the intense bombardment of their senses. Clearly, the amount of information necessary to create psychological overload varies greatly from situation to situation. Conceivably, our electronic age is altering characteristic human responses to certain types of complex physical environments—thereby redefining the significance of information overload. We will return to additional aspects of this complex problem in a later section of this chapter.

Diversity and Rate. The concept of information load deals with the number of incoming signals, but it does not take into account the diversity of sensory data or the rate at which they appear. Again, no hard-and-fast rules apply, either to diversity or to rate. Caution is in order, partly because of growing evidence that people who live in an electronic age increasingly are required to respond to diverse bits of information presented in a rapid-fire manner. Surely, the phenomenon of rock music is a case in point, but others abound in the performing arts. Producers of motion pictures, for example, are experimenting as never before with rapid flash-back techniques, dissolves, and other strategies of film composition. The same applies to television commercials. The trend toward shorter ads stems in part from the viewers' ability to "get the message" in shorter amounts of time. Many viewers even show signs of heightened interest toward those commercials in which scenes flash successively at less than one-second intervals.

In one intriguing study of the effects of diversity and rate on information processing, a group of four subjects is given a complex task in the form of a game: A model of a volcanic island is held by a military enemy about whom no information is given; the group attempts to discover enough about the situation to make moves and decisions which will secure the island. The role of the enemy is played by experimenters who give the group feedback they would receive in an actual test of the operation. Results show that as environmental complexity increases (as measured by the units of information supplied to the group), the more group interaction shifts from simple decisions to high-level, abstract choices—amounting to what was earlier described as the maximum level of integration. Soon, however, as information load surpasses the optimum level for information processing, high-level decisions disintegrate, performance suffers, and the group reverts to more restricted decision making based upon compartmentalized units of information. In practical terms, the group "warms up" to the task of handling an increasingly complex environment, only to find that the very complexity, diversity, and rapid flow of information prevents them from an efficient transfer of their social experience into meaningful thought patterns.

Psychological Factors

The impact of environment is only one part of the theory of information processing advanced by Schroder et al. Another is the role of psychological factors as they mediate the imprint of external cues on the activity of the nervous system.

People differ greatly in the levels at which they characteristically process information. It is true that certain events tend to force all individuals to think at the most abstract, highest levels of integration. Questions dealing with politics and religion, philosophy or the arts, and any matter of personal conviction usually require complex thought processing, whereas the routine choices of daily experience can usually be resolved at a simple, almost automatic level of decision making. Clearly, then, no one operates at any fixed level of information processing. At the same time, however, most people do exhibit characteristic patterns of processing over extended periods of time and circumstance. Some people think in integratively complex ways; others use relatively simple rules and structures for transferring the imprint of events on the critical higher activities of the brain.

In a variation of the tactical game just described, it is possible to compare the information processing of group members who tend to think in abstract terms with those who favor thinking at low integration levels. Those with abstract orientations take in more information, attend to more diverse forms of information, and generate a higher number of new ideas and ways of looking at tasks and problems than do teams composed of more concretely oriented people. The latter process information in relatively simple, compartmentalized ways, preferring to focus on one item at a time and on the most practical concerns of the moment. They interact without any overall strategy for attacking problems, resolving conflict, making decisions, or understanding the task at hand (Streufert et al., 1965). Of further relevance is the finding that abstract thinkers are better able to integrate new information into their attitudinal framework (Janicki, 1964; Streufert, 1969; Streufert and Schroder, 1965).

A Word of Caution. We have discussed integration levels as a way of viewing the larger structure of information processing. Many specific questions remain unanswered. Therefore, in shifting our focus now to specific aspects of the *different stages* of processing activity, we must be prepared to deal with a picture that is not as neat and tidy as the theory just discussed. Remember that we are dealing with units of covert behavior that are not readily available for public inspection. While the internal dynamics of processing can be traced with reasonable confidence, many of the internal workings of the nervous system resist simple explanation. Not surprisingly, then, the burgeoning literature appears at times to be a crowded clearing house for the interests of investigators who bring quite dissimilar assumptions and approaches to their study. For example, the work in perception alone reflects no less than a dozen or more competing theoretical viewpoints. And this holds also for the larger province of information processing generally. Some units of measurement consist solely of exacting physiological data; others fall under the more equivocal labels of "thinking," "cognition," "thought," and so forth. In one sense the disarray and the many gaps in knowledge should not be surprising, particularly with the enormous difficulties entailed in discovering the major determinants of behavior which cannot always be observed directly. The difficulties can be exaggerated all too easily, however; they must be interpreted within the context of rapidly advancing knowledge.

DECODING-ENCODING

As we have seen, information processing involves a set of complex and interrelated physical and psychological functions. These fall into various stages of activity that are known as *decoding* and *encoding*. Decoding includes all the activity required to transfer raw sensory data into what we experience as meaningful information. Correspondingly, encoding includes all activity necessary to transform information into some behavioral response. Decoding and encoding are interdependent rather than separate processes. Occurring simultaneously and continuously, they therefore constitute the major components of the human processing system. It is tempting but misleading to think that one begins where the other leaves off. In actuality, they are so interdependent that it is impossible to specify exactly what is unique to each.

The remainder of this chapter contains a general survey of the decoding-encoding process and explores some of its major determinants. In the main we will examine a chain of events that links the entire nervous system simultaneously and concurrently in four stages: (1) the acquisition of sensory data, (2) the activity of central processing units, (3) information storage, and (4) recall. The acquisition of sensory data centers in the activity of the sense organs as they register and transform incoming signals into a form that the brain can decipher. As the central processing units complete the work of transforming physical energy into interpretable form, the signals are integrated into the higher regions of the brain where they go through the stage of memory, technically known as storage, and finally the stage of recall, where they can be reused—or reconstructed—at a later time. Figure 3.4 depicts the four stages of information processing in relation to the decoding-encoding activity that occurs at the various integration levels discussed earlier.

RECEPTOR UNITS: THE ACQUISITION OF SENSORY DATA

We naturally think of the physical world in terms of objects and classes of events. Chairs, tables, trees, lakes, freeways, and apartments exist "out there in time and space"; consequently, we suppose that what we know of the stuff of our physical surroundings constitutes a mirror image of what really exists. In this commonsense view, the work of the senses is strictly a passive

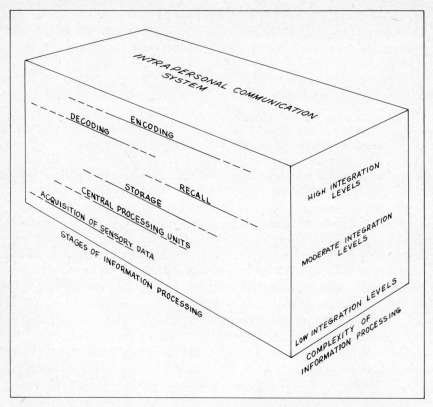

Figure 3.4   *The intrapersonal communication system. This system consists of four interrelated stages of decoding and encoding activity that vary from simple to complex levels of integration. Broken lines indicate the absence of a fixed beginning and end; presumably all dimensions of the system function simultaneously and concurrently.*

and mechanical affair. The eyes function like the zoom lense of a TV camera, the ears like a tape recorder, the skin like the weighing operations of a scale, and the chemical senses like variegated litmus paper. The tendency, then, is to think of our picture of the external world as matching physical reality, or if not an exact matching, at least closely approximating the way "things really are." So viewed, information processing is simply a dispassionate recording of sensory activity for the purpose of further automatic editing, sorting, storing, and recalling of relevant items. In actuality, of course, there is nothing truly automatic about the intricate and finely tuned sequence of activity that links our sensory organs and the critical activity of our brains.

The main energy sources that impinge on our senses are either light waves or sound vibrations. In fact, the eyes and ears are almost entirely responsible for our composite picture of the external world. Olfactory and chemical senses serve mainly to supply overtone and to integrate what is experienced through the eyes and the ears, both of which are capable of making an incredible number of barely noticeable discriminations among light waves and sound vibrations in the environment. For example, the eye can handle 5 million such discriminations per second. In the area of color discrimination alone, it is estimated that the average human being can differentiate 7½ million color shades (Triandis, 1964). Likewise, the ear is enormously sensitive to rapid oscillations of air (Miller, 1951). A person with normal hearing can distinguish about 340,000 separate tones (Stevens and Davis, 1938). If the ear were any more sensitive, it would oscillate simply because of the normal displacement of molecules in the air and would result in a constant case of "ringing" ears.

Despite its enormous capacity, the human receptor system is limited in how much physical energy it can monitor at any point. One clearly documented pair of findings is that we can react to only a small proportion of the environment, and this information is not a random sample of what is objectively available (Berelson and Steiner, 1964). The explanation for the strategic and selective nature of the human receptor system is greatly a result of (1) the nature of arousal thresholds, (2) the capacity of the system, and (3) the effects of stimulus analyzing mechanisms.

Arousal Thresholds

An essential characteristic of the receptor system is its ability to transmit physical energy to the brain by means of an electrical, all-or-nothing principle of nerve conductance. Here the parallel between man and machine is striking indeed, for both human nerve conductance and mechanical processing depend largely on the transfer of current that operates in the manner of a light switch. The key to what Woolridge (1963) called "nature's on/off switch" is the special nerve cells, known as *neurons*. These building blocks of the nervous system operate in a manner well illustrated by studies of the muscular movement of frogs. Consider a situation in which the legs of a frog are artificially stretched to varying amounts of elongation. Electrical equipment measures the current that flows between nerve cells at a point near a main muscle. Starting from a relaxed condition, the muscles are stretched, first the slightest distance, then farther. With minimal amounts of stretching, nothing happens. The electrical apparatus shows no neural activity. Then, at some point of elongation, the attached nerve registers a response to the muscle movement. Thereafter, whenever there is sufficient movement, a pulse of electrical energy flows through the nerve. What is happening is that the receptor units fail to register the change in muscular action until a lower limit, or *arousal threshold*, is reached. After that point, the current rises to a maximum level of activity. In a sequence lasting about one-thousandth second, a pulsating flow of electrical energy passes the point of measurement and continues as long as the stretching is kept above the arousal threshold. No matter how far the muscles are stretched, individual pulses continue. Further pulling of the muscle increases the flow of current but does not alter the nature of the individual pulses; they are identical. The all-or-nothing principle of nerve control in a frog leg is the same for all adjusting organs of man. In the comparison of different sense organs, Woolridge (1963) observed:

> Whether the nerve is one that indicates stretch, touch, chemical composition, warmth, cold, sight, or sound, it transmits its information by means of a train of pulses of electricity, all of approximately the same magnitude and duration, regardless of the intensity of the stimulus, with only the rate of generation of the pulses indicating whether the sensation is trivial or intense [p. 5].

Generally, a great deal more physical energy must register on the receptor organs than what is strictly necessary to reach a minimal arousal threshold, because much energy is lost in the process of acquiring sensory data. The eye, for example, loses about 4 percent of the energy from incidental light waves because of reflections from the cornea. Another 50 percent is lost through scattering and absorption of light that takes place between the outer surface of the cornea and the retina. For that portion of light which remains, another 80 percent fails to be picked up by the receptor cells (cones and rods) at the base of the eye. This means that the original stimulus must be some 90 percent greater than the minimal threshold level to stimulate the receptor cells of the eye (Smith et al., 1967).

Similar evidence of thresholds exists for the other sense organs. In hearing, most people are insensitive to sound vibrations of less than 10 to 15 cycles per second or much above 23,000 cycles per second (Corso, 1963). For the tactile system, the classical work of Woodworth (1938) demonstrated dramatic differences in the energy required to register on the different regions of the skin. As might be expected, the tip of the tongue and fingers have the lowest arousal threshold (approximately 2 to 3 grams per square millimeter). Next in sensitivity is the front of the forearm, then the back of the hand, the calf of the leg, the abdomen, the back of the forearm, the loin, and finally, at 250 grams per square millimeter, the thick parts of the soles.

One additional property of arousal thresholds needs to be mentioned. The fact than an incoming signal registers on the receptor cells does not guarantee that the signal will be transmitted to the brain. For the most part, receptor cells transmit messages along the network of nerve cells at speeds ranging from 2 to 200 miles an hour. At each link in nerve conductance, known as the *synapse*, the impulse pauses for recharging, though never for longer than a thousandth of a second. Little is known about how the recharging occurs, except that the change involves an interaction between sodium ions at one end of the nerve fibers and potassium ions at the other. The recharging of the nerve endings makes it possible for the current to arrive at its destination with as much force as it had when it left the receptor cells. However, certain "inhibitory" nerve fibers may impede the transmission of energy from one neuron to another. At times, then, the signal must be stronger than the arousal threshold to trigger a complete transfer of sensory activity to the higher corticals of the brain.

Channel Capacity

Despite its enormous capacity, the human information processing system can do only a few things at a time and can attend to only a small proportion of the available information. There is a clear and definite limit to the amount of information which the human organism can identify accurately; in recognizing a series of numbers, for example, the span of absolute judgment lies somewhere in the neighborhood of seven items of information (Miller, 1956). For more difficult types of material, there is evidence that man is able to monitor five features simultaneously, but rarely more (Bruner et al., 1962). Generally, even slight increases in the difficulty of material or the rate of presentation can adversely affect the capacity of the receiving system.

Most social situations test our processing capacity by what Cherry (1953) called the "cocktail party" problem. Each guest stands in a crowded room, amidst the din of conversation and background noise. Every voice in the room, each physical movement, every background noise, and all the features of the physical surroundings are available for inspection. The problem: How can each person select one voice for conversation from a host of sounds and still shut out all remaining sounds? Cherry's immediate interest was how a person separates two messages simultaneously. As a test of the problem, he devised a technique called *shadowing*, whereby a subject is asked to repeat word by word a message presented through an earphone while ignoring another message presented through an opposite earphone. Under a variety of circumstances, subjects reported no difficulty in listening to one message while rejecting the other. The same results occurred with two speeches which were mixed together so that the subjects had to "switch" from one ear to another in order to unscramble the relevant message. Cherry found that people were able to track the desired message in the easiest manner when the material was selected from a novel; technical material was more difficult to shadow. Tracking one message became even more difficult with a series of randomly arranged English words and, even harder, with nonsense words. After Cherry had switched speaking voice or language during the middle of the passage, subjects were asked to describe the message they had "ignored."

Results showed that the subjects almost always noticed changes in pure tone and switches from male to female voices, but they did not recognize the language or content from the ignored channel. The problem with the shadowing strategy was that subjects were not asked to report what was heard until after each trial. Since recall requires skill in short-term memory (see p. 115), the subjects may have been aware of the "ignored" message when it was presented, but they rapidly lost their awareness. To test whether people can remember an ignored channel for at least a moment before its trace disappears, Norman (1969b) quickly interrupted those who were shadowing a message; he found evidence for the existence of temporary, but not long-term, recognition of ignored items. Even rapid interruption does not ensure that the message is uncontaminated by the effects of short-term memory. However, despite the possible confounding effects of short-term memory, Cherry's findings are consistent with the larger evidence that people do depend heavily on physical cues when attempting to separate relevant from irrelevant messages. Furthermore, even without physical cues, it is known that subjects can separate items presented from multiple sensory channels when there is a sufficient grammatical context in which to make the discriminations (Hirsh, 1950).

On the basis of shadowing research and related evidence, Broadbent (1958) hypothesized that the capacity of the organism to process information is limited to a single-channel system in which a "selective filter" focuses on one item at a time. Hence, Broadbent views man as reducing the complexity of his environment to manageable proportions by tuning in one desired message and avoiding all others. Broadbent's model defines the system as having limited capacity and using physical cues as the basis for filtering or accepting information from one channel or another. The model explains the "cocktail party" problem by positing that at any given moment the filtering mechanism blocks all undesired inputs except those coming from the one most relevant stream of sensory experience.

Despite its heuristic value in stimulating research, the filter theory leaves unresolved the difficult question of how we are able to turn attention away from a competing channel if we are truly unaware of it. Recent evidence seems to indicate that recognition and rejection of incoming signals is not determined, as Broadbent supposed, by physical cues alone. Generally, the more relevant the incoming item and the more complex the linguistic context, the greater is the probability of recognition—irrespective of any selective filtering (Grey and Wedderburn, 1960; Oswald et al., 1960). In addition, most people seem to switch their attention momentarily from one channel to another, particularly at strategic points, without being aware of what they are doing.

An alternative possibility is that similar processing occurs with both relevant and rejected messages, the difference being that the one channel is amply monitored at a more gross level of attention. Moreover, the receptor units, according to Treisman (1964), perform a hierarchy of tests on sounds entering all channels whether they are attended to or not. The initial tests in the hierarchy distinguish among the flow of incoming signals on the basis of sensory or physical cues; later tests deal with phonetic patterns, word usage, and finally grammatical organization and meaning. In the case of the "cocktail party" problem, sounds such as the clinking of glasses and distant voices can be separated at a very early stage of sensory activity. In other words, on the basis of physical cues alone, some signals—though not completely ignored or filtered—are attended to but are readily downgraded in importance. From the range of competing sounds in an immediate conversation area, further tests of voice quality, grammatical context, and meaning permit detection and separation of relevant and irrelevant signals. As a modification of the early view, all incoming signals are attended to, provided they fall within flexible threshold levels, by a hierarchy or sequence of operations which involves the integration of the entire nervous system, rather than simply by the sorting action of the sensory units themselves.

It appears that the acquisition of sensory data involves selectivity, to be sure, but not in a way which can be accounted for apart from the critical functions of the brain. The framework advanced by Duetsch and Duetsch (1963) and elaborated by Norman (1968) proposes that selectivity occurs at a two-level information processing, as suggested by the schema outlined in Figure 3.5. Accordingly, every incoming signal above arousal threshold passes through an early stage of analysis performed by the sensory system. Then, as Norman (1969a) explained,

> The parameters extracted from these [receptor] processes are used to determine where the representation of the sensory signal is stored. Thus . . . all sensory signals excite their stored representation in memory. Now, at the same time, we assume that an analysis of previous signals is going on. This establishes a class of events deemed to be *pertinent* to the ongoing analysis. The set of pertinent items also excites their representation in memory. The item most highly excited by the combination of sensory and pertinence inputs is selected for further analysis [the shaded item in Figure 3.5]. Given the selected item, the attention process now completes its analysis, adding newly acquired information to what has come before and bringing the pertinence judgments up to date [pp. 33, 35].

Thus, it appears that the acquisition of sensory experience occurs at two levels. The first centers in the sensory system itself; the other occurs in the sorting and grouping action of a central storage system, where selection and attention to signals is modified by expectations, grammatical meaning, and pertinence of incoming signals as determined by past experience. Before we turn to the complex problem of how the incoming signals are actually separated for further processing by the storage system, it will be useful to examine the role of stimulus analyzing mechanisms in the acquisition of information.

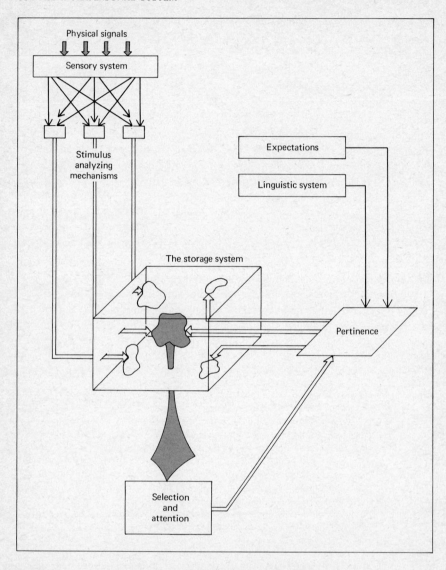

Figure 3.5   *The selection process. Both the physical inputs and the pertinence of information determine what will be selected for further processing. Physical inputs pass through the sensory system and stimulus analyzing mechanisms before exciting their representation in the storage system. Simultaneously, the analysis of previously encountered material, coupled with the history of expectations and the rules of perception, determine the class of events assumed to be most pertinent at the moment. That material which receives the greatest combined excitation is selected for further attention. (Reprinted with permission from Norman, 1968.)*

Stimulus Analyzing Mechanisms

In the incessant effort to transmit data to the brain, the sensory system trans-
forms sensory elements into a form acceptable for further processing. The
transformation of raw sensory data is a peripheral form of data processing, one
exhibiting considerable computerlike sophistication. The first important clue
to the general feature of stimulus analyzing came from two classic studies on
lower animals. At the Massachusetts Institute of Technology researchers
observed the details of processing that occur in the eye of a frog by devising a
technique that tapped the signals sent to the brain by individual nerve fibers in
the frog's optic nerve (Mantuana et al., 1959). The aim was to determine how
visual information was rearranged in the optic nerve before the signal was
transmitted to the brain. A major discovery was that the optic nerve rearranged
the visual signal not into one "picture," but rather into four distinct pictures,
each carried by a layer of fibers. In later interpretations of the findings at M.I.T.,
Woolridge (1963) compared this transformation to the operation of a color
television set, where separate pictures in different color modalities are simultaneously transmitted and then recombined in the receiver to produce a
"single" picture. Unlike the TV receiver, however, the four sets of fibers do a
considerable amount of rearranging of the sensory data before transmitting the
signal to the brain. One set of fibers, for example, seems to accentuate the
detection and maximum response to dark objects. For a hungry frog in search
of flies, this special adaptation is most fortunate: The fibers aid in noticing bugs
at the very distance to which a frog can extend its tongue. Consequently, when a
color photograph of the frog's natural habitat was waved 7 inches from the eye,
the fibers specializing in detection of dark objects failed to respond. When the
same background was held constant and a dark object moved around it, the
detecting fibers in the optic nerve responded rapidly.

Parallel findings demonstrated that a cat also has a set of stimulus
analyzing mechanisms. The cat, it turns out, has cells which are specially
adapted to analyze line segments, visual orientation, and movement (Hubel and
Wiesel, 1959, 1962). The major difference between the cat and the frog is in the
point at which the stimulus analyzing mechanisms operate. In the more intelligent of the two, the cat, the transformation of raw sensory data occurs further
back in the nervous system. What the research on both organisms illustrated
is the remarkable extent to which even the "intelligence" of lower animals
resides outside of the brain (Frishkopf, L. S., and Goldstein, M. H.).

Growing evidence indicates that man—in ways differing mostly in
the complexity of that found in lower animals—also has powerful detectors for
analyzing those stimuli most pertinent to his biological and social needs (Abbs
and Sussman). Without conclusive evidence, there is disagreement about how

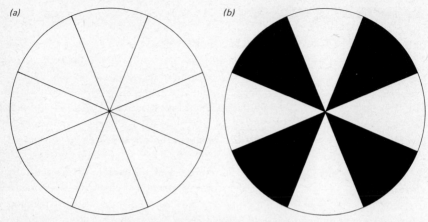

Figure 3.6 *Alternating figure and ground. What is perceived as figure in (a) tends to shift, whereas in (b) it tends to remain constant.*

the analysis takes place; but not in dispute is that the sensory system does rearrange raw sensory data. It is also clear that the analysis of incoming signals does not occur instantaneously, even though it occurs too rapidly for a person to know what is happening. Most people experience great difficulty in identifying objects exposed for 1/10 second or less. In a series of rapid exposures to an object or event, people are first conscious of something "out there," some *figure* or *object* which is distinct from the surrounding *background* or general field of view. A fraction of a second later comes an awareness of matters of outline and contour, then attention to the main internal features of color and intensity, and then further classification of details. No differentiation of an object or figure from its background, or *ground*, is possible in an environment that is homogeneous or undifferentiated.

Generally, the centralized features of an object, or anything vivid or novel, tend to be perceived as the figure in a visual field. Sometimes the figural configuration changes as the eyes sweep across parts of the total field of view. For example, chances are much greater that what is perceived as the figure portion in Figure 3.6a will shift if a person stares long enough, whereas the black cross in Figure 3.6b tends to be invariably maintained as figure. Moreover, where two parts of the perceived object are equally important, as in Figure 3.7, the tendency is for figure and ground to alternate. Although no hard-and-fast rules apply, the analysis of figure and ground in an object takes more time when either the intensity of light decreases or the stimulus object is a complex form.

In addition to shape and form, stimulus analyzing mechanisms deal with other features of an object. Some decisions extract information about the intensity and movement of stimulus objects, colors, contour, form, size, and depth of field. Nor is the peripheral analysis limited to visual objects. The tactile system analyzes the sensation of surfaces and textures in contact with

Figure 3.7 *The Peter-Paul goblet. What appears first, the famous twins or the goblet? After locating both, try to shift your perception back and forth between the two forms.*

the skin in terms of whether they are rough, smooth, bumpy, velvety, slippery, and so on. The auditory channel extracts information about pitch, loudness, timbre, and direction of acoustical signals, and it aids in determining the temporal and spatial relation of visual and acoustical signals. All the sensory transformations are greatly important to the nervous system's handling of inflowing information that must be transmitted and further analyzed by the high-level storage system shown in Figure 3.5. The act of transforming sensory data simplifies operations, but at a loss of efficiency. "Transformations waste information," wrote Norman (1969a), "for aspects of the signal that are combined with one another at one level of processing cannot be separated at higher levels." The composite picture of the sensory system is one in which information about incoming signals is abstracted and combined at increasingly higher levels of processing. Once the peripheral analysis of sensory data is complete, the finely tuned work of the central nervous system begins.

CENTRAL PROCESSING UNITS

At the cost of time and energy losses, the receptor units complete their wondrous task of transforming raw sensory data into an economical form for transmission to the spinal cord and then to the brain. The spinal cord is an intricate cable consisting of several million fibers, each a few ten-thousandths of an inch in diameter, bringing information either to or from the brain. Nature's input/output cable does more than keep the maze of wires straight. It also groups and rearranges data received from the input receptors. This power to modify neural impulses gives the spinal cord its capacity to alter the thresholds imposed by the sensory system. The arrangement of fibers is also needed to sort the nature and source of incoming impulses. Data concerning light and darkness, sound and pain, pressure and internal irritation are generated from the particular arrangement and connections of independent pathways leading to corresponding control sections of the brain.

What happens beyond the managing function of the spinal cord is much less clearly understood. The cortex of the brain is an elaborate storage system of connected cells and fibers containing approximately 10 billion neurons. Some regions of the storage network have fibers so small that more than 100 million are packed into each cubic inch. The brain can handle several streams of independent activity simultaneously, each major stream taking place in a distinct subsystem that is organized around a large number of inter-connected electrical circuits. The interdependence of the major subsystems suggests that the brain's activity is not simply a composite of individual cells acting in a "click-click" cause-effect manner. Rather, as Lashley (1954) cited in Chapter 1, noted: "Even the simplest bit of behavior requires the integrated action of millions of neurons; . . . Differential behavior is determined by the combination of cells acting together rather than by cells which participate only in particular bits of behavior [p. 116]."

The organization of the brain into an orderly set of connecting cables, pathways, and distinct subsystems of activity corresponds with a far more primitive logic employed in the design of computer equipment. The largest area of the brain, the mass of grey matter known as the *cerebral cortex,* transfers electrical impulses from the sense organs to the appropriate pro-cessing units housed within its boundaries. Some units route information, others store it, still others analyze reports from the outside world or the internal environment and make decisions, monitor directives to the rest of the body, stabilize the movements of muscles or sense organs, and cross-check for errors against other streams of activity. Some regions of the body and all sensory units receive priority in the allocation of circuitry. As suggested by the distor-tions of the little man in Figure 3.8, the subsystems receive priority on the basis of their complex activities rather than on the size of the organs or muscles for which they are responsible. From the incredible cross-currents of activity—data gathering, sorting, integrating, decision making, monitoring, controlling, cross-checking, storing, and recalling of memory traces—the control head-quarters of the nervous system transfers the only language it can understand into the integrated and synchronized activity which is known as conscious human experience.

The central processing units first perform the extraordinary activity we know as perception and then further integrate all perceived information into a form suitable for storage and recall. It is impossible, in the matter of perception, to separate the exact roles of the brain and sensory organs, partly because the transformation of sensory data into final form is a complex transac-tion between forces that are both external and internal to the organism. From the external world comes the force of the stimulus object with its variable properties of form, intensity, duration, and frequency. And from the nervous system are the mediational factors that transform impressions of the physical world into the only language that is acceptable to the nervous system. The fascinating range of correspondence between stimulus object and the organism constitutes the central processing stage of decoding-encoding.

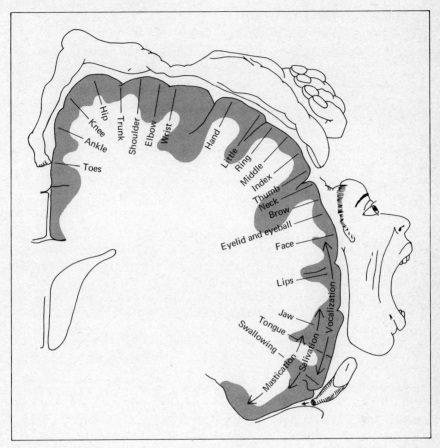

Figure 3.8 *The homunculus of man. (Reprinted with permission from Wooldridge, 1963.)*

Stimulus Properties

A major discovery of gestalt psychology is that our interpretation of sensory signals depends upon the surroundings in which they are imbedded. In the gestalt view, the fundamental unit of perception is not a given material object or stimulus; rather it is the total configuration of the outside world as it is interpreted by the individual. In everyday experience we know that our interpretations of size, movement, depth, and distance of material objects depend upon the nature of the background in which they are cast (Figures 3.9 and 3.10). Without a contextual backdrop, accurate perception becomes impossible. A stationary point of light in an otherwise dark room appears to move because the perceiver lacks a field in which to judge the location of the light and to affirm that it is not, in actuality, moving. Sitting at the window of a stopped train while another train rushes by often creates the impression that the stationary train is moving and the other is not. In a partially clouded moonlit sky, the moon

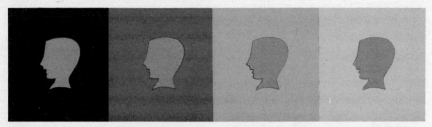

Figure 3.9 *These four heads were cut from the same paper; yet note how the surrounding context influences perception of the shade of gray in each section. (Reprinted with permission from Krech and Crutchfield, 1958.)*

often appears to be moving against a backdrop of fixed cloud formations when in fact it is the clouds which are moving.

    The contextual field is not limited to matters of background. The location of a perceiver in relation to a visual field makes a critical difference in the way things appear. There is, for example, a major difference in how one interprets a visual field from a side location and how he interprets it from an approaching, frontal view. Looking straight ahead at a landscape from a fast-moving car at night or from a cockpit of a plane taking off resembles the pat-

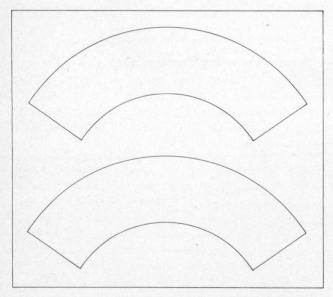

Figure 3.10 *Though these two figures are the same size, the one below appears larger because of the surrounding context.*

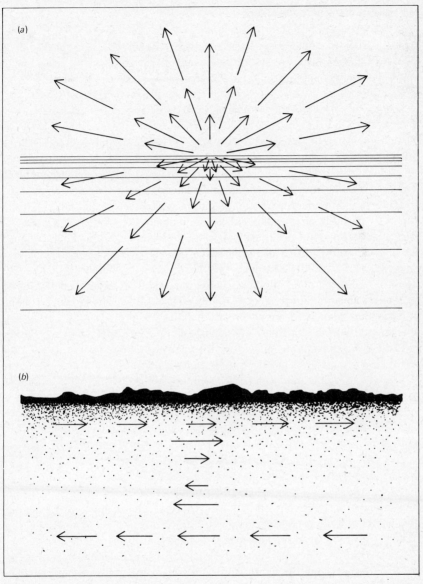

Figure 3.11 *Direction of flow of the textured field. (Reprinted with permission from Bartley, 1969.)*
(a) *A field composed of land and sky as seen during an observer's forward motion, particularly when above the ground, as in an airplane.*
(b) *A field made up of land as seen when an observer looks to the left and fixates a point midway between himself and the horizon as he moves along.*

terned field illustrated in Figure 3.11a. The same landscape viewed from an angle—either to right or left of the direction of motion—more closely approximates the pattern in Figure 3.11b. Looking straight ahead at approaching objects rushing by changes the retinal image of the landscape. The surroundings appear to expand in front of the car or plane, then to "flow" around the sides and contract in back of the visual field. In sharp contrast is the effect of looking to the side of the same landscape and fixing on a point midway between the observer and the horizon. In the former context, the positions below the horizon appear to be flowing up, and those representing the sky appear to be coming down. In other words, the flow is greatest near the observer and least near the horizon. The contrasting effects produced when objects approach from the side and from the front can be explained only by the interaction of the visual field and the particular orientation of the observer in that field.

In addition to contextual background and the location of a perceiver in relation to the object, another important determinant of our impressions is the internal configuration of the stimulus object. In judging matters of size, intensity, and depth, we depend heavily on internal details as cues. The slightest detail can often affect our perception of the total field. Being fooled by a visual illusion, for example, is usually a result of some superficial conflict in detail that keeps us from accurately judging the entire configuration. This often can be remedied merely by breaking the figure into its component parts; in so doing we prevent any given detail from distorting the overall appearance of the stimulus object. Consider the illusions shown in Figure 3.12. In Figure 3.12a, no matter how hard one tries, the upper horizontal line with turned-out edges appears longer than the lower one with turned-in angles. In the two-dimensional context of this book page, the overall configuration produces what we know to be illusionary by breaking the figure into its components. If one considers the two horizontal lines as part of a three-dimensional perspective formed by looking down at the figure from the top, the two lines will again appear to be equal.

In Figure 3.12b, geometrical perspective keeps the diagonal lines from forming a continuous straight line. A ruler placed on a perpendicular plane close to the two line segments restores the appearance of a straight line. Another way to resolve the illusion is to assume that the rectangle stands erect and that the lines forming the horizontal structure extend away from the observer. Again, once the figure is viewed from a three-dimensional perspective, the illusion disappears.

Finally, Figure 3.12c suggests a three-dimensional figure in which the horizontal lines appear to be farther apart at the center than they are at the outer sides of the rectangle. The key to the illusion is again the context, which includes a series of lines radiating from a fixed point. Our tendency is to regard this point as the center and the edges as the outer rim. In this instance the figure must be broken down into a two-dimensional plane. Presto! The horizontal lines appear straight.

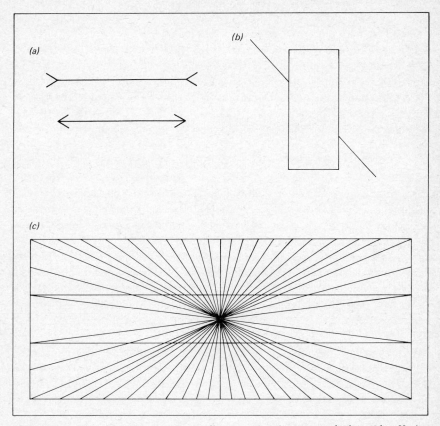

Figure 3.12   *Three illusions. (a) After Muller-Lyer. (b) After Poggendorf. (c) After Hering.*

Rules of Perceptual Organization

All contacts with the physical world entail some form of perceptual organization. Even the simplest of experiences requires some characteristic means or
strategy to superimpose order on what otherwise appears as a blur of disconnected elements. The way in which we attempt to order our sensual experience
is neither arbitrary nor randomly determined. On the contrary, we use certain
learned rules—some say "laws"—to organize all perceived experience. The
rules of perceptual organization apply to all sensory systems but can be best
illustrated by considering our visual strategies.

The most basic rule is that an individual organizes in ways which
give priority to what is striking. We alluded to this principle earlier as the
figure-ground relationship. Major distinctions between figure and ground, as
noted by Rubin (1958), revolve around our tendency to identify figures by
borders, edges, and shape—all of which the ground does not have. Moreover,
the ground seems to extend behind the figure, which, unlike the ground,

appears to be a particular object or distinct form. Furthermore, figures have more substantive color and appear to be closer and more dominant. These figure-ground distinctions account for the way in which we interpret many features of each changing event in the physical world: our detection of form, shape, depth, stability, and constancy. Generally, the less contrast between figure and ground, the less apt we are to focus constantly on any one aspect of a visual configuration (Figure 3.13). In the reversible cross shown in Figure 3.14, the figure and ground components appear to be interchangeable parts of the overall form.

Another general principle is that we prefer "good" configurations or "good" figures. In the gestalt sense, "good" may be equated with simplicity or balance of form. The notion that we tend to perceive objects in as good a form as possible suggests a tendency to see more regularity, continuity, or symmetry in complex forms than what actually exists. Nonetheless, our bias of perceiving the environment so that it appears as simple and orderly as possible is one way to reduce a complex visual field to manageable proportions. The "goodness of form" principle stems in part from the tendency to classify events and objects by labels with which we are most familiar. Hence, for complex forms like Figure 3.15, our first tendency is to organize the configuration by ignoring internal detail, discontinuous lines, and asymmetrical shapes in favor of the more familiar classification of connected squares or a symmetrically formed cross. Notice how difficult it is to find Figure 3.16a in Figure 3.16b through d.

One corollary of the goodness-of-form principle is known as the principle of *closure.* To close is to strive for completion. We cause incomplete forms to be "complete" by filling in the gaps or missing details. Though Figure

Figure 3.13 *An ambiguous figure. Is the woman you perceive old or young? (Reprinted with permission from Boring,* American Journal of Psychology, *1930.)*

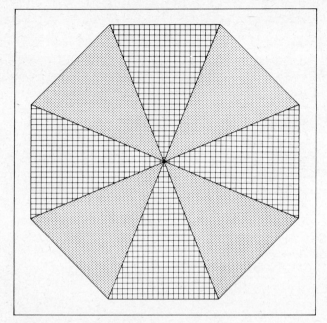

Figure 3.14 *A reversible cross. (Reprinted with permission from Newman, 1948.)*

3.17 is obviously incomplete, it can be readily identified; when flashed briefly on a screen, observers typically identify it as a circle. The pressure for closure is not so much a matter of filling in the blanks in an idiosyncratic manner as it is an attempt to organize in the most *meaningful* way. Few people would identify Figure 3.18 as discrete patches of black on a white background. The most meaningful way of filling in detail is to find a dog—perhaps even a certain breed comes to mind.

Gestalt pyschologists assume that the laws of perceptual organization come from innate abilities of the nervous system, whereas those with a behavioral orientation tend to emphasize the importance of what we learn through social experience. On one hand, those who favor the gestalt view point to the well-documented fact that human beings and lower animals share certain primitive and innately determined powers of visual discrimination (Weisstein, 1969; Wiesel, 1967). On the other hand, human beings require considerable time to learn how to organize complex visual form (Hubel, 1949). In the absence of conclusive evidence supporting one view or the other, only this is clear: The rules of perceptual organization have far-reaching implications for decoding communicative behavior; in fact, they provide an explanation for the way in which we interpret the significance of human speech. In a conversation between two people, for example, we know that the meaning of their verbal behavior depends on the same factors at work in the visual discrimination tasks

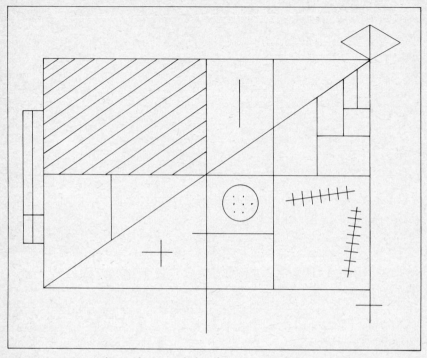

Figure 3.15 *Internal complexity and the absence of familiar or "good" organization make it difficult to readily classify this figure.*

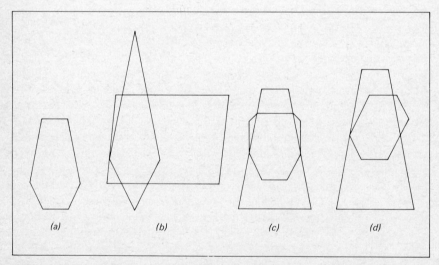

Figure 3.16 *Note how the asymmetrical form makes it difficult to locate (a) in the other three figures.*

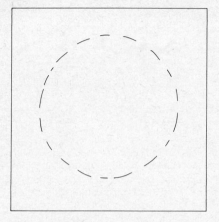

Figure 3.17 *It is easy to recognize the broken lines as a circle, despite gaps and missing details.*

discussed earlier, namely, impact of social context, the location of each person vis-à-vis each other (a problem to be discussed in more detail in Chapter 7), and the defining aspects of their physical surroundings. Moreover, each interactant will attempt to attend to what is most important in the other's speech by unconsciously relying on a primitive form of figure-ground discrimination; that is, he focuses on sounds that most stand out from the larger backdrop of sound and noise. Closely related is the tendency to filter sound according to the rule of simplicity and closure; inevitably, details are ignored in favor of an overall impression of what the other is saying. In short, the rules of perception act as a psychological filter, enabling each person to focus on what he considers to be the most strategic aspect of the interaction.

Figure 3.18 *We tend to add details to forms so that they correspond with our experience.*

Attitudinal and Motivational Determinants

A clue to the importance of attitudes in perceptual organization is found in a well-known case study of events surrounding an infamous football game between Dartmouth and Princeton on November 23, 1951. The immediate incident, which touched off a spectacular sequence of events, is recorded by Hastorf and Cantril (1954) in the following understated description:

> A few minutes after the opening kickoff, it became apparent that the game was going to be a rough one. The referees were kept busy blowing their whistles and penalizing both sides. In the second quarter, Princeton's star left the game with a broken nose. In the third quarter, a Dartmouth player was taken off the field with a broken leg. Tempers flared both during and after the game. The official statistics of the game, which Princeton won, showed that Dartmouth was penalized 70 yards, Princeton 25, not counting more than a few plays in which both sides were penalized [p. 129].

In the heated controversy following the game, partisans loyal to their respective universities hurled insults and accusations at the opposing team, blaming it for injuries, penalties, and combative conduct. Hastorf and Cantril investigated the perceptions of the respective sides by means of questionnaires and a film of the game shown to some one hundred students. The reports were so divergent that it seemed each side witnessed separate events. For example, Princeton students who watched the film "saw" the Dartmouth team commit over twice the number of infractions reported by the Dartmouth students. Spectators from the respective teams "saw" more than twice the number of "flagrant" violations made by the members of the opposing team. Hastorf and Cantril concluded:

> The "same" sensory impingements emanating from the football field, transmitted through the visual mechanism to the brain, obviously gave rise to different experiences in different people. The significances assumed by different happenings for different people depend in large part on the purposes people bring to the occasion and the assumptions they have of the purposes and probable behavior of other people involved. . . .
> It is inaccurate and misleading to say that different people have different "attitudes" concerning the same "thing." For the "thing" simply is not the same for different people whether the "thing" is a football game, a presidential candidate, Communism, or spinach. We do not simply "react to" a happening or to some impingement from the environment in a determined way (except in behavior that has become reflective or habitual). We behave according to what we bring to the occasion, and what each of us brings to the occasion is more or less unique [p. 133].

This incident is not unique. The central nervous system by and large separates the torrent of incoming signals on the basis of whatever feelings, needs, attitudes, and motives happen to be dominant at the moment. The very existence of an attitudinal framework for perception virtually precludes the possibility that the signals will be separated in an arbitrary or mechanical way. Attitudes, after all, constitute a predisposition or readiness to respond to message cues in stable and consistent ways. Typically, the state of readiness is grounded in a judgmental bias, either positive or negative, toward classes of ideas, events, or objects of perception. Attitudes, then, enable each observer to respond to whatever features of an environment he regards as pertinent while ignoring or discounting items he views as having little or no import. The question, then, is: How free are we to perceive what we want to perceive? Do we automatically discount those aspects of an environment for which we do not have strong favorable attitudes? And, conversely, do positive attitudes necessarily entail ready recognition? These and other related matters raise a more general question of the role of selectivity in perception.

Part of the case for the selective nature of perception rests on what has become known as the controversy over *selective exposure*. One representative finding is that exposure to mass-media political campaigns—rallies, newscasts, pamphlets, magazine articles, and editorials—is partisan, often highly so, despite the fact that the welter of political propaganda is open to virtually everyone. Even with equal access to disparate views, voters go out of their way to avoid conflicting information and seek instead those situations where the propaganda reaffirms their political views. Generally, the stronger the partisanship, the greater the selectivity of exposure (Klapper, 1960). In a series of field studies, Greenburg (1965) reported that voters who favored passage of school voting issues exposed themselves to significantly more campaign information than those who did not. Interestingly enough, the more partisan the voter was, the stronger was his tendency to seek those forms of information which could be most easily screened in a selective manner. Moreover, partisans showed a greater preference than did nonpartisans for newspaper articles, pamphlets, and other printed information; presumably, television and social gatherings offer less opportunity for selective exposure to operate. Such findings are typical of research on patterns of exposure to campaigns (Lowin, 1967; McGinnies and Rosenbaum, 1965).

Research on selective perception in political campaigns is consistent with conclusions on a number of topics. One common finding is that media campaigns designed to create public interest on a topic are most apt to reach those whose interest is highest to begin with (Star and Hughes, 1950). Closely related is the finding that health campaigns attempting to link smoking and cancer are far more often viewed by nonsmoking male adults than by an equivalent-sized sample of male smokers (Cannell and MacDonald, 1956). Another example of selective exposure to mass rallies comes from Wolfinger (et al., 1964); he studied the composition of audiences at a Christian anti-Communist crusade organized and controlled by politically conservative white Protestants. Over 75 percent of the audience was found to be Protestant; 66

percent were Republican (only 8 percent were Democrats); and only a "handful" were nonwhite. In political, religious, and racial features the audience grossly misrepresented the social composition of the local neighborhood and the surrounding communities.

Similar data could undoubtedly be gathered on virtually any meeting arranged for a particular political or social cause. Republicans favor Republican-sponsored meetings; Democrats attend a disproportionate number of Democratic rallies. Religious radio stations mainly reach church members. Liberals are more apt to read the *New Republic* than the *Reader's Digest*. Advertisements from discount stores reach customers in the middle and lower income brackets. *Playboy* caters to the single adult, mostly under thirty, and the *Ladies Home Journal* draws most of its followers from young and middle-aged housewives. Indeed, it would be difficult to find many interpersonal contacts that follow a pattern that is inconsistent with the idea of selectivity. Of course, there may be many reasons why people seem to be exposed to congenial information more than to the contrary. Hence, the evidence for selective exposure does not prove that man perceives selectively in an automatic way; rather it can only be taken as indirect support for the idea that we tend to avoid incompatible information. As Freedman and Sears (1966) argued, selectivity may be quite incidental to the real reason why people seem to seek out those situations that are the most consistent with their own attitudes.

Since we have no way to ensure that selective exposure itself indicates a general psychological tendency to favor supportive information, other types of evidence must be consulted. One source is the now-classic study of rumor transmission where Allport and Postman (1945) found considerable support for selectivity and distortion of messages by people who transmitted a message in a face-to-face situation. In the most famous part of this study, subjects were required to describe a picture of a white man holding a razor while arguing with a Negro on a train. As the narrative was passed successively from subject to subject, the message changed in a direction that was consistent with the characteristic attitudes of each person. Allport and Postman observed, among other findings, that information which is inconsistent with the perceiver's views is apt to be

> recast to fit not only his span of comprehension and retention, but, likewise, his own personal needs and interests. What was outer becomes inner; what was objective becomes subjective [p. 81].

More recently, studies using a technique known as *visual search* shed much additional light on the mechanics of selectivity in perception. In a typical visual search task, subjects are given an assortment of information and required to locate one particular unit, or more technically, a *target* of information. The task is not unlike being asked to find a given file in a crowded drawer, to spot a particular card in a shuffled deck, or even to find a name in a telephone directory. Subjects may simply be asked whether or not a given array of information contains a target, or they may have to remember the identity of several targets from a larger store of information. In a typical task, subjects scan vertical lists of fifty alphabet letters in which a target letter is embedded. Subjects are first given several days of practice in which to reach a stable level of performance.

A number of findings from visual search tasks are relevant to the question of selectivity in perception (Neisser, 1963, 1967; Neisser et al., 1963). Subjects report that they do not actually see each irrelevant letter in each master list; they scan the list, causing a blurring effect, until the target seems to jump out in a burst of recognition. Equally important, subjects show no recognition of the irrelevant letters on the list. After each trial, subjects are given a set of words, only half of which appeared on the master list; recognition of list words does not exceed chance expectation.

Since visual search tasks require an examination of every letter on all lines before the target item is reached, the task is a more representative test of selectivity than the typical investigation of mass-media campaigns or social gatherings. It is noteworthy that the evidence on visual search fits a hierarchial system of decision making that is quite similar to the viewpoint advanced early in this chapter by Schroder, Driver, and Streufert (see p. 72) and also to the discussion of the detection features of stimulus analyzing mechanisms (p. 87). In a search for a target letter, elemental tests for openness, angularity, and the like seem to be performed on *all* letters. Those items which pass the early analyzing tests are then selected for further testing. The others are passed by; rejected items are neither classified nor further identified. The initial sorting takes only a fraction of a second. Note that the initial stage of visual scanning appears to be nondiscriminative, or nonselective; only after initial tests are performed on *all* letters are target items identified for further testing. Apparently, then, selectivity does occur, but only in the later stages of information processing. It is quite consistent with the notion of selectivity that people report seeing only a blur when searching over the master list, then they find that target items seem to jump out at them. Also consistent with the notion of selective perception is the finding that only items identified as targets are remembered. In short, visual search suggests a finely tuned process of undifferentiated scanning followed in turn by selective testing of items judged most salient to the perceiver.

Findings from visual search tasks might seem to imply that the role of attitudinal factors in selective perception is free of emotional or affective overtones. The eyes seem to blur over irrelevant items and then suddenly key in on the targets. There is, however, ample evidence that attitudes have much to do with the affective coloring of perception. For example, Smith (1970) designed a study to find out if people's perceptions of faces judged to be friendly differs in any significant way from those judged to be unfriendly. Results showed a tendency for observers to perceive friendly faces as being larger than unfriendly faces. Smith concluded:

> Ss [subjects] responded to the meaning which faces elicited in this situation; and . . . this meaning emerged out of the assumptions, attitudes, expectations, purposes, and special sensitizations which Ss had acquired through experience. . . . The fact that "pleasant" or "liked" faces were made larger (closer) than others indicates that attributed meaning, rather than size of retinal image alone, determined the responses. . . . Perception of a human face literally changed before the eyes of the Ss as a function of alterations in beliefs, assumptions, etc. [p. 134].

The demonstrated relationship between attitudinal factors and selective perception does not imply that people who feel strongly about events invariably warp the significance of what they observe. Intensely held attitudes markedly increase the risk of distortion in perception, but there is nothing automatic about the possible outcomes. The same holds true for selective perception in general. It is a mistake, therefore, to think of selectivity as something which invariably governs the dynamics of perceptual activity. The evidence typically indicates that varying degrees of selectivity occur among some given percentage of those in the study. "The selective processes," wrote Joseph Klapper (1960), "appear to function at times imperfectly or not at all, and on some occasions to serve, atypically, to *impel* opinion change [p. 25]."

In reference to de facto selectivity, Freedman and Sears (1965) suggested somewhat cryptically that the evidence shows only that "man is a little selective all the time" or "man is very selective only sometimes." Since the evidence for selective exposure is not nearly as strong as that for selective perception, a more temperate conclusion would be that *selectivity occurs with great regularity, under an enormous range of tasks and social conditions*; and when it does so operate, it functions in ways which protect the dominant needs and attitudes of the moment.

Innumerable everyday experiences testify to the role played by motives in perception. In interpreting the deluge of TV commercials, billboards, glances, handshakes, news headlines, and the countless other cues of daily experience, we are prone to make judgments on the basis of whatever needs and drives we experience at the time. In earlier sections we mentioned the close tie between perception and the signals that are of greater importance to the observer. The schema on page 86 uses the term "pertinence of incoming information." Whatever the term, to say that we are intent on perceiving an object or event is to imply some strong and persistent motivation for doing so.

Motivation contributes in characteristic and striking ways to the perception of vague or ambiguous stimuli. For example, it has been known for some time that people who have been deprived of food differ from those who are not hungry in the degree to which they are predisposed to "see" food-related meanings in ambiguous stimuli. When compared with rich children, poor children are more apt to overestimate the size of coins pictured for a moment on a screen. Laboratory studies also indicate that the perception of moving lights, line lengths, and names of objects follows a pattern that is in part or in whole determined by an individual's momentary needs and drives. In some cases hungry people have achieved the illusion of seeing a food-related object when in fact none existed.

Generally, the stronger the motivational state, the more motivational factors will determine what is to be perceived and how much perceptual distortion occurs. In one of the earliest studies (Levine et al., 1942), subjects deprived of food for varying lengths of time were shown blurred pictures of food-related and household-related objects. In periods of food deprivation ranging up to six hours, subjects reported they "saw" an increasing number of food-related objects as need increased. Thereafter, they grew less responsive to food-related objects as well as to household objects (Levine et al., 1942). In a parallel investigation using three groups of naval trainees who had been deprived of food for one, four, or sixteen hours, McClelland and Atkinson (1948) found that the number of food-related responses increased progressively with need. Of additional relevance is the discovery that as hunger increases, the imagined size of food objects grows larger. Later studies confirmed the tendency to perceive food-related objects more readily up to a point; thereafter a period of frustration and indifference set in (Lazarus et al., 1953). The overall picture is that the effects of time and motives work in the direction where individuals report "seeing" relevant objects in ambiguous stimulus configurations, even to the point of overestimating their size. In other words, a hungry person may prefer not to think of a beef steak at all, but if he sees one it may appear larger and juicier than normal.

It is also clear that fear-related motives can have a marked bearing on perception. Because of the difficulties of inducing fear conditions in laboratory settings, little experimental evidence is available to demonstrate what most people experience, particularly in childhood, in moments of isolation or in unfamiliar and threatening surroundings. In one remarkable study of the gripping effects of fear, Weintraub and Walker (1966) discussed a situation involving a training exercise:

> As a part of a military training exercise, troops were to be placed in trenches very close to the point at which an atomic explosion was to be produced. The position was closer than men had voluntarily occupied before, or since, and the setting was one in which distances appear extremely short. The net effect was that the participants, including the writer, felt that they were sitting virtually beneath an atomic bomb when it was to be detonated. In this setting, it was possible to carry out an experiment in which men were asked to write stories about characters in ambiguous pictures containing human figures. Furthermore, a similar task could be asked of the same or similar individuals removed in time both before and after the experience, and removed in distance from the site of the explosion [p. 85].

After conducting the experiment, Walker concluded that fear-related stories were written with unusual frequency by the group located near the site of the bomb explosion.

The effects of motives on the perception of ambiguous events and objects cannot be assumed to apply in an identical way for situations involving unambiguous objects of perception. Typically, motives yield grossly distorted perceptions only when the event or object is ambiguous or when the motivation level is usually high (Berelson and Steiner, 1964). The change from an ambiguous stimulus situation to a clear-cut one alters the effects of motivation; warping and distortion of interpretations gives way to a greater concern for determining what is *pertinent* to further information processing. The distinction between ambiguous and clear-cut stimuli is important for a number of reasons. For one thing, most social situations require each participant to try to interpret events in a realistic way. An obvious and important fact is that certain sanctions and penalties exist in most social situations for those who make grossly inaccurate interpretations of what goes on. It is hardly surprising, therefore, to find that the presence of a reward for accurate perceptions on various tasks, and some form of punishment for inaccurate responses, soon produce a marked increase in perceptual accuracy. In one study, the tendency to overestimate the size of objects disappeared by the twelfth trial under conditions of reward and punishment (Smith et al., 1951). In related research, subjects were shown sets of juxtaposed faces (Figure 3.19) in a tachistoscope for 1/3 second. Initially, only a single face was shown at a time; subjects were asked to learn the names that went with each face. They also knew that when one face was to be shown, say Figure 3.19a, they would receive a money reward. When the other face appeared (Figure 3.19b), money would be taken away. Attention was not drawn to the connection between the reward and the need to learn names; observers later reported that they did not even suspect such a relationship existed. After trial tests, the combined faces, Figure 3.19c, were shown. In the great majority of cases, the name that was immediately called out was the one figure that had been previously rewarded. From such a spectacular finding we conclude that motives do not influence perception independently of the utility of the task. Hence, the risk of distortion is greatest for items which are not highly valued or for which motivation is low (Tabu, 1965).

INFORMATION STORAGE

Information storage is an awkward and embarrassingly complicated problem for any mechanistic view of human thought. In an electrical apparatus, once the central processing units complete their activity, the business of data storage can almost be taken for granted. The organization and storage

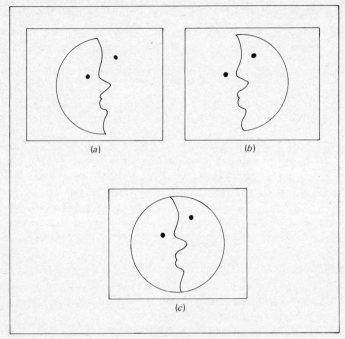

(a)   (b)

(c)

Figure 3.19   *Faces used in studies of perception under conditions of reward and punishment. (Reprinted with permission from Smith et al., 1951.)*

of information in computers resembles a file cabinet with its orderly set of drawers, files, and compartments, each serving as a depository for processed information. The storage is an orderly and passive matter; more importantly, the rules which govern the storage of data by a computer must be established beforehand by a programmer. In the human beings, however, information storage is neither passive not automatically controlled. Through experience, we acquire our own set of ground rules for organizing and storing information, and reorganization and change are the rule rather than the exception. The constructive or transformational nature of human information processing begins with the detecting features of stimulus analyzing mechanisms, continues through the complex sorting, grouping, and monitoring operations of the spinal cord and higher regions of the brain, and then extends to the various stages of storage. An early advocate of a constructive view of remembering, Bartlett (1932) observed:

> The description of memories as "fixed and lifeless" is merely an unpleasant fiction . . . memory is itself constructive. . . . I have regarded it rather as one achievement in a line of the ceaseless struggles to master and enjoy a world full of variety and rapid change. Memory, and all the life of images and words which goes with it, is one with the age-old acquisition of the

distinct senses, and with that development of constructive imagination and constructive thought wherein at length we find the most complete release from the narrowness of present time and place [pp. 311, 312, 314].

An active, constructive view of information storage denies all attempts to explain memory as a complicated filing system into which specific signals are imprinted in a form that can be stored and recalled. In criticism of the view that one recalls on the basis of stored copies of finished mental events, Neisser (1967) suggested that recall follows an elaborate process of reconstruction. In describing the nature of reconstruction in memory, he remarked:

> There are no stored copies of finished mental events, like images or sentences, but only traces of earlier constructive acitivity . . . we store traces of earlier cognitive acts, not the product of those acts. The traces are not simply "revived" or "reactivated" in recall; instead the stored fragments are used as information to support a new construction [pp. 285–286].

Since the organization, storage, and reconstruction of events are closely intertwined, it is misleading to think of information storage as somehow separate from the higher mental processes of the brain. Information storage does not in any strict sense begin where thinking leaves off. Hence, before discussing the specific stages of memory, it will be useful to return to some larger matters which govern the activity of both the central processing units and information storage.

Hierarchies

The concept of hierarchy, mentioned earlier in connection with integration levels and the "cocktail party" problem, has important implications for understanding the basis on which information is organized and stored. We have seen that human beings execute a sequence of tests, ranging from the simple to the most complex, in the course of processing incoming signals. These tests determine what gets stored and, more importantly, what type of organization is superimposed on the stored information. The hierarchies, or schemas of thought organization, control the fate of stored information in large measure because they are themselves a type of information. Recall that incoming signals attain meaning only in relation to their place at various levels of thought integration. In discussing the importance of informational hierarchies, Lashley (1960) remarked:

> Every memory becomes part of a more or less extensive organization. When I read a scientific paper, the new facts presented become associated with the field of knowledge of which it is a part. Later availability of the specific items of the paper depends on a partial activation of the whole

body of associations. If one has not thought of a topic for some time, it is difficult to recall details. With review of discussion of the subject, however, names, dates, references which seemed to be forgotten rapidly become available to memory. . . . I believe that recall involves the subthreshold activation of a whole system of associations which exert some sort of mutual facilitation [pp. 497–498].

It is easy to see why the completeness of the hierarchy has so much to do with what is stored. We tend to recall specific details of past experiences best when the details are imbedded in a more or less complete hierarchy of thought. Young children seem ever inclined to recall in minute detail the elaborate rules governing games and pastimes, the daily batting averages of baseball heroes, and the whereabouts of distant hiding places—but not the facts of geography or spelling. And adults show a capacity to recall specifics where money and professional interests are concerned. Most people, for example, need only recall a few specifics to reconstruct the larger schema associated with filling out their income tax return from some distant year. A given detail triggers not only recall of payment but also the larger context of the experience: the relative importance of medical bills for the year in question, the number of personal deductions, moving costs for the year, circumstances surrounding the dispute over storm damage, the importance of inflation, and so on. The larger hierarchy or schema serves as a frame of reference for recalling a seemingly unending number of facts not germane to the immediate question at hand.

Routines, Plans, and Strategies

If the hierarchial nature of information processing can be taken as axiomatic, the question that arises is this: How does the organism establish and maintain the hierarchy in the first place? The very notion of a hierarchy implies an underlying order, a means of organization, or some deliberate means of structuring and storing incoming signals. A pile of bricks need not indicate deliberate planning, but a wall of bricks does. In answer to the problem of cognitive organization, a traditional school of psychology seeks to find in all organized thought patterns, however complex, some underlying network of connections or associations between stimuli and response. Appearance, the argument goes, is deceptive; what seems to be a deliberately arranged hierarchy is in actuality a result of an existing response to associations. How the specific connections are organized and stored is said to be the result of the amount of past experience, the consequence of a chain of reinforcement and inhibiting effects, and the mediating influence of other sources of learning. For years the only alternative to "nickel-in-the-slot, stimulus-response" interpretations of thought organization seemed to be the ghostly assortment of appeals to the existence of mental images and other subjective and intangible elements. The choice, in other words, seemed to reduce itself to mechanistic reflex theories or subjective interpretations which reduced the higher intellectual activities of the brain to the control of a little man inside the head who reads maps and makes decisions. One cognitive psychologist (Neisser, 1966) held that "if we do *not* postulate some agent who selects and uses the stored information, we must think of every thought and every response as just the momentary result of an interacting system, governed essentially by laissez-faire economics [p. 293]."

Today, a concept borrowed from computer programming seems to offer an alternative to explanations which reduce behavior either to "click-click" associations or to a "little man in the head." The general notion views the higher integrative functions of the brain as an *executive routine,* or plans and strategies. The metaphor of an executive routine springs from the fact that advanced computers have a complex set of independent parts, or "subroutines." In the sequence of tests performed by the computer, the order in which the routines operate varies from one step in the operation to the next. The simplest routines are handled in rather automatic fashion. However, under more complicated circumstances, the decision must be evaluated by a master, or executive, routine. The executive routine is the highest level of control; all other operations are subordinate. The executive function is not a miniature of the entire program. It is rather the highest level in a hierarchial structure of operations. According to Neisser (1966), the executive

> does not carry out the tests or the searches or the constructions which are the task of the subroutines, and it does not include the stored information which the subroutines use. Indeed, the executive may take only a small fraction of the computing time and space allotted to the program as a whole, and it need not contain any very sophisticated processes. Although there is a real sense in which it "uses" the rest of the program and the stored information, this creates no philosophical difficulties; it is not using itself [p. 296].

The role of the executive routine is akin to what Miller (et al., 1960) called "plans of behavior." In computers and humans alike, a *plan* is a hierarchy of instructions, some overall process which controls the order in which a sequence of organization and storage is to be performed. Plans suggest a sequence of testing operations that determine which operational phase is appropriate for processing incoming signals. The minimal number of steps of a given plan are known as a *TOTE* and include (1) some preliminary or anticipatory test, (2) a sequence of operations, (3) further tests of the operations in stage two, and (4) a final exit stage. The two testing stages permit the organism to decide whether to complete some initial operation, take corrective action, or abandon the activity altogether in favor of some other plan. As an example of a relatively simple two-stage plan, Miller gives the example of hammering a nail. The act of hammering is a hierarchy of operations which occurs in two stages—lifting and striking. Preliminary tests center on the positioning of the nail and lifting the hammer. Further testing continues at each stage of operations. If one part of the sequence is unsuccessful—if one hits one's thumb—corrective action is taken. If successful, the operation and tests continue until the exit stage is reached, when the nail is flush against the surface of the work. All information processing, however complicated, proceeds in a parallel manner which involves a hierarchy of activity. What differentiates complex plans from simple ones is the number of stages in the hierarchy and the complexity of testing and operations.

A plan, then, is more than a chain of actions. Plans are central to every act of behavior. So long as people behave, they execute some plan, however sketchy or incomplete it may be. This does not mean that all plans are completed. Revision and changes in planning routine are implicit in the very act of executing any action or thought. As the course of our daily interests changes, some preparatory plans are inevitably abandoned in favor of other routines. Hence, plans are flexible and interchangeable. Some plans are compatible; others are not. Some are executed in a systematic and painstakingly accurate manner; others are sloppy and haphazard. Finally, some plans recur; others are strictly temporary, one-shot affairs.

Plans characteristically involve the execution of strategies and tactics. Ordinarily, a person does not try to solve a problem in the most systematic and exhaustive way. The whole point is to devise a solution to the problem as efficiently as possible. We therefore look for shortcuts, hedges, hunches, schemes, strategies, and tactics that focus on whatever operations must be performed to get to the exit stage of a given plan. Generally, the greater the number of alternatives, the more we rely on strategies and tactics in problem solving. Strategies increase the likelihood of performing appropriate operations, reduce the stress inherent in information processing, and regulate the amount of risk one assumes in executing a plan.

Research into concept formation has revealed much about how we use strategies and tactics in problem solving. In a typical situation, subjects are given an array of eighty-one cards that vary in shapes of figures, number of figures, colors, and borders. Each subject must select all cards which share a particular attribute—all red cards, all those with a given number of figures, and so forth. With a particular concept in mind, subjects sort through the cards to determine what the described concept is. At each step in the process, the experimenter tells them whether their selections are in line with the correct answer.

Typically, subjects use discernible strategies and tactics in their search. By *simultaneous scanning* they use each instance to determine which outcomes are tenable and which have been eliminated; since so many possibilities exist, this strategy requires an accurate memory and considerable accuracy when thinking through many independent outcomes at one time.

Successive scanning, on the other hand, tests single possibilities. For example, if the subject believes red cards with common borders to be the solution, he chooses only those instances which provide a direct test of his hypothesis before he tries some other tactic. This strategy is ordinarily ineffectual, since it places a premium on guessing; but apparently some people favor the approach because it lessens the strain on memory. With another strategy, *conservative focusing,* the subject starts with any card that puts him on the right track; then he tests the secondary attributes to see whether he is still moving in the right direction. For example, if blue is the focus card, all blue cards with one, two, or three figures can then be tested. If those with one and two figures lead him in the wrong direction but three is the right course, the subject is then certain that the solution involves a blue card with three figures. This strategy is highly effectual, places slight strain on the memory, and demands little complex thinking. Finally, with *focus gambling* the subject finds a particular correct focus card and then changes more than one attribute at a time—presumably in the interest of hitting upon two additional aspects of the solution at once. This strategy is risky. If the initial hunches are correct, the subject can solve the problem quickly; but if the initial trials are not correct, the subject has no way of knowing which of the two additional attributes is responsible for the incorrect course, and he must abandon his strategy. Since focus gambling is hedging, rather than a systematic search of possible outcomes, it places considerable strain on the memory in those instances where initial moves are incorrect.

By varying the complexity and circumstances of the testing procedures, Bruner (et al., 1962) discovered that each subject tends to rely on some set of strategies and tactics in problem solving. Each strategy has its own advantages and disadvantages, and each tends to produce certain types of systematic error. As a whole, though, strategies contribute efficient problem solving. After conducting a battery of tests, Bruner concluded:

> In general, we are struck by the notable flexibility and intelligence of our subjects in adapting their strategies to the information, capacity, and risk requirements we have imposed on them. They have altered their strategies to take into account the increased difficulty of the problems being tackled, choosing methods of information gathering that were abstractly less than ideal, but that lightened pressures imposed on them by the tasks set them. They have changed from safe-but-slow to risky-but-fast strategies in the light of the number of moves allowed them. They have shown themselves able to adapt to cues that were less than perfect in validity and have shown good judgment in dealing with various kinds of payoff matrices. They have shown an ability to combine partially valid cues and to resolve conflicting cues [p. 238].

Memory and Plans

The relationship between routines, plans, and strategies is so fundamental to information processing and storage that it is difficult, if not impossible, to specify the relative importance of the hierarchies to each. Remembering, after all, is a form of thinking, not merely the final and incidental step in decoding. Information storage is central to both decoding and encoding behavior, and it should be regarded as an integral link between the two. Plans and strategies are not mere products of the moment. Rather, by deciding to execute a plan, we bring some existing hierarchy of thought from dead storage and place it in the control of the central processing units. Remembering, in short, is implicit in the very act of executing plans and strategies. Sometimes gathering data and remembering facets of a plan involve the use of several possible plans which compete to enter the mainstream of our conscious behavior. In this vein, Miller (et al., 1960) remarked:

> The parts of a Plan that are being executed have special access to consciousness and special ways of being remembered that are necessary for coordinating parts of different Plans and for coordinating with the Plans of other people. When we have decided to execute some particular Plan, it is probably put into some special state or place where it can be remembered while it is being executed. Particularly if it is a transient, temporary kind of Plan that will be used today and never again, we need some special place to store it [p. 65].

Miller uses the term *working memory* to refer to the memory we use when executing our plans. This concept suggests an active, constructive form of memory that offers quick access to the completion of behavior. Working memory is also instrumental at those times when we have difficulty deciding which plan to use. As Miller explained:

> There may be several Plans, or several parts of a single Plan, all stored in working memory at the same time. In particular, when one Plan is interrupted by the requirements of some other Plan, we must be able to remember the interrupted Plan in order to resume its execution when the opportunity arises. When a Plan has been transferred into the working memory, we recognize the special status of its incompleted parts by calling them "intentions" [p. 65].

The ancient study of memory techniques known as *nmemonics* serves as dramatic testimony to the role of plans and strategies in information storage. The history of man's search for aids to improve his retentive power can be traced back at least to Cicero's writings on rhetoric. Contrary to popular belief, a strong memory is not simply a result of determined practice. In fact, William James was so opposed to this idea that he conducted a time-consuming experiment in remembering by establishing a rigorous daily program to learn poetry. He first took eight consecutive days to learn 158 lines of Victor Hugo's *Satyr*. Next, he spent thirty-eight days learning Book I of Milton's *Paradise Lost*. Such an effort surely should have tested the notion that practice alone improves memory. But alas! When James tried to memorize the next 158 lines of Victor Hugo, he found that it took at least as long as, if not longer than, the first 158 lines did. Not trusting his own effort, James repeated the whole procedure on several friends, only to find that rote practice did nothing for their ability to memorize on the whole. A later test of James's discovery under laboratory conditions (Woodrow, 1927) confirmed what students of rhetoric had known for centuries: namely, that certain techniques improve memory where blind practice does not.

Miller (et al., 1960) illustrated the close tie between the process of remembering and the use of plans and strategies in a delightful anecdote that is worthy of the following detailed, admittedly unscientific, lapse:

One evening we were entertaining a visiting colleague, a social psychologist of broad interests, and our discussion turned to Plans. "But exactly what is a Plan?" he asked. "How can you say that memorizing depends on Plans?"

"We'll show you," we replied. "Here is a Plan that you can use for memorizing. Remember first that:

> one is a bun,
> two is a shoe,
> three is a tree,
> four is a door,
> five is a hive,
> six are sticks,
> seven is heaven,
> eight is a gate,
> nine is a line, and
> ten is a hen."

"You know, even though it is only ten-thirty here, my watch says one-thirty. I'm really tired and I'm sure I'll ruin your experiment."

"Don't worry, we have no real stake in it." We tightened our grip on his lapel. "Just relax and remember the rhyme. Now you have part of the Plan. The second part works like this: when we tell you a word, you must form a ludicrous or bizarre association with the first word in your list, and so on with the ten words we recite to you."

"Really, you know, it'll never work. I'm awfully tired," he replied.

"Have no fear," we answered, "just remember the rhyme and then form the association. Here are the words:

> 1. ashtray,
> 2. firewood,
> 3. picture,
> 4. cigarette,
> 5. table,
> 6. matchbook,
> 7. glass,
> 8. lamp,
> 9. shoe,
> 10. phonograph."

The words were read one at a time, and after reading the word, we waited until he announced that he had the association. It took about five seconds on the average to form the connection. After the seventh word he said that he was sure the first six were already forgotten. But we persevered.

After one trial through the list, we waited a minute or two so that he could collect himself and ask any questions that came to mind. Then we said, "What is number eight?"

He stared blankly, and then a smile crossed his face, "I'll be damned," he said. "It's lamp."

"And what number is cigarette?"

He laughed outright now, and then gave the correct answer.

"And there is no strain," he said, "absolutely no sweat."

We proceeded to demonstrate that he could in fact name every word correctly, and then asked, "Do you think that memorizing consists of piling up increments of response strength that accumulate as the words are repeated?" The question was lost in his amazement [pp. 134–136].

Such results, however spectacular, are not characteristic of all plans on tasks involving memory-associated items. Most complex social situations cannot be reduced to simple, ready-made plans. Ordinarily, it takes a person a considerable length of time just to formulate the preliminary mapping strategy and tactics. Then too, immediate memory tasks are not always analogous to the requirements of information storage over extended lengths of time. Therefore, we must separate problems associated with short-term memory from those concerning long-term retention and recall.

Short-term Memory

The human storage system is bound roughly by the existing moment—one's awareness of the present—and the dimmest recollection of past experience. In distinguishing between memory of just-occurring events and the distant past, William James (1890) remarked:

> The stream of thought flows on; but most of its segments fall into the bottomless abyss of oblivion. Of some, no memory services the instant of their passage. Of others, it is confined to a few moments, hours, or days. Others, again leave vestiges which are indestructible, and by means of which they may be recalled as long as life endures [p. 643].

From the bond formed between the "instant" and "the indestructible vestiges," we strive ever to transform a succession of fleeting sensory segments into a sense of continuity between the past and the present, a stable and permanent record of the stream of consciousness. No one knows exactly how long it takes for our sense of the present to slip into the outer recesses of what we perceive as the past. Ordinarily, the fleeting moment lasts no more than a second or two; in that brief span we make several different discriminations, shifting and refocusing and monitoring the objects of our attention on different aspects of the encompassing visual and auditory field. In the matter of speech recognition alone, Miller (1962) estimated that at a rate of 150 words per minute we make a dozen phonemic decisions and approximately one hundred phonetic decisions. However, short-term memory does not deal primarily with objects of momentary focus; they are more of a problem in attention than true memory.

In the immediate, or short-term, storage of information, we recognize far more information than what can be recalled only an instant later. The process seems to involve the fleeting recognition of an enormous array of incoming signals, as a first stage in the processing hierarchy, then a grasping after pertinent segments and a slipping away of all others from retention. In an important series of experiments, Sperling (1960, 1963) had subjects watch a series of tachistoscopic exposures of a set of twelve letters, arranged in three rows of four letters:

```
M   D   B   W
L   Y   M   T
C   D   Z   F
```

Sperling's idea was to systematically vary the amount of information to be recalled and thereby to provide some basis for estimating the total capacity of immediate memory. As expected, subjects reported they could "see" all the letters, yet on the whole they could recall only a few of them at exposures of 1/20 second. In the case of the first four or five letters, subject recall was immediate and accurate. From then on, the letters seemed to slip rapidly to the border of consciousness. Sperling argued that the sensory system records far more fleeting information than what can be reported within the span of short-term memory.

Ordinarily, only a fraction of a second is required for a rapid loss of information. Sperling's ingenious studies suggest that accuracy of recall falls off sharply in a fraction (0.3) of a second. The matter is complicated, however, by the *rate and sequence* in which incoming signals appear and the *strategies* used in storing and recalling them.

Rate. Rate influences our capacity for short-term memory in a manner not unlike the effect of speeding up the action of a slide projector. The more rapidly the slides appear, the greater are the odds that one slide will blur the image of those that occur just before it. And just as one slide may interfere with the impression of earlier ones, so also may one signal mask or obscure the immediate memory of earlier items. Much depends, of course, on the similarity of a given sequence of incoming signals. In general, the rate of presentation becomes increasingly important as the appearance of a given sequence of items becomes more similar (Averbach and Coriell, 1960; Eriksen and Collins, 1964).

Consider the risk of distortion with the visual pattern presented in Figure 3.20. Suppose the line segments are seen first, only briefly, then the square; anyone who reports actually seeing the lines is then eliminated from a second part of the experiment. Using this procedure Smith and Henriksson (1955) found that those who remain tend to distort the square and report it as a trapezoid whenever the lines and the squares are presented in rapid succession. Additional confirming evidence of distortion effects were reported by Guthrie and Wiener (1966) and Smith (et al., 1959).

In addition to influencing the chances for distortion, rate of presentation is also known to have a direct bearing on the degree to which information *fades* in short-term memory. Unfortunately, the evidence is far from conclusive. Some studies advance the argument that a slow rate of presentation gives the receiver more time to encode stimulus information. For instance, Pollack (1952) found the percentage of accurate recall to increase as the presentation rate of a list of digits and letters decreased from 4 to 0.25 items per second. The studies of Norman (1966) and Aaronson (1967) also report better short-term memory at slow rates than fast ones. Other studies indicate

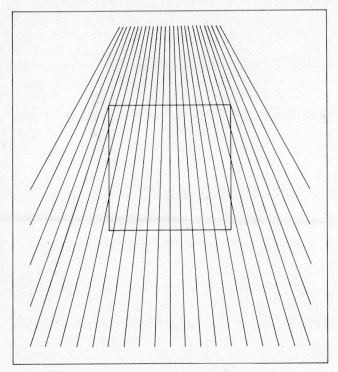

Figure 3.20 *The effect of exposure to radiating lines followed a fraction of a second later by presentation of a square. (Reprinted with permission by Smith and Henrikson, 1955.)*

that the supposed advantage of a slow presentation actually allows more time for the incoming signals to be forgotten. Research by Conrad (1959), Conrad and Hille (1958), Fraser (1958), and Posner (1964) favors increased presentation rates.

In an attempt to reconcile conflicting findings, Aaronson (1967a, 1967b) suggested the import of a third factor in short-term memory—intelligibility or complexity. Intuitively we would expect that the difficulty of interpreting a signal would have much to do with the rate at which the stream of information can be retained accurately. In support of the importance of intelligibility, widely documented findings favor slow presentations under conditions having a great deal of interference or static in the presentation (Fairbanks and Kodman, 1957; Klump and Webster, 1961). At this point, it can only be said that the advantage of slow presentation rates increases under conditions of low intelligibility or where there is maximum interference with the reception of the signal.

Sequence. The notion of sequence (see pp. 103–106) reveals much about how an organism recalls just-occurring events. If information loss did not depend upon the types of strategies people use to recall the stream of incoming signals, we would expect to find that people simply remember events in the order of their presentation. It is plausible, of course, that memorizing items in the order of their presentation is itself a deliberate strategy. If so, we would expect that with a short list of items, say digits or numbers, people would recall the items in their presented sequence. Sometimes this is exactly what happens. At the same time there is considerable evidence that our ability to recall items in sequence is often poor. In a study requiring subjects to recall items from a list of eight digits, Conrad (1959) found that at least 50 percent of the mistakes in identification were due to "order errors." It is also known that the closer the items appear in succession, the less accurate are the powers of discrimination and recall. Schmidt and Kristofferson (1963) argued that poor recall of ordered events is a result of the notion of "psychological time." According to their theory, our sense of time and order is not perfectly continuous; instead we tend to think in momentary sequences that last but a fraction of a second. Hence, people can switch attention from item to item only at the end of a "moment" and cannot as readily differentiate between events within moments. Of relevance to this idea of psychological time are data which led Stroud (1955) to support the notion that discrete moments last about 100 milliseconds. It should be noted, however, that we are talking about errors which occur with only a very fleeting succession of events. Most sequential errors in short-term memory disappear when the time separating two signals is greater than 100 milliseconds (Ladefoged and Broadbent, 1960).

Strategies. Whether psychological time is discrete or continuous, it is clear that we perceive and store items in strategic ways which often differ from the sequence of a presentation (Harley, 1965a, 1965b). Again, we return to confirming evidence of an active, constructive view of the human storage system. Consider as a case in point studies in word association. In the typical word-association task, subjects are asked to memorize a list of words presented in random order from a set of categories—animals, objects, cities, numbers, and the like. Typically, subjects do not try to repeat the items in the order presented. Instead they organize the words in appropriate categories first, then recall some from one category, then some items from another category, and so forth (Bousfield, 1953; Tulving, 1962). Moreover, some people adapt characteristic strategies of reception and recall; that is, they do not pause but maintain a consistent tracking of incoming signals at a rate which approximates the presentation. Others use an alternate strategy of holding back, delaying by a fraction of a second certain decoding operations until more information in a sequence is available (Miller, 1962; Moray and Taylor, 1958). The more redundant the incoming signals, the more apt a person is to employ some delayed strategy which focuses on groups and clusters of words.

In a direct test of the use of strategies in short-term memory, Aaronson (1967b) asked a group of subjects to memorize and recall an auditory sequence consisting of a list of 7 items present at a rate of 3 digits per second and a comparable list presented at a rate of 1.5 digits per second. Subjects then assigned scale values to the type of strategy they employed in both presentations. The four statements used in the test were:

1. You passively waited for all 7 digits to be presented and then actively listened to them.
2. You passively waited for the first few digits to be presented and then actively listened to those as a group. You passively waited for the rest of the digits to be presented and actively listened to them.
3. You actively listened to one digit at a time at a slight delay after its presentation.
4. You actively listened to each single digit as it was presented.

Aaronson found that subjects did employ different strategies: They relied more on listening to one digit at a time for the faster presentation and used more deliberate strategies for the slower rates. It is also known that the more well-developed the strategies of memory become, the more people rely on them in subsequent tasks; these ingrained strategies seem to persist even when the type of presentation changes appreciably.

These findings further substantiate the constructive, inventive aspects of short-term memory. The use of alternative strategies, in accordance with the demands of the situation and the psychological makeup of the respective parties, fits well into a transactional view of decoding-encoding. To fill in the rest of our survey we need to understand the dynamics underlying the transformation of information, once processed, into an encoded response.

RECALL

Of all the concepts in this chapter, the notion of memory system serves as the most direct link between the decoding and encoding stages of information processing. Recall that only a small proportion of incoming signals are retained in consciousness for more than an instant or so. The fleeting sense of the moment suggests that those segments of experience which pass to long-term memory act as a ceiling or upper limit on what is potentially available for later recall and encoding. Hence, the real bottleneck in pinning down the link between decoding and encoding is the difficult question of long-term memory and retention. Just-occurring events can be explained as being the most readily available for immediate response, but the matter of how vestiges of past experience manifest themselves is another, far more difficult problem.

The most striking difference between short-term and long-term memory is the rate at which information is lost, wasted, or otherwise rendered unusable for future experience. In a famous study by Peterson and Peterson (1959), subjects memorized a list of single verbal items and, after intervals ranging from three to eighteen seconds, attempted to recall the items. In the interim, subjects engaged in irrelevant tasks to prevent rehearsal of items heard during the interval. Yet despite the fact that a maximum of only eighteen seconds lapsed between presentation and recall, less than 10 percent of the subjects could recall the items. Further research indicated that the more difficult the intervening task, the less accurate subsequent recall (Posner, 1964). The obvious implication is that the first few seconds are critical in determining what is available for future use in encoding.

It is not clear exactly how segments of just-occurring events pass into long-term storage. Most explanations can be divided into variations of *decay*, or *disuse*, and *interference* theories. Decay theories assume that each incoming signal leaves a neural impression or trace which weakens with time. Forgetting continues over time unless repetition or rehearsal occurs. In decay theories of retention, time, rather than the nature of events, is the critical factor said to account for information loss. In sharp contrast are interference theories, which assume that previous memory traces interfere with traces of just-occurring events. The greater the degree of confusion, the greater the amount of forgetting.

This dispute over forgetting seems largely a result of the difficulties inherent in setting up an unequivocal test of the effects of time on long-term memory. The ideal situation would be to present a sequence of information, followed by a period in which the subjects do nothing, and then to complete a test of their retention. If the subjects could actually do nothing, there would be no confusion between prior events and present experience. Therefore, the interference theorist would predict no loss, whereas the decay theorist could predict an appreciable loss—the greater the time lapse, the greater the loss predicted. The chief obstacle is that the brain cannot "do nothing"; it is constantly at work monitoring and rehearsing, analyzing and recalling, past experience. So, short of any definitive conclusions, we can only observe with Jung (1968) that decay theories seem to fit best into the narrow confines of results on short-term memory, and interference theories best conform to results on long-term memory. The reasoning is that the rapid loss of memory which immediately follows a presentation seems to fit the assumptions of rapid decay. However, information that passes into long-term storage appears to be subject to a host of confusions and errors of interference rather than to a decay rate (Conrad, 1964; Hintzman, 1965, 1967; Posner, 1964).

The complex problem of information retrieval, or recall, is central to determining what is available for the purposes of encoding. Miller (et al., 1960) likened the retrieval problem to the task of a librarian seeking to locate a book. The library represents the storage system, the book the target item, the shelves and catalog the organizing system. Seen in this perspective, the question of how to locate the book is a matter more of the organization and operation of the entire system than storage of one detail. The matter of locating the book is dependent upon the efficiency of the storage system and the plans and strategies available for retrieval. Failure to locate the book does not mean it is missing; it may merely be misshelved, or the plan for retrieving it may be inefficient or inaccurate. What gets recalled (after being located) depends upon the larger capacity of the organism not only to remember but to restructure the past experience relevant to the designated item (Bower, 1967; Norman, 1966).

A remarkable series of experiments in the late 1950s underscored the tremendous power of the human organism to recall past events. While working on techniques to stimulate the speech centers of the cortex, Penfield (1959) accidentally discovered something quite spectacular. When he probed certain portions of the cortex with electronic instruments, subjects suddenly recalled—with astonishingly accurate detail—events ranging from early childhood. Most patients recalled these events with such naturalness that they seemed to experience all the original emotions. One patient, with vivid recall of the details and circumstances, appeared to see herself as she gave birth to her child; another saw himself in his early home in South Africa, complete with recollections of relatives laughing and talking; and still another was deeply moved by a Christmas song she had heard on a distant Christmas Eve in her church at home in Holland.

All the reports have several things in common. Although the electronically triggered events are often trivial, each appears to the subject as a real event. Seldom are the patients conscious of having carried the event in their memories. None of the recollections appears to be based on fantasy. And in contrast to ordinary memory, all the recollections are intense and vivid. Never are the reports vague. Penfield commented: "The patients have never looked upon an experiential response as a remembering. Instead of that is a hearing-again and seeing-again a living-through moments of past time." Perhaps most striking is the overall organizational quality and structure of the recollections. According to Penfield,

> When, by chance, the neurosurgeon's electrode activates past experience, that experience unfolds progressively, moment by moment. This is a little like the performance of a wire recorder or a strip of cinematographic film on which are registered all those things of which the individual was once aware—the things he selected for his attention in that interval of time. Absent from it are the sensations he ignored, the talk he did not heed.
>
> Time's strip of film runs forward, never backward, even when resurrected from the past. It seems to proceed again at time's own unchanged pace. It would seem once one section of the strip has come alive, that the response is protected by a functional all-or-nothing principle. A regulating inhibitory mechanism must guard against the activation of other portions of the film. As long as the electrode is held in place, the experience of the former day goes forward. There is no holding it still, no turning back, no crossing with other periods. When the electrode is withdrawn, it stops as suddenly as it began [p. 53].

The phenomenal discoveries of Penfield's research fit nicely into earlier findings from techniques devised by Sir Frederic Bartlett (1932) to study recall of complex events. Bartlett employed a variety of tests in which subjects were asked to examine and later reproduce some designated material, usually a story or a drawing. By varying the time intervals, Bartlett was able to isolate the effect of increasing time lapse on remembered material. Seldom do subjects give an accurate report of what they see. So great is the distortion from the original material that subjects actually reconstruct the material rather than remember it. The longer the time lapse, the more evident becomes the constructive aspect of the recollections. Bartlett was particularly fascinated by the extent to which recall of specific details hinged on each subject's overall frame of reference. He proposed that long-term recall is more a matter of reconstruction than memory, and he advanced a theory based on the notion of *schema*, or organization imposed upon stored material. A schema is an active organization of past reactions or past experience. The notion of schema places a premium on the constructive aspects of recalling complex events. Without being aware of it, we use schema, according to Bartlett, to integrate past events with present experience into a framework that is constantly being modified and reconstructed in light of our concerns of the moment.

The concept of schemata does not coincide with the present-day interest in the storage and recall of particular memory traces. Most recent work, we have seen, focuses on recall of digits or isolated words and items. Bartlett, however, was interested in the reproduction of complex events. His conception fits best into ideas about the larger fabric of information processing, particularly the interest in the dynamics of integration levels, thought heirarchies, and processing rules and tests, executive routines, plans, strategies, and tactics. Such a tradition rejects attempts to reduce human information processing to the operations of a gigantic and enormously complicated filing system. Instead, the reconstructive view of man assumes particular memory traces have meaning within the context of an individual's preconceptions. What we reactivate is not simply a sequence of memory traces, but rather an active mass of images. In any attempt to recall past events, we recreate the processed information on the basis of all relevant schemata or rules, both past and present. And in the process of recalling or recreating past events, we continue the cycle from self to world and back again.

INFORMATION PROCESSING
AND PERSONAL AWARENESS

So far we have traced the complex sequence of events that begins with the imprint of physical energy on the sense organs and culminates in a complex set of interrelated functions performed by the nervous system. Through it all, the organism always seeks to impose a sense of order on the ceaseless deluge of impressions that impinge both from the physical world and from internally generated activity. The process of transforming sensory data into recognized form, we discovered, is wholly unlike the dispassionate and objective recordings of a tape recorder or TV camera. What we have examined is rather a fascinating and intricate set of adaptive functions designed to register, sort out, transform, monitor, integrate, store, and recall information. Through the complex hierarchy of tests and time delays, many incoming data are lost or selectively classified from the very time they pass from the threshold of awareness to the final stages of storage and recall.

The larger question, then, is whether the four stages of processing adequately account for what we experience when engaged in an act of communication. The answer is that while information processing may be a *necessary* condition of communicative experience, it is not a *sufficient* condition in itself. The components of information processing are the physical and psychological building blocks that make consciousness or personal awareness possible. Yet, just as counting the bricks in a pile does not account for the end product of a completed wall, so also this description of the fundamental building blocks of human information processing does not fully account for what we experience as communication. Hence, another dimension of study, one that deals directly with the problem of personal awareness, must now be explored to account for the dynamic forces underlying the intrapersonal system of communication.

SUGGESTED READINGS

Aaronson, D. "Temporal Factors in Perception and Short-term Memory," *Psychological Bulletin,* 67:130–144, 1967.

Atkinson, R. C., and **Shifrin, R. M.** "Human Memory: A Proposed System and Its Control Processes," in K. W. Spence and J. T. Spence (eds.), *The Psychology of Learning and Motivation: Advances in Research and Theory,* vol. 2. New York: Academic, 1968, pp. 89–195.

Bartlett, F. C. *Remembering.* London: Cambridge, 1932.

Broadbent, D. E. *Perception and Communication.* New York: Pergamon, 1958.

Bruner, J., Goodman, J. J., and **Austin, G. A.** *A Study of Thinking.* New York: Science Editions, Wiley, 1962.

Cherry, C. "Some Experiments on the Recognition of Speech with One and with Two Ears," *Journal of the Acoustical Society of America,* 25:975–979, 1953.

Deutsch, J., and **Deutsch, D.** "Attention: Some Theoretical Considerations," *Psychological Review,* 70:80–89, 1963.

Egeth, H. "Selective Attention," *Psychological Bulletin,* 67:41–57, 1967.

Freedman, J., and **Sears, D.** "Selective Exposure," in L. Berkowitz (ed.), *Advances in Experimental Social Psychology,* vol. 2. New York: Academic, 1965, pp. 57–97.

Hastorf, A. H., and **Cantril, H.** "They Saw a Game: A Case Study," *Journal of Abnormal and Social Psychology,* 49:129–134, 1954.

Johannsen, D. E. "Perception," *Annual Review of Psychology,* 18:1–40, 1967.

Miller, G. A. "The Magical Number Seven, Plus or Minus Two: Some Limits on Our Capacity for Processing Information," *Psychological Review,* 63:81–97, 1956.

Miller, G., Galanter, E., and **Pribram, K.** *Plans and the Structure of Behavior.* New York: Holt, 1960.

Neisser, U. *Cognitive Psychology.* New York: Appleton-Century-Crofts, 1967.

Norman, D. *Memory and Attention: An Introduction to Human Information Processing.* New York: Wiley, 1969.

Schroder, H. M., Driver, M. J., and **Streufert, S.** *Human Information Processing.* New York: Holt, 1967.

Vernon, N. "The Nature of Perception and the Fundamental Stages in the Process of Perceiving," in L. Uhr (ed.), *Pattern Recognition.* New York: Wiley, 1966, pp. 61–73.

Woolridge, D. *The Machinery of the Brain.* New York: McGraw-Hill, 1963.

four
psychological
orientation

Communication may result as much from what we expect to happen in a social situation as it does from what we find. This is a critical distinction, for if man has an interest in making sense of communicative events, he wants even more to make *a certain kind of sense,* one constructed along lines that follow his prior expectations. However, the problem is not simply finding what we expect. Some situations match our expectations; others do not. As Kelley (1963) noted,

> Man looks at his world through transparent patterns or templets which he creates and then attempts to fit over the realities of which the world is composed. The fit is not always good. Yet without such patterns the world appears to be such an undifferentiated homogeneity that man is unable to make any sense out of it [p. 9].

However close the match between what we expect and find, the process of interpreting events within one's frame of reference is a central dimension of human communication. Of the many concepts in the scientific literature which deal with matters of orientation, the notions of "predisposition," "set," "frame of reference," "personal construct," "social schema," and "state of mind" are representative. Common to all these hypothetical constructs is the recognition that psychological orientations may influence our interpretation of events in many ways. The concept of *psychological orientation* is synonymous, then, with attitudes toward communication, our readiness or predisposition to respond to message cues in characteristic ways.

These most pervasive orientations are not developed in a social vacuum but are acquired gradually, often painfully, from birth on (see Chapter 2, Figure 2.4). Through his interpersonal contacts, man learns to approach every opportunity for communication with characteristic feelings of openness or defensiveness, trust or suspicion, commitment or detachment. Barnlund (1968b) noted:

> Every success or failure contributes in some way to [man's] accumulating experiences about the world and how it operates. Such cognitive predispositions are learned unconsciously, and most people are only vaguely aware of their profound effects. Yet they are, in the view of Roger Harrison, "the most important survival equipment we have" [p. 25].

It is hardly surprising, given the array of learning situations, that we should attempt to survive in unique and distinctive ways.

If it is important to acknowledge the most enduring of orientations, it is equally significant to note the influence of those most transitory. In every daily contact—from the fleeting recognition of strangers to the enriching exchange of lifelong friends—each party to communication seeks to impose a frame of reference, a semblance of order and stability, on the succession of his experience. In some encounters a person may be only faintly aware of his orientation: He may only sense a twinge of apprehension, a vague sense of uncertainty or discomfort, a fleeting sense of depression or anxiety. In others, his orientation may be firmly grounded in joy or despair, compassion or contempt, openness or reserve. The more intense the inner feelings, the stronger our sense of anticipation, the less apt we are to be objective about what is said and done. We use our frame of reference to color the subjective interpretation of an interpersonal event. If we expect an encounter to be dull and uninteresting, it is not likely to be otherwise. The congenial manner of others present, their feelings of excitement and personal involvement, will go unnoticed—or even be distorted—if we approach the situation with mistrust.

Transitory feelings of interpersonal encounters necessarily reflect the influence of immediate and recent psychological states. Since an infinite number of factors may color the meaning of verbal interchange, even the most uncomplicated and straightforward interaction between strangers may reflect the accumulative impact of forces that work to make a particular kind of sense out of the event. Consider a student who introduces his roommate to a friend one morning at breakfast. Though the two persons being introduced are considered by a mutual friend to be much alike in personality and temperament, the roommate appears distant and remote while the friend seems congenial and friendly. The difference in their behavior may result from any number of transitory factors which, had they not been operating, would have led to a different personal orientation and tone in the exchange. Probably many factors were involved: The roommate's alarm clock didn't work, his shower unexpectedly turned cold, he was irritated over the heavy starch in his shirt, or he had difficulties with a term paper the night before. Little wonder that two people so much alike would appear to be so different!

Such a case indicates something important about the psychological orientation of the respective parties and how they are subject to change. Psychological orientation refers in the broadest sense to one's frame of reference; it consists of three types of consciousness that we may characterize as *self-directed, other-directed,* and *cooriented.* In differing social circumstances any one psychological state may assume more or less importance but will never be experienced in isolation or in a psychological vacuum. As communicators we cannot undergo a change in orientation without experiencing some change in the meaning we attribute to the verbal activity of others or to aspects of our relationships. In this chapter we will examine how these crucial components work to become our most valuable survival equipment.

SELF–DIRECTED ORIENTATION

It is possible to conceive of the slippery notion of self in a number of acceptable ways. Self may connote a set of feelings or personal attitudes (an internalization or introspection), or it may be viewed simply as a process involving self-awareness (an externalizing examination). Since our interest is the relationship of self-awareness to communication, the concept may be most fruitfully approached as a psychological state characterized by awareness both of self and toward self which can occur either in the presence or in the absence of others. For our purposes, then, *self-awareness includes any behavior in which a sense of self is central to the meaning that is attributed to the event.*

Among living creatures, only man can act socially toward himself by imagining how others view him. An inner dialogue is implied when we refer to a person "arguing or reasoning with himself," "kicking himself," "reassuring himself," "consoling himself," or "making a pact with himself"; or when we say he has set for himself goals, plans, schedules, deadlines, timetables, standards, pledges, promises of reward, or countless other expected acts. "The conscious life of man," wrote Blumer (1967), "from the time that he awakes until he falls asleep, is a continual flow of self-indications—notations of the things with which he deals and takes into account [p. 140]."

The capacity to act toward oneself does not require another person. Nonetheless, the power of self does come strongly into force in all interpersonal contacts. Man is again unique among animals because he can address himself from the standpoint of others. In all of his dealings with others, man is both object and subject. Admittedly the ability to see ourselves as others do is often poorly fashioned, but there is little doubt that we can. Mead's (1934) famous phrase, "taking the role of the other," designates self as an integral facet of all interpersonal conduct. Man, in Mead's view, is not innately self-conscious, yet he can experience other people as objects of his thinking, and they in turn—through communication—give him reactions that make him the object of their conscious experience. Through social interaction, a person learns to think of himself from the standpoint of others. By taking the position or role of others, man can get out of himself, so to speak, and look back on his own actions. Only where there is social communication, Mead argued, can man become "a self insofar as he can take the attitude of another and act towards himself as others act [p. 171]."

Not only does communication fashion one's self-directed orientations, it also serves to guide future behavior. Thus, a change in self-orientation implies that some sort of social interaction has influenced the way a person views himself. Though more than a single event is typically required to alter one's self-concept, rather dramatic changes can occur in a short time. Note the intertwined relationship between communication, self-orientation, and changes in behavior by the participants in this anecdote from Kinch (1967):

> A group of graduate students in a seminar in social psychology became interested in the notions implied in the interactionist approach. One evening after the seminar five of the male members of the group were discussing some of the implications of the theory and came to the realization that it might be possible to invent a situation where the "others" systematically manipulated their responses to another person, thereby changing that person's self-concept and in turn his behavior. They thought of an experiment to test the notions they were dealing with. They chose as their subject (victim) the one girl in the seminar. The subject can be described as, at best, a very plain girl who seemed to fit the stereotype (usually erroneous) that many have of graduate student females. The boys' plan was to begin in concert to respond to the girl as if she were the best-looking girl on campus. They agreed to work into it naturally so that she would not be aware of what they were up to. They drew lots to see who would be the first to date her. The loser, under the pressure of the others, asked her to go out. Although he found the situation quite unpleasant, he was a good actor and by continually saying to himself "she's beautiful, she's beautiful . . ." he got through the evening. According to the agreement it was now the second man's turn and so it went. The dates were reinforced by the similar responses in all contacts the men had with the girl. In a matter of a few

short weeks the results began to show. At first it was simply a matter of more care in her appearance; her hair was combed more often and her dresses were more neatly pressed; but before long she had been to the beauty parlor to have her hair styled, and was spending her hard-earned money on the latest fashions in women's campus wear. By the time the fourth man was taking his turn dating the young lady, the job that had once been undesirable was now quite a pleasant task. And when the last man in the conspiracy asked her out, he was informed that she was pretty well booked up for some time in the future. It seems there were more desirable males around than those "plain" graduate students [p. 235].

Our story does not directly prove that the young lady changed her self-orientation because of the reactions reflected in the others' behavior. Yet if it is reasonable to assume some consistency between overt behavior and inner psychological states, then surely her determined effort to improve her appearance supports the notion of socially defined self. It is interesting, too, that the behavior of the male conspirators changed even though they were engaged in what they regarded merely as an experiment. Their reactions suggest that not all changes in self-orientation occur through a process of unconscious change. The fact that man happens to be fully aware of "stepping out of himself" (as these young men were) does not diminish the potential for change.

Much of what is known about the dynamics of self-oriented psychological states can be integrated around a single working proposition: *The self-directed orientations of people engaged in communication tend to make each interactant unique, integrated, internally consistent, and active.* In the remainder of this section, we will examine these four attributes of self and see how they work.

Uniqueness

With so much emphasis on the social, shared aspects of self, it may be easy to forget that the very notion is one of the most personal and subjectively interpreted aspects of human consciousness. From the standpoint of self-orientation, people differ in a number of respects. We are each unique in the type of communication we experience, the range and succession of our social events, and the roles we maintain while engaged in communication. We also differ in the particular sense of anticipation and remembrances we have, the level of involvement we experience, the sense of risk and trust we feel, and the sensitivity we show toward others. And through it all, we learn, adapt, and thereby define our unique sense of self.

Fortunately, adults have no monopoly on a richly developed sense of self. Though infants have little or no self-awareness, children readily learn to act toward themselves from a perspective supplied by the reactions of others. Not surprisingly, the matter of self-concept is known to be one of the factors that correlates most closely with student achievement at all grade levels. In his work with students at a large, integrated urban high school Borton (1970) used the question "Who am I?" Students came to him "thirty . . . an hour, five hours a day—each a bubbling volcano crusted over with self-consciousness. . . ." Among the many voices Borton described was that of "a loose-jointed Negro boy in [his] slow section, who had written [the following] loose-jointed but beautiful description of himself":

> I am Charles Thomas a law ablie citizen who should have right. I know who I am because there no other one like me, though I Belong to another and I may not stand a gost of a chance, But I tell the world of Charles, Because He a victim of circumstance. If I said I was the only Boy who act this way, then that would be a sin. Im a boy who dream dreames, shall have vision, think, love, enjoy everythink, I am a boy who to self consence, who respect mother father, and other people [p. 6].

Another student wrote about his expectations:

> In ten years from now I will probably be wishing my past was not true. In ten years from now I would gladly pledge all of my material wealth, to erase certain events, that have not as yet, taken place. And I will be truely sorry for what has happened then, but as I approach these problems I will not give them a second thought but now I have a future, in ten years I will have a past [p. 9].

And finally, in testimony to the desperation that can engulf one's self-orientations, Borton described a girl who had watched a swan and later spoke of it as a part of her personal dream, as "locked away in her mental 'jewel box' where no one could get at it." She then wrote:

> I am like a crazy, complicated maze.
> I never cry, never love
> I am like egotistical egotists

> I am fear, constant fear that they might find out what I really am. I'm not really fear but fear the blanket that protects and prohibits what I really am. I've locked it all away in a jewel box. I'm afraid that it might be hideous. I'm afraid that there won't be anything at all. I'll be disgusted if it's beautiful.

> My only request is to know it.
> When I am dying. Or dead [p. 67].

However reasonable the idea of uniqueness as a leading aspect of self-orientation may appear, a troublesome question arises. Namely, if individual differences are so marked, and if these differences are of such a personal and private nature, how can they be shared with another? The question raises an issue of enormous import, one that has no obvious or intuitive answer.

A disturbing possibility is that self-oriented thought cannot *always* be the object of meaningful communication. Perhaps there are gaps between individuals that cannot be bridged by the spoken word. Conceivably, at a certain point each party's uniqueness may work against the power of words to create understanding.

The possibility that intensely personal aspects of self cannot be shared runs counter to some prevailing American attitudes about individual initiative and work. There is a tendency for Americans—particularly those who adhere to the work ethic—to equate the requirements of authentic communication with those of physical labor. Thus, the popular conception goes, if people are sincerely motivated to work at it hard enough, they can express themselves about anything. So conceived, the task of achieving common understanding with another person is reduced to a matter of will and resolve. When difficulties are encountered, a whole battery of work-centered rules for improving communication are available. Many popular ideas about how to communicate amount to little more than sophisticated versions of an injunction to "work at it." Thus, if you do not find it easy to listen to another person, you should "strive to become more conscious of what they say," "really concentrate on listening," "get motivated," and so on. Similar advice is available to the student of public speaking, where the model of effective interaction is often reduced to equations for working hard on outlines, gathering an elaborate ream of supporting material, practicing delivery religiously, and displaying a "sincere desire" to communicate. The notion of work is, of course, only one step removed from motivating audiences with long lists of appeals and the like. When all else fails, the communicator can always fall back on projecting an image of sincerity and honest intent. While there may be nothing wrong with the principle of "working at communication" per se, there is something quite errant and injurious in relying on rules that reduce the incredible complexities of human interaction to the work habits required for laying bricks or digging foundations in a rainstorm. The numerous references in popular literature to "communication barriers" (see Chapter 1) conjure up images of the difficulties encountered by a demolition crew or by athletes on an obstacle course.

But any number of social situations exist where no amount of determined effort will bridge the gap between interested parties. As Rogers (1951) noted, much of what we experience of self is "for each individual, in a very significant sense, a private world [p. 484]." It is impossible to conceive of a communicative situation with a one-to-one relationship between what we each experience of self and what we share. Inevitably, much of the meaning we construct must remain within the private domain of our inner thoughts.

It is not possible, wrote Kelley (1963),

> for one to express the whole of his construction system. Many of one's constructs have no symbols to be used as convenient word handles. They are therefore difficult, not only for others to grasp and subsume within

> their own systems, but also difficult for the person himself to manipulate or to subsume within the verbally labeled parts of his system. The fact that they do not readily lend themselves to organization within the verbally labeled parts of the system makes it difficult for a person to be very articulate about how he feels, or for him to predict what he will do in a future situation which, as yet, exists only in terms of verbal descriptions [p. 110].

To the limits of self-expression must be added countless problems of interpersonal interpretation. It is most difficult, often impossible, to create understanding where there is no basis of shared experience. The greater the divergence in matters of past experience, value system, and life style, the greater are the liabilities of trying to communicate the unique aspects of personality. Hence, any appeal to work-centered rules is apt to be futile and pernicious when applied to people with unique and divergent outlooks, say a member of the Black Panther Party and a white separatist or a member of the John Birch Society and a communist.

Recognition of the limitations associated with self-oriented thought does not fully resolve the question of uniqueness raised earlier. Were uniqueness the only characteristic of self, the possibility for mutual understanding of individual differences would be truly impoverished. Fortunately, some forces work to facilitate mutual understanding. The very existence of language constitutes a mechanism for sharing, however imperfectly, the private domain of human experience. The resources of language serve as an enormous wellspring for establishing shared meaning and common ground. What is important about the potential to share is that it is based not only on commonly available tools for expressing inner experience but also on common forces that work to frame "self-hood." An analogous biological process produces fingerprints that are unique to each person yet share similar patterns and characteristics. In the remaining section we shall examine several aspects of self-orientation that, to a large degree, work in the interest of shared orientation.

Integration

It is tempting, and in some quarters fashionable, to reduce self-awareness to a bundle of sensations and responses to stimuli. One factor this automistic view ignores is man's enormous ability to organize his private thoughts into a totally integrated sense of self-consciousness—often independent of the imprint of physical events. The organization is not a result of differences between signals taken in and those given out, an operation Boulding (1966) cryptically referred to as a "sausage machine grinding out instructions from messages received." It occurs, rather, because of the characteristic ways each person has of integrating intermittent and fleeting impressions of self into meaningful patterns which are filtered through an elaborate and active principle of internal organization. We encountered evidence for the hierarchial and holistic nature of information processing in Chapter 2, and there is every reason to believe that the same principles apply to the larger matters of psychological orientation. We must remember, however, that man's heightened sense of self-awareness, as contrasted to lower animals', is not merely a result of the *amount* of information he can process. The explanation for what Boulding called "the chief glory of our species" lies rather in the *greater capacity of the organism to integrate impressions of self into extended and larger patterns of self-directed thought.*

Amid the constant struggle for self-perspective is an urgent need for structure and order. The importance of a unified and integrated sense of self is widely recognized in the writings of personality theorists. Lecky (1945) spoke, for example, of the craving for a sense of unification and underscored his idea with phrases such as "living unit," the "unity and integrity of the organism," and the "self-consistency" of inner thought. In reference to each individual's need to "come to terms with the environment," Goldstein (1939) grounded his organismic theory of personality on the principle of equalization, which emphasizes the need for balance, centering, consistency, and orderliness. So great is the need for an integrated sense of self that Angyal (1951) viewed man as striving to submerge his sense of individuality in the interest of forming a harmonious union with the environment. In Angyal's holistic view, "The human being is both a *unifier,* an organizer of his immediate personal world, and a *participant* in what he conceives as the superordinate whole to which he belongs [p. 133]."

The interest of personality theorists in the notion of self-actualization also underscores the view that man strives for what Hall and Lindzey (1957) termed "the fullest, most complete differentiation and harmonious blending of all aspects of man's total personality [p. 96]." Thus, Erich Fromm (1955) considered self-actualization the integrated unfolding of "one's own inner activity . . . and the mystical experience of union [pp. 31–32]." Likewise, in the schema advanced by Abraham Maslow (1954), all human needs are organized along an integrated hierarchy of potency or priority that regards self-actualization as a master motive. As the most potent *physiological needs* like hunger and thirst are satisfied, the organism turns increasingly to concerns Maslow categorized as *safety, love and belongingness, esteem,* and finally *self-actualization.* The five categories in the hierarchy form a kind of ladder. Only after the satisfaction of lower needs does the person turn to the higher needs of self. By realizing his unique potential, man places ever greater emphasis on the attainment of esteem—the need for a stable, firmly based, and usually high sense of self and a regard for others. And with the experience of self-actualization comes greater self-awareness, acceptance, spontaneity, independence, and capacity for intense interpersonal relationships.

The seemingly universal need for an integrated and stable sense of self has important consequences for communication. For one thing, the nature of self-orientation makes a considerable difference in some of the larger attitudes a person has about himself (Kuhn and McPartlund, 1954). Persons who have a stable and fully integrated sense of self are better able to become oriented to problems outside of themselves. They are more likely to attain an increased measure of autonomy, a freshness of perspective, more creativity, and greater ability to resist pressures to conform (Maslow, 1954).

Self-related attitudes also have a marked bearing on the nature of the communication process. When compared with people who lack a stable and well-developed sense of self-regard, those who are high in self-esteem tend to show less anxiety and hostility and greater tolerance for uncertainty; they also manifest greater spontaneity and are better able to express feelings of sympathy, concern, and affection. Those lacking in self-regard tend to communicate in ways that are disorganized, unrealistic, and ineffectual (Cohen, 1959). There is additional evidence that the attitudes a person holds about himself help to define the meaning he attributes to others' behavior, particularly to their attempts to influence his attitudes and overt actions. In the main, research indicates that high esteem protects a person from social influence; the exact degree of resistance depends, among other things, on personality attributes (Appley and Moeller, 1963), the complexity of the message (Levonian, 1968; Nisbett and Gordon, 1967), the attention and comprehension of what is said (McGuire, 1968c), and the interaction context (Gergen and Wishnow, 1965). We will return to other fundamental aspects of the complex relation between self-orientation and interpersonal behavior after considering the role of *internal consistency* and *activity* in self-oriented conduct.

Consistency

To claim that self-orientations grow from the need for a stable and integrated sense of self is to give an accurate but incomplete picture. A remaining and crucial problem is *how* the integration takes place and along what lines. Undoubtedly the notion of consistency provides a valuable clue. Admittedly, the doctrine of consistency is not relevant solely to the topic at hand, namely the role of psychological orientations in human communication. Nor for that matter are consistency theories confined to research in the behavioral sciences —though the consistency theories of Heider (1946), Osgood and Tannenbaum (1955), and Festinger (1957) have as much right as any to the claim of offering the dominant focus in psychology during the 1950s and most of the 1960s. In a general sense some argue that the underlying consistency in the universe makes the very existence of science possible. Yet even if consistency in man is evidence of universal consistency, it has a special application in explaining how notions of self are organized along lines that seem free of ambiguity and inconsistency.

The one consistency theory that most closely fits communication is Newcomb's A-B-X theory (1953, 1959, 1961). In the simplest possible communicative act one person (A) transmits information to another (B) about something (X). The degree of consistency in the relationship between A and B depends on the interplay among certain minimum components of the system, namely the attraction of A toward B and B toward A plus their respective attitudes toward X, the object of their interaction. Though the system is presumed to be in a state of equilibrium, changes in any one aspect or their orientations may lead to further changes that follow what Newcomb called the "strain toward symmetry." The notion of symmetry is similar to the idea of cognitive consistency, or balance. The tension associated with a lack of symmetry creates pressures to interact in ways that restore the sense of symmetry. For example, suppose that A and B are strongly attracted toward one another, yet manage to get into a heated dispute. Since consistency theory predicts that people will want people they like to approve of the ideas they endorse, both A and B presumably should experience considerable psychological tension. Therefore, Newcomb predicted that they will alter their interaction along lines that reduce the strain produced by inconsistent orientations. Among the options are changes in the strength of attraction (A feels less attracted toward B) and adjustments in the relevance of X (either A or B decides the topic is not worth fighting over) or in the perceived importance of X to the other person (either A or B concludes that the other does not really mean what he says). Another outlet for tension may be a change in attitude toward the topic or, if all else fails, withdrawal from the situation.

Newcomb's predictions were all based on the assumption that the very existence of inconsistency is a noxious state which people tend to avoid. However, the problem for balance theories is that the sense of inconsistency is a very personal matter. Each person has his own standard for judging what, for him, is congruent with the orientations he maintains toward himself and others. Admittedly the forms taken to ensure self-consistency may not always be obvious to the independent observer, as can be seen from the following conversation cited by Allport (1954):

Mr. X: The trouble with Jews is that they only take care of their own group.

Mr. Y: But the record of the Community Chest shows that they give more generously than non-Jews.

Mr. X: That shows that they are always trying to buy favor and intrude in Christian affairs. They think of nothing but money; that is why there are so many Jewish bankers.

Mr. Y: But a recent study shows that the per cent of Jews in banking is proportionally much smaller than the per cent of non-Jews.

Mr. X: That's just it. They don't go in for respectable business. They would rather run night clubs.

So nature abhors inconsistency. In the realm of self-orientation, this rarely if ever entails a psychological state devoid of tension or conflict.

Inconsistency is not like a light switch—either on or off. Rather, the noxious effect of incompatible information is one of degree or magnitude and is more akin to the sensation of watching houselights being brightened or dimmed. Thus, the pressure to resolve inner conflict increases in direct proportion to the strength of a given cluster of inconsistent associations or ideas. Let us represent the strength of any cognitive elements along a continuum where 1 is weakest and 5 is strongest and where $+$ is positive and $-$ is negative. It is unlikely, then, that a person who vaguely views himself as prompt $(+1)$ will feel inconsistent for being thirty minutes late to an appointment (-1). Another person in an identical situation would feel considerably inconsistent so long as he places a premium on promptness $(+5)$ and also regards a thirty-minute delay as a serious matter (-5). In a countless number of ways every communicative situation requires each party to align aspects of self-orientation and experiences of the moment against the rule of compatibility. There is apt to be strong pressure to resolve inconsistency when a person who is confident of his leadership ability $(+4)$ suddenly has reason to believe that he will not be elected to an important office by his closest friends (-5). A person whose self-orientations center on the idea that he enjoys talking with people $(+4)$ would have difficulty admitting that he is at fault for carrying on a dull and meaningless conversation (-5). Along similar lines a person who sees himself as fluent and articulate $(+3)$ is not apt to be comfortable in a situation where he acknowledges that he cannot think of what to say or do (-3).

Another important qualification is that inconsistency is not uniformly at work in all communicative situations. Generally, the strongest pressures to resolve inconsistency arise only when a person commits himself to a particular decision or mode of *active* participation. Hence, it is one thing for an interested bystander to admit that a student protest rally is being badly managed, but it is quite another for the persons in charge to acknowledge the same. Typically, people feel most bound to commitments made in public; highly visible social acts are far more apt to engender sensitivity to matters of incompatibility than are actions made in private, however well-intended the person may be at the time. Moreover, the less the sense of personal justification a person feels toward his public commitment, the more intensely he is apt to feel a sense of inconsistency over his actions. We will have more to say about the important role of participation and justification of one's commitments to communication in Chapters 8 and 9.

Selective Exposure and Avoidance. The tendency to be self-consistent functions to delimit communication in two important ways. The first has to do with the kind of communicative situations people place themselves in—whenever they have a choice. One way to act in accordance with the principle of selective exposure (see pages 372–373) is simply to avoid situations where marked inconsistencies in one's psychological orientation are most apt to occur. Selective exposure may assume a number of forms. A score of studies support the idea that given a choice people will avoid information which is inconsistent with their attitudes (Brodbeck, 1956; Cohen et al., 1959; Festinger, 1957; Mills, 1965a; Mills et al., 1959). One representative finding is that people are far more likely to express interest in reading advertisements for products they endorse than for those they reject (Mills, 1965a). The question is complicated, however, both by the many failures to support the notion of dissonance avoidance (Adams, 1961; Ehrlick et al., 1957; Feather, 1962, 1963, 1964) and by evidence that willingness to seek out incompatible information is consistent with a sense of self-confidence, an individual's sense that he "can handle it"; people are known to differ, sometimes dramatically, in both their confidence and their capacity for dealing with opposing information (Canon, 1964; Festinger, 1964a; Mills, 1965b; Mills and Ross, 1964).

Another instance of the consistency principle is evidenced when people choose to interact largely with those they judge most like themselves. There is enormous scientific support for the idea that people seek those whose thoughts and actions they regard as compatible with their own. One study by Backman and Secord (1962) reported that sorority girls interact most often with those whom they regard as supporting their own self-concept. And a raft of investigations have noted that feelings of psychological stress are greatest whenever people find themselves acting in ways they consider incompatible with their private view of themselves (Gross et al., 1958; Hanson, 1962; Merton, 1957; Schwartz, 1957; Stone, 1962). Another matter, the frequently noted tendency to favor familiar surroundings and established routines, seemingly indicates a need for stable, predictable, and, hence, consistent social surroundings.

The bent toward self-consistency delimits not only matters of exposure to information and situations but also the range of interpretations that can be imposed on the information. It is well known that people engaged in communication tend to evaluate their behavior and others' against standards stemming from the need for self-consistency (Goffman, 1959; Harvey et al., 1957; Howard and Berkowitz, 1958; Stone, 1962). Some responses are attempts at self-enhancement, where people try to anticipate which actions lead others to think highly of them and then act accordingly (Combs, 1959). Others seek protection of self against the unfavorable responses of their interactants (Backman and Secord, 1959; Gerald, 1961).

Selective Forgetting and Discounting. *Selective exposure* and *avoidance* are not the only ways of dealing with dissonant information. In many communicative situations there is simply no way to "tune out" the source of inconsistency—for reasons as diverse as the lack of control over a situation or a sense of deference toward a speaker. Under such circumstances, the odds favor some form of perceptual distortion of incompatible information. Herein the arsenal of the human mind is formidable indeed: The simplest tactics are either *selective forgetting* or *discounting* of the material. It should not seem too surprising to discover that debators tend to remember those arguments which strongly favor their stand and to forget their weakest arguments as well as the strongest arguments of the opponent (Jones and Kohler, 1958). Discounting is a corrective psychological measure that renders contradictory information less plausible, less acceptable, or less important than it would otherwise be. Usually discounting is simply a means of minimizing the impact of some incompatible information (Hastorf and Cantril, 1954; Kendall and Wolfe, 1949). That persons do discount information they find incompatible has been demonstrated in a variety of settings (Brehm, 1960; Cronkhite, 1966, 1969; Festinger, 1957). Moreover, receivers are known to attach less significance to their opponents' evidence and reasoning than to their supporters' (Delia, 1970; Lefford, 1946; Thistlethwaite, 1950; Waly and Cook, 1965). As we will discover in Chapter 5, the greater the personal involvement, the less people are able to judge opposing information in an objective and detached manner.

A person may discount incompatible information in a number of ways. One consists of devaluating everything associated with a given set of related ideas. For example, a person may be uncomfortable because he views himself as extremely high in self-esteem and confidence ($+4$) and yet cannot bring himself to feel secure (-5) when speaking before large groups, an activity he also values. One option is to restore self-consistency by depreciating or deemphasizing the importance of speaking as an indication of self-confidence. "After all," he tells himself, "what's so important about public speaking —it's got little to do with professional advancement, social standing, or my contribution to the community." If this decision is not feasible, there is a selective form of discounting which Heider (1958) called "differentiation." This is used when inconsistency arises in matters associated with some global aspect of self-orientation: Rather than discounting the entire cluster of associations, a person separates them into those he continues to value and those he does not. To return to our example, the person may differentiate between self-confidence in public speaking and confidence in a one-to-one situation. By making the distinction between self-confidence$_1$ and self-confidence$_2$ and by devaluating the former, self-consistency can be readily restored. It may be, as Brown (1965) noted, that the process of differentiation is a basic pattern underlying personal attitudes generally.

A Warning. Before turning to another aspect of self-orientation, a final word of caution is in order. We have discussed the consistency principle as a means of gaining added perspective on the concept of self-orientation. In so doing, we have deliberately avoided mentioning the particular theoretical underpinnings of various consistency positions, which are themselves open to criticism. Since the criticisms are discussed in detail elsewhere (Brown, 1965; Chapanis and Chapanis, 1964; Cronkhite, 1966; Freedman, 1968; Zajonc, 1968b, 1970), they need not be spelled out here. Nonetheless, it is important to note that *man does not absolutely avoid psychological states that produce dissonance.* In fact, in countless situations he seems to seek them. Some people, in addition, are known to have a high tolerance for internal stress, while others do not. So while man may avoid inconsistency and may even make decisions aimed at resolving it, he also has an inclination to seek inconsistency in situations where he is confident that he can handle it. The very fact that man often seeks and then copes with inconsistent information limits the extent to which we can generalize the consistency principle. So the larger question is not the truth of the tendency but its extent and the circumstances under which it operates. Given the existing state of knowledge, we can only conclude that the doctrine of consistency is a necessary and useful, but not sufficient, basis to account for self-orientation.

Activeness

Since the incessant need to know who we are comes mainly by gauging the reactions of others, the very act of communicating entails a rather personal risk. Risk is psychological in nature and amounts to nothing less than a required change in the way we view ourselves. The stakes in most communicative situations may seem fleeting and inconsequential, but there is always a risk of nonrecognition or outright disapproval. Each success or failure contributes, in however minute a fashion, to the ever-unfinished work of self-definition. Few men can withstand, or remain unaffected by, a single important situation in which they find themselves received with indifference, disrespect, or (worse) outright contempt. Usually, however, the cumulative record of minute pinpricks to the self take the greatest toll. Self-doubt may result from hearing one's name mispronounced often, from a speech defect, from feelings of personal inadequacy, or from general difficulties in finding something worthwhile to say. Even another's silence or unresponsiveness may trigger self-doubt. Conversely, actions that suggest approval and respect can be the touchstone for reassessment and restoration of self-regard. From the effects of a single situation—good or bad—most people recover quickly. Only after a succession of events are the most pervasive of self-orientations imprinted and categorized under the headings of acceptance, recognition, respect or—on the painful side of the ledger—rejection, threat, or self-inadequacy.

If communication can render such profound changes on matters of self-orientation over time, why then do so few people appear to be altered by the course of their everyday lives? Why the gap between the potential for change and the change itself? These two questions are important ones. In any given day, most of us confront a host of unfamiliar people in new social situations with unpredictable outcomes. Even the routines of a typical working day can engender feelings of tension, inferiority, recognition, approval, isolation, frustration, self-importance, esteem, and doubt. Yet, amid the panorama

of a changing social environment and an evolving set of interpersonal relationships, most of us maintain a frame of reference that remains reasonably stable
and free of ambiguity. At issue, then, is the degree to which self-oriented
stability can be maintained in an age of ever-increasing velocity and interpersonal entanglements.

In large part, we choose not to abandon or drastically alter our
sense of self because we have a vested interest in preventing radical change.
For most of our waking hours, we are actively engaged in maintaining a framework of orientations that is uniquely integrated to be consistent with our
inner chemistry. Therefore, in any verbal interaction—where there is always
the potential for self-risk—any view of man as a passive interpreter of stimuli
is, once again, patently inadequate. To enjoin the word *active* is simply to
stress with Bertalanffy (1968) that "internal activity rather than reaction to
stimuli is fundamental [p. 106]." The basis for such personal activity is not so
much a conscious need to make a dispassionate measurement of the reactions
of others as a need to make an active effort at constructing a significance that
is personally acceptable. The difference between the measured reaction and the
constructed one is critical in most communicative situations. For it is man's role
as active agent that enables him, as Kelley (1963) rightly insisted, to chart any
course of behavior, "whether explicitly formulated, or implicitly acted out,
verbally expressed or utterly inarticulate, consistent with other courses of
behavior or inconsistent with them, intellectually reasoned or vegetatively
sensed [p. 9]."

The human organism has a formidable repertoire of stratagems for
pursuing a stable interpersonal environment. We have already discussed
certain decoding stratagems in connection with information processing
(Chapter 2). Consider how some options might work in tandem for a coed who
faces the bleak prospect of having no date for the most important social event
of the school year. It is possible, but highly unlikely, that a young lady with a
high self-regard, a frequent dating record, and a strong desire to attend the
event would go through the affair without the slightest sense of self-doubt.
Probably uppermost in her arsenal of tactics is the use of selective perception.
As the deadline approaches, she begins to anticipate an invitation from one of
her former dates. Every ring of the telephone heightens her sense of expectation. Privately she selectively perceives the significance of conversations
between her roommates and their dates; without realizing it she attaches less
significance to their chatter about the event than she would otherwise. Then
there is the matter of selective interaction. As the event looms near, the coed
unwittingly gravitates to the conversations of those in a similar plight, rather
than to those of the elect. If necessary, she may go through a private dialogue
to quell moments of greatest uneasiness: "After all," she may tell herself, "I've
had to work when most of the dates were being set up." An alternative and more
drastic technique is to discount the importance of the event itself—and

thereby restore consistency. Probably the most dramatic change comes when our unfortunate coed begins to alter the tenor of her conversation with others. She seems to go out of her way to be congenial and friendly, encouraging and approving the sort of comments from the eligible that she might well ignore otherwise.

There is abundant evidence that threats to self-orientation lead to the active changes in perception and overt behavior just described. In the formulative stages of interpersonal relationships, the participants do tend to be highly selective in the behavior they display (Jourard and Laskow, 1958). If they anticipate future interactions, the respective parties are far more apt than they would otherwise be to screen the aspects of self that they are willing to place on public inspection (Gergen and Wishnow, 1965). There is also evidence for certain reciprocal aspects between communication and self-regard. For instance, a person who holds negative attitudes toward himself tends to actively construe negative meaning in the action of others (Diggory, 1966; Phillips, 1951). Conversely, consistent feelings of self-approval tend to be projected in interpersonal situations and to be met with approval, resulting in heightened feelings of self-regard. Experiments by Haas and Maehr (1965) indicate that people are normally quite sensitive to the degree of approval or disapproval they receive and that the resultant changes in self-ratings last for several weeks. The extent to which communication leads to reciprocal changes in decoding activity and overt behavior corresponds with the number of interactions, the significance or regard each person has for the other, the intensity of the interpersonal climate, and the self-involvements of each (Videbeck, 1960).

It now should be apparent why the sense of self plays such a strategic role in the psychological make-up of people engaged in verbal interaction. The ability to act toward oneself is the central mechanism the human organism uses to interpret the actions of others. Self defines who we are and how we judge others in relation to us. It influences, as we discovered in Chapter 3, the meaning we attribute to the torrent of impressions we get from the physical world, and it serves as a barometer for our inner world of thought. Through the full gamut of human dealings—verbal wranglings, idle banter, heated confrontation, intimate disclosure, subterfuge, and innuendo—the self adds to our storehouse of defining information. Hence, the individual sense of self is constantly taking on new shape. It is neither fixed nor capricious, yet in some elastic and dynamic way it permeates all facets of the unfolding moment and brings a wondrous sense of immediacy to human experience.

OTHER-DIRECTED ORIENTATION

Communicating fully with another entails a distinct shift in one's psychological orientation. In essence the required change is away from the comfort and safety of self-preoccupation and toward a more inclusive frame of reference that embraces the experiential field of another person. To be experienced fully, an interpersonal orientation requires a willingness to go beyond the claims of self to share in an intensely personal and subjective relationship.

Regrettably, most interpersonal contacts involve only a sporadic and uneven sense of mutuality. Part of the problem is the risk of self-disclosure. To focus on others' behavior is to attend to reminders of what they directly or indirectly say we are, and to reminders of what we are not—our failures, misplaced commitments, erroneous assumptions, self-delusions, and misguided intentions. When the reminders become too painful, we may resort to the protective strategies discussed earlier, especially to distortion, selective recall, disassociation, and avoidance.

Even more volatile is the risk that we may have to change our self-concept. The risk of disclosure may stem from misunderstanding, from threats to one's status, from questioned motives, flat-out rejection, and a host of other psychological inquiries; often it is easier to withdraw, to establish social distance and fall back upon a battery of other personal defenses. Little wonder, then, that the act of communicating fully should have prompted Barnlund (1968) to suggest that it "may be the most courageous of all human acts [p. 37]."

Imperfections and personal risks notwithstanding, the human organism still has an enormous capacity to interact with others in profound and moving ways. So the central question is how communicators are able to maintain a stable and integrated personal frame of reference while also attending to the actions of those who charter the course of their day-to-day experience. In one sense, this entire book deals in some way with more inclusive aspects of interpersonal orientation. However, where later chapters are addressed to specific influences, the remainder of this chapter deals with the underlying aspects of interpersonal impressions.

Source Credibility

Not until quite recently have phrases such as "projecting the right image," "credibility," "prestige," and "credibility gap" come so prominently to public attention. In the political arena, for example, journals and newspapers made hardly any reference to political credibility until the 1960 Presidential race between John F. Kennedy and Richard M. Nixon. Recall the controversy over Kennedy's alleged lack of political experience and the furor over the supposedly anemic appearance of Nixon during the first of the famous TV debates. Then there were the subsequent "crises" over the credibility of what Kennedy revealed about his handling of incidents in Berlin and the Bay of Pigs. Two years later came the controversy over ethical issues raised by the 1964 Presidential TV campaigns. By 1967 a whole generation of young people had witnessed unprecedented social ferment—precipitated largely by Viet Nam—over not only the credibility of Lyndon Johnson but the integrity of the office of the President. With its rapid popularization, credibility has been expanded in meaning to include images of persons, public statements, platforms, offices, and institutions. Even the mass media engender questions of credibility—and most people place greater faith in visual media than in print and radio (Greenburg, 1966; Westley and Severin, 1964).

Underlying the many uses of the term *credibility* are a number of common elements. The term corresponds roughly to impressions or images people hold toward a message source—whether a person, a medium, or an institution. Moreover, the impression is largely evaluative and general. A person may have good credibility or bad credibility, or it may be conceived as high, moderate, or low with few precise distinctions in between. Also, it is tempting to think of credibility as something one possesses, much like sex or weight. However, the scientific meaning of the term is closely tied to what persons perceive to be the characteristics of a source. Ordinarily, there is no one-to-one relationship between *actual* and *perceived* source characteristics. Technically, however, it is as misleading to think of credibility as "whatever is in the eye of the beholder" as it is to conceive of it in terms of the inherent attributes of a source. Rather, we should think of credibility as a result of the interaction between source-related attributes and perceived attributes that are held by receivers.

In rhetorical theory, interest in credibility goes back 2,300 years to Aristotle, who used the term *ethos* to refer to a "favorable disposition" held by listeners toward the intelligence, goodwill, and character of a public speaker (Cooper, 1932). In current parlance, credibility refers to *the image of a source in any communicative situation*. Much of what is known about the dynamics of source credibility centers around three propositions which we will consider in turn.

Credibility Is a Multidimensional Construct

Though it may seem that credibility is a single, unitary variable, the concept is actually a rather loose assortment of factors that, taken together, produce a total impression of a source. This is not to imply that people gain their impressions of credibility in a fragmentary or disconnected way. The impression of credibility, after all, constitutes an event that is holistic and organized, an event that is a gestalt.

Only a moment's reflection is necessary to note the range of factors that can influence the image of a communicator: style of clothes, posture, tone of voice, diction, length of hair, social distance, and myriad factors associated with personal demeanor. Some people "sound" or "act" highly credible (Harms,

1959). People who sound unsure of what they are saying tend to be judged nonauthoritative (Bettinghaus and Preston, 1964; Greenburg and Tannenbaum, 1962). Also, some statements contribute to impressions of authority, others do not (McCroskey, 1966; Ostermeier, 1967; Wenburg, 1969). And where there is marked inconsistency between impressions of a speaker and what he says, receivers respond by revising their estimates of the speaker's credibility. For example, when a message is judged to be high in credibility but the personal manner of a speaker is not, receivers lower their impressions of the person rather than the content (Atwood, 1966; King, 1966). Sometimes, even irrelevant and subjective aspects of communication may alter estimates of credibility (Zimbaro et al., 1965). For instance, even when an audience is given objective proof that a speaker is an unusually gifted engineer with impeccable professional credentials, they still tend to permit such features as black skin to influence their impressions of his authoritativeness on a subject in which he is well versed (Aronson and Golden, 1962).

Factor Analysis. If so many factors can influence credibility—even objectively irrelevant ones or subjective feelings—the question is whether any one set of factors consistently covaries as personal images of communicators are formed across dissimilar social situations. The best available insight comes from research into what is technically known as factor analysis, in essence a study of the commonalities in meaning in a stipulated list of items. In the typical research situation, people are asked to rate a speaker on a continuum of personal characteristics where the possibilities range from two extremes through a middle ground. One sample of items might well consist of the characteristics listed below.

```
       sincere _ _ _ _ _ _ _ insincere
     admirable _ _ _ _ _ _ _ contemptible
        honest _ _ _ _ _ _ _ dishonest
   intelligent _ _ _ _ _ _ _ unintelligent
      informed _ _ _ _ _ _ _ uninformed
    openminded _ _ _ _ _ _ _ closeminded
      rational _ _ _ _ _ _ _ irrational
          safe _ _ _ _ _ _ _ dangerous
```

The use of factor analysis assumes that the most important factors will comprise those items which respondents check in consistent ways. For example, if a group of respondents consistently checks "intelligent," "informed," and "sincere" to designate high credibility, while not checking other items in any uniform way, we may reason that these three items constitute an underlying factor, whereas the others do not. Though this explanation is simplified, the logic of the procedures is used in a number of investigations which indicate that some factors do operate in predictable ways across a spectrum of situations, speakers, and audiences (Anderson, 1961; Berlo, 1961; King, 1966; Lemert, 1963; Markham, 1966; McCroskey, 1966; Schweitzer and Ginsburg, 1966; Whitehead, 1968).

From the various studies two underlying factors of credibility emerge: *authoritativeness* and *trustworthiness*. One who ranks high on authoritativeness would be perceived as reliable, informed, qualified, intelligent, valuable, and expert; conversely, one who ranks low would be viewed as unreliable, uninformed, unqualified, unintelligent, worthless, and inexpert. Clearly, not all items apply to all situations and speakers.

The second factor, trustworthiness, operates independently of authoritativeness and has to do with the "nice guy" image: A person is viewed as honest, friendly, pleasant, selfless, and so on. A person may rank high on trustworthiness and score low on authoritativeness and vice versa. For example, a well-meaning, friendly person could also be regarded as a bungler, a professional incompetent; and on the other hand, a person can be respected for his technical ability but disliked because he has an unpleasant personality.

Dynamism, too, is sometimes cited as a factor underlying impressions of credibility. Dynamism relates to matters of presentation and appearance. A dynamic communicator may be described as emphatic, aggressive, forceful, bold, active, and energetic. A low rating on dynamism indicates that a speaker is perceived as timid, reserved, forceless, passive, and shy. Dynamism is the least stable of the three factors, holding up in some investigations (Berlo, 1961; Lemert, 1963) and not in others (McCroskey, 1966). One plausible explanation is that dynamism simply functions less uniformly across diverse situations than do authoritativeness and trustworthiness.

Not surprisingly, other factors besides trustworthiness, authoritativeness, and dynamism are sometimes reported as contributing to rankings of credibility. One study (Markham, 1966) identifies extroversion, skill, and openness as important factors, while another (Whitehead, 1968) concludes that openmindedness also influences impressions of credibility. The list could readily be expanded to include professionalism and safety, among others.

Source Credibility Is Positively Correlated with Attitude Change

The effect of source credibility on attitude change can be tested in a straightforward fashion. An investigator divides a randomly drawn sample into two groups judged beforehand to hold comparable attitudes toward the topic of a persuasive speech they hear via tape recording in equivalent situations. The versions of the speech are identical but their sources are different. The speech one group hears is attributed to a person regarded as high in credibility, and the other group hears a low-credibility version. By comparing questionnaires administered before and immediately after the presentation, the investigators determine if there is any difference in the average attitude shift between the two groups. If attitudes change more in a favorable direction under conditions of high source credibility, the difference presumably results from the greater persuasive impact of a source held in higher regard.

A well-known study by Haiman (1949) employed this basic paradigm of equivalent audiences, identical messages, manipulated source credibility, and immediate test of attitude change. Three groups heard a tape-recorded speech on socialized medicine, and each group thought a different person had delivered the speech: Thomas Parran, Surgeon General of the United States; Eugene Dennis, Secretary of the Communist Party in America; and a student at Northwestern University. The version attributed to Parran was rated significantly more competent than the other two, and it also was more effective in changing attitudes toward the topic. Similar results occurred when Hovland and Weiss (1951) used a written message attributed both to institutions and to individuals, for example, to *Pravda* and to J. Robert Oppenheimer. Additional confirming evidence was reported under conditions where the medium was a film (Kraus, 1959, 1960), a picture (Farnsworth and Misumi, 1931), and a small-group discussion (Cole, 1954).

Although there is little reason to doubt that a highly credible source is more persuasive than one which is not, the standard finding must be interpreted with caution. Heightened credibility does not bring about either an automatic or a constant gain in persuasiveness. Remember that the basic paradigm does not incorporate anything even remotely akin to a linear relationship between persuasive influence and degree of credibility. There is no evidence that a given gain or loss in personal standing leads to a *proportionate* change in interpersonal influence. Furthermore, the standard research design does not take into account any of the factors now known to interact—often so notoriously—with source credibility.

Consider a situation where the speaker's views are markedly discrepant from those of his audience. If credibility does not interact with the discrepancy factor, we have reason to expect that any increase in credibility will yield a proportionate gain in the attitude change on the part of listeners *independently of how discrepant their views are from the speaker's.* Yet, in actuality, quite the opposite holds true. Research by Bochner and Insko (1966) demonstrated that credibility and discrepancy are not independent influences but rather act in tandem in determining how much an audience will be influenced by a speaker.

Credibility also interacts with other variables when receivers feel coerced to comply with the speaker's recommendations. Sometimes nice guys do finish last. One controversial study (Zimbaro et al., 1965) centered around an amusing situation where a communicator tried to make army reservists eat objectionable food—fried grasshoppers, no less. Surprisingly, though the speaker's credibility did not affect the degree of compliance, the attitude change toward eating grasshoppers was significantly less when the source was perceived to be a nice guy than when he was judged to be cold, tactless, bossy, egotistical, and snobbish. Apparently, the need to comply was greatest when credibility provided little or no justification or incentive for engaging in an unpleasant task. Along another line, the state of Kansas designed a lecture program to warn teenagers of the dangers of drug abuse. They found that a distinguished criminologist from a renowned university was an effective persuader only in schools attended mainly by students from families with professional backgrounds. In inner-city schools attended mostly by those from socially deprived neighborhoods, people responded more favorably to the personal testimony of a young man on parole from a charge of drug abuse. Clearly, the person who was high in credibility in one situation fared less well in others. Such evidence on discrepancy and forced compliance should be taken as representative of a larger number of factors that interact with or mediate the effects of credibility.

Credibility Is Bound by Time and Situation

It was earlier thought that we form our impressions of credibility in a stable and fixed way. Some people seem to have high credibility while others do not. For students, the names of John F. Kennedy and Martin Luther King, Jr., score consistently high in credibility over time, and George Wallace ranks low. Huey Newton ranks high among members of the Black Panther Party and low among those in the John Birch Society. Some people enjoy lasting esteem, while others never outlive the stigma of incompetence or untrustworthiness. This fixed model of credibility ignores the dynamic interplay and intertwined effects of time and situation on impressions of credibility. In few communicative situations are the defining factors of credibility fixed or static. Even when we have years to form impressions of someone, our judgments are still subject to sudden and dramatic change.

As a rule, during the initial stages of a relationship we use all available information to form personal impressions, even data not encountered during the course of a communicative exchange. In reality, most initial impressions of credibility are formed *before the interactants actually come into direct contact.* Ordinarily, the mere anticipation of contact is sufficient to trigger some sketchy and generalized impression of a person. People tend to personalize all incoming data associated with anticipated encounters—even fragmentary items that have little direct bearing on the actual make-up of new acquaintances. Often the mere thought of meeting a stranger in a given social setting is sufficient to trigger vague feelings about what a person will be like. Some situations and events color our expectations about people, too. One set of expectations may be associated with people we might meet at a local pub, and another with those in a motorcycle club, sensitivity group, and so on.

The urge to personalize is even stronger when something is known about the views of an expected acquaintance. Knowing nothing more than the opinions held by a stranger, subjects in one study formed feelings of attraction that correlated positively with the similarity between them and the other person (Bryne, 1961). Also relevant is an investigation in which Mortensen and Sereno (1970) asked students to fill out a questionnaire to determine their interest in current social topics. Five days later, the students were told that volunteers were needed for another phase of the study, in which they would discuss their views about one of the topics with a student from another class. Each student examined sample scales supposedly completed by three subjects who had endorsed stands different from his own. They were told that final pairings would be made on the basis of their reactions. Results showed that the subjects did form impressions of credibility which were based solely on their knowledge of others' positions and, more importantly, that the rankings were positively correlated with discrepancy. The rankings were highest where the other person had taken a stand *closest* to that of their own.

If people form impressions of credibility by personalizing information they associate with anticipated social encounters, the question arises: "When can a person enter a communicative situation with no credibility—or technically—neutral credibility? Are there conditions, in other words, where a person *cannot not* form impressions about others which he associates with the meaning of that situation? The issue may seem rather speculative, but it is by no means trivial. At the heart of the matter is the larger question of neutrality in communication. For years investigators assumed that the initial level of credibility of an unseen, unknown, tape-recorded speaker in an experimental situation was strictly neutral. The assumption rested on the argument that since nothing was known directly about the communicator, receivers had no basis for feeling anything other than neutrality. The prevailing view was that each respondent functioned, in Burt's (1962) words, as "a stimulus-response machine: You put a stimulus in one of the slots, and out comes a packet of reactions [p. 232]." Conversely, no inserted stimuli must equal no packet of reactions. More recently, however, investigations ranging from information processing to experimenter bias clearly dispel any notion of neutrality, either in research with unknown and unseen speakers or in that with public figures. It is now certain that the very presence of a person in an experimental setting triggers feelings and emotions that are tied up with one's attitudes toward science, toward volunteering and testing, and toward the experimenter and his prior performances in research experiments (Friedman, 1967; Jourard, 1968; Kelman, 1967; Orne, 1962; Rosenthal, 1966). Moreover, some of the work on source credibility also undermines the notion of neutral credibility (Dresser, 1962; Holtzman, 1966; McCroskey and Dunham, 1966; for a rejoinder, see Tompkins, 1967).

It now should be apparent why impressions of credibility are as much a function of subjective expectations as is the meaning receivers attribute to the verbal behavior of a given source. From the moment each interactant enters a communicative situation, a deluge of personal cues pours in for classification and interpretation. What is impersonal soon becomes personalized, and what would otherwise seem to be neutral in emotive overtone soon becomes heavily evaluative. Minute fluctuations in manner and mood, attentiveness and expectations, combine with impressions gained from the environment—seating arrangement, background, noise, furniture design, lighting conditions, and color scheme—to define the affective tone of the interchange. Even before an unknown speaker begins to talk, receivers start to form personal hunches, according to the dictates of the situation, about what he might be like. A poor introduction, or a laudatory one, may further add to initial feelings of approval or disapproval. Even minute details of content may heighten or discount the regard receivers hold toward a source (Kersten, 1958).

In most situations, however, receivers will not make fixed judgments about a source at the outset, only hunches and tentative estimates. If his presentation turns out to be hesitant and nonfluent, his image may undergo marked revision—particularly if the presentation becomes increasingly more halting (Miller and Hewgill, 1964; Sereno and Hawkins, 1967). Even moderate variations in delivery are known to alter impressions toward a speaker. One study (Bowers, 1965) indicated that an extroverted voice (characterized by strong vocal emphasis and varied vocal quality) tends to produce more favorable attitudes toward a source than does an introverted style (characterized as a flat, tense, and breathy vocal quality with little emphasis). Similarly, the details of what is said are also clues to impressions gained about the trustworthiness or competence of a source. For instance, the more frequently a speaker makes references to his first-hand experience, the more likely he is to be judged as competent and trustworthy (Ostermeier, 1967). If the details of what is said run counter to the expectations of receivers, credibility tends to undergo further revision (Wyer and Schwartz, 1969). Ordinarily, only a few moments of speaking time are required to alter impressions of a given source (Andersen and Clevenger, 1963). One investigation reported that revisions in attitudes take place in as little as thirty seconds (Brooks, 1970).

The momentary fluctuations in credibility may vary to a spectacular extent. An illustrative study made by Brooks and Scheidel (1968) is worth examining in detail. A group of predominantly white college students listened to a tape-recorded address in which Malcolm X, late spokesman for the Black Muslims, argued for black separatism. Editing permitted the insertion of silent periods so that receivers could rank the speaker at specific moments, each of which occurred at a natural break in the content of the speech. While prior attitudes toward Malcolm X changed in a favorable direction, his credibility actually declined during portions of the speech (see Figure 4.1). The most dramatic and unexpected change occurred between the pretest and the first ranking made (time interval 1). Then several distinct changes in impressions of credibility took place. Note the relationship between what was said and the rankings of credibility:

> An increase in favorable evaluations toward Malcolm X was observed at Time 4. The speaker had just argued that the Black Muslim movement had restored pride in the Negro race and diminished hate the Negroes allegedly bear toward their blackness. In the interval preceding Time 6, Malcolm X had argued thus: A Negro who wants integration thinks ". . . that he should have your *house*; he thinks he should have *your* factory; he thinks he should have *your* school; and most of them think that they should have *your* woman, and most of them are *after your women*." The measurement (Time 6) revealed a negative shift in evaluation in contrast to the relatively favorable measurements achieved at Time 4 and Time 5. The measurements did not increase in favorableness after Time 6; Times 7, 8 and the post test revealed decreasing evaluations. The content following Time 5 and preceding Time 6, then, may well provide the most significant data about the speech [p. 6].

Not all changes in source credibility are dramatic or lasting, for credibility is as much bound by the effects of time as by situational influences. An experiment by Hovland and Weiss (1951) showed that the advantage of high credibility is often transitory. Although the greatest immediate shifts in rankings occur under conditions of high credibility, a reversal to original positions occurs over a span of four weeks. Moreover, even those exposed to a source low in credibility tend to accept his recommendations over the same four-week period. In the absence of reinforcement, Hovland posited the idea of a "sleeper effect," where initial agreement with a credible source diminishes and agreement with a source low in credibility increases because of the tendency to forget information more rapidly about a source than about what he says. Hence, repeated playback of personal items from a message is necessary to sustain effects associated with high credibility. Also consistent with the notion of a sleeper effect is evidence that those who initially dislike a communicator tend to become more favorably inclined toward him over time (Cohen, 1957).

Individual Differences. The extent to which situational and temporal factors limit the effect of credibility varies widely from person to person. Therefore, in predicting effects of credibility, much can be gained by knowing just how sensitive receivers are toward the credibility of a communicator. People with strong authoritarian tendencies, for example, seem particularly sensitive to *who* is

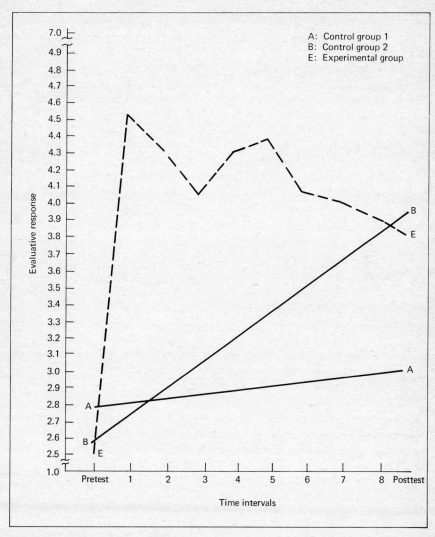

Figure 4.1 *Evaluative responses toward a source over time. (Reprinted with permission from Brooks and Scheidel, 1968.)*

talking and less attentive to the content of what is said (Johnson and Steiner, 1967). Those who are not especially authoritarian tend to perceive messages independently of who the source is. It is significant that highly authoritarian individuals have been found to accept recommendations from a high-status source more easily than do those who are less authoritarian. Also, the highly authoritarian seem less able to recall the content of a speech (Harvey and Beverly, 1961; Paul, 1956). Consistent with this line of reasoning is evidence leading to what Siegal, Miller, and Wotring (1969) called "credibility proneness." A person is prone to perceive credibility to the extent that he is sensitive to differences between sources. Accordingly, one who perceives great differences among those he regards as most and least acceptable is more influenced by credibility factors than one who is not so sensitive to such differences. The notion of credibility proneness may be useful in discovering more about the degree to which the effects of credibility are not bound by time and situation.

Credibility and Related Aspects of Orientation

Credibility has proved useful to our description of the global impressions which interactants maintain vis-à-vis one another. It does not, however, offer much insight into the particular grounds upon which the respective judgments are made. Even the knowledge that impressions of credibility tend to be made along lines of authoritativeness, trustworthiness, and often dynamism does little more than refine the description. Ordinarily, the factors associated with credibility function only within the larger context of interpersonal orientation. Moreover, there is reason to believe that factors commonly associated with credibility may not always be important determinants of impressions maintained toward other interactants. In certain situations such factors as dynamism and authoritativeness may function in secondary, even negligible, ways. For example, an intimate conversation between an engaged couple about marriage is not apt to hinge on their impressions of one another's expertise or dynamism. In such a situation a sense of mutual trust, feelings of common bond, and confidence in each other's expressed intentions are the factors most apt to apply. In another situation, the central factor may be simply the amount of social power which any given person wields over others. Cases in point might include a labor-management dispute, a negotiation between a student protest group and university administrators, or the attempt of an employee to talk his boss into giving him a raise. Since the significant factor in one's perception of a person may be virtually anything, we must confine our discussion to two concepts which are representative of larger forces at work in face-to-face encounters.

Trust. Recall that most of the factor analysis of credibility uncovered something like trustworthiness or honesty as measured by impressions of a person's reliability, friendliness, pleasantness, and the like. The matter of trust is now known to be a good deal more complicated than what is typically accounted for by the honesty or trustworthiness dimension of credibility ratings. Deutsch's imaginative research indicates that trust is not defined solely by one-sided, internalized impressions about others. Rather, the trusting orientation grows out of a *reciprocal* pattern of interrelationships. What is internalized is the result of orientations toward oneself and toward another, including expecta-tions which prescribe what each expects from the other and norms of how to act toward the other (Deutsch, 1960).

Before two strangers can establish a trusting relationship, they must perform certain moves that have to do with the type and sequence of choices each makes toward the reactions of the other. If neither is willing to make initial choices that entail some degree of self-risk or personal loss, a trusting relationship is not apt to be forthcoming. As Deutsch (1958) wrote, "Risk taking and trusting behavior are thus really different sides of the same coin [p. 266]." Bennis (et al., 1964) held that feelings of mutual trust come about after the parties go through an early period of testing and commitment where their expectations are realized through a sequence of exchanges aimed at increased self-disclosure:

> If the response is disapproval or rejection, the relationship freezes at that point, is terminated, or testing begins anew. If each exposure is met with acceptance, there is continual build-up of trust, a growing confidence that they will not hurt each other intentionally. The process is mutually rein-forcing, since when one person trusts enough to make himself vulnerable by exposing himself, trust is generated in the other person [p. 217].

It is not easy for new acquaintances to create an atmosphere which meets all the complex conditions required to promote trust. The intricacies are reduced to their minimum when two people play a *non-zero-sum game.* The game consists of moves leading to an imaginary money payoff that varies with the risks assumed in the moves. The exact payoff depends upon the total choices made by both parties, rather than by what any one person does. Person A makes a choice that determines part of the risk in the payoff—namely, how much each stands to win or lose. One may decide, for example, to go for broke— one wins all, the other loses all. Similarly, B makes his decision; this completes the combination of choices necessary for the first payoff. Since neither knows what the other is going to do, each must rely on his own *expectations* of whether the other will choose to maximize the chance for mutual gain, mutual loss, or individual gain. In short, each person makes a decision—plays a hunch, really—about whether he trusts the other or not. The alternatives are so arranged that both must act in a way that signals a trusting orientation or one of suspicion. For the payoff to be mutually beneficial, both parties must be willing to make an initial choice that entails the possibility of mutual gain through risk of personal loss.

When given a choice, only a small proportion of players make an initial choice that signals a willingness to risk personal loss with the prospect of later reaching mutual gain. In one study only 11 percent initially signaled trust on their first move (Swinth, 1967). A far larger percentage (52.8) showed a willingness to respond in a trusting manner only after the other took the initiative of a trusting choice. However, where the players are led beforehand to feel they should show concern for the welfare of the other person as well as for themselves, they are far more apt to establish a trusting relationship from the outset. In sharp contrast are the results obtained where players begin with a competitive orientation: They are led beforehand to feel they should do as well as they can for themselves and to assume that the other person feels the same way (Deutsch, 1958). Significantly, once players learn to act reciprocally in a trusting manner, that atmosphere almost invariably continues for subsequent payoffs (Loomis, 1959). Though the conditions required to establish mutual trust are undoubtedly complex, they tend to promote lasting and mutually binding alliances once recognized by the respective parties (Giffen, 1967a, 1967b).

Even slight fluctuations in a trusting atmosphere can produce dramatic effects in the course of communication. In the early stages of a relationship trust is rather fragile and must be handled with sensitivity. The effects

	A	B
X	(+30, +30)	(-30, +40)
Y	(+20, +10)	(-10, +20)

	Your DECISION	Your Partner's DECISION	MONEY YOU WON OR LOST
Game #1	————	————	————

Figure 4.2 *A non-zero-sum game used to study trust-destroying behavior. (Reprinted with permission from Leathers, 1969.)*

The Money Game

During the next few minutes you will be playing a money game with two different partners. The objective of each game is for you to win money. In each of the ten games you play Person I is to choose between rows X and Y; Person II is to choose between columns A and B. The amount of money each person wins or loses is determined by the box they get into as a result of their respective choices. For example, if Person I chooses row X and Person II chooses column A, they get into the AX box, and they each win $30. If Person I chooses row Y and Person II chooses column B, Person I loses $10 and Person II wins $20 (the person choosing first wins the amount of money on the left-hand side within the parentheses).

of gross violations of trust can be readily documented by Leathers's (1970) attempt to measure the effects of trust-destroying and trust-building communication. His study was designed around a discussion in which a trust-building relationship was established between participants and their partners, who were secretly trained to act consistently competitive or cooperative. After trust was established in a series of non-zero-sum games (Figure 4.2), subjects engaged in a sixty-minute discussion of a campus controversy over the black student union. In the first thirty minutes the cooperative plant tried to reinforce the subject with positive comments such as "You're right—I agree with you completely"; "Very good. Yes, that's very good"; and "I like that idea so much I wish you'd expand on it. Will you?" Then the cooperative plant suddenly began to destroy the subject's sense of trust by systematically violating the prior agreement to work in a cooperative manner. His comments became negative: "I don't understand why I ever agreed with you"; "You're wrong. Dead wrong"; and "That's a ridiculous statement. I disagree." Two judges recorded the subject's reactions to the trust-building and trust-destroying comments. They found that subjects reacted in highly characteristic ways to the two phases of the interaction. In the main, the trust-destroying condition produced communication that was markedly tense, inflexible, and personal in affective tone. Leathers offered these examples of feedback responses.

1. *Tense*   The selected subject suddenly begins to rub his hands together very vigorously, his neck muscles begin to constrict, his eyes appear to open very wide. Meanwhile, the other discussants begin to squirm in their seats while they avert their eyes from the selected subject and the plant.
2. *Inflexible*   "Oh, you think so huh. OK, you think that way. Why? You think I'm wrong; I don't think so. Why can't you recognize that ethnic studies centers just give right-wingers more ammunition to claim that whites and blacks are different. I am convinced that that is the way it is."
3. *Personal*   "Man, you are a strange cat. Oh wow, you can't be real. Are you kidding me. You are nothing but a white racist [p. 187]."

Clearly, the requirements of building a trusting relationship are a good deal more complex than the notion of trustworthiness measured by credibility ratings. A trusting relationship requires active participation, adherence to rules of exchange, mutual sensitivity to each gesture of self-disclosure, and, most importantly, a willingness to engage in trusting acts of self-disclosure.

Similarity. The impressions interactants form toward each other are tied to judgments of the similarity between their respective stands on a topic (Simons et al., 1970). Similarity heightens a sense of mutuality and common ground;

dissimilarity accentuates a feeling of individual differences. There is psychological comfort in hearing others express views that coincide with one's own. Hence, the probability of social influence increases markedly when a speaker announces at the outset that his personal view is similar to those of his audience (Ewing, 1942). Closely related is the audience's tendency to more readily accept a speaker's view on an issue if common ground has already been established on previous issues. Moreover, once receivers decide that the intentions of a communicator are consistent with their own self-interests, they become even more susceptible to his subsequent recommendations (Mills and Ellison, 1968).

Similarity also has far-reaching implications for impressions about appearance, personal demeanor, and a mélange of other nonverbal cues. The personal characteristics that interactants notice about each other include even minute aspects of nonverbal behavior. Impressions of similarity or dissimilarity are gained from nuances of posture, body position, physical distance, eye contact, and—if reclining—the degree of body angle (Mehrabian, 1969). Other clues are amount of head nodding, the frequency of verbal reinforcers like "uh-huh," the length of communication, the frequency of speech disturbance, the facial expressions, and the amount of gesture and body movement (Mahl and Schultz, 1964; Mehrabian, 1965, 1969; Rosenfeld, 1966a, b). The only limit to the discovery of links between impressions of similarity and nonverbal cues seems to be the time and ingenuity investigators devote to such research.

If similarity affects how a person interprets the cues of others, it also functions as a gauge to one's own communicative conduct. A number of references were made earlier to the expectations a person has when he approaches and interacts with another; recall the links between such factors as motivation and selective perception (Chapter 3) and between personal expectations and presituational influences on source credibility (p. 147), and the complex problems associated with forming a trusting relationship (p. 152). Common to all these matters is the relationship between one's expectations and one's own communicative conduct.

As a rule, people are more willing to interact with those they expect to exhibit a manner and attitude like their own. The concept of similarity, therefore, does as much to explain why people do or do not interact in the first place as it does in accounting for how they maintain personal impressions during the encounter. There seems to be no limit to communicative situations in which perceptions of similarity influence the course of verbal interchange (Brock, 1965; Byrne and Griffitt, 1966; Byrne and London, 1966; Byrne and Nelson, 1965a, 1965b; Sheffield and Byrne, 1967). The link between perceptions of similarity and degree of interpersonal attraction even holds when there are major personality differences (Byrne, 1965), prestige differences (Byrne, et al.,

1966), and racial prejudice (Byrne and Wong, 1962; Rokeach and Mezei, 1966). In addition, the relationship also assumes central relevance in a host of problems we will examine in connection with nonverbal communication (Chapter 6), interpersonal contact (Chapter 7), and communication networks (Chapter 9).

As a final word of caution, similarity is best considered a barometer of interpersonal encounters, not an exacting ruler. If we adhered strictly to its predictions, no one would interact with people unlike themselves. Apparently the need for order and stability—the real psychological basis for similarity—is balanced by the need for novelty and unpredictability. Unfortunately, little information is available on how these two needs are related.

Power. The notion of power may seem out of place in a discussion of the psychology of personal orientations in communication, for in everyday terms *power* has a decidedly mechanical ring. We are apt to associate power with the sheer physical force of missile thrust or horsepower. In human affairs, the term triggers political and institutional images: we think of power elites, power blocks, and political power. In communicative situations, however, the word is synonymous with *the potential for social influence.* More particularly, a person may be said to have power insofar as he has the capacity to influence the interactive behavior of others. Not all social situations elicit such feelings of social dependence among participants. People walking past a soapbox orator may feel no compulsion to stop and listen—they even may catch part of the message without feeling the slightest bit obligated. Such a speaker has, in other words, little social power. In sharp contrast is the degree of power operating in a university classroom, a corporation boardroom, or any other situation where the behavior of the receivers depends upon the directives, sanctions, and evaluations of another interactant.

Social power probably comes closest to a situation of *total dependence* when one person controls the very possibility of communication. Such control may stem from the physical aspects of the environment in which communication takes place—usually the medium or instrument that links participants and messages. For instance, at a public rally a person may turn off a loudspeaker system or drown out the voices of others with a bullhorn. Probably no situation gives a person a greater sense of helplessness than when he uses his last dime in an isolated pay phone to dial the operator and plead with her to contact someone who can bring assistance. Less dramatic, perhaps, but impressive, is the power exhibited by those deciding who will have the opportunity to interact with people in high station, say the president of a large corporation. Others have total control over the course of communication because of their *position* or *role* in an organization. At the opposite end of the power continuum is the sort of *self-designated control* whereby a person initiates an act which prevents communication among others. Disruptive tactics are clear cases in point. We will return to a particular form of total control over communication in connection with the concept of the "gatekeepers" in Chapter 9. And in Chapter 8 we will discover that the possibility of total control increases as the number of interactants decreases. In essence, as size decreases, each person can have more influence over the course of a discussion; in fact, where only two are present, each interactant has—by exercising the threat of withdrawal—a veto power that amounts to full control over the life of the interaction.

There are few ways of influencing the process of communication more dramatically than by exercising the full measure of the powers to *coerce* and to *reward*. Ordinarily people easily recognize authority and adjust their verbal behavior accordingly. A person tends to use whatever power he has. In numerous situations, the correlation between having power and using it runs up to .90 (Hurwitz et al., 1968; Zander et al., 1957). Nonetheless, a certain amount of calculation always accompanies the decision to risk using one's power. Rarely does a situation permit one to use power without considering its cost. Usable power, therefore, is the amount of power which is convenient and practical to use (Thibaut and Kelley, 1959). The leader of a group may have the authority to veto any group decision and still not find it wise to constantly remind opposing group members of his rights. To do so would risk continuous resentment among other group members and undercut the chances of reaching long-range objectives.

Power in interpersonal relations has much bearing on the level of participation and the flow of verbal interchange from one member to another. It can decide who talks, how much, and about what. The subtle nuances of assigned or self-designated powers of coercion and reward also affect matters of style and personal manner. Predictably, those with greatest social power are likely to talk most often; they direct comments to others as a whole, initiate directives and announce decisions, and assume a manner that rewards those who show deference and punishes those who do not. Moreover, communication from both low-power and high-power individuals tends to be directed more often to those with greatest authority. Low-power individuals recognize the coercive power of those in higher station by approaching them in a noncritical, deferential manner.

Low-power individuals tend to assign characteristic meanings to messages from those in high station. For example, powerless group members are apt to find, in messages of whatever content, evidence of personal threat, hostility, and other signs that give them feelings of insecurity and anxiety. They also tend to perceive power figures in negative terms and avoid contact with them. In addition, low power is associated with low motivation, aggression, and ineffectual work (Cartwright, 1959; Thibaut and Gruder, 1969). Even in situations characterized by a strong supportive climate, prolonged exposure to coercive power figures often results in distrust and hostility. On the other hand, those with a great amount of social power tend to feel a high sense of self-esteem and exhibit a greater willingness to accept messages from their peers.

Trust, Power, and Credibility Revisited

It should now be apparent why the concepts of power and trust are necessary adjuncts to the idea of credibility. Impressions of another communicator entail far more than authoritativeness and trustworthiness. This is not to say that credibility is of incidental importance. On the contrary, factors associated with credibility certainly *influence* interpersonal impressions, but they do not, as previously thought, invariably *govern* them. Many communicative situations exist wherein personal impressions result not so much from credibility, as the term has been used, but rather from social standing, role, and power. Furthermore, trust—unlike credibility—is needed to account for effects associated with the *sequential* aspects of an encounter. The back-and-forth, unfolding nature of an exchange contributes much to impressions of risk, self-disclosure, and the expressed willingness of each party to establish a trusting relationship. Power, like trust, may also function independent of the effects commonly associated with credibility; for unlike credibility, the potential for social power often functions in an all-or-nothing manner. People exercise power in an absolute sense, as we have seen, and even rule out the possibility of further interaction. Rarely, if ever, would impressions of credibility per se lead to such extreme degrees of social control among interactants. Finally, the logic which argues that the effects of power and trust go beyond those of credibility can be extended to still more concepts. In short, our picture is open-ended and incomplete. Clearly, interactants maintain impressions of each other on grounds too complex to be accounted for by any single concept or even by any specified set of concepts. Therefore, this account of other-directed orientation, like most matters in communication, must remain an unfinished picture.

COORIENTATION

In any interpersonal encounter the boundary between the self and the world becomes very blurred; the cycle from world to self and back again has no clear cut-off point, no fixed beginning or end. Simultaneously, each participant in the communicative act maintains more or less continuous orientations toward himself, toward others, and toward selected aspects of their common surroundings. Even the simplest exchange involves a mixture of personal and interpersonal that blends into the larger totality of conscious experience. The fluid interplay between self and world has been described in terms of "flow processes" (Platt, 1968), "perceptual transactions" (Kilpatrick, 1961), "correspondence" (Jones and Davis, 1965), "linkages" (Kibler and Barker, 1969), or simply "coorientations" (Newcomb, 1953).

The term *coorientation* is used to establish the minimal condition necessary for interpersonal communication. To say that participants A and B maintain coorientations is simply to assert that their respective psychological orientations are in some way interdependent. The nature of this interdependence depends upon the combinations of possibilities outlined by Newcomb (1953) and summarized here:

1. A's orientation toward whatever functions as the object of communication—the message cues, designated X—including both the intensity of orientation and the way relevant items are interpreted (all the particulars of information processing).

2. A's orientation toward B, in exactly the same sense.

3. B's orientation toward X.

4. B's orientation toward A.

This simple system has a number of implications and testable propositions. What is of relevance to this discussion is the assumption that coorientation is essential to all social interchange. Presumably, then, the orientation of A toward B rarely, if ever, takes place in a social vacuum. However A responds to B is inevitably due in part to their awareness of and dependence upon common surroundings. In other words, because each person must orientate himself toward environmental objects, including other people who are orientated toward some of the same objects, communication is inevitable ("you cannot not communicate"—see Chapter 2).

The significance of coorientation depends, above all, on the degree to which A and B are personally involved in an object of common concern. The concept of involvement, or personal relevance, is admittedly rather abstract and elusive. Yet we recognize the importance of involvement in virtually all aspects of contemporary public life. Our vocabulary is filled with its language. We speak of "getting involved," "telling it like it is," "laying the cards on the table," "breaking through" to someone, "becoming relevant." Critics decry what they judge to be lack of personal involvement in the entire fabric of society. Virtually no institution, from politics to religion, education to entertainment, is free from charges of irrelevancy in content and activity. Likewise, the Peace Corps, VISTA, Women's Liberation, and ecological issues gain much of their credence because their adherents long for a sense of personal relevance and involvement—a search that may indeed be the primary concern of our time.

Unfortunately, the public's sensitivity to involvement has not yet been matched by our social scientists. Until recently little scientific attention has been aimed at determining how personal relevance influences the conduct of human talk. Consequently, the bulk of findings in psychology, sociology, and communication textbooks rests on conditions of low involvement: estimating the number of beans in a bottle, undertaking laboratory games, judging line lengths, performing trivial tasks for 50¢ an hour, arriving at decisions in transitory groups whose lifespan is seldom more than thirty minutes, and listening to five-minute taped speeches by unknown speakers on remote topics. Such conditions, needless to say, hardly foster high psychological stakes. Nonetheless, a recent surge of interest in certain aspects of involvement provides the broad outline of forces which determine the intensity of coorientation in interpersonal settings.

Peripheral Involvement

A substantial proportion of talk takes place without engendering any distinct personal involvement. Much interpersonal contact begins and ends with idle punctuation points. "How are you?" "So nice to see you again." "How are you feeling?" "You're Don's roommate." "Nice day." "OK." "Looking good." "See ya soon." "Let's get together." Most of what happens at lunch counters, in elevators, at informal gatherings, or in public lines functions mainly as a form of adult babble. The semantic meaning of the words assumes less importance than the act of talking. This is not to dismiss conversation and small talk as inconsequential. Spontaneous talk, for all its repetitive and ritualistic overtones, serves many functions. It acknowledges others, eliminates tension, fills time intervals, and permits us to orient ourselves to the surroundings. Moreover, small talk is its own reward, at times both stimulating and fun.

Even idle conversation can create involvement of sorts. It is altogether possible to begin a conversation in a highly ritualistic fashion and a second later become caught up, spontaneously, in the moment. "When an individual engages in an encounter," wrote Goffman (1961), "his conscious awareness can bring certain shared things to life and deaden all other matters. By the spontaneous involvement in the joint activity, the individual becomes an integral part of the situation, lodged in it and exposed to it, infusing himself into the encounter . . . [p. 31]." The beauty of such spontaneous involvements is that they can be enjoined without participants' revealing their innermost values and beliefs. Spontaneous involvement is strictly peripheral to the human belief system. The only thing required is the willingness to follow the unfolding moment in all its ambiguity and unpredictability.

As participants become increasingly involved in personal communication, a number of important changes take place in their psychological orientations. Some changes can best be understood by seeing how organized sets of beliefs, values, and attitudes are formed and maintained, for the centrality and intensity of the belief system determine what each individual will regard as most personally involving.

Central Involvement

In Rokeach's (1968) approach to the human belief system, matters of personal involvement are viewed as differing solely in terms of their *connectedness*. The more a given belief is interwoven with other beliefs, the more implications and consequences it has for other beliefs, and therefore, the more important it is. Furthermore, the more central the belief, the more resistant it is to change. And when changes do occur, central beliefs have a greater implication for the rest of the belief system. From a communication standpoint, we can say that the more interaction bears on matters which the participants find highly involving, the more the beliefs of personal relevance function as the central determinant of coorientations. The movement from peripheral to central involvement can be summarized by using Rokeach's continuum of five classes of belief:

1. *Inconsequential beliefs* are matters of judgment and individual taste. They have few connections with matters of self-identity and self-esteem. When they are changed, they have little or no influence on a person's view of himself.

2. *Derived beliefs* come second-hand from the acceptance of someone else's authority. Derived beliefs are closely tied to the credibility of sources—persons, textbooks, and news media are all sources of derived beliefs.

3. *Authority beliefs* are controversial items learned through direct social contact and identification with groups—family, class, peer, ethnic, religious, political, and national. Authority beliefs are relatively enduring and thus are more difficult to change than derived or inconsequential beliefs.

4. *Primitive beliefs (zero consensus)* are incontrovertible beliefs that are closely tied to personal existence and self-identity. They are learned through direct encounters, but they do not depend on others for their continued validation. Since their credibility does not depend upon shared acceptance, they are impervious to change through interpersonal communication. Examples include items of faith and those personal identifications learned through social experience, such as "I know I am an honest and sincere person" and "No one really understands me."

5. *Primitive beliefs (100 percent consensus)* are the most central of beliefs, for they are learned through communication with others and are reinforced by unanimous social support among all of one's personal contacts.

These beliefs are primitive in the sense of being the most fundamental under-pinnings or axioms of the person. As Rokeach (1968) wrote,

> "A person's primitive beliefs represent his "basic truths" about physical reality, social reality, and the nature of the self; they represent a subsystem within the total system in which the person has the heaviest of commit-ments. In the ordinary course of life's events, they are so much taken for granted that they do not come up as a subject for discussion or controversy. "I believe this is a table," "I believe this is my mother," "I believe my name is so-and-so" are examples, respectively, of primitive beliefs about the physical world, the social world, and the self—supported by a unanimous consensus among those in a position to know [p. 6].

These five classes of belief have far-reaching implications for under-standing the coorientations people maintain and alter throughout their inter-actions with others. Primitive beliefs with 100 percent consensus are least apt to be the object of communication. Rarely is there any reason to mention what one accepts as a given or what can be taken for granted. The same holds for primitive beliefs with zero consensus; they, after all, are also considered to be incontrovertible and independent of others for validation. However, both types of primitive belief form the basis by which other, less central beliefs are represented in interpersonal encounters. For example, two people suddenly engage in a heated argument over the risks of smoking. On the surface their differences center on derived beliefs having to do with the actual harm caused by smoking. Yet underlying the flare-up are more central differences in the values each assigns toward such matters as health, physical fitness, and the desirability of prolonging life. An even greater difference is reflected in their primitive beliefs about the inevitability of death, immortality, and so forth.

There is also much significance in the notion that the more central a belief, the more it resists change. From a communication standpoint, by knowing how central an object of discussion is to a participant one often can predict what the outcome of an interaction will be. However, central beliefs influence more than simply the outcomes of communication. Generally the more involving the interaction, the greater is the probability that the sense of personal involvement will become the central determinant of other facets of the encounter.

Ego Involvement: Latitudes of Acceptance, Rejection, and Noncommitment.
The notion of ego involvement advanced by Sherif and his associates (Sherif and Hovland, 1961; Sherif, Sherif, and Nebergall, 1965; Sherif and Sherif, 1967) deals in a complementary way with many matters relevant to the organiza-

tion of human beliefs. Specifically, ego involvement refers to the relevance, significance, or meaningfulness that an issue or topic has for an individual. Sherif was primarily interested in how a person determines what is of utmost importance and how his evaluative judgments define the orientations he forms and maintains in interpersonal situations. One fundamental assumption of Sherif's approach is that individuals differ widely in the degree to which they tolerate opposing viewpoints. Generally, the more involved one is in his position, the less tolerant and, hence, the less discriminative his evaluative judgments become. Observations of these differences can be determined by studying certain latitudes of rejection and noncommitment. Latitude suggests a range or breadth of tolerance. *Latitude of acceptance* refers to whatever range of positions a person is willing to accept, including all positions he tolerates and the one he finds most acceptable personally. *Latitude of rejection* refers to all items that are objectionable or unacceptable to the individual, including the most objectionable as well as all unacceptable positions. *Latitude of noncommitment* includes all positions that are excluded from the other latitudes. *Noncommitment* centers on ambiguous items, positions of uncertainty and those for which a person has no definite response of acceptance or rejection. Thus, the degree of one's involvement depends upon how he organizes his latitudes.

Sherif further proposed that people highly involved in their stands use fewer categories than do those who are less involved. In the main, high

Responses of person A

good	___	___	___	___	___	X	___	bad
warranted	___	___	___	___	___	X	___	unwarranted
necessary	___	___	___	___	___	___	X	unnecessary
desirable	___	___	___	___	___	X	___	undesirable

Responses of person B

good	___	___	___	___	___	X	___	bad
warrented	___	___	___	___	___	X	___	unwarranted
necessary	___	___	___	___	___	X	___	unnecessary
desirable	___	___	___	___	___	X	___	undesirable

Figure 4.3 *An example of responses that show latitude of most acceptance in studies of ego involvement.*

Response of person A

good	U	U	U	U	U	X	A	bad
warranted	U	U	U	U	U	X	A	unwarranted
necessary	U	U	U	U			X	unnecessary
desirable	U	U	U	U	U	X	A	undesirable

Response of person B

good	U					X	A	bad
warranted	U					X		unwarranted
necessary	U					X	A	unnecessary
desirable	U					X		undesirable

Figure 4.4 *Examples of responses that show latitudes of most acceptance, rejection, and noncommitment in studies of ego involvement. The pattern of person A shows evidence of high involvement, while that of person B indicates low involvement.*

ego involvement is revealed by a broad latitude of unacceptance and a narrow latitude of acceptance and noncommitment. For example, persons A and B are asked to indicate their latitudes on the topic of abolishing all university entrance requirements for minority groups. Both start by indicating their rejection of the idea by aligning the "Most acceptable" category as shown on the scales in Figure 4.3. At this point we would be tempted to say they both find the idea bad, unwarranted, unnecessary, and undesirable. However, when asked to indicate which positions they find acceptable or unacceptable, a different pattern emerges (Figure 4.4). Though both appear to equally disfavor the idea, person A conforms to all the requirements of high involvement, while person B fits the pattern of low involvement. According to the theory, these differences in judgment lead to major differences in the way the two parties will interact on the topic.

First of all, ego involvement affects the expectations or predispositions which people have about the prospect of engaging in future communication with another on the topic. A representative finding was reported by Mortensen and Sereno (1970) in a study designed to compare the predispositions toward communication which people with varying levels of ego involvement have toward those who endorse stands that differ in varying degrees from their own. Subjects were led to believe that they would be engaged in a short discussion with someone who took a different position on a topic of common interest. Each person completed a questionnaire from which the pairing would be made. Subjects who differed in level of involvement also differed systematically in their judgments of the attractiveness of future communication and the expectations they had for the situation's possible outcomes. Highly involved subjects were not so interested as less involved persons in discussing a topic with someone who endorsed a position that was maximumly discrepant from their own. Also, highly involved subjects had significantly lower expectations of reaching a mutually satisfactory resolution.

In a related investigation, Sereno and Mortensen (1969) asked people who differed in involvement to engage in a discussion with those who endorsed an opposing view. Subjects were told to persuade their partners to accept what they considered to be the most acceptable stand. Comparisons were made between pairs who took opposing and highly involved stands with those who were equally far apart but lowly involved. While nine of ten pairs in the highly involved condition failed to reach agreement, only two of the eighteen lowly involved pairs failed to do so. This again is consistent with the notion that the more involved a person is in his stand, the more he resists change.

Ego involvement also influences one's orientations toward others. In the study dealing with the attraction individuals feel toward future communication with persons who take stands that differ from their own, highly ego involved persons formed significantly less favorable impressions of the people they expected to come in contact with than did those who were lowly involved. The relationship between ego involvement and credibility also operates in communicative situations. Sereno (1968) asked subjects to read newspaper articles about the use of contraceptive pills by unmarried females. Depending on whether the subject's response was favorable or unfavorable, one of two messages was presented by a source each regarded as high in credibility: "Salk calls for wider birth control use" or "Salk sees birth control dangers." Results showed that highly involved subjects were significantly less influenced by reading the discrepant message than were lowly involved ones. Moreover, highly involved subjects lowered their evaluations of the source's credibility, while lowly involved subjects did not. The results support the finding that attitudes shift more under conditions of high source credibility and low ego involvement than under any other combination of credibility and involvement (Johnson and Scileppi, 1969).

Clearly, the concept of personal involvement is critical to an understanding of how individuals establish and then maintain simultaneous orientations toward all aspects of a communicative situation. High ego involvement functions as the basis for judging all other aspects of the social situation. Hence, it affects not only resistance to change but also one's predisposition, impression of credibility, susceptibility to attitude change, and a host of matters affecting the outcomes of the encounter.

CONNECTEDNESS

The factors comprised by our psychological orientations, when taken together, present a picture of exceeding complexity. Some constituent influences seem common to all daily experiences, while others flare and wane with the moment. Some result from man's urge for order and consistency; others seem attributable to a bent toward novelty, risk, creativity, play, or solitude. Some orientations testify to man's need to be an active creator and participant in all of his dealings; others owe their credence to the dynamics of a given social situation or to the idiosyncratic nature of a particular conversation. In any situation where man's psychological survival equipment is involved, there are no constants, no isolated or singular influences. No sooner is one concept reduced to manageable proportions than there is reason to go beyond it. Thus, orientations centered in self-consciousness lead to those centered in the experiential field of others; and those, in turn, require notions of interdependence and coorientation.

Yet despite this complexity and variability, it is inconceivable that all these factors operate in an unorganized and purely chaotic fashion. On the contrary, the thread that binds the relevant literature is *connectedness*. Man has an active and vested interest in seeing that everything fits together; where it does not, pressure is exerted to restore order to the cycle of self to world and back again. Technically, it is necessary to think of different orders of connectedness. There is the orderly aspect of cognition—what goes on inside the nervous system. Certainly the principle of connectedness underlies the dynamics of self-orientation—particularly matters of internal consistency and integration of thought, the structure of the human belief system, and ego involvement with its interdependent latitudes of acceptance, rejection, and noncommitment. In the interpersonal domain, too, things work toward an orderly fit. A high degree of trust-building behavior on the part of one person leads to reciprocal behavior by others. Impressions of high credibility lead to perceived power, which, in turn, is correlated with characteristic levels of performance and message content.

The principle of connectedness applies to the larger aspects of orientation as well as to the relation between specific variables. That which alters the subjective experience of self invariably has far-reaching implications for other-directed objects of orientation and for the reciprocal aspects of coorientation. In the interface between personal, interpersonal, and situational forces, interdependence is the rule and not the exception. There is little reason to question the view that man somehow fashions a deluge of impressions into an orderly system with describable properties and predictable consequences to his verbal dealings with others. In the next two chapters we will discover more about how the principle of connectedness functions in nonverbal and verbal behavior.

SUGGESTED READINGS

Andersen, K., and **Clevenger, T.** "A Summary of Experimental Research in Ethos," *Speech Monographs,* 30:59–78, 1963.

Boulding, K. E. *The Image.* Ann Arbor, Mich.: University of Michigan Press, 1966.

Brooks, R. D., and **Scheidel, T. M.** "Speech as Process: A Case Study," *Speech Monographs,* 35:1–7, 1968.

Cartwright, D. (ed.). *Studies in Social Power.* Ann Arbor, Mich.: University of Michigan Press, 1959.

Chapanis, N. P., and **Chapanis, A.** "Cognitive Dissonance: Five Years Later," *Psychological Bulletin,* 61:1–22, 1964.

Deutsch, M. "Trust and Suspicion," *Journal of Conflict Resolution,* 2:265–279, 1958.

Giffin, K. "The Contribution of Studies of Source Credibility to a Theory of Interpersonal Trust in the Communication Process," *Psychological Bulletin,* 68:104–120, 1967.

Kelley, G. *A Theory of Personality.* New York: Norton, 1963.

Leathers, D. G. "The Process Effects of Trust-destroying Behavior in the Small Group," *Speech Monographs,* 37:180–187, 1970.

Mortensen, C. D., and **Sereno, K. K.** "The Influence of Ego-involvement and Discrepancy on Perceptions of Communication," *Speech Monographs,* 37:127–134, 1970.

Platt, J. R. "The Two Faces of Perception," in B. Rothblatt (ed.), *Changing Perspectives on Man.* Chicago: University of Chicago Press, 1968, pp. 63–116.

Rokeach, M. *Beliefs, Attitudes and Values.* San Francisco: Jossey-Bass, 1968.

Sereno, K. K. "Ego-involvement: A Neglected Variable in Speech-Communication Research," *The Quarterly Journal of Speech,* 55:69–77, 1969.

Sherif, C. W., Sherif, M., and **Nebergall, R. E.** *Attitude and Attitude Change.* Philadelphia: Saunders, 1965.

Simons, H. W., Berkowitz, N., and **Moyer, R. J.** "Similarity, Credibility, and Attitude Change: A Review and A Theory," *Psychological Bulletin,* 73:1–16, 1970.

Swinth, R. L. "The Establishment of the Trust Relationship," *Journal of Conflict Resolution,* 12:335–344, 1967.

three

---

the
inter-
personal
system

Five

verbal

interaction

The study of verbal interaction is one of the most engrossing and elusive dimensions of human communication, for its province embraces the multitude of ways that we use language to deal with ourselves and our environment. Though the potential uses of language may be limitless, common patterns that underlie the range of possibilities are not. Our interest, then, is not in the effects of words or in their combinations, but rather in the common denominators of *large classes of verbal activity*. All interaction through language hinges on common denominators in matters of syntax, organization, style, logic, appeal, reasoning, imagery, semantic considerations, and many more. Some underlying aspects of verbal interaction pertain to form, others to content, and still others to pragmatic considerations; some touch upon self-expression and speech production, and others relate more directly to interpersonal matters.

   With such an inclusive range of potential subject material, the topics of this chapter should be approached as suggestive, and hopefully representative, of larger forces at work whenever we interact through spoken or written word. Much of what is known about the underlying fabric of verbal interaction can best be illustrated by examining research into *verbal appeals, message order and organization,* and *patterns of argument.* The complicated matter of verbal appeal covers any situation where men attempt to influence the attitudes, feelings, and action of others. Message order and organization may be taken as a barometer of the import of language structure, however disjointed it may appear at times. Finally, patterns of argument deal with the larger promise and hazards of basing one's appeals on logic and reasoned evidence.

VERBAL APPEALS

The daily bombardment of television commercials, political announcements, sermons, and editorials constantly enjoins us with appeals to our feelings and emotions: anxiety, guilt, sympathy, psychological well-being, physical comfort, sex, security, pleasure, joy. A plethora of injunctions are aimed at attributes of loyalty, generosity, devotion, compassion, dedication, and patriotism. Some appeals arouse only fleeting and transitory attention, while others evoke the most enduring concerns of human experience. Verbal appeals differ in degree and intensity as well as in kind: Some messages arouse a strong sense of guilt, for example, while others prompt only a twinge of remorse or misgiving. Indeed, it is as much the *range* as it is the *kind* of appeals that makes the possible combinations virtually limitless.

Given this enormous range of potential verbal appeals, one might expect great variety in the research literature. Unfortunately, the existing material touches on only a small sampling of those we commonly experience in a single day. Equally disappointing is that the findings are all too often fragmentary and inconclusive. In part, these deficiencies result from the very complexity of appeals. So much depends on factors that are more or less unique to each interaction that ordinarily there is no way to equate the type and degree of a given appeal in one communicative situation to another. How, for example, can an investigator be sure that a mild plea for a charitable donation can be equated with a mild appeal to join the Peace Corps, though in each case a feeling of guilt has been aroused specifically to engender a sense of obligation? Even if we are fortunate enough to find *comparable* situations and identical topics, there is no way to standardize, say, two units of mild and strong appeals and then merely to compare their respective outcomes. Yet, until recently, appeals were manipulated in a manner that resembled the pushing of a button or the turning of a dial: Show the gory details of three-car accidents in a film about seat belts and—presto!—out comes a message arousing a high degree of fear; show no details and only one accident and label it mild fear arousal. Such research strategy, not surprisingly, yields results from which it is truly difficult to generalize. Notwithstanding the problems of poorly conceived research, it is instructive to examine representative material on verbal appeals in the interest of clarifying some key problems of communication research. An additional objective is to explore the sorts of discoveries that have come about only from the willingness of investigators to grapple with persistent and thorny problems over extended periods of time.

Fear-arousing Appeals

No appeal has been the object of more scientific interest than has fear arousal. But the topic is worthy of detailed consideration for reasons other than interest alone. For one thing, the dynamics of fear-arousing messages are typical of those at work in verbal appeals generally. Thus, at only minimal risk of over-simplification, we may explore the concept of fear arousal as an approximation of forces at work in any number of verbal appeals.

Much interest in fear arousal stems from an early investigation by Janis and Feshbach (1953) designed to test the effect of three levels of fear appeals. In their experiment, an illustrated lecture on dental hygiene was presented to three groups of high school students. The lecture was identical in each presentation except for the amount of threatening material. A *high-threat* treatment consisted of a great deal of information on tooth decay and accompanying pain. Realistic photographs vividly portrayed bleeding gums and rotted teeth. This strong appeal also contained a high number of personal threats. For example:

> If you ever develop an infection of this kind from improper care of your teeth, it will be an extremely serious matter because these infections are really dangerous. They can spread to your eyes, or your heart, or your joints and cause secondary infections which may lead to diseases such as arthritic paralysis, kidney damage, or total blindness [p. 79].

The *mild-threat* presentation made fewer references to the consequences of neglecting teeth and contained more factual material. Photographs tended to be less dramatic than those used in the first presentation. Finally, the group exposed to the *low-threat* message heard the fewest personal references and only a rare allusion to the consequences of tooth neglect. In place of vivid photographs, the mild-threat presentation consisted solely of x-rays, diagrams of cavities, and photographs of healthy teeth. One week before the lectures, and immediately after, the students were asked about their feelings regarding hygienic practice. With choices ranging from "very worried" to "not at all worried," they responded to the following:

1. When you think about the possibility that you might develop diseased gums, how concerned or worried do you feel about it?
2. When you think about the possibility that you might develop decayed teeth, how concerned or worried do you feel about it?

In addition, students were asked about the feelings they had while watching the presentation.

Results showed that the greatest amount of worry and concern was produced by the high-threat presentation with its strong fear appeal. But surprisingly, the greatest acceptance of recommendations occurred under conditions of *mild* and *low* threat. A change of attitude toward the recommendations occurred in 8 percent of the high-threat group, whereas a change of 36 percent characterized the low-threat condition. Janis and Feshbach explained the results by claiming that students who watched the high-threat presentation made a determined effort to escape the vivid reality of the message by an *avoidance reaction,* a strategy enabling them to deny the personal relevance of the event. In other words, the students seemed to say, "It may be so but it doesn't apply to me." The emphasis on "avoidance" caused a great deal of controversy and attention in subsequent research. One supportive study by Nunnally and Bobren (1959) dealt with people's willingness to respond to a persuasive lecture on mental health. Again, resistance to the recommendations was found to be highest among those exposed to a very personal message designed to arouse strong anxiety. Related evidence of a negative relationship between attitude change and fear arousal has been reported in studies by Goldstein (1959), Haefner (1956), and Janis and Terwilliger (1962).

On the strength of early findings, some investigators mistakenly accepted the unqualified conclusion that appeals containing highly threatening material produce less attitude change than bland appeals (Berelson and Steiner, 1964; Hilgard, 1962; Krech, Crutchfield, and Ballachey, 1962; Morgan and King, 1966; Secord and Backman, 1964). More recently, however, the many failures to replicate early findings, together with additional conflicting evidence, triggered heated controversy and speculation over the entire theoretical underpinnings of the issue of fear arousal.

In one study that is representative of the contrary evidence, Powell (1965) had male subjects listen to variations of a recorded message calling for a national program of community fallout shelters. The only difference in the presentations was the degree of threat material and the *object* of the threat; in one case the object was the listener or his family, and in the other it was more generalized and referred to matters of national security. One finding was that a strong-threat message aimed at a person's family produced significantly greater attitude change in the recommended direction than that evoked by a milder personal threat. In other words, when the object of the menace was very personal, an increased amount of threatening material had a facilitating effect on the willingness of the individual to follow recommendations. In apparent confirmation of these findings, research by Niles (1964) and Leventhal and Niles (1964) reported a greater tendency for subjects exposed to a high-threat message about cancer to express an *intention* to act in accord with recommendations than for those in a low-threat situation. Similar support for the facilitating effect of fear arousal on attitude change has been reported in studies by Dabbs and Leventhal (1966), Darley (1966), McGuire (1968), and Millman (1968).

The inconclusive state of affairs certainly points to the futility of searching for "universal" effects of fear appeals. It is one thing to label variations of a message either "high" or "low" in fear arousal; it is quite another to specify precisely how much concern each message will arouse once the labels are attached and furthermore to specify how much attitude change will occur as a result. The lesson, then, is that it is no more reasonable to expect uniform effects of variously labeled appeals than it is to assume a one-to-one relationship between any type of message and its subsequent effects. In short, the very question of whether fear appeals—or for that matter any verbal appeals— facilitate or interfere with attitude and behavior change is itself simplistic and misleading. For one thing, it takes too much for granted. By reducing the problem to simply one message attribute, we ignore the dynamic interplay among factors that reside only partly in the presentation of the verbal appeal itself.

Variables That Affect Fear Appeals

The factors that have the greatest impact on the effect of fear appeals are known to fluctuate greatly from situation to situation, from topic to topic, and from person to person. Among the most important are (1) the nature of the situation itself, (2) the type of recommendations contained in the message, and (3) the psychological make-up of the receivers.

The Nature of the Situation. The setting of communication wields tremendous power over the potential effects of fear appeals. Generally, people regard familiar surroundings as less menacing than strange situations. If a person delivers a presentation filled with highly threatening material in an environment that itself evokes a sense of fear, the results are apt to differ markedly from those achieved by the same message presented in a low-threat setting. For example, a man's response to a film designed to maximize his concern over the failure to wear seat belts may well depend on whether he responds from the comforts of his living room or within the confines of a courtroom or hospital. Clearly, fear arousal involves more than the power of words to trigger feelings of anxiety.

The participants' own perceptions of a threatening communicative situation may have a strong influence on the effect produced by fear appeals. Any number of factors may exert an influence: Some work in the direction of engendering an acute sense of immediate threat; others rouse more distant and long-range feelings of fear and anxiety. Most people, for example, regard the act of brushing their teeth as posing less of an immediate concern than the thought of having a dentist take an x-ray or fix a decayed tooth. And for most, the topic of seat belts poses less immediate anxiety (but perhaps more of an ultimate threat) than the thought of getting a shot for the prevention of a cold virus. Leventhal and Watts (1966) found that those smokers who felt most threatened at the prospect of having a chest x-ray responded more consistently to messages involving low or moderate amounts of threat material.

Type of Recommendations. There is little doubt that the effect of verbal appeals depends in large part on the type of recommendations that accompany the presentation. This is particularly true of fear-arousing messages. The two most important determinants of the effects of recommendations have to do with the nature of the *consequences* of a threat and the *likelihood* of its occurrence. Both of these factors have been ignored, confounded, or left uncontrolled in much of the relevant literature. Part of the difficulty stems from the sheer impossibility of equating consequences on topics as diverse, for example, as smoking (Stern et al., 1965), fallout shelters (Powell, 1965), population growth (Frandsen, 1963), syphilis (Duke, 1967), roundworms (Chu, 1966), safety belts (Berkowitz and Cottingham, 1960), grades (Cohen, 1957), and fear of viewing the sun (Kraus et al., 1966). On some of these topics, the consequences are apt to be well known and avoidable, on others they are not. Some are personal, others are impersonal. Still, there are lessons to be learned from the very proliferation of dissimilar types of recommendations. Generally, the findings indicate that the more threatening the consequences, the greater is the likelihood of social influence (Higbee, 1969). Also, the effectiveness of the recommendations could reasonably be expected to increase as the likelihood of the consequences increases. Incidentally, it is worth noting that the relation of consequences to likelihood of occurrence may explain in part the many failures to replicate the original findings of Janis and Feshback discussed above. Recall that the high school students were shown graphic photographs of several diseases of the teeth and gums. It is not likely that young people in generally good health would interpret the sight of older people's abscessed gums as much of an immediate personal threat.

It is important to note, however, that under some circumstances the severity of consequences can increase while the likelihood of the occurrence decreases. For example, most people would regard the consequences of having no life insurance to be most severe, yet put off purchasing it on the grounds— perhaps only subconsciously experienced—that "it's not very likely to happen to me in the immediate future." The opposite type of relation between consequences and likelihood of occurrence exists on matters such as looking into the sun and failure to get good grades.

In both matters of consequences and likelihood of occurrence, recommendations differ widely in the extent to which their acceptance can eliminate the sense of threat, however strongly they may be felt by the receivers. Most people, for example, would place more faith in the effectiveness of a shot as an antidote for an infection than they would in the power of a tooth-brush over bleeding gums and abscessed teeth. A study by Leventhal (et al., 1965) used the typical high-versus-low fear conditions in urging college students to get a free shot at a campus health service. Half the students in each threat situation received detailed instruction on how to comply most readily with the recommendations: The information included a map locating the campus health service, suggestions for the best time of day for the trip, and so forth. The other half received identical recommendations about the importance of getting a shot, but no information about how to comply with the instructions. As pre-dicted, those in the high-fear condition reported more tension and anxiety and stronger intentions to get the recommended shot than did those in the low-threat condition. Even more striking was the finding that those who received specific instructions were significantly more apt to get the shot (28 percent in both threat conditions) than were those in either threat group who did not receive the particulars (3 percent of both threat conditions). There is, in short, no known evidence to conflict with the reasoning that led Leventhal to conclude that fear works in the direction of compliance whenever the dynamics of the situation "make action seem highly possible and effective."

Psychological Make-up of Receivers. Also relevant to the effect of fear arousal is the psychological make-up of receivers. It is well known that people differ widely in their tolerance of threatening situations and that they differ about the types of statements regarded as highly threatening (Miller, 1963; Miller and Hewgill, 1966). Consequently, a person highly sensitive to fear-inducing mes-sages may interpret a low-threat presentation much as a person with less tolerance would react to one designed to maximize fear. Likewise, the one who is highly sensitive would react to a mild fear appeal, whereas the other might not even recognize the threat value of the message. The recognition that people differ significantly in their tolerance for anxiety has importance in explaining the lack of uniformity in the literature we discussed earlier. If one study happens to contain a large proportion of individuals who are highly sensitive to threatening material and another does not, it would hardly be surprising to find the two investigations reporting different effects of fear arousal. In the original study by Janis and Feshback (discussed on pp. 175–176), it is most significant that those who scored high on tests of neurotic anxiety were very resistant to high-threat material. In sharp contrast was the tendency of nonanxious subjects to accept equally all variations of fear arousal.

Persons who harbor neurotic feelings of vulnerability to disease have been found to comply with almost any recommendation for improving their health, even when it is couched in the mildest possible warnings. Niles (1964), for example, found that people who are most sensitive to health-related warnings are increasingly apt to comply with recommendations as threatening material increases from low to mild levels; thereafter, however, any further increase in the menace only serves to inhibit their acceptance. Moreover, those who do not view themselves as particularly vulnerable to disease tend to be unresponsive to low and mild levels of threat but are increasingly accepting as appeals reach high levels.

In one subsequent investigation, Leventhal and Watts (1967) divided subjects into groups of heavy smokers, light smokers, and nonsmokers; each was then divided into those who believed themselves vulnerable to disease and those who did not. All subjects viewed a variation of a film linking smoking to cancer under a condition of high, moderate, or low threat. The results, shown in Figure 5.1, confirmed expectations. Note that the amount of perceived threat correlated highly with feelings of vulnerability to disease. Of added relevance is the fact that light smokers with vulnerable feelings experienced considerable fear even under a low-threat treatment consisting entirely of statistics and other factual material.

Another personality factor, self-esteem, also influences the meaning people assign to fear-arousing messages. Ordinarily, one who ranks high in esteem is best able to deal with threat; as a consequence, he is also better able than one low in esteem to give an objective reading to potentially threatening messages; thus he is not so subject to the persuasive appeal of a presentation (Dabbs and Leventhal, 1966; Higbee, 1969; Kornzweig, 1968; Leventhal and

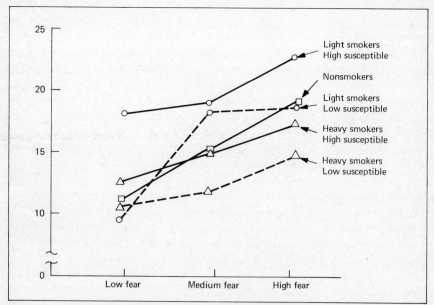

Figure 5.1 *The emotional response to fear-arousing films used in a study of smoking and lung cancer. (Reprinted with permission from Leventhal and Watts, 1967.)*

Trembly, 1968; and Zemach, 1966). In short, the psychological make-up of a person acts to mediate the meaning he attributes to fear-inducing messages. Given enough concern over external threats, a person will be sensitive to the mildest hint of threat. However, for those with more normal sensitivity to fear-inducing events, a higher amount of threat potential is necessary to trigger acceptance of the message (Gollob, H. F., and Dittes).

Though the findings may be far from conclusive, recent work on fear arousal yields a clearer picture than that which was available just a decade ago. The larger question of the impact of fear appeals is now known to be most complicated, for in the very failure to find uniform effects of threatening material, a number of important discoveries have emerged. The most important is the knowledge that *there is no single optimum point at which fear-inducing material maximizes the chances of attitude change.* Furthermore, it is now known that there is no necessary conflict in discovering that fear facilitates social influence at some times and at others actually hinders it. The early notion of a one-to-one relationship between appeals and outcomes has gradually given way to the assumption that *there are a number of optimum points for fear arousal, depending upon the interplay of message, situational factors, and the psychological make-up of the receivers.* This recent view, best represented in different form in the work of McGuire (1968a) and Janis (1967), rests on what is technically known as an inverted U-relationship, or a family of relationships, between level of fear arousal and subsequent performance (Figure 5.2).

Neurotic and Reflective Fear

To establish the optimum effect of fear appeals, it is important to know whether the respective receivers are largely influenced by *neurotic* or *reflective* fear. Neurotic fear is one of intense inner conflict and heightened anxiety. It causes the individual to project his sense of conflict on his interpretation of external threats and thereby to distort the reality of the situation. As suggested by the discussion about the psychological make-up of receivers, neurotic fear is not readily modified by fear appeals. The characteristic responses of the chronically anxious person are all maladaptive: denial, repression, perceptual distortion, and an assortment of other defensive reactions (Janis and Leventhal, 1968). Regardless of the fact that a neurotically fearful person may stop thinking about actual external danger, the threat remains. In contrast, reflective fear also triggers a sense of vigilance, and the individual makes an active effort to seek out informational cues that give a sense of reassurance against external threats. In short, reflective fear is unlike neurotic fear in that it is firmly grounded in careful thought and sensitivity to slight changes in the intensity of external dangers.

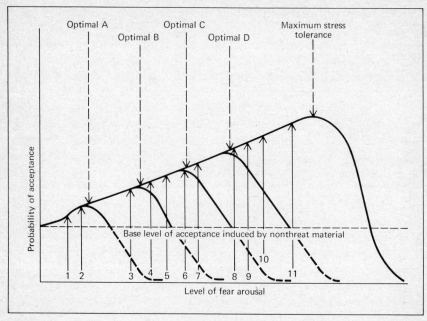

Figure 5.2 *The impact of fear-arousing messages on attitude change. Note that as the level of fear arousal increases, the degree of threat material needed to maximize the change of acceptance is lessened. (Reprinted with permission from Janis, 1967.)*

With these distinctions between neurotic and reflective fear in mind, we are in a position to examine the major consequences of anxiety-inducing messages under conditions where reflective fear prevails. According to Janis (1967), the message first gives rise to feelings of *heightened vigilance*. A person in a state of vigilance suddenly becomes alert to signs of threat, searches the environment for new signs of danger, and reflects on alternative courses of action to deal with the emergency. Vigilance, then, is a keying-up process, a heightened sensitivity to menacing aspects of external events. The second possible consequence of reflective fear is evidenced when a person experiences a *need to seek reassurance* as a means of coping with emotional tension. Reassurance usually takes the form of an effort to minimize the danger, more of a shoring-up process, an attempt to regain confidence in one's own ability to respond to the impending danger. In more extreme cases the need for reassurance results in behavior shown by those suffering from neurotic fear. Thus, the endangered person resorts to a fatalistic outlook and often experiences feelings of invulnerability or believes that the danger is somehow not real. In the case of what Janis termed "blanket reassurance," there is a feeling of compliance and a willingness to be less vigilant. Thus, in pure form reassurance and vigilance are opposing forces, a set of extremes that compete rather than complement. A third possible consequence of anxiety-inducing messages a *compromise attitude*, stems from the competing nature of the two extreme needs of vigilance and reassurance (Figure 5.3). The formation of a compromise attitude, Janis (1967) noted,

> combines discriminative vigilance (seeking further information about the threat, remaining alert to signs of oncoming danger) with discriminative reassurances (expecting to be able to cope successfully, or to be helped by others, if the danger becomes extreme). Outstanding examples of compromise attitudes are seen among victims of heart disease who learn to live with their illness. Realizing they might be subject to another heart attack, they make specific plans for carrying out protective actions that will help them to survive if such an attack happens to materialize. For instance, after his first heart attack, a man will go about his business carrying a well-labeled bottle of digitalis in a prominant pocket and a legible note in his wallet stating the appropriate dosage to give in case he is found unconscious. Such an individual displays a mixed attitude, because he remains vigilant to possible signs of worsening of his illness and worries about being incapacitated or killed by it, and yet is able to gain some reassurance by adhering to a medical plan that could actually save his life in an emergency [p. 172].

The three consequences of fear appeals seem to clarify much of the confusion over the lack of uniform effects of threat material. Some failure may be due to insufficient emotional stimulation, others to an excessive amount of vigilance; but the most important point is that the schema advanced by Janis gets away from any single optimum point of fear arousal. Instead, *any given level of arousal, from mild to maximum, is assumed to have its own maximum*

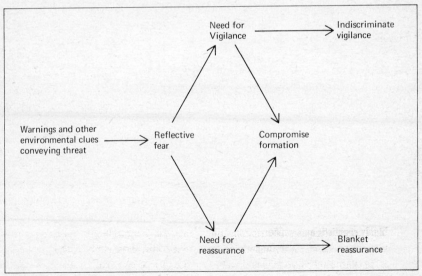

Figure 5.3 *The probable consequences of reflective fear arousal. (Reprinted with permission from Janis, 1967.)*

point of influence, depending on the nature of the compromise that is reached between the competing needs for assurance and vigilance. At a very low level of fear arousal, mild warnings in a message are apt to go unnoticed. At successively greater levels of emotional arousal, the optimum use of threat material decreases in like proportions. And once a person is in a maximum state of arousal, the chances are reduced that fear appeals of any magnitude will be, in Janis's words, "correctly understood and assimilated into the person's system of beliefs and plans for action."

Janis's work does not resolve, nor was it intended to resolve, all inconsistencies in the literature on fear arousal. That would be too much of an obligation for any explanatory system. Nor can it be said that the notion advanced by Janis is without problems in its own rights. In fact, the idea of a family of inverted U-shaped curves is so complicated that it suffers from problems exactly opposite to those of the explanations it is designed to replace. Moreover, Janis's framework is theoretically unwieldy and almost impossible to disprove. Since there is no way of knowing exactly what level of fear arousal is under investigation, one can use the system to explain virtually any outcome. Where appeals are effective, one can hold that the optimum level of arousal has been tapped; where they are not, the result can always be dismissed as lack of stimulation or an excessive need for reassurance. It must be quickly added, however, that Janis was able to marshall indirect support for his position from findings in the diverse fields of fear arousal, social stress, neurophysiology, and information processing. As a fringe benefit, his insightful work illustrates the hazards of oversimplifying complex problems in interpersonal communication and highlights the value of working with persistent and fundamental problems through phases of investigation dominated by initial confusion and fragmented speculation.

MESSAGE ORDER AND ORGANIZATION

From the historical standpoint alone, the parallels between message organization and verbal appeals are numerous and striking. And the lessons and major discoveries of each are much alike in their relative importance to the larger dynamics of verbal interaction. Initial interest in both topics may be traced to testing some commonsense notion about what makes a difference and what does not, usually to matters of attitude change. Moreover, the early research into both began with what in retrospect seems to have been a set of highly simplistic assumptions, questions, and procedures governed by a pointless search for an underlying "universal" law about attitude change. Then, through a painstaking and halting succession of investigations—often characterized chiefly by controversy, gaps, and inconsistencies—the outlines of a clearer but more complex picture emerged. In the process some seemingly important factors turned out to be inconsequential, and others, presumably quite straightforward, proved to be inordinately complicated. While a few factors seemed to operate in more or less uniform fashion, most turned out to rest on an assortment of variables, the majority of which were discovered accidentally. But finally, the potential import of both verbal appeals and message organization can be seen to range from that which barely qualifies as trivial to that which assumes first-rate importance in the communication process.

Message organization is a dimension of verbal interaction that we take very much for granted most of the time. Words often come easily; they are the product of the moment, the result of reactions that tend to be spontaneous, fragmentary, and free-wheeling. So effortless is the business of producing human speech that we are seldom even conscious of the organizational aspects of language. To some extent our inattention to organizational matters is understandable and quite natural. To a point we are free to say or write anything, in any order or sequence, that suits the impulse of the moment. And yet we can never totally escape the requirements of organization in language, not even in the most idle moments of conversation. For without the ability or willingness to impose some semblance of structure on the flow of words, we reduce human talk to nothing more than gibberish.

The organizational fabric of a given message influences virtually every aspect of its meaning. Both the syntactical features of individual letters, words, and sentences and all the larger units of thought are involved. Consider the syntax of this page as a case in point. The smallest unit of measure is the arrangement and grouping of individual letters on the page. The arrangement is exact, uniform, continuous, and linear: The letters and groups of words are centered, sequential, and placed on lines reading from left to right and top to bottom with an elaborate set of rules governing matters such as the separation of clauses, sentences, and paragraphs.

So dependent are we on the arrangement of the printed page that even minor violations of the rules of space can play havoc with the meaning of a message. Some violations cause only minor distraction:

PEACECA NNOT BEBOUGHTBY WORDSAL ONE

Other violations bring disastrous consequences:

P EAC EC ANN OTB EBOU HTB YW OR DSA LON E

Few aspects of the organization are arbitrary, and of those that are, we may gloss over some but not others. In some instances, the very act of changing the rules or ignoring conventions may contribute to the meaning of the message.

The following poem by E. E. Cummings is a case in point:

```
                          r-p-o-p-h-e-s-s-a-g-r
                    who
          a)s w(e loo)k
          upnowgath
                    PPEGORHRASS
                              eringinto(o-
          aThe):1
                eA
                  !p:
          S
                                              a
                      (r
          rIvInG           .gRrEaPsPhOs)
                                     to
          rea(be)rran(com)gi(e)ngly
          ,grasshopper;
```

Our dependence upon rules of organization seems closely tied to the characteristic thinking patterns of Western man; thus, it should not seem coincidental that people from Western cultures are known to think and be better able to reason in linear, sequential terms (De Soto, 1960, 1961; De Soto et al., 1965; Woodworth and Schlosberg, 1954). Westerners are known to be more capable of judging the validity of syllogisms when they are arranged in a linear pattern than when the equivalent thought is expressed in nonlinear form (Miller, 1968). Note the difference in the linearity of these two syllogisms:

> A is to the left of B
> B is to the left of C
> Thus, A is to the left of C

> A is to the right of B
> B is to the right of C
> Thus, A is to the right of C

Despite the fact that the syllogisms are logically equivalent, the second one is more difficult to validate. Seemingly, the linear consistency of symbols designated "to the left of" reduces problems in making a judgment, while the consistency of symbols "to the right of" makes it more difficult to arrive at the correct conclusion.

So far we have considered the organizational features of only the smallest units of language. In ordinary conversation, problems of quite a different order come into play. These wider considerations of organization are roughly analogous to the concerns of a person working a jigsaw puzzle; despite an interest in finding the exact match of individual pieces, he must not lose sight of the problems associated with the overall organizational form of the puzzle. In like manner the bulk of research on message organization deals with the larger fabric of message structure. The following questions are typical. Should the message be organized so that the strongest material is presented first, last, or in the middle? To what extent does organization make a difference in such factors as attention, credibility, comprehension, and attitude and behavior change? Is there any difference in using explicit or implicit conclusions? Are two-sided or one-sided presentations more persuasive? Should favorable material be presented first or last? Do first impressions really count most? In the remaining part of this section we will examine representative findings on all these questions.

Primacy-Recency

In a pioneering effort to determine the most effective organization of material, Lund (1925), a social psychologist, raised the issue of primacy-recency. He presented a "law of primacy" which states that when both sides of a controversy are presented successively, the side presented first (primacy) has the advantage over the side presented later (recency). The issue originally drew credence from such intuitive judgments as "first impressions count most," and "first things first." Lund examined the issue by presenting two sides of an argument to a group of students; the first presentation advocated one side, the next defended the opposite position. He discovered that no matter which side came first, pro or con, the initial argument was most effective in producing immediate attitude change on the topic. Lund formalized the results in what was to become a most controversial "law of primacy."

Follow-up investigations at first seemed to confirm the principle of primacy. In one early study Knower (1936) varied the order of presentation in two different messages and found evidence favoring primacy. Subsequent investigations reported primacy effects under some conditions (Janis and Feierabend, 1957; Lana, 1961, 1963a, 1963b) and recency under others (Anderson, 1959; Cromwell, 1950; Hovland and Mandel, 1957; Insko, 1964; Miller and Campbell, 1959; and Wilson and Insko, 1968). By the mid-1960s, amidst growing interest and controversy, the state of affairs was best described by the title of an article by Rosnow (1966b): "Whatever Happened to the Law of Primacy?" The question is open to a number of interpretations. One possibility is that the so-called evidence for primacy does not result directly from message organization after all. Perhaps primacy is a special case of people's larger tendency to persist in whatever direction they take at the outset of any activity. Often it is easier to act or think along set lines than it is to change. When people are assigned problem-solving tasks, for example, if they begin by using some complex strategy of problem solving, they resist any change to a simpler and more direct technique even when later presented with a succession of increasingly easier tasks.

What is significant about human persistence is that the evidence cited for primacy effects has been reported by and large in situations where there is great pressure to think along characteristic lines. Lund's study, for example, took place in a classroom between teacher and students. Since the students had from past experience strong reason to believe in the importance of whatever material the teacher presented first (as a key to understanding later and often more difficult material), it is not earth-shaking to find them most accepting of initial material on a subject. Nor is it difficult to see why their confidence in the believability of the information and the situation would be shaken when their teacher, a high authority figure, suddenly presented information that stood in direct opposition to what he had said at the outset. It is note-worthy that when Hovland (et al., 1957) attempted to replicate Lund's proce-dures in all respects except that outsiders presented the rival material, he did not confirm evidence of primacy effects. In three of four instances, in fact, the results favored recency. Likewise, Luchins (1957) found that he could greatly weaken the impact of primary information by cautioning students beforehand to be on guard against forming snap judgments until all information was pre-sented. If our hunch is correct, then, initial material may have an advantage only to the extent that the receivers are *already* predisposed to think along set lines.

A second possible explanation of the primacy question may be attributed to a principle of learning theory. If two segments of a message or two separate messages are equally well learned, learning theory would predict that the most recent of the two items will be better remembered. Exactly how much better depends largely on the time lapse between the two presentations and the length of interval before the subject has to recall the items. According to a forgetting curve advanced by Ebbinghaus, the advantage of recent events over the remote diminishes rapidly over time. If today's conversation with a friend can be recalled in more detail than a comparable event from yesterday, the edge in recalling from today over yesterday will diminish by next week and within a few months it will scarcely be noticeable. Hence, if we are to be given an immediate recall test, any impact primacy may have is apt to be offset by the power of recent recall.

We can generalize from the example and say that in any research situation where there is an immediate recall of two items or messages equally well learned, learning theory will predict a recency effect. Since immediate test of recall is used in virtually all research on primacy-recency, the cards are clearly stacked against the possible advantage of primacy material. Thus it is significant that when Miller and Campbell (1959) varied either the amount of time between the presentations of opposing views or between the presenta-tions and the test of recall, the power of recency diminished greatly. The findings of Miller and Campbell are consistent with larger evidence that delays in time work against the optimal impact of recency (Bossart and Di Vesta, 1966; Luchins, 1957, 1958; Mayo and Crockett, 1964; Rosenkrantz and Crockett, 1964; Wilson and Miller, 1968).

A third possible explanation for the inconsistent findings on primacy begins with the assumption that any difference in what comes first and last in a presentation is apt to be determined by other factors in the situation. One relevant discovery comes from research on *order effects*, which has to do with the impact of placing the strongest arguments or material in various places in a presentation. In a *climax* order the most important material comes first; in an *anticlimax* order it comes last; and in a *pyramidal* pattern it is placed in the middle. It is thought that either climactic or anticlimactic orders are preferable to the pyramidal arrangement (Gulley and Berlo, 1956), with the preponderance of evidence favoring climactic order (Cromwell, 1950; Gilkinson, et al., 1954; Sponberg, 1946). One dissenting study, however, reported no significant differences in message order (Thistlethwaite, et al., 1956). There is an important implication in the discovery that message order does make a difference but that no one pattern is invariably successful. Perhaps some factors work to maximize the impact of what comes first and others what comes last. Where this is the case, the outcomes may be as much the result of these "other factors" as they are of the effect of the position itself. The very same logic would suggest that some situations would work to *cancel out* the effects of either primacy or recency. Such *multiple outcomes* may be far more typical than what has been assumed previously.

Free Variables Affecting Primacy and Recency. This plausibility of multiple outcomes draws much support from what is known about the intervening impact of certain "free" variables that favor neither primacy nor recency yet have much to do with the outcome of message organization. Examples of free variables include *reinforcement, strength, involvement,* and *commitment.* The relevance of reinforcement stems from the commonly accepted notion that receivers most accept whatever aspects of a message they regard as most personally rewarding and satisfying. Attitudes change in the direction of whatever material is *most reinforcing* to the receiver (Corrozi and Rosnow, 1968; Golightly and Byrne, 1964; Rosnow, 1965, 1966a; Rosnow and Lana, 1965; Rosnow and Russell, 1963; Rosnow et al., 1966). Now suppose the information presented first is interpreted as most satisfying because of a striking use of language or the heightened interest aroused by the potential usefulness of some comment in the presentation. In such circumstances the order of material is apt to be less important than the effects of reinforcing material. Since the satisfying material may appear in any segment of the message, and since it is the receivers themselves who determine what is the most rewarding, the effects of the reinforcing material could work for or against either primacy or recency.

What applies to reinforcement holds equally well for other free variables. Consider the matter of *commitment*. Most people are not apt to change their attitudes on an issue after they have made a personal commitment to one side of the controversy. The commitment can be made in any number of ways: signing a pledge, going to the front of an audience at a revival, making a New Year's resolution, or sharing a decision in confidence with a close friend are all varieties of commitment. The point is that the nature of the commitment alters the significance of the message presentation itself—including, presumably, matters of order and organization. To change what one says in public is not the same as altering a stand made privately.

When the commitment is made is also important. If a test of primacy permits people to make a commitment after hearing only the first side of an argument, and if that action leads to some positive identification with the initial material, the second part of the message will have a markedly diminished ability to change the subject's attitude. On the other hand, if the opportunity for commitment comes only after the entire presentation, the odds—according to learning theory—clearly favor recency effects. Thus, it is significant that the act of making an *anonymous* commitment has been found by Hovland (1957) to have no impact on the effects of some later and opposing side of a controversy. When a *public* commitment was permitted before hearing the second side of an issue, however, receivers were found to resist views subsequently expressed about the opposite side of an issue. The matter of commitment has, then, implications for the effect of message organization and, as we will discover in Chapter 7, a host of other aspects of the communication process.

One additional example of a free variable's interacting with primacy-recency is *ego involvement*. Despite an absence of research, there is reason to believe that ego involvement may work against *either* primacy or recency, and often in a brutally impartial way. Stated as a hypothesis, we may say that the more highly involved one is on a belief-discrepant topic, the less is the chance for either a primacy or recency effect. Recall that to be highly involved is to be preoccupied and committed to one's own stand on a topic. The more absorbed a person is in his own position, the less sensitive he is apt to be to matters of order and organization. On questions involving matters of self-identity, people generally care little about what comes first or second. Therefore, ego involvement tends to eliminate sensitivity to the internal details of messages that would be required to make them effective. The case for viewing ego involvement as impartial to matters of order and organization is implied by the failure to find any consistent effects of primacy-recency on matters of great personal importance (Lana, 1961, 1963b; Lana and Rosnow, 1963; Rosnow and Goldstein, 1967).

Obviously not all variables in the primacy-recency question operate in a nondiscriminating manner. Some factors work more or less consistently in favoring material positioned either at the beginning or at the end of a message.

In the case of *two-sided presentations*, for example, the highly controversial side of a debatable topic seems to favor the impact of whatever is presented first. After receivers have heard one side of any controversy on which they have not taken a personal stand beforehand, their tendency is to disregard the appeal of subsequent material because it stands in direct opposition to the side presented first (Hovland, 1957). Moreover, studies by Lana (1961) and Rosnow and Lana (1965) report evidence that familiarity with a topic is one factor that favors the positioning of material; they find that familiarity heightens the impact of primacy, while strange or new material favors recency. However, their own findings may be due to the confounding influence of recall on familiarity with a topic. Since we remember best that information which was best learned, any lack of familiarity under conditions of immediate test of recall would naturally tip the scales in favor of what comes last.

Most scientific interest in the problem of recency employs the use of either two successive messages or one message divided into two equal and opposing sections. Unfortunately, such gross differences in arrangement shed little light on the effect of finer gradations of message structure and organization. The question that arises, then, is whether organizational detail has any impact on such factors as attention, interest, comprehension, and attitude change. Although the question is still open (Beighley, 1952, 1954), there is some support for long-standing admonitions about the import of orderly arrangement and organization. In one early study, Smith (1951) found that rearrangement of two main parts of a speech had the effect of decreasing the level of attitude change when all introductory material, transitions, and concluding information were in proper sequence. Darnell (1963) went farther than Smith into the matter of organizational detail by casting several variations of a fifteen-sentence speech into a logical, deductive order. The first version was in intended order; the second was identical to the first except the thesis sentence was placed in the middle. By making an increasing number of transpositions in sentence order in each of five other versions, Darnell was able to measure the effect of disorganization on the reactions of the audience. Each group was tested for comprehension and interest in the message. Darnell concluded that organization made no difference in *interest* but did have a slight impact on *retention*. Other investigations have confirmed the importance of organizational detail on matters of recall (Thompson, 1960, 1967) and audience attitudes toward the speaker (Sharp and McClung, 1966).

Strategic Considerations of Message Organization

Strategy is concerned with patterns of order and arrangement that maximize the impact of a message. One relevant issue is whether there is any advantage in structuring a message around those elements which *arouse* a need before presenting those which satisfy existing needs. Such strategic considerations abound in advertising. In the award-winning television commercials for Alka-Seltzer, for example, all initial material, visual and spoken, is designed to trigger concern over the condition of one's stomach. Then, after fifty-five seconds of scenes showing stomachs in sundry shapes, sizes, and conditions, the ad switches to a mere five-second mention of the product. Another commercial spends twenty-nine seconds depicting children of various nationalities in states of extreme poverty before the camera holds for one second on the words "Join the Peace Corps." Obviously, many factors lead an advertising man to spend most of the time arousing needs before even mentioning a product's name. Some advertisements, in fact, devote the entire segment to demonstrating how a product will satisfy a want or need. But with prime time costing up to 65,000 dollars a minute, the decision to withhold all mention of a product until completion of need arousal could prove costly indeed. The work of Cohen (1957) provided some support for the need-arousal strategy so prominently at work in TV commercials.

One further illustration of strategic considerations in message organization was reported in a study that McGuire (1957) designed to test the effect of pleasant versus unpleasant information on attitude change. McGuire used principles of learning theory to reason that if message organization does not evoke pleasant reactions to initial material, receivers will be less receptive to subsequent information, *even if it coincides closely with their opinions.* Furthermore, if a person agrees with initial information but does not feel personally rewarded (that is, has pleasant feelings in listening to the material), any tendency he might have had to agree with later information will be severely weakened. Therefore, McGuire predicted greater acceptance if message information of a rewarding nature preceded that which was not. After he determined what a group of subjects held to be pleasant and unpleasant about a series of topics, he asked them to listen to the messages and fill out a shift-of-opinion questionnaire. As predicted, the strategy of placing rewarding information first proved superior. Apparently, those who listened first to unpleasant information avoided what followed, *even though it was consistent with what they held to be personally satisfying.*

The work on strategic considerations in message organization is important for two reasons: First, the findings are not intuitively obvious. It is not immediately apparent why people, on strategic grounds alone, would resist information they otherwise find personally satisfying. Second, these strategic factors are now known to interact, sometimes notoriously, with the impact of purely formal matters of message organization and arrangement. This being so, it would not be difficult to understand why the search for uniform effects has proved so difficult. The impact of message organization is obviously a complicated matter. Even the seemingly simple question of the sequence of organization is known to be dependent upon the larger context of the message presentation.

What is true of strategic considerations holds as well for the larger questions of message order and organization. The existing knowledge about primacy-recency has already been cited as being strikingly close to that reflected in the literature on verbal appeals. Despite the solid advances of more than a decade, the picture is still far from complete. There is no body of uniform effects, and certainly nothing that remotely qualifies as a "law" of message organization or verbal appeal. And even if the basis of comparison is the level of generalization common to the literature on communication, the results are still disappointing. In the case of primacy-recency in particular, there has been, as Rosnow (1966) rightly noted, "no success to date in embracing all of the different findings with any one explanatory system." If the reasons already cited do not seem sufficient to rule out the chance, much less the necessity, for a single explanation, it is hoped that additional clues will be forthcoming in the following discussion about the crucial matter of human rationality.

PATTERNS OF ARGUMENT

It should now be clear that the complications of verbal interaction are quite unlike the transactions of a desk calculator or an automatic change-counter. Word meanings and their arrangements are never fixed; there is no assurance that a given presentation will have an additive impact; and there is ordinarily no one-to-one relationship between the face value of words or messages and their interpreted value. Indeed, the gap between assigned and intended meanings can be enormous. What one person recognizes as moderate threat, another interprets as mild, and still another misses entirely. For a time one person remains attentive to the details of message organization, when suddenly, for reasons he may not be fully aware of, he cannot follow even the largest threads of the presentation. This state of affairs may seem to reduce communication to a level of barnyard intelligence. After all, one might convincingly argue, if a message is well organized, why shouldn't it be effective? Or if a string of sentences is arbitrarily shifted around, why shouldn't it be more difficult to follow them? And why should free variables cancel out the effects of primacy in one situation and recency in another? Why should the average amount of anxiety differ so markedly in what appear to be comparable situations? These and other quite legitimate questions are important both in their own right and also in the way they all reflect the acceptance of a critical assumption about human nature. If man is viewed from a rationalistic framework, then expectations of his behavior will necessarily differ markedly from those based on a less reflective and complementary bias.

Assumptions about human rationality, though relevant to all aspects of communication theory, are critical to any attempt to deal with the effects of the reasoned dimension of verbal interaction. In one discussion of contemporary views of rationality, Scott (1968) cited this delightful passage from Tolstoy's *War and Peace:*

> What impressed Prince Andrey as the leading characteristic of Speransky's mind was his unhesitating, unmovable faith in the power and authority of the reason. It was plain that Speransky's brain could never admit to the idea—so common with Prince Andrey—that one can never after all express all one thinks. It had never occurred to him to doubt whether all he thought and all he believed might not be meaningless nonsense. And that peculiarity of Speransky's mind was what attracted Prince Andrey most.

Though the positions of Speransky and Prince Andrey seem overdrawn, most people find greater personal affinity with the view that endorses the power and authority of reason. Most people manage to maintain a picture of themselves as men of reason rather than as adherents of meaningless nonsense. Fortunately, wholesale acceptance of Prince Andrey's spirit is not a requirement for raising questions about the efficacy of reason in controversy. One such question deals with the all-important matter of the receivers' ability to recognize and make judgments about the reasoned aspects of controversy. Another deals with the effects of presenting two sides rather than one side of an issue. Still another potentially fruitful question attempts to determine the effect of basing one's claims on sound evidence and reasoning rather than on an assortment of psychological devices. Before turning to a discussion of these questions, it will be useful to examine what is meant by the concept of argument and its components.

Toulmin's Model of Argument

Arguments differ tremendously in form, complexity, and detail. The dominant classical mode of argument, the syllogism, assumes the simple structure of two premises and a conclusion:

> College students favor tuition-free education.
>
> John Blake is a college student.
>
> John Blake favors tuition-free education.

In sharp contrast are the technical arguments that govern the affairs of science and the courts, running several pages or an entire volume in length. Yet no matter how complex the form or how great the number of details, all arguments have three common characteristics. These may be regarded as the minimum requirements for the existence of an argument, the irreducible attributes which Toulmin (1958) referred to as *data (D)*, *warrant (W)*, and *claim (C)*. Data are whatever information leads through some mode of reasoning (known as a warrant) to a conclusion, or claim. In other words, the claim depends on data for its support, and the warrant serves as a reasoning principle to justify or certify the soundness of the move from data to claim. In simplest form, then, the layout of the minimum requirements of an argument can be diagrammed as follows:

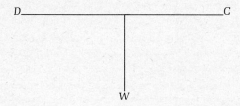

Note that the move from data to claim is the only direct connection in the chain. Since warrants serve to show the connections between data and claim, they are designated as indirect and supporting links underlying the main line of argument. The usefulness of the layout can readily be viewed in the sequence of the following statements:

> The majority of United States citizens, according to leading opinion polls, now favor a substantial increase in social security benefits. The government has a responsibility to take whatever steps necessary to fulfill the will of the people. The government must pass legislation to increase markedly the monthly social security benefits of all qualified citizens.

The main features of the sample argument can be represented in this form:

(D) The majority of citizens favor increased social security benefits.
(W) Since government is obligated to act in accordance with the expressed will of the people,
(C) The government should take steps to increase social security benefits.

Of course, most arguments are far more complicated than this. Many contain a number of characteristics other than the sequence from data through warrant to claim. Some depend, for example, on claims that have accompanying *backing* for warrant, and on *reservations* that stipulate conditions under which the claim does not apply. These secondary features of argument are discussed at length in many articles and texts written on the subject (Bettinghaus, 1966; Brockriede and Ehninger, 1960; Ehninger and Brockriede, 1963; Toulmin, 1958). For the purposes of this discussion, the only focal point of interest in Toulmin's schema is its relevance to the concept of argument.

Effects of Argument

It may seem sensible to expect reasonable men to accept messages grounded in reasonable argument. Though the question is still open, the research evidence has yet to confirm this commonsense view of the effects of argument. What sketchy evidence is available indicates that the use of sound argument does not necessarily constitute an advantage in matters of factual controversy. An early study by Knower (1935) compared two variations of a speech, one based on a logical arrangement and the other ordered in a different fashion, and found no significant differences in the effect the two forms had on immediate attitude change. Knower interpreted his data as indicating that the nature of original commitment on the topic was a far more important determinant of the outcome than was the type of arrangement used. Later work on a related issue of "logical versus emotional" appeals also led to inconclusive and sometimes contradictory findings (Becker, 1963; Clevenger and Knapprath, 1966; Cohen, 1957; Hartman, 1936; Hovland et al., 1953). Since failure to discover statistically significant differences does not rule out their possibility, the only conclusion is one that acknowledges a gap between the long-standing claims of what the persuasive value of argument *should be* and what, in fact, its value *is* as empirically demonstrated by the literature.

Any number of factors may mitigate the potential authority of well-reasoned messages. Some of these have already been discussed in connection with the problems associated with verbal appeals and message organization— matters of reinforcement, situational differences, strength of prior attitudes, time factors, recall, and so on. Two factors that bear most directly on the authority of reasoned messages are those of perception and ego involvement. It is now apparent that much early research falsely assumed too much about the receivers' ability to recognize matters of argument and, in so doing, to respond to their authority. Yet it is obvious that receivers cannot follow what they do not perceive. The problem of perception is not far removed from the consequences of slapping the labels "high threat" and "low threat" on variations of a persuasive message and then assuming that people will perceive the messages in accordance with the labels.

While it may be hazardous to make unqualified generalizations about people's ability to recognize the force of reasoned ideas, it is clear nonetheless that receivers differ notoriously in the conditions under which they can consistently separate that which qualifies as argument and that which does not. The research of Morgan and Morton (1944) and Lefford (1946) indicates that even students of logic often experience difficulty recognizing formal deductive syllogisms. Furthermore, when asked to judge the validity of a syllogism ("All men are mortal. Socrates is a man. Therefore, Socrates . . ."), students made *mistakes that followed the direction of their own personal biases on the subject.* In Lefford's research, for example, subjects judged the validity of two different types of syllogisms; one was based on content the investigator had judged to be emotionally loaded, the other on material he had held to be neutral in tone:

An emotionally loaded argument

Given: If peace is desirable at all costs, then negotiation to end war is desirable. If peace is important, then the United States should not capitulate to the pressure of warmongers who would destroy any chance for peaceful coexistence with Communists.

Therefore: If peace is desirable, the United States should not capitulate to the pressure of warmongers who would destroy any chance for peaceful coexistence with Communists.

A neutral argument

Given: If prompt payment is important, then this month's bills must not be ignored. If prompt payment is important, then it would be a mistake to ignore the bills that are now in the mailbox.

Therefore: If prompt payment is important, it would be a mistake to ignore the bills that are now in the mailbox.

Subjects more consistently misjudged invalid syllogisms *when they were in agreement with the argument* than when they were not. Strikingly, it proved more difficult to recognize the errors in the emotionally loaded material than in that whose content was more neutral. In an extension of Lefford's work, Bettinghaus (1968) trained students to judge the validity of syllogisms and found further evidence that mistakes follow individual bias. In fact, Bettinghaus noted, "Almost 20 percent more mistakes were made when the subject agreed with the conclusion of an invalid syllogism or disagreed with the conclusion of a valid syllogism than when the subjects' biases did not conflict with his judgments [p. 158]."

What is so striking is not that people fail to agree in their recognition and judgment of argument but rather the frequency and flagrance of their disagreements. Several examples of national disagreement were dramatically documented in the television campaign of the 1964 presidential race. A few incidents are worthy of recall because they underscore the research findings with exacting fidelity. Some may recall Barry Goldwater's statement: "Sometimes I think this country would be better off if we could just saw off the Eastern seaboard and let it float out to sea." Shortly thereafter, an enterprising Democratic party showed a cartoon commercial with someone sawing off the Eastern section of the continental United States while Goldwater's comment played in the background. The Democratic campaign also featured the famous daisy-girl spot. While a male voice soberly counted down to zero, a beautiful girl was shown plucking petals from a daisy. With the simultaneous disappearance of the last petal and the countdown to zero, a spectacular atomic explosion filled the screen. The voice of President Johnson then provided the words, "These are the stakes. To make a world in which all of God's children can live, or go into the dark. We must either love each other, or we must die." As a finishing touch the announcer reminded the voters to vote for President Johnson before intoning, "The stakes are too high for you to stay home." The Republicans counterattacked with singing choruses and documentaries. One sample script recorded by Mortensen (1967) featured a chorus chanting:

> Go with Goldwater. Go, go with Goldwater. You know where Goldwater stands. Clap your hands and go with Goldwater. Go, go with Goldwater. Let's go with Goldwater's plan. Clap hands and sing our song. He's the man for you and me. Clap hands and sing out strong. Let's show the world that we agree and go with Goldwater. Go, go with Goldwater. You know where Goldwater stands. Clap your hands and go with Goldwater. Barry's the man for our land . . . [p. 226].

Determined not to be outclassed by the Democrats, the Republicans authorized the design of a documentary entitled "Choice," sponsored by the Mothers for a Moral America. The scenes of violence and lawlessness aroused such intense emotional reaction that the documentary was withdrawn from its scheduled bookings.

In retrospect we might have expected the emotional outcry against "Choice" to typify the larger public reaction to the 1964 TV campaign. Quite the contrary. The reactions ran the gamut from unqualified endorsement of the drive as a deftly planned and highly reasonable appeal to voters all the way to vehement condemnation of what some authorities regarded as the low-water mark in presidential campaign strategy. Some saw the campaign as eminently reasonable, while others dismissed the whole affair in what one political scientist (Rubin, 1967) termed "hit-them-below-the-belt productions that demean democratic standards . . . [and] play with people's emotions and sensibilities and capacities to reason [p. 187].

The risk of misinterpretation is high in political persuasion mainly because of the intensity of public attitudes. In fact, we may generalize and say that campaigns are still another instance in support of the notion that the more ego-involved a group of receivers is on an issue, the greater will be the disparity in their perception and judgment of matters of argument. Recall the evidence in Chapter 4 suggesting that highly involved people are least likely either to resolve their individual differences or to interpret the meaning of messages in an accurate and objective manner (pp. 163–166). Of relevance also is Knower's (1935) finding on the importance of commitment in judging logical arrangement (p. 196) and the related evidence that mistakes in judging the validity of syllogisms follow subject bias and the degree of emotionally loaded content (p. 197). Moreover, research by Feather (1964) and McGuire (1962) indicates that the decision to accept or reject formal argument is positively correlated with the intensity of a person's attitude toward the conclusion.

The problems of recognizing and interpreting sound logic and well-reasoned argument should not suggest that logical structure is of incidental importance in verbal interaction. People may have difficulty in judging the validity of a given syllogism or in recognizing the details of an argument from a lengthy controversy, but they are normally quite sensitive, as we will see in the next section, to the grosser aspects of argument and evidence. What seems to be most important is that a message must pass the test of reasonableness but not necessarily tests of formal validity or soundness for each specific argument.

In one test of the importance of appearing "reasonable," Bettinghaus (1968) designed two variations of a persuasive message. One audience listened to a version where each argument started with the phrase, "Isn't it only logical that . . ." while the other audience heard a speech identical in every respect except for the absence of the phrase indicating that the speaker believed in the logical worth of what he was saying. A significant difference in degree of attitude change was found to favor the speech with the logical signposts. Apparently, the audience was sensitive to the overall dimension of "logicality" even in the absence of any specific bases for distinguishing between valid and invalid content. In such a finding we have additional testimony that what is important in matters of reasoned controversy is not so much the face value of each specific component of argument as the overall impression of the reasonableness of what is said. Once the larger impression is established, receivers may rely on subtle shifts in meaning to make the particulars fit their judgments of the basic logic of the message.

Two-sided versus One-sided Messages

One of the important characteristics of argument is the matter of whether or not a given presentation is grounded in more than one side of the issue. The risk of a two-sided presentation is that it invites comparison, doubt, and the chance that the opposing idea will appear the stronger. Not willing to invite comparison, the bulk of TV advertising concentrates on claims vaunting only the sponsor's product. Only rarely does a commercial carry more than a hint of a competitive product. On the other hand, the risk of a one-sided presentation is that an audience will attribute weakness to a presentation that neglects relevant and opposing views.

One of the earliest and best-known experiments on the topic was conducted during World War II by three social psychologists working with the War Department: Carl Hovland, Arthur Lumsdaine, and Fred Sheffield (1949). Their assignment was formidable. The surrender of Germany to Allied forces had led American soldiers to expect a similar and early end to the war with

Japan in the Pacific. A campaign was needed to impress upon American troops the magnitude of the task and the likelihood of a long and hard-fought combat with Japan. The question confronting Hovland and his associates was how best to design a campaign that would replace the excessive optimism with a more realistic view of the war effort. Should the appeal contain only the Army's view, or should it also represent some of the arguments backing the more optimistic interpretation of the war?

In order to compare the effects of two-sided and one-sided presentations, one experimental group was given a talk containing only arguments that supported the idea of a protracted war; this treatment discussed such factors as the great length of United States supply lines to the Pacific, the enormous resources and military strength of the Japanese empire, and the determination of the Japanese people. The two-sided program discussed identical points but included factors favoring a short war: the United States' naval superiority, the United States' progress despite a two-front war, the internal problems of Japan, and the impact of our expanded air war. The messages were presented only to soldiers whose previous attitudes on the topic were known; in this way comparisons could be made immediately after the presentation.

The principal discovery was that the messages had a different effect on various groups of people. The one-sided presentation was more effective with those who were less well educated, and the two-sided presentation had a greater impact on those with more education. When previous attitude and education were considered together, the two-sided treatment was more effective with all except the less well-educated men whose initial attitudes favored the view expressed in the material.

Counterarguments: Mentioning versus Refuting

Most social controversy cannot be resolved by a mere mention of opposing views. Does it make any difference, then, whether an advocate handles a two-sided issue by merely mentioning opposing views rather than by actively refuting them? If time is at a premium, the dilemma is clear. Every minute spent on an opponent's case leaves less time to establish one's own. On the other hand, mere mention of opposing arguments may not satisfy those audience members who will be influenced only if the weaknesses of the opponent's position are systematically exposed.

Unfortunately, research into the problem of refutation is disappointing and equivocal. The typical approach has been to compare the effects of speeches which simply allege that an opponent's arguments are not true against those which first present a supporting argument, then mention and actively refute counterarguments (Ludlum, 1958; Thistlethwaite and Kamenetzky, 1955;

Thistlethwaite et al., 1956). While some groups do not react differently to the two patterns of argument, others seem to be slightly more accepting of the active refutation. Apparently, the willingness to refute counterarguments contributes to the appearance of being logical and reasonable, as mentioned earlier. However, one factor overlooked in the investigations on refutation is the rather obviously important matter of the relative *skill* in refutation. If the advocate does not deal effectively with opposing arguments, or if he appears to be going through the motions of refutation in a half-hearted way, it would be no surprise to learn that his own credibility is adversely affected in the process. Then, too, insufficient skill in refutation may produce a boomerang effect wherein the other side's views are made to appear the stronger. Generally, the decision to actively refute counterarguments seems to work best for well-educated listeners.

From the findings on primacy-recency (pp. 187–191), we would expect the issue of refutation to hinge somewhat on such factors as which information comes first, prior attitudes, degree of commitment to the topic, and the likelihood that receivers will later be exposed to counterarguments. It is known that two-sided messages generally work best whenever an audience is to be subsequently exposed to counterarguments. Therefore, if the receivers commit themselves to the advocate's position *before* hearing any refutation of the opposition, or if they are expected to hear subsequent appeals from the opponent's side, the risks of active refutation are lessened.

On the strength of early research findings, Cronkhite (1969) suggested that if a group of listeners is aware of both sides of a controversy before the presentation, the organization with the least risk is the one that mentions and refutes opposing arguments at the outset, then shifts to the advocate's own arguments, followed in turn by an attempt to gain immediate commitment on the issue. Conversely, if the receivers are not particularly aware of all sides of the controversy, then the risk of refutation is lessened if the active refutation comes only *after* an attempt is made to gain commitment together with a warning about opposing arguments. Clearly, additional knowledge is needed to determine the extent to which the effects of active refutation hinge on such factors as prior attitudes, skill in refutation, education level and commitment of listeners, and expectation of subsequent counterargument.

Inoculating Effects of Two-sided Arguments

The very risk of refutation suggests that two-sided messages may have an unexpected consequence of inoculating the subject against attitude change. The phrase *inoculating effect* is analogous to the medical term which refers to the administering of a small dose of a disease to help the patient withstand a stronger impending attack. Dramatic testimony to the inoculating power of two-sided messages was reported in an early experiment by Lumsdaine and Janis (1953). College students listened to two-sided and one-sided versions of an alleged radio program devoted to arguments concerning the ability of Russia to produce atomic bombs. After determining that both versions produced significant attitude change, the experimenters had students listen, at a later date, to a tape that advocated the opposite point of view. The groups differed radically in their responsiveness to the counterarguments. Whereas only 2 percent of the group initially exposed to the one-sided message retained agreement in the views expressed in the initial message, 67 percent of those who heard the two-sided message did so. Apparently the very exposure to the two-sided message helped to inoculate students against the effects of subsequent counterarguments. In other words, counterarguments had no effect on those who were exposed to the two-sided messages but had a substantial effect on those exposed to the noninoculating, one-sided presentation.

Though there is much support for a general principle of inoculation, the effects are not uniform from situation to situation. Some factors heighten the inoculating influence of two-sided messages while others work in an opposite way. For example, there is reason to believe that the power of refutation can be heightened by delaying its presentation by two to three days after the initial message is heard (McGuire and Papageorgis, 1961). Such a finding is consistent with evidence on recency effects discussed earlier (p. 191). Recall that the more time which elapses between two segments of a presentation, the greater is the chance that what comes last will have the advantage. Much depends, of course, on what receivers do with the available information during interim periods. Time provides an opportunity for the receivers to construct their own "belief defenses" against anticipated counterarguments. The longer the time lapse, the less effective inoculating activity is apt to be (McGuire 1962).

When given sufficient time to build psychological defenses, virtually everyone seems to do so. In the interim, the more *actively* a person thinks about a controversy, the greater his resistance to counterarguments is apt to be, even though he has serious doubts about the entire issue during the interim. Only when a person runs into unanticipated counterarguments is the active effort to build personal defenses apt to be less effective than more passive efforts, such as simply reading about the topic (McGuire, 1961a, 1961b, 1962). There is also additional evidence that the very act of forewarning a person that he will soon hear opposing views sometimes aids him in his efforts to resist opposing presentations (Freedman and Sears, 1965; Manis, 1965; Manis and Blake, 1963). Forewarning also offers a risk that the receivers may be predisposed, that is more receptive, to counterarguments as they begin to anticipate and think about them (McGuire, 1968; McGuire and Millman, 1965). The complexities of forewarning and inoculation underscore the dynamic and unpredictable nature of the process by which people assess the reasoned worth of messages.

EVIDENCE

As we might suspect from the early sections of this chapter, the research into evidence encounters all the problems associated with the organizational details of message structure and content. The bulk of research deals with gross considerations relating to the consequences of using or not using evidence in persuasive communication. In the most comprehensive review of the subject, McCroskey (1969) found a marked disparity between the *presumed* and the actual, or *verified,* import of evidence. Studies by Cathcart (1955) and Bettinghaus (1953) found that the use of authoritative evidence produced significantly more attitude change than what was obtained in an identical presentation without citing authorities. On the other hand, Gilkinson (et al., 1954) and Ostermeier (1966) did not find any advantage accruing for the citation of authorities in support of claims.

Moreover, there have been a repeated number of unsuccessful attempts to find any advantage on a host of matters including use of statistical evidence (Costley, 1958); authoritative quotations and pictures (Wagner, 1958); augmentation of the number of citations (Anderson, 1958); increase in the amount of commentary designed to establish the qualifications of cited authorities (Anderson, 1958); alteration of the proportion of satisfactory evidence (Dresser, 1963); or the number of irrelevant or internally inconsistent pieces of evidence (Dresser, 1963). Even in situations such as formal debates and political campaigns, which supposedly place a premium on the skilled use of evidence, the manner of handling such material is known to typically fall short of acceptable standards (Anderson and Mortensen, 1967; Dresser, 1964; McKee, 1959; Mortensen, 1968a, 1968b).

Much of the reason for the apparently incidental impact of evidence is underscored in an inciteful analysis of the literature by McCroskey (1969). Evidence assumes importance, reasoned McCroskey, mainly as it interacts with other factors in a communicative situation—particularly source credibility and manner of presentation. His thesis is that the inclusion of evidence has little effect on immediate attitude change when presented by a highly credible source but does have an impact when it comes from a source perceived as moderate to low in credibility.

Underlying such a rationale is the notion that a law of diminishing returns quickly sets in when evidence is presented by a highly credible source. Since the credibility of the speaker's statements are initially high anyway, the inclusion of supporting material can have little further impact on the perceived authoritativeness of an already-respected communicator. However, the person who is low or moderate in credibility has much to gain by the inclusion of evidence because, McCroskey reasoned, the act of citing evidence has a potentially greater effect on audience attitudes toward him and the ideas he favors. Generally, the interaction between credibility and evidence holds so long as the material is well presented and insofar as there is some consensus by the respective parties as to what constitutes sound support (Arnold and McCroskey, 1967; McCroskey, 1967).

VERBAL INTERACTION AND THE INTERPERSONAL SYSTEM

The explanation advanced by McCroskey (1969) on evidence applies to, and is fully consistent with, the dynamic interplay of factors we saw operating in the perception of logical arrangement, order effects, fear arousal, and related matters. What is striking is how few lines of investigation have yielded results that point to any uniform or universal effects of the spoken or written word. This is not to say that messages cannot have effects independent of other influences. It is not difficult to imagine situations where the message seems to be the only major cause of subsequent behavior. For example, if a stranger suddenly runs into a room with people engaged in conversation and frantically announces the danger of an imminent explosion, there is little doubt that his announcement will have a uniform effect—one that is independent of the details of logical arrangement in the manner of presentation or the level of emotional arousal of the listeners. At the same time, however, we have seen how seldom the meaning of verbal interaction is akin to something that is fixed.

Clearly, the significance of verbal interaction does not center in a process even slightly analogous to a transaction like counting change or exchanging poker chips. The meaning of the verbal message is not fixed or stamped on the face of the words themselves. In ways that often prove to be most baffling to investigators, receivers have a way of attaching meaning to verbal cues that invariably reflect the unique dynamics of their own intuitive sense of logic. Usually, the meaning results as much from the receiver's psychological orientation as it does from any conventional interpretation of what the words—spoken or written—mean. In reiterating that the explanation for verbal interaction rests ultimately in the eye of the beholder, we are not denying the reality of verbal messages. Nor are we denying the possibility that messages can have characteristic and highly consistent effects on any given group or receiver.

To press the matter of message effects one step further, it may be well to try to pin down the conditions that favor the maximum impact of verbal message cues. When, in other words, does the verbal dimension of communication make the most difference? At the risk of overextending a rather mechanical-sounding analogy, we may compare the determinants of verbal interaction with the factors underlying the changing lighting conditions of a room. The typical living room in any house has a number of light sources originating outside and inside the room. The outside light and artificial light can blend in any number of ways. During daytime, when no electrical lights are being used, natural light streams in from outside. As twilight approaches, any given source of artificial electrical light will have greater relative impact on the total atmosphere of light in the room. Moreover, each electrical light, like most variables in verbal interaction, potentially has both *independent* and *interacting* effects on the overall lighting conditions. At night, when no other lights are on, a single 60-watt bulb is the major determinant of the lighting effect in the room. Likewise, virtually any aspect of verbal interaction can be a major determinant so long as there are *no other competing or mediating influences* at work. The rub, of course, is that the forces at work in most social situations are so complex as to simply rule out the probability that any one factor will dominate in a way even remotely akin to the effect of a single light in a room at night.

To say that ordinarily there is no one-to-one relationship between the details of messages and the response of receivers to those details is not to imply that the details have no influence. A single light may not have as much effect when sunlight floods the room, but this is not tantamount to saying that its light energy is in the slightest way diminished by the dominant effects of sunlight. Unfortunately, much of the research into message order and organization assumes too much of factors that function in a secondary way, much like the false expectations one would have about the influence of a 60-watt bulb at noonday if he had studied its effect only at night. As a case in point, the knowledge that the details of message structure have little relative impact under conditions of high ego involvement does not amount to a wholesale denial of the potential import of these details under certain ideal conditions. The lack of correspondence between the face value of an argument and its assigned value does not mean that the rigor of a well-reasoned presentation is a trivial matter in all social situations. In many social contexts, such as a public hearing on air pollution or a convention of scientists, sound argument may be the critical prerequisite of a presentation. In short, *the sorts of internal details of messages cited in this chapter typically influence but do not determine the outcome of verbal interaction except in those instances where a host of other factors serve in an instrumental way to accentuate and complement their impact.*

There is another important sense in which the mechanics of lighting conditions in a room resemble the larger fabric and tenor of the interpersonal system. One cannot adequately explain the effect of lighting in a room merely by focusing exclusively on the sources of light themselves. Factors such as the size of the room, color scheme, angles and textures of floors and walls must also be taken into consideration. These indirect influences are roughly akin to nonverbal influences on verbal activity. Verbal interaction is a dimension of a communicative act, but it does not constitute the total act. Therefore, verbal interaction must be approached in *relationship* to other dimensions of communication in the very same way in which specific verbal influences must be seen in the particular context of other mediating variables. Hence, the relative impact of verbal activity must always be interpreted within the larger context of other dimensions of communication, both those already discussed and the four we have yet to examine. We turn in the next two chapters to the dynamic interplay of nonverbal and interpersonal dimensions of the communicative act.

SUGGESTED READINGS

Darnell, D. K. "The Relation between Sentence Order and Comprehension," *Speech Monographs,* 30:97–100, 1963.

Duke, J. D. "Critique of the Janis and Feshbach Study," *Journal of Social Psychology,* 72:71–80, 1967.

Higbee, K. L. "Fifteen Years of Fear Arousal: Research on Threat Appeals, 1953–1968," *Psychological Bulletin,* 72:426–444, 1969.

Hovland, C. *The Order of Presentation in Persuasion.* New Haven, Conn.: Yale University Press, 1957.

Hovland, C., Janis, I., and **Kelley, H.** *Communication and Persuasion.* New Haven, Conn.: Yale University Press, 1953.

Janis, I. *The Contours of Fear.* New York: Wiley, 1968.

Janis, I. "Effects of Fear Arousal on Attitude Change: Recent Developments in Theory and Experimental Research," in L. Berkowitz (ed.), *Advances in Experimental Social Psychology,* vol. 3. New York: Academic, 1967, pp. 166–224.

Janis, I. L., and **Feshbach, S.** "Effects of Fear-arousing Communications," *Journal of Abnormal and Social Psychology,* 48:78–92, 1953.

Lana, R. "Three Theoretical Interpretations of Order Effects in Persuasive Communications," *Psychological Bulletin,* 61:314–370, 1964.

Leventhal, H., and **Watts, J.** "Sources of Resistance to Fear-arousing Communications on Smoking and Lung Cancer," *Journal of Personality,* 34:155–175, 1966.

McCroskey, J. C. "A Summary of Experimental Research on the Effects of Evidence in Persuasive Communication," *Quarterly Journal of Speech,* 55:169–176, 1969.

McGuire, W. "Personality and Susceptibility to Social Influence," in E. Borgatta and W. Lambert (eds.), *Handbook of Personality Theory and Research.* Chicago: Rand McNally, 1968.

Miller, G. R. "Some Factors Influencing Judgments of the Logical Validity of Arguments: A Research Review," *Quarterly Journal of Speech,* 55:276–286, 1969.

Miller, G. R., and Hewgill, M. A. "Some Recent Research on Fear-arousing Message Appeals, *Speech Monographs,* 33:377–391, 1966.

Powell, F. A. "The Effect of Anxiety-arousing Messages When Related to Personal, Familiar, and Impersonal Referents," *Speech Monographs,* 32:102–106, 1965.

Rosnow, R. L. "What Happened to the Law of Primacy?" *Journal of Communication,* 16:10–31, 1966.

Rosnow, R. L., and Robinson, E. J. (eds.) *Experiments in Persuasion.* New York: Academic, 1967.

Six

nonverbal interaction

The form of communication that has generated the most extensive scientific interest is the spoken or written word, primarily because verbal performance can be tested and, of course, because of the obvious import and immense power words have in the conduct of human affairs. Yet, this emphasis, or perhaps overemphasis, on verbal signs has caused the richness and subtlety of the nonverbal mode to remain, by comparison, unexplored territory. The lack of systematic, long-standing study of nonverbal behavior should remind us to resist the temptation to oversimplify the complexities of communication by reducing them solely to aspects of the verbal code. Nor, as a corollary, should we accept any model which assumes that man interacts primarily through words. The less charted realm of nonverbal interaction must be approached and understood as a significant, often central means by which people communicate.

There are several reasons for considering nonverbal interaction an important object of study. One stems from the recognition that communicative behavior cannot be separated from the psychological make-up of the human organism generally. It is often said that communication is not something which is done *to* a person; rather it is an interchange which is *engaged in* by consenting parties. To respond openly to another person is to react to the total dynamic of his behavior, not simply to the words that accompany his presentation. Moreover, each gesture, facial expression, and body movement is a potentially rich source of information about internal emotive states. Nonverbal cues also have a special symbolic value. They invariably reveal, sometimes unconsciously, impressions of self, feelings of worth, denial, esteem, guilt, doubt, confidence, status, social power, and so on. Furthermore, the nonverbal lexicon is a gauge to the status of interpersonal relationships; the stream of behavior constitutes a visible record of each party's impressions toward the objects of their coorientation. Finally, and most importantly, nonverbal cues form a large part of the meaning that is assigned in any face-to-face encounter.

RELATIONSHIP BETWEEN VERBAL AND NONVERBAL INTERACTION

The essential reason for drawing a distinction between verbal and nonverbal interaction is hueristic; that is, it is useful in conducting a probing action that otherwise would go unnoticed. The distinction should not be taken to imply, however, that the two dimensions are mutually exclusive. In actuality they are complementary aspects of a communicative act. The nonverbal includes all nonlinguistic or extralinguistic aspects of behavior that contribute to the meaning of messages: body movement, gesture, proxemics, facial expression, eye contact, posture, and certain paralinguistic cues associated with vocal quality and intonation.

The rules of logic underlying nonverbal expression are quite unlike those governing verbal interaction. Words are discrete entities, akin to coins and numbers in the way they function in an all-or-nothing fashion. Words have little meaning in part or as fractions; as a rule they must be uttered completely and in an intermittent, digital sequence that can be readily controlled by the speaker. Though a person may decide to stop talking, he cannot stop behaving. And it is behavior itself, the very presence of a person, that provides an uninterrupted stream of information and a constant source of emotive overtone. Nonverbal data are neither discrete units nor intermittent forms of expression. They function quite unlike the all-or-nothing operations of a desk calculator. The nonverbal sequence is continuous, visible, and beyond ready concealment or manipulation.

NONVERBAL BEHAVIOR: UNDERLYING CONSIDERATIONS

To specify how nonverbal cues influence any communicative act, it is necessary to know something about each of the following: (1) the unit of behavior under observation, (2) the type of awareness, (3) the type of conveyed information, and (4) the origin of each unit.

Unit of Observation

When dealing with a dimension of human behavior as complex as nonverbal interaction, it is often necessary to specify exactly what unit measure is being observed. It is clear that no one element has meaning in isolation, and yet it is also apparent that nonverbal behavior is not a single undifferentiated process. In some instances the meaning of nonverbal behavior can be accounted for in quite specific terms: for example, the proportion of time spent in eye contact. In other circumstances more inclusive activity must be regarded as the proper focal point: for example, the significance of how a person walks or sits in a chair while engaging in communication. Moreover, we will later discover the import of certain types of units that focus not simply on some aspect of individual behavior but on the activity of one person in relation to another.

Also cutting across the problem of the units of measurement is the question of whether the proper frame of reference is an *act* (movement of head, hands, shifting of body) or a *still position* (a particular facial expression, gesture, body position, and so on). We will also discover that studies which emphasize body positions yield results that differ markedly from those dealing with body movements and acts. Also, the *area* of the body position or action where the cues occur makes a difference in assigned meaning. For example, head movements convey more information about the *nature* of an emotion such as joy, anger, or frustration, and body movements indicate more about the *intensity* of whatever emotional state is being expressed. The complex relationships between nonverbal activity and the various units of observation should again remind us of the import of viewing the dynamics of nonverbal behavior in a multidimensional frame of reference. In short, no one attribute of nonverbal behavior can provide a sufficient basis from which to standardize units of observation.

Type of Awareness

A fascinating but baffling aspect of nonverbal interaction stems from differences in the level of awareness that people maintain toward nonverbal message cues. The problem of awareness, or sensitivity, applies both to the range of awareness about self and to the nonverbal activity of others. Ordinarily, people are more apt to assign significance to the nonverbal activity of others than they are to their own actions. It is, of course, easier to view others as acting intentionally and deliberately than it is to attribute the same degree of intent to one's own nonverbal behavior. Most people, observed Ekman (1968),

> do not know what they are doing with their bodies when they are talking, and no one tells them. People learn to disregard the internal cues which are informative about their stream of body movements and facial expressions. Most interactive nonverbal behavior seems to be enacted with little conscious choice or registration, efforts to inhibit what is shown fail because the information about what is occurring is not customarily within awareness [p. 181, Italics added].

In face-to-face situations it is tempting to view the person who stands too close for comfort and waves his hands wildly in the air while talking loudly as being overbearing and self-assertive, even though he may not be at all conscious of how his own action is being interpreted. Likewise, the person who suddenly turns away from a conversation appears most often to be deliberately giving the "cold shoulder," even though others present would rarely define comparable action on their own part as cold and impersonal. The inclination, then is to define personal action as natural and spontaneous and to view the nonverbal acts of others as deliberate and intentionally motivated.

In most interpersonal encounters, a high proportion of potentially meaningful cues go unnoticed. The recordings made by investigators trained in observing nuances of nonverbal movement, a field known as kinesics, underscore the level of awareness that can be obtained through rigorous powers of observation. Consider the level of awareness demonstrated in the following sequence of actions observed by the pioneering kinesiologist Birdwhistell (1952) while riding on a bus:

1. This situation was observed on a street bus at about 2:30 P.M. The little boy was seated next to the window. He seemed tired of looking out the window and, after surveying all of the car ads and the passengers, he leaned toward his mother and pulled at her sleeve, pouted and vigorously kicked his legs.
2. The mother has been sitting erectly in her seat, her packages on her lap, and her hands lightly clasped around the packages. She was apparently "lost in thought."
3. When the boy's initial appeal failed to gain the mother's attention, he began to jerk at her sleeve again, each jerk apparently stressing his vocalization.
4. The mother turned and looked at him, "shushed" him, and placed her right hand firmly across his thighs.
5. The boy protested audibly, clenched both fists, pulled them with stress against his chest. At the same time he drew his legs up against the restraint of the mother's hand. His mouth was drawn down and his upper face was pulled into a tight frown.

6. The mother withdrew her hand from his lap and resettled in her former position with her hands clasped around the packages.
7. The boy grasped her upper arm tightly, continued to frown. When no immediate response was forthcoming, he turned and thrust both knees into the lateral aspect of her left thigh.
8. She looked at him, leaned toward him, and slapped him across the anterior portion of his upper legs.
9. He began to jerk his clenched fists up and down, vigorously nodding between each interior-superior movement of his fists.
10. She turned, frowning, and with her mouth pursed, she spoke to him through her teeth. Suddenly she looked around, noted that other passengers were watching, forced a square smile. At the same time that she finished speaking, she reached her right hand in under her left arm and squeezed the boy's arm. He sat quietly [pp. 27–28].

Note that within a brief time span the mother and the child went through twenty-six distinct movements, most of which occurred in the absence of verbal cues. Yet the meaning is still unmistakable. Clearly, the complex matter of awareness contributes in no small measure to the potential meaning of the nonverbal repertoire.

Type of Conveyed Information

The gap between potential and actual significance of nonverbal cues entails more than differences in levels of awareness. Early work in kinesics presupposed that all nonverbal movement had some significance within the larger context of behavior. Hence, no facet of movement could be taken as accidental or meaningless (Birdwhistell, 1952; Renneker, 1963). The question, of course, is what *type* of significance does a movement have? There is a need to distinguish among three distinct levels of significance.

Some nonverbal acts are purely *random* movements; they have no regularity, no recognized meaning, not even for a single person. The only requirement of random acts is movement itself. All situations, private and social, contain an enormous range of random activity; a person squirms deeper into his chair, he moves his neck muscles to lessen the pressure of a tightly fitting tie, he blinks his eyes, and he makes countless other adjustments that are beyond the range of personal or social awareness. The important point about random movements is that the persons need not be aware of their occurrence and, where minimally aware, attach no particular significance to them. For other persons present, random movements are the ones that go unnoticed. In short, they have significance only as part of the autonomous functioning of each individual but do not influence the meaning assigned to communicative behavior.

There is also a class of movements which carry information that

Ekman and Friesen (1969) labeled *idiosyncratic*. An act is idiosyncratic if there is some lawfulness or regularity associated with its occurrence but the association is peculiar to a single individual. Mannerisms and personal quirks fit this pattern. One person has a characteristic way of shrugging his shoulder. Another looks at the floor whenever a social situation suddenly becomes strained and tense. Still another suddenly starts to nod his head or tap his fingers on a table whenever someone begins to disagree with his expressed opinion on a topic. Every person has a repertoire of characteristic recurrent patterns of walking, sitting, and looking and a host of patterns related to facial expression, posture, hand movements, lip pursing, head nodding, eye contact, and so forth. Unlike random movement, idiosyncratic acts have potential communicative significance, particularly in long-standing, personal relationships. As two or more persons spend more and more time in each other's presence, they gradually acquire insight into the personal mannerisms of the other, investing each act with significance that comes only through repeated association in a way that is beyond the range of what others judge as meaningful.

An act has *shared* significance if the information associated with its occurrence is common to a class of individuals (Ekman and Friesen, 1969). The degree of sharing may refer to the number of people who attach common importance to it or to a range of situations in which particular patterns are recognized as meaningful. This distinction between people and situations is important because of the range of possibilities it incorporates. A person may act in common ways and with a high degree of predictability across dissimilar social situations whenever confronted by high stress or tension; however, his nonverbal acts have shared significance only for himself and possibly his wife. In short, they are limited not by situation but by the number of people present. On the other hand, there is growing evidence that large classes of people, often an entire culture, may respond in predictable ways to matters of physical space, overcrowding, and other nonverbal behavior.

Clearly, to say that a nonverbal act has significance is to allow for any of the combinations, among others, designated in Figure 6.1. The level of significance can be ordered roughly from simple to complex as shown by the numbers. The simplest type of significance, type 1, is purely random movement, the only requirement being some autonomous act of behavior. Next in level of complexity is idiosyncratic meaning, level 2, which is lawful but restricted to the actions of a particular person. If the awareness is known to at least one other person, say a wife who knows how her husband will act after an exhausting day of work, it qualifies as shared (type 3). Those acts which are shared by the initiators and respondents alike constitute a higher level of complexity (type 4) that comprises the attributes of regularity, awareness, and also mutuality, or coorientation. Both type 3 and type 4 may include any number of communicators, from two to a class of people, an organization, or even a culture. The greater the number of people who share common meanings, the higher

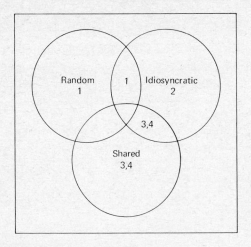

Figure 6.1 *Nonverbal cues; four levels of significance. Level 1 = random, intrapersonal significance; level 2 = lawful, intrapersonal significance; level 3 = lawful, interpersonal significance; and level 4 = shared significance.*

the level of significance. In Chapter 8 we will discover evidence that some nonverbal acts have common meanings which are applicable even across cultures. The four levels of significance have considerable overlap and certainly do not exhaust the possibilities, but they do represent broad distinctions necessary in most communicative situations.

Origin of the Behavior

The source of nonverbal acts, that is, their underlying basis, is so fundamental and yet so elusive that it is necessary to consider the problem in detail. At its heart is a host of fundamental assumptions about the basis of human actions generally. It obviously makes a difference, for example, whether one builds an explanation of human emotion on the assumption that nonverbal cues are mere surface manifestations of inner psychological states or whether one regards their origin as social and experiential in nature. The problem of origin is one of those persistent and fundamental considerations which can neither be dismissed nor be fully resolved. The justification for even raising the question is the potential insight that comes from a willingness to grapple with a thorny issue which has far-reaching implications for our study.

At least two possible types of origins need be distinguished. One is *biological*, and the other is *social*. The former emphasizes the relationship between nonverbal cues and activity built into the nervous system. The latter focuses instead on the accumulative impact of social experience, rather than inheritance.

The biological tradition interprets emotive states as surface manifestations of *internal physical activity*. The term *activity* covers varying degrees of activation, arousal, or drives which trigger given levels of feeling and emotion. The stronger the drive, the higher the level of activation, the more intense will be the subjective experience of emotion. Since internal functioning of the organism is essentially a matter of physiology, the biological school of thought does not emphasize the role of psychological and social influences in the experience of emotion. However, since a person may experience more than one emotive state for any given level of physiological activation, the higher, critical faculties of the central nervous system are used to explain the particular blend of emotive overtones that accompany the experience of emotion. The biological viewpoint, with its emphasis on internal levels of activation, is advanced in most recent form by Malmo (1959), Duffy (1962), and Schachter and his associates (Schachter and Singer, 1962; Schachter and Wheeler, 1962).

According to the biological tradition, the emotional meaning of a gesture or muscular movement has significance only insofar as it signals information about the internal state of the individual. The expectation is that a person who experiences an intense, highly activated state is more likely to engage in highly expressive forms of communicative behavior (Ax, 1953; Davitz, 1964; Schachter, 1957). For example, a person who expends a great deal of physical energy is apt to speak in a loud voice, use intense gestures, show animated facial expression, reveal rapid movements of all surface muscles and heightened skin tone. In sharp contrast is the person whose outward passivity belies minimum internal arousal. Both cases, in other words, do not so much result from such social factors as positive feedback, stimulating surroundings, or the expressive behavior of others as they do from some intense or minimal level of internal arousal.

To their critics, the adherents of physiologically based explanations of emotion have two shortcomings. They take into account only the *intensity* of emotion and, therefore, cannot adequately explain *various types* of emotive states (Schlosberg, 1954). Equally damaging, particularly from a communication standpoint, is the charge that notions of activation provide only general explanations of emotional activity. As a consequence, the difficulty is in accounting for particular types of emotional expression that accompany a particular level of arousal. As an alternative explanation, some social scientists approach the problem of emotion from a different perspective—one that is socially based rather than one that stresses a more visceral level of activation.

Typical of the social school of thought is the position advanced by Tomkins and McCarter (1964). These investigators made two assumptions: first, that the *primary* human emotions are all *affective*, or *expressive*, in nature; second, that human affects are primarily a matter of *facial expression* and only secondarily indicators of inner arousal. The crux of the issue is the relationship between what can be observed and what can be inferred about emotional arousal. Tomkins and McCarter reasoned that whatever is observable is primary. And the most visible expressor of emotion is undoubtedly the face. Hence, they regard the face as the primary and leading expressor of human emotion, one that is the most capable of rapid and complex activation, far more so than the slower-moving internal visceral organs.

The essential difference between the biological and social theories of emotion is not one resulting from an exclusive, either-or position but rather one of degree of emphasis. The notion of internal arousal is useful in underscoring the fact that overt expression is not solely determined by surface appearance. The meaning of any expressive act is neither self-contained nor fully evident to an observer. At the same time it must be acknowledged that the social tradition is useful in underscoring the fact that the face has through time been the principal organ for transmitting emotive information from one person to another. While both traditions have supporting evidence, little research has been conducted to sort the comparative importance and interplay of social and internal factors governing the nature of human emotion. In subsequent discussion we will return to the problem of origin in more specific detail.

THE NONVERBAL REPERTOIRE

The remainder of this chapter consists of a framework for describing the inner workings of the nonverbal repertoire. Throughout the discussion it is necessary to keep the matters of units of observation, awareness, type of information, and origin all in perspective. In so doing we acknowledge that nonverbal interaction includes quite dissimilar forms of behavior that can be best understood in a multidimensional framework. The schema borrows from the work of Efron (1941), Ekman and Friesen (1969), Mahl (1968) and our earlier discussion of communication models. It focuses on the major types of nonverbal cues as they in turn contribute to the meaning of communicative behavior.

Affect Displays

Nonverbal cues are the principal means of expressing basic affective or emotive states. The concept of affect display is synonymous with expression of emotion: interest, excitement, joy, surprise, anguish, fear, shame, contempt, and anger, together with countless number of blends. A display may be expressed unconsciously or consciously, with minimal or high awareness in any gradation from specific to general, that originates either in the inheritance of the past or the contingencies of the moment. Affect displays communicate the most personal of all types of information, primarily because of the visibility of the face and the regularity with which the human body makes its most intimate self-disclosures. Affect displays have consequences for the meaning assigned to personal and social events; in addition, they color the interpretation given to situations that are supposedly neutral in tone. Hence the pervasive dimension of affect coincides with the assumptions underlying our discussion of the proactive nature of psychological orientation (pp. 16–18).

Facial Expression as Affect Display

The most complex and fascinating aspect of affect display is the composite of meanings conveyed by the human face. The face is at once a visible and transparent focal point of interpersonal events. It is also the key to self-identity and the main vehicle for personal recognition. No other feature of the human body is as richly expressive of inner feelings nor as readily subject to misinterpretation and ambiguity. As an object of wonderment and mystery, the variety of facial expressions result from a composite of minute muscular movements which, in turn, form visual impressions as complex and unique as the number of individuals who produce and interpret them. Yet individual differences notwithstanding, facial expressions are also learned, culturally defined patterns of behavior which, by their very patterning, elicit shared, conventional meaning. And it is upon this patterning that all who engage in face-to-face relations must rely in interpreting the reactions of others to their own affect displays.

The research literature on facial expression, spanning some sixty years, is in itself an indication of the elusiveness of the face as an object of scientific study. Even in early investigations, there was no real disagreement over the importance of facial expression as an expressor of affect. Initially what was in question was the accuracy with which people judged the emotions depicted by facial expression and the relative import of various facial features in those judgments. On the problem of accuracy, inconclusive and conflicting findings abounded, even when the same stimulus materials were used. For example, Langfeld (1918) used retouched photographs of an actor and found judges able to identify accurately from 17 to 58 percent of a set of emotional meanings; but in a subsequent study, Allport (1924)—even after selecting the best (least ambiguous) photographs—was unable to obtain better than about 50 percent accuracy in matching emotions with photographs. Related lines of investigation differed on matters ranging from the relative import of various facial features to the overall significance of individual differences in judging facial cues (Carmichael).

The Importance of Context. Why did early studies yield such inconclusive and confusing results? As is often the case in scientific investigations, failure to discover important findings is as important as identifying substantive successes. In essence the problem resulted from the many faulty attempts to isolate the communicative value of each facial movement independent of other cues. Eventually investigators accepted the suggestion of Frois-Wittman (1930) that the meaning of facial cues is not to be found in momentary movements or in isolated facial positions. Rather, meaning could only be interpreted as part of the larger, ongoing stream of nonverbal behavior.

Osgood (1966) underscored the importance of context, pointing out that if people are asked to *name* the emotional meaning conveyed by a particular facial expression, they usually do poorly. Yet, in everyday situations, where people are judging the dynamics of a total communicative act, not just the face, they are confident of their ability to judge the emotional state of a person on the basis of his facial expression. There is now abundant evidence that accuracy of communication increases as information is gained about the context in which facial expression occurs (Cline, 1956; Frijda, 1958; Frijda and Philipszoom, 1963; Munn, 1940; Rump, 1960; Schachter and Singer, 1962; Vinacke, 1949). One study (Argyle, et al., 1968) supports the notion that full visibility of another person is itself an important determinant of the mutual orientation of the interactants. Closely related is the finding that any information concerning the situation, even the sketchiest of details, improves accuracy of communication.

The importance of context is underscored in a study (Cline, 1956) showing that the affective meaning of a smiling face depends upon the type of contextual cues available for comparison. When paired with a glum face, for example, the smiling person is regarded as dominant or vicious. However, when the identical smiling face is paired with a frowning face, the smiling face is typically regarded as friendly, good-natured, or peaceful. Closely related is the tendency to judge what otherwise would be judged as a neutral facial expression in a film as lustful when preceded by a shot of a girl in a bathing suit, and as horror when immediately preceded by a shot of an auto accident. Moreover, judgments of affect display change markedly if the person who makes the judgments happens to know the other person on a personal basis (Bruner and Taguiri, 1954; Woodworth and Schlosberg, 1954). The findings on context are consistent with the view that facial expression constitutes a *general dimension* of affect display and that contextual cues supply more specific variations of the type of state—anger or impatience, satisfaction or contentment—depicted by the facial expression (Frijda, 1958).

The analysis of emotion by Schlosberg and his associates (1952, 1954, 1957, 1958) provided much insight into the general dimension of the face as a source of affect display. Using the assumptions of the biological tradition discussed earlier, Schlosberg rejected any notion of emotion as a special state, one differing qualitatively from other states, in favor of considering it on a continuum of arousal (Figure 6.2). When viewed in this light, the affective meaning of facial expression can be conceived of as differing on the general dimensions of *pleasantness to unpleasantness, attention to rejection,* and *level of activation or arousal.* Though more general than most category systems, Schlosberg's schema has effectively accounted for gross differences in the judgments of facial expressions through a variety of social settings (Abelson and Sermat, 1962; Frijda and Philipszoom, 1963; Osgood, 1966; Triandis and Lambert, 1958).

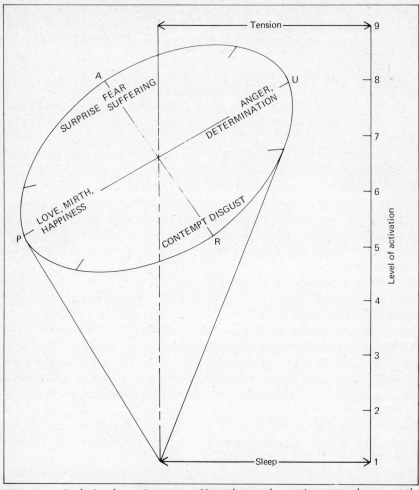

Figure 6.2 *Analysis of emotive states. Note that each emotive state shown on the solid figure is placed in relation to its maximum level of activation. The top surface is sloped to show that anger and fear can reach higher levels of activation than can love, contempt, etc. (Reprinted with permission from Schlosberg, 1954.)*

Primary Affect Displays

If the face is the main expressor of affect, it is more than incidentally important to establish what particular affective states can be reflected with greatest fidelity. A long-standing tradition of writing since Charles Darwin is based on the reasoning that distinctive muscular movements of the face are closely associated with certain basic affective states that can be recognized by most everyone. Tomkins and McCarter (1964), the adherents of the social school of thought discussed earlier, advanced their position by differentiating among eight primary affects:

1. *Interest-Excitement:* eyebrows down, eyes track, look, listen
2. *Enjoyment-Joy:* smile, lips widened up and out, smiling eyes (circular wrinkles)
3. *Surprise-Startle:* eyebrows up, eyes blink
4. *Distress-Anguish:* cry, arched eyebrows, mouth down, tears, rhythmic sobbing
5. *Fear-Terror:* eyes frozen open, pale, cold, sweaty face, trembling, with hair erect
6. *Shame-Humiliation:* eyes down, head up
7. *Contempt-Disgust:* sneer, upper lip up
8. *Anger-Rage:* frown, clenched jaw, eyes narrowed, red face

In a test of the theory of primary affect, subjects examined photographs of models who were instructed to depict emotional neutrality and each of the eight primary affects. Results indicated that the subjects could identify the eight primary affects far above chance expectations. The greatest error in judgment occurred with photographs of emotional neutrality; however, even those subjects who made the inaccurate judgments of emotional neutrality were still able to recognize, almost without exception, the particular meaning of each primary affect.

The eight affective states differ in only small respects from the tentative categories of primary affect advanced by other investigators working in different decades with dissimilar methods on various nationalities (Boucher and Ekman, 1965; Ekman and Friesen, 1967, 1969; Frijda, 1963; Osgood, 1966; Plutchik, 1962; Schlosberg, 1941). Though the search for primary affects will always be an open question, there is surprising consistency in the evidence supporting the following as primary: surprise, happiness, sadness, fear, anger, disgust, and interest.

Blends and Microfacial Displays. The range of possible blends of affect displays is analogous to the spectrum of a color chart. The primary affects are akin to primary colors; the infinite variety and blends of facial expressions compare with the various combinations of possible color blends. Cutting through the spectrum of affect displays are factors pertaining to the amount of physical movement, contextual considerations, and the length of expression. All the factors are capable of an incalculable number of blends and fluctuations in expressive overtone (Tomkins, 1964, Plutchik, 1962). There is even recent evidence that some facial displays are so fleeting that they are beyond conscious awareness. Using slow-motion film techniques, Haggard and Isaacs (1966) found that certain *micro* expressions occur between 1/5 and 1/8 of a second. Microfacial expressions cluster around moments of general expression when an individual attempts to conceal or disguise any visible indication of his internal emotions. Some fascinating confirming evidence for the existence and import of micro displays (Ekman and Friesen, 1967, 1969; Huenergardt and

Finando, 1969) attest to the difficulties of concealing affective states. Despite all efforts to the contrary, the face is a visible source of leakage. For example, the microfacial expressions shown in Figure 6.3 occurred in completed form within 1/5 of a second (Huenergardt and Finando, 1969). The subject, watching a film designed to arouse emotional stress, was instructed not to show any emotion. When interviewed later, he felt that he had been successful in not giving the slightest visual hint about how he reacted to the film sequence. The photographs are graphic testimony to the subtlety of visual cues and the complexity of facts that contribute to the meaning of affect display. Also relevant to the details of affect is a study (Stritch and Secord, 1956) based on a series of retouched photographs of a face, altered in subtle ways to change the shading of brow wrinkles, the brightness of the eyes, and the position of the mouth. Results showed that the slightest alteration of these facial features was sufficient to change the judged meaning of the facial expression. For example, the act of shading the eyebrows was itself sufficient to have the person judged as having darker skin, coarser features, and disarranged hair. In sum, the record of the last two decades is one impressive testimony to the ever-changing, richly expressive nature of affect displays, both in primary form and in the countless blends and micro fluxuations as they are modified by body movement and context.

Body Movement and Affect Display

The relationship between the face and other regions of the body as affect display may appear at first glance to be altogether obvious. After all, one might reason, if the face expresses a given affect, then the body should do nothing other than convey more of the same information. And yet, the question remains. For if the face is primary and has distinct characteristics, perhaps the significance of body movement is not so obvious. Some body movements, it is true, seem to display affect—trembling and startled responses—but these are exceptions.

The only systematic work on the relation of facial expression and body movement is that of Ekman and Friesen (1968, 1969). They reasoned that since the rate of facial expression far exceeds the rate of body movements, judgments concerning affect can more frequently be made from head cries than from body cues. Moreover, body movements do not so much express

Figure 6.3 *Microfacial expressions. The key to the meaning of momentary facial expressions lies not so much in how rapidly the face changes but in the degree of similarity in a given expression before and after the "leakage" occurs. Note that the first couple of frames in the sequence of photographs are virtually identical to the last frames. What we see depicted in between is a squelched expression of disgust at a moment when the subject saw a gory accident in a film for driver education. Even though he was instructed to conceal all signs of emotional reaction, the subject was unable to control his expressions completely. (Taken with permission from Huenergardt and Finando, 1969.)*

affect as they do a *response to affect;* they are relevant mainly to the way a person copes with the primary affect displays. Body movements, in other words, "are the behavioral consequences of the affect, rather than the display of affect itself . . . [1969, p. 71]." Said still another way, the body conveys information concerning the adaptive and regulative efforts of an organism responding to affect display. We will consider some of the particulars of nonverbal regulators later.

One way to test the notion that distinct types of information are conveyed by the head and the body is to create a situation that requires subjects to match a person's body movements with what he is saying. Ideally, the situation should be one of stress or tension, thereby increasing the probability of creating affect display. The more frequent the interruptions, personal attacks, and unkind criticism, and the more negative the tone of the conversation, the more likely it is that a person will react unequivocally in an emotional manner. The next step is to film the interaction, creating segments in which people try to match nonverbal segments with other aspects of behavior. Using variations of this procedure, Ekman (1964, 1965b, 1967) found that body movement and facial expression can be reliably matched with verbal statements and, more importantly, that the head and the body convey distinct types of information. With striking regularity receivers rely on head movement for information about someone independently of what is communicated by his body. Whereas head cues and facial expression convey information about the type of emotional feeling expressed (joy, anger, fear) and little about the degree of emotional arousal, the body indicates something about the intensity or depth of emotional involvement. Hence, the body may be regarded as a part of the context of affect display, modifying and amplifying information about the intensity of expressed states.

Ekman's findings are consistent with larger evidence about body movement. As stress becomes more intense, the frequency of body movement is known to increase (Dittmann, 1962; Sainsbury, 1955). Moreover, as a person's emotional mood changes from a relaxed to a tense state, his body responds in kind by becoming increasingly active, particularly with regard to greater shifting movements, twitching, and so forth. Even in clinical settings, for example, particular hand movements are known to convey characteristic reactions to given types of psychological stress. Typically, the more intense the stress, the less various hand movements are displayed. By comparing hand movement with other aspects of behavior, the trained investigator can read the significance of movement with considerable accuracy. As an illustration, "hand shrug" motions typically cluster around verbal expressions of uncertainty; "open hand reach" motions occur early in attempts to answer direct questions; and "hand rubbing" seems to be associated with verbal expressions of fear and conflict (Ekman and Friesen, 1969). Though it is not known whether these findings apply in nonclinical settings, it is known that in everyday situations people can rely on the physical movements of others to indicate matters of mood (Dittmann, 1962),

Figure 6.4   *Stick-figure test. (Reprinted with permission from Rosenberg and Langer, 1965.)*

stress (Sainsbury, 1965), affect, and a host of other affect displays that occur in the absence of any verbal statement (Ekman, 1965b).

Further evidence for what is termed the "relative uniform, albeit rudimentary, meaning" of body movement was reported by Rosenberg and Langer (1965) in a study dealing with the communicative value of various body postures. Subjects watched a sequence of twenty-five stick figures (Figure 6.4) projected on a screen for twenty seconds at a time and then were asked to rank the meaning of various body positions on scales of affect-related terms such as "feeling," "stability," and "direction." The subjects matched the figures and descriptive terms with a high degree of accuracy. The highest agreement among subjects was obtained for those stick figures associated with most intensive affective states. The least consistency occurred for figures designed to depict passive or relaxed states such as sensitivity to the communicative significance of physical movement. The studies of Levitt (1964) and Beldoch (1964) indicate that a person's ability to interpret the meaning of body language depends on the degree to which he is sensitive to his own feelings and emotions.

Whatever the extent of individual differences there is much evidence that people can consistently interpret the meaning of body cues over time. Those who are most accurate in judging body movement tend also to be most effective in communicating their own feelings by vocal, musical, or graphic means of communication. Some people tend to be very selective in the modes of nonverbal expression to which they respond most accurately. For some, tone of voice, manner, facial expression, and body movement are most important in judging the inner states of others. Others seem to respond almost exclusively to the spoken or printed word. This range of differences accounts for many difficulties in specifying how well classes of people agree about the meaning of physical activity. The findings of Dittmann et al., (1965) indicate that past experience plays a part in one's ability to evaluate nonverbal cues; clinical therapists have been found to be less able to judge body cues than trained dancers. Finally, research by Guilford (1929), Levy (1964), and Shapiro (1968) indicates a positive relationship between the judgment of nonverbal meaning and the degree of consistency with which people respond to either facial or body movement.

Physical Contact as Affect Display

The human capacity to express an infinite number of emotional states and to judge the emotional feelings of others would be greatly minimized were it not for the skin's sensitivity to touch. Without the experience of tactile stimulation, social relationships often would be bare and meaningless, lacking richly expressive power and intensity of emotional stimulation. In human communication the contraction of blood vessels, the changes in respiration and glandular secretion, the twitching of muscles, and the dilation of the pupils do not in themselves constitute discriminative, symbolic message cues. Rather they are immediate, nonpurposive signals, carried out largely by the autonomic nervous system and stimulated both from the internal activity of the organism and from the physical environment around it. Nonetheless, tactile stimulation is *overlaid* with motor activity, visual signs, and verbal symbols; thereby it is capable of transforming human consciousness into the most intense of all human experiences.

It is little wonder, then, that physical contact plays such an important part in defining the emotional dimensions of social relations. In a comparison of emotional reactions to physical contact with other people and with physical objects, McBride (et al., 1965) reported that the very act of touching another person produces a far more intense reaction (as measured by galvanic skin response) than what typically occurs with inanimate objects. Moreover, physical contact has enormous power to convey a gamut of richly expressive meanings.

Three stages of learning influence the meaning which we assign during the course of our physical contacts with others (Frank, 1957). The first stage, accomplished during infancy, is one of *orientation to spatial dimensions* of the physical world. Largely out of the earliest tactile exploration with his fingers and mouth, an infant unravels the mysteries of the gross physical characteristics of objects—qualities, shapes, and textures. Subsequent physical contact with human beings is largely brought about by the tactile stimulations of nursing, cuddling, patting, stroking, and other forms of physical comforting. Gradually, a child's early tactile experiences become further differentiated and overlaid with higher forms of symbolic recognition.

During the second stage of development, which Frank considered to be critical, the infant learns to recognize *restrictions on physical surroundings* as he gropes for meaning and accommodation in an increasingly social world. From the socially defined rules of physical contact, the child then enters the third stage, wherein he learns *rules that apply to affect display* in face-to-face situations—particularly religious rituals (laying on of hands), contact between sexes, social decorum, etiquette, and all the elaborate provisions governing the way people approach and relate to others in communicative situations.

Evidence for the cultural patterning of physical contact in the United States is suggested by studies (Jourard, 1964; Jourard and Rubin, 1968) in which students kept track of when they were touched and by whom. Their self-reports showed that the most frequent physical contact occurred with their mothers and friends of the opposite sex. The least amount of contact occurred between students and their fathers, for many such contact was restricted to the touching of hands, mostly in the form of handshaking. The import of cultural patterning is evident both in the predictability of these findings and the fact that a different result would have undoubtedly occurred in other cultures, particularly among Mediterranean people, who are accustomed to a great deal more physical contact, even among members of the same sex. Clearly, then, there is little reason to dispute Frank's (1957) conclusion that tactile experience is indeed both "highly complex and versatile, with an immense range of functional operations and a wide repertory of responses [p. 219]."

Paralanguage as Affective Overtone

The human voice in communicative situations has a twofold function in that its effects are both verbal and nonverbal. Its verbal function is linguistic, stemming from the primary role of the speech mechanism in speech production. Its nonverbal function is extralinguistic, or paralinguistic. Paralanguage is based on the meaning associated with vocal intonation and cues of vocal quality —pitch, rate, timbre, and volume. The distinction between linguistic and paralinguistic approximates the difference between *what* is said and *how* it is said.

In the paralinguistic realm, we are all victims of our voice. People depend upon our vocal quality and intonation to indicate our mood, personality, and affect displays. Those who suffer from a flat and monotonous vocal quality may be regarded as boring and uninteresting. Long-standing conventions and social stereotyping dictate that certain types of husky, gutteral male voices are a liability for a political candidate. There is also a tendency to associate certain pitch and timbre qualities as feminine and to regard others as masculine (Markel and Roblin, 1965).

One of the earliest problems investigated scientifically concerned the relation of the voice to stable or fixed physical characteristics of a speaker. Evidence suggested that matters of age, sex, height, body type, intelligence, political preference, and occupation could be judged consistently by vocal quality alone. Critics pointed out that many such findings could have resulted from the existence of vocal stereotypes rather than from the meanings actually conveyed by a person's vocal characteristics. In the case of vocal features associated with certain professions, for example, critics showed that people judged the vocal qualities of certain professions purely on the basis of a stereotype of what they *thought* a person in that profession should sound like. A minister suggested a loud, booming voice; a radio announcer a resonant, deep, bass voice; a male dancer was apt to be associated with a high-pitched, vocal quality; and so forth. The problem, then, was that any voice which triggered the stereotype would be sufficient to produce consistent rankings, even though the speaker was in a different profession. Such mixed or negative results occurred in many attempts to associate selected vocal qualities with tests of dominance-submission and a host of social and personality traits. An additional shortcoming of the early studies resulted from the crudity of measurement and the research procedures employed, as well as from the use of untrained judges. Nonetheless, a review of the early literature by Kramer (1963) argued convincingly that the very evidence of social stereotypes was in itself important. Insofar as people associate certain vocal qualities and other characteristics of an individual in question, the stereotype becomes relevant in determining their expectations and the actual perceptions.

By far the most fruitful line of investigation concerns the relationship between changes in vocal quality and given affective states. A study by Dusenbury and Knower (1939) was among the first to demonstrate that judges can consistently determine eleven emotive states on the basis of vocal tone alone. The same ability to discriminate among emotional states has since been shown to apply to speech samples lasting less than one second (Pollack et al., 1964) and to extended passages (Boomer, 1963; Davitz, 1964). As with judgments of any nonverbal cues, great allowances must be made for individual differences (Mahl and Schultz, 1964).

The most important paralinguistic cues appear to be speech disruptions and hesitations (Dittmann and Llewellyn, 1967, 1968a; Mahl, 1956; Panek and Martin, 1959) in addition to variations in pitch and tempo (Kramer, 1963; Mahl and Schultz, 1964). One representative finding stems from research that required people to read paragraphs in ways to communicate intense anger, contempt, indifference, love, grief, and other emotional states (Costanzo et al., 1969). Untrained judges then rated the test passages for pitch, loudness, and tempo before matching each voice with vocal cues and emotional states. The tendency is to associate grief with an intense pitch, loudness with anger and contempt, and "peak tempo" with indifference. The link between affect and vocal cues, taken both in transitory states and over time, provides convincing testimony of the role of paralinguistic cues in providing affective overtone (Markel, 1965, 1969; Markel and Roblin, 1965; Markel et al., 1967).

REGULATORS

All face-to-face encounters require some orderly means of regulating the ebb and flow of speaking and listening between respective parties. Most acts which regulate the back-and-forth nature of interaction are nonverbal. Since almost any nonverbal cue can have some regulative value, it is impossible to sharply divide those which regulate from those which do not. Nor is it feasible to isolate any one unit of measurement, though it is clear that most regulators are interactive rather than independent. Moreover, the cues tend to be on the periphery of self-awareness: one usually does not deliberately regulate another's verbal behavior by means of nonverbal cues. Deliberate and intentional regulators are mostly verbal in nature. Examples include such statements as "Hey, you've talked long enough," "Let me get my two cents' worth in," or complaints about not being able to "get a word in edgewise." At a nonverbal level, most regulators are emitted involuntarily or unconsciously, and yet they are required acts that designate a need to speed up, continue, repeat, elaborate, slow down, allow someone else to talk, and so forth. Though a large variety of nonverbal cues can serve regulative functions, it will be most useful to focus on two types of cues in detail: body movement and proxemic factors.

Body Movement as Regulators

The most recurrent and common regulators are small nonverbal acts: head nodding, eye contact, shifting body positions, punctuating hand movements,

eyebrow motions, and so on. Most striking is the moment-by-moment correspondence between simultaneous aspects of nonverbal and verbal activity.
Head and hand movements, for example, regulate the flow of speech; that is,
they perform an *accentuating*, or punctuating, function (Ekman, 1965*a*, 1965*b*;
Freedman and Hoffman, 1967; Kendon, 1967). Most people are highly sensitive
to head movements, perhaps because they are highly visible and closely related
to the face as the focal point of attention. The slightest up-and-down head movement, for example, as little as 5°, according to Birdwhistell (1963) is all that is
necessary to elicit awareness. Body movement tends to occur in clusters, punctuating the stress points of speech, particularly the beginning of phonetic pauses
and the end of sentences and main ideas (Dittmann, 1962). Small head movements toward another person, particularly forward motions, tend to occur most
frequently at the end of sentences and with the completion of phrases. Among
the most important regulative functions associated with head movement is
its usefulness as what Kendon (1967) termed "change-over signals which
assist in the smooth progression of verbal interactions." Other body movements, particularly jerking and repetitive tapping motions, cluster around
points of verbal hesitation and mispronunciation (Boomer, 1965; Dittmann
and Llewellyn, 1967, 1969). Also, the more rapidly a person talks, the more
frequent is the amount of punctuating movement he displays (Boomer, 1965).

For the observer trained in kinesics, the regulative meaning of
nonverbal behavior extends to the slightest units of such varied movements
as head nodding and shifting, brow motion, and variations in other parts of the
body, particularly the fingers, arms, and mouth. Any movement which accompanies or modifies the meaning of the spoken word is referred to in kinesics
as a *body marker*. Certain types of *proximal* markers characterize self-refer-
ences, and *distal* markers accompany references to other people (Birdwhistell,
1966). Still other variations in body movement, such as a backward jerking of
the head, punctuate prepositional phrases, and a host of these accompany the
use of adverbs, plurals, and verbs of action. In the case of markers which
accompany active verbs, the trained investigator can distinguish among various
body activities on the basis of the amount of verbal stress. Of course, this is
not to say that *all* movement is necessarily *coordinated with* verbal activity; at
least two studies (Boomer and Dittmann, 1964; Levitt, 1964) suggest that some
movements seem to be unrelated to the stream of words in social interaction.
Nonetheless, the degree of synchronization among body movements and speech
is strikingly high (Condon and Ogston, 1967).

The interactive basis of body regulators can be illustrated in a
number of ways. One is the tendency of people to "dovetail" their speaking
and listening patterns to the pace of another's speech. If one person in a group,
for whatever reason, starts to talk at a rapid rate and interrupts others at an
increasing rate, the remaining group members will tend to follow suit. Moreover, there is a strong tendency for the regulative acts of each person to fit
together over time in an ever more exacting match. The stronger the feelings

of attraction, the more congruent become matters of posture, hand movement, head nodding, and other regulative acts of two persons (Charney, 1966). In clinical settings, people are known to go through distinct stages of an interview, with each successive change in verbal activity being matched by distinct body movements (Scheflen, 1964, 1965). For example, during introductory stages, there is a tendency to lean back while "free associating" verbally. Later the nonverbal cues level off to a more controlled and less flexible pattern of change through periods of active, disciplined participation. Variations in head movements, eye blinking, gesture, and seating posture also vary during successive points of an interview, particularly those in which an interviewer is shifting from listening to speaking and vice versa. Once each individual is familiarized with the other's physical movements, each increasingly relies on nonverbal cues as a signal before shifting into a new phase of the interaction.

An investigation by Scheflen (1964) indicated that the affect display of a participant in informal social gatherings is largely a function of the actions of others present—particularly as they effect matters of posture such as the folding of arms and the crossing of legs. The tendency to follow the lead of others may be reversed, however, when there are important differences in status or authority. At staff meetings of psychiatrists in hospitals, Goffman (1961) found that those in high-status positions, notably the psychiatrists themselves, adopted relaxed postures and assumed an informal air while junior staff members observed more formal personal carriage.

The context of body movement is largely influenced by the type of interaction and the nature of the interpersonal relationships that exist among those present. For example, Baxter (et al., 1968) suggested that people rely on frequent and vigorous body movement when discussing topics familiar to them, whereas their movements are more restrained when the material of discussion is not familiar. Generally, positive and close interpersonal relationships are associated with relaxed and uninhibited body language, while the opposite holds true in encounters between strangers or those who are not held in high regard. In one study (Mehrabian, 1968), subjects were told to imagine themselves in several communicative situations with people they "liked intensely," "liked moderately," "neither liked nor disliked," "disliked moderately," and "disliked intensely." As predicted, several facets of body movement and posture—eye contact, physical distance, orientation of body, degree of relaxation, angle of posture, and angle of physical movement—were found to be significant indexes of interpersonal affect. More tense, inhibited movements and body stances were found to be associated with communication under conditions of personal disharmony. Mehrabian also found that male communicators generally exhibited more tenseness and what he called "vigilance" in the presence of men they disliked than did females who found themselves confronted by women they disliked.

Body language is further complicated by the nature of the relationships which individuals *attempt* to establish in communication. A series of investigations by Rosenfeld (1966a, 1966b) shed light on the extent to which common facial and gestural movements are emitted by individuals instructed to either seek or avoid approval in conversation with another person. A comparison of data from the two conditions revealed far more nonverbal activity— in the form of head nodding, gesturing, smiling, and verbal reinforcing—under the approval-seeking condition. Supplementary information showed that communication which avoided approval engendered a highly critical attitude toward the other person. In contrast was the tendency of those in the approval-seeking condition to perceive their counterpart to be friendly, lively, interesting, willing to engage in questions, and contributing to what was termed "free conversation."

Normative Basis of Regulators

Implicit in any social situation are well-recognized norms or expectations governing regulative acts. These conventions or rules influence the physical movement of people as well as what they say or think. Some situations require a set of highly formalized, even stereotyped forms of personal conduct; others are associated with uninhibited, unconstrained modes of body movement. Social encounters in cathedrals or libraries and processions, reception lines, and public ceremonies are consistent with conventionalized modes of affect display. In each situation people tend to be highly conscious of their movement and stance, making sure that each facet of their activity is consistent with the total demands of the situation. In sharp contrast are the loosely defined conventions and norms associated with informal social gatherings, private lodges, public parks, recreation areas, and family rooms and patios.

The normative influence on body language is nothing short of an obligation, as Goffman (1963) noted, to present oneself in ways which carry acceptable social impressions. Correspondingly, it provides a basis for judging the behavior of others. In familiar surroundings, people typically have enough information to regulate their body movement and to react fully to those who violate accepted social standards of personal conduct. These normative influences are closely related to culturally defined patterns of behavior. Through experience and conventions passed from one culture and one generation to the next, we develop—often quite unconsciously—a set of expectations which govern matters as diverse as how far apart to stand from others and how much free rein to give to movements of head and hands, footshuffling and head nodding, eye contact, posture, and physical contact.

Proxemic Factors as Regulators

The regulation of communication is influenced in no small measure by how the interactants physically orient themselves. People can regulate the flow of speech and listening most readily when they feel that they are interacting at a "comfortable" distance. Within certain limits, distance connotes remoteness and detachment, while proximity engenders feelings of solidarity and attraction. The pioneering studies of physical distance by Sommer (1959) concluded that subjects engaging in conversation tend to maintain a distance of about 5 feet. In a related investigation, Goldring (1967) examined the effects of varying distances upon judgments of interpersonal attraction in dyads. Undergraduate female subjects were asked to rate four sets of line drawings; the figures were placed either close together or at some distance and were shown in an upright or reclining seated position. Subjects ranked the "near-reclined" figures as warm, accepting, natural, and responsive and viewed the "far-upright" figures in opposite terms.

Sex and personality factors also influence the distance individuals maintained toward each other. Kuethe (1962, 1964) used felt figures (a woman, a man, a child, a dog, and rectangles of various sizes) and asked students to position them on a felt board. The subjects positioned the woman and child closer together than the man and child and placed the dog in closer proximity to the man than to the woman. In all cases they placed the rectangular objects farther apart than the groups of people. As for personality factors, there is evidence that introverts view themselves as interacting at greater distances than do extroverts (Williams, 1963) and that both introverts and extroverts favor greater proximity in person-to-person conversation under a condition of praise than under one of anxiety (Leipoid, 1963).

Physical distance has been found to interact not only with the degree of attraction between people but also with the type and purpose of the interaction. The anthropologist Hall (1964) held that interaction becomes more intimate as distance decreases, but only within certain limits governed by the type of relationship maintained by the respective parties. People who interact in dyads tend to operate at distances which are considered comfortable for social activity ranging from intimate conversation, where distance is shortest, to the increasing distance associated with casual conversation and more formalized types of discussion. Within each distinct type of exchange, physical distance tends to remain uniform. People engaged in intimate discussion, for example, tend to maintain uniform distances which typically vary 1 foot or less. As distance increases, the activities of the senses change correspondingly. Vision, for example, according to Hall, is less important than physical contact or olfactory and thermal senses in intimate relationships, whereas vision and hearing assume greater relative importance among the senses for casual conversation which commonly occurs at a distance of 5 feet. The voice also is important. A soft whisper is most common for intimate interactions (3 to 6 inches) while a full voice is used for interaction of a less personal nature (4½ to 5 feet), and a loud voice is employed for the public zone of people talking across a room to a group.

Moreover, people meeting for the first time typically "keep their distance" or "stay at arm's length." The more established the friendship, the greater is the tolerance for proximity and physical contact. An interesting test of the relationship between friendship and physical distances is reported in an investigation of personal space by Little (1965). Subjects were informed that the investigator was interested in the types of interactions that they thought would occur between two people in three different settings: an encounter between good friends, another between casual acquaintances, and a third between strangers. Based solely on information provided for three situations, subjects were instructed to place felt figures representing the respective parties on a board before relating what they thought the persons would talk about. While the word distance was never mentioned in the instructions, a camera recorded how far apart the students placed the felt figures in each trial. As predicted, the average distance between the two persons was greatest when they were depicted as strangers, closest in the good-friendship situation. Similar results occurred in follow-up studies using real people under a variety of circumstances (Gotheil et al., 1968; Little, 1965).

Despite evidence of stability in the distance maintained under varying degrees of friendship, everyday experiences suggest that a dynamic interplay often occurs between distance and interpersonal relationships. For example, when people talk while engaged in physical action, there is apt to be a fluid change in spatial relations, as in the case of friends who stop and chat while window shopping or couples who converse while strolling through a park or museum. Parties and receptions also exhibit an interplay between space and people. Lyman and Scott (1967) observed that at informal social gatherings, the spatial relations among people tend to be quite mobile and fragile. After remaining in one place for a certain time, people become restless, moving erratically, perhaps interrupting a group of guests engaged in conversation in a remote corner of the room. Even one intrusion on the personal space of a clique or faction may disrupt the flow of words, thus threatening the very existence of the conversation. Whereas the inclusion of a person who does not fit the shared space may break the flow of the conversation, the inclusion of a person who fits may only stimulate new interest.

The importance of maintaining proper distance suggests that space may be misused in social interactions. People who are insensitive or unaware of the dynamics of space may unwittingly contribute to what Sommer (1967) called the "friction of space," a term associated with the tensions aroused by intrusions or violations of space which an individual feels "belongs" to him. In reference to the consequences of intruding into another's personal space, the most incisive commentary of Simmel (1961) is worthy of detailed consideration:

> In regard to the "significant" [i.e., "great"] man, there is an inner compulsion which tells one to keep at a distance and which does not disappear even in intimate relations with him. The only type for whom such distance does not exist is the individual who has no organ for perceiving distance.

. . . The individual who fails to keep his distance from a great person does not esteem him highly, much less too highly (as might superficially appear to be the case); but, on the contrary, his importune behavior reveals lack of proper respect. . . . The same sort of circle which surrounds a man—although it is value-accentuated in a very different sense—is filled out by his affairs and by his characteristics. To penetrate this circle by taking notice, constitutes a violation of personality. Just as material property is, so to speak, an extension of the ego, there is also an intellectual private property, whose violation effects a lesion of the ego in its very center [p. 320].

Simmel's view coincides with Hall's claim that people show deference to important figures by keeping their distance, typically 25 feet or more. He cited the following example from Theodore White's *Making of the President* as a case in point. The setting is a "hideaway cottage" used by John F. Kennedy and his staff:

Kennedy loped into the cottage with his light, dancing step, as young and lithe as springtime, and called a greeting to those who stood in his way. Then he seemed to slip from them as he descended the steps of the split-level cottage to a corner where his brother Bobby and brother-in-law Sargent Shriver were chatting, waiting for him. The others in the room surged forward on impulse to join him. Then they halted. A distance of perhaps 30 feet separated them from him, but it was impossible. They stood apart, these older men of long-established power, and watched him. He turned after a few minutes, saw them watching him, and whispered to his brother-in-law. Shriver now crossed the separating space to invite them over. First Averell Harriman; then Dick Haley; then Mike DiSalle, then, one by one, let them all congratulate him. Yet no one could pass the little open distance between him and them uninvited, because there was this thin separation about him, and the knowledge they were there not as his patrons but as his clients. They could come by invitation only, for this might be a President of the United States [p. 171] .

Those who persistently violate the personal space of others may experience any number of consequences. Whatever the form, these violations of personality deeply affect interpersonal relations by incurring the risk of being perceived as tactless, unnecessarily familiar, aggressive, or simply "too personal." A study by Felipe and Sommer (1966) disclosed no one set of reactions by people whose spatial territory has been infringed upon. When a person comes too close to another, Felipe and Sommer noted that certain individuals simply turn their heads away from the encroaching person, while others place an elbow or some part of their body between themselves and the intruder. Still others respond by treating him as a "nonperson," often showing indifference or even leaving the room. Not surprisingly, McBride (et al., 1965) found that galvanic skin response is greater when a person is approached directly and frontally than when he is approached from a side or rear angle.

Argyle and Dean (1965) investigated the relationship between visual orientation and physical distance by inviting subjects to stand as close as they comfortably could to look at various life-sized photographs; when the subjects were placed only two feet from the photographs, they maintained less eye contact with the pictures than when separated by greater distances. They were also found to engage in proportionately less eye contact when gazing at photographs of life-sized pictures of people with open, staring eyes than when confronted with pictures that depicted individuals with closed eyes. These findings are consistent with much everyday experience. When people are forced into too great a proximity with another person, their immediate defense is to lessen eye contact and to change the directness of their body orientation. It is, for example, a common practice for people who stand directly next to others in crowded subways or buses to manage always to look at some distant object. The lessening of eye contact serves as a way of regulating the friction of excessive proximity.

Probably the most interesting and dramatic way of regulating the effect of intrusions upon personal space is the instantaneous reaction of people who unknowingly pull back physically or even break off interaction altogether. There is ample evidence that friction of space is sufficiently powerful to alter the posture or even the overt behavior of someone who is the unwitting victim of spatial intrusion. So powerful is the urge to retreat, particularly among Americans, that rather dramatic reactions often take place. In this regard, Hall (1959) commented:

> "I have observed an American backing up the entire length of a long corridor while a foreigner whom he considers pushy tries to catch up with him. This scene has been enacted thousands and thousands of times—one person trying to increase the distance in order to be at ease, while the other tries to decrease it for the same reason, neither one being aware of what was going on [pp. 160–161]."

In response to Hall's view of the impact of personal space on interpersonal relations, Brown (1965), a social psychologist, recalled that he once had occasion to express skepticism over the supposed importance of space while talking to Hall personally. As Brown recounted the discussion,

> While we talked, having the sort of impersonal, professional discussion that is supposed to go on at a neutral distance of four or five feet, Dr. Hall occasionally moved his chair forward. Whenever he did so I moved mine back. He somewhat shook my skepticism when, as we concluded our discussion, he pointed out that he had moved me a considerable distance across the room by repeatedly crossing a zone boundary [p. 81].

Most instances of body regulation fall short of these dramatic consequences. There is also reason to question the assumption that people are willing to respect proxemic norms in the exacting manner implied by the reaction of Kennedy's staff and the image of the "great man" described earlier by Simmel. Perhaps the slackening of respect for authority, coupled with the readiness of young people to question the long-standing deference shown to people in high station, has already made inroads on the regulative power of proxemic norms. Perhaps the current call for social relevance, personal involvement, and "intimate" communication already is working against the sanctity of proxemic zones. Nonetheless, distance and body regulators still interact in powerful ways across dissimilar social situations. We will return to the related aspects of physical orientation in Chapter 8, when dealing with the spatial dynamics of communicative situations.

INDICATORS

All message cues influence the sort of psychological orientations which various interactants maintain toward each other. That which distinguishes nonverbal cues from the verbal—particularly their greater transparency, continuity, and nonsusceptibility to manipulation and concealment— also makes nonverbal cues ideal indicators of personal evaluation, feelings of attraction, and impressions of status. For example, proximity is an ideal indicator of liking (Mehrabian and Ferris, 1967; Mehrabian and Wiener, 1967). So also are leaning movements, frequent eye contact, certain primary affect displays, body orientations, and spontaneous gestures (Argyle, 1967; Mehrabian, in press). Since no nonverbal cue is immune from subjective interpretation, it would be possible to review the dynamics of affect display and regulators for their overlapping value in indicating the personal attitudes of respective communicators. Instead, it will be more instructive to use one type of nonverbal cue, namely eye contact, as a basis for an in-depth case study into the workings of nonverbal indicators generally. There are two reasons for focusing especially on eye contact. First, eye contact has a more specialized communicative value than most other nonverbal cues; hence, little has been said about the fascinating literature on eye contact as nonverbal cues. Second, and more important, is the uniqueness of eye contact as an indicator of the personal attitudes defined and maintained in an act of communication. No other cue is as significant a gauge of personal and social orientation. Eye contact, in Simmel's (1924) view, is the purest form of reciprocity, the highest form of psychic union. Yet, however direct the bond of mutual glance, it is also exceedingly transitory. Simmel wrote:

> So tenacious and subtle is this union that it can only be maintained by the shortest and straightest lines between the eyes, and the smallest deviation from it, the slightest glance aside, completely destroys the unique character of this union. No objective trace of this relationship is left behind, as is universally found, directly or indirectly, in all other types of associations between men, as, for example, in interchange of words. The interaction of eye and eye dies in the moment in which directness of the function is lost [p. 358].

Patterns of Eye Contact

So complex is mutual eye contact that a whole vocabulary is necessary to distinguish among the ways people look at each other. We think not of a simple act of looking, but rather of staring, glowering, peeping, piercing, glancing, watching, gazing, scanning, and so forth. Within each type of eye contact are the many variations of looking: directly or indirectly, overtly or covertly, critically or kindly, boldly or bashfully, sternly or mildly. We refer to the qualitative aspects of looks as being cold, hard, intense, shifty, cunning, nervous, timid, tender, affectionate, sinister, sly, sexy, hostile, calculating, and even blank. Among the many idiomatic expressions are "catching one's eye," looking a person "up and down," allowing the eyes "to wander," giving the "evil eye," or looking "down" on someone. Some looks are fixed; others are blank or guarded. Before examining the significance as nonverbal indicators of such a bewildering variety of looking patterns, it will be useful to determine first what principles of eye movement apply to all patterns of eye contact.

The first factor in a person's looking behavior is *centering*. To be the object of another's gaze is to perceive that his pupils are relatively well centered in the sclera, or "whites," of the eyes. Whenever the eyes are off-centered in either direction, the impression gained by the receiver is that he is not the object of eye contact (Figure 6.5). In reality, however, the principle of centering holds only for the general case where the confronting parties meet head on—that is, when the head and eyes of each are directed squarely at the other. Since mutual eye contact varies from frontal to profile angles, the perception of being looked at depends upon the movement and centering of the eyes in relation to the larger context of facial expression and head movement (Figure 6.6).

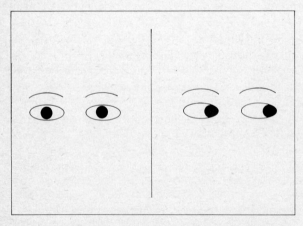

Figure 6.5 *Stimulus used in study to test perception of eye gaze. (Reprinted with permission from Gibson and Pick, 1963.)*

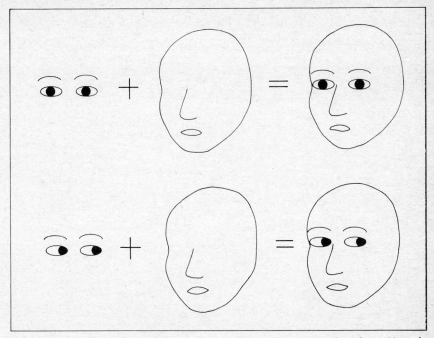

Figure 6.6 *Eye form shown in Figure 6.5, with the inclusion of a face form. Note the shift in the apparent direction of the eye gaze; eyes formerly gazing forward now gaze to the left, and those formerly gazing to the right now seem to gaze forward. (Reprinted with permission from Gibson and Pick, 1963.)*

Amidst the constant shifting and moving of people who are in proximity to others, the eyes normally turn in a direction that is opposite from head movements (Nachshon and Wagner, 1967). This compensating adjustment between eye and head movements has been found to be a reciprocal and invariant type of relationship (Figure 6.7); as the head turns to one direction, the eyes turn roughly in direct proportion to the opposite direction (Gibson and Pick, 1963; Nachshon and Wagner, 1967). The reader can prove this point conclusively by noting his eye movements while reading, and by looking up, turning to the right, then to the left. As the head orientation moves closer to what a receiver would view as the profile position, the more clearly is the impression of being looked at "out of the corner of the eye." In short, then, the impression of being looked at depends not simply on the directness and centering of the pupils of the eyes, but on the interplay between eye movements and the facial and bodily orientations of the respective parties.

The degree to which people perceive themselves to be the object of another's gaze was reported in a study by Gibson and Pick (1963). Subjects made a series of judgments about whether they were in the direct gaze of someone who had been trained to maintain passive facial expressions while focusing

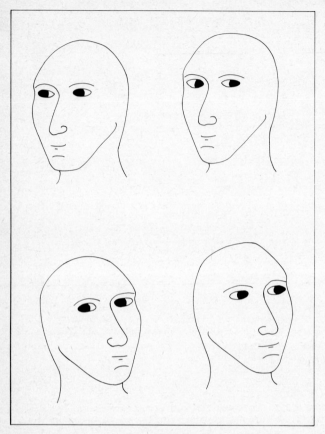

Figure 6.7   *Stimulus used in eye-gaze research. (Reprinted with permission from Nachshon and Wagner, 1967.)*

both her head and eyes directly on a series of seven positions located at the back of the room (Figure 6.8). Throughout a series of random trials the subjects noted the appearances of the looker and then decided whether or not they thought they were directly in line with the other's eye gaze. The number of affirmative judgments for all subjects was clustered closely to the center, most direct position, with only minimal differences reported. These findings indicate that the subjects were in close agreement in their perceptions of being in or out of the range of eye contact; this ability is at least as sensitive as that required to read fine print of an eye doctor's acuity chart.

Eye contact is *reciprocal* in the sense that the eyes are both the *agents* of looking and the *objects* of the look. This process of reciprocity is akin to what Tagiuri (1958) called a "double interaction." The stimulative function of the eyes is well demonstrated in animal studies which report that monkeys undergo measurable changes in brain activity when they become aware of

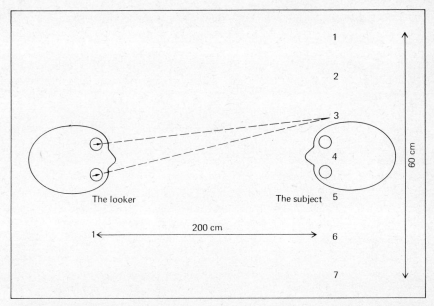

Figure 6.8 *Experimental arrangement used by Gibson and Pick in study of eye gaze. Note that the horizontal distance is shortened relative to the vertical distance. (Reprinted with permission from Gibson and Pick, 1963.)*

being looked at by humans (Wada, 1961). Furthermore, in a number of studies cited by Gibson and Pick (1963), children were found to be highly conscious of whether or not they were being looked at by adults and for what proportion of the time.

Mutual looking begins with people's widely noted tendency to arrange themselves so that full eye contact can readily be established with others present. Full visibility is important for purposes other than simply the maintenance of eye contact. Yet people's choices in seating, body orientation, and proximity to others all seem to be influenced by the desire to avoid the discomforting feelings associated with not being able to look at another person or with being in the direct gaze of someone who is not a part of the interaction. Once initial eye contact is under way, each person looks only intermittently in the region of the other's eyes. While some people have been reported to look at another's eyes anywhere from none to virtually all of the total interaction time, most establish eye contact 30 to 60 percent of the time (Argyle and Kendon, 1967). The length of each glance varies also, of course—typically from one to seven seconds. Naturally, not all eye contact is mutual; in fact, only about 10 to 30 percent of the total interaction time of members in a dyad is spent in mutual looking behavior, for periods averaging one second in length (Argyle, 1967).

When people listen, they spend more time engaged in eye contact, look for longer periods of time, and spend less time looking away from the other person (Argyle, 1967). During a sequence of interaction, eye contact is also more apt to occur just before a person begins to speak and at the end of a verbal utterance (Figure 6.9). From the standpoint of the sender, eye contact is lowest during pauses and hesitations that occur in the natural breaks of the conversation.

Typically, the longer individuals talk, the deeper their mutual involvement becomes and the more intensive and lengthy will be their mutual eye contact. The question, then, is why eye-to-eye contact does not simply increase until it is maintained throughout a conversation. One possible explanation, offered by Argyle and Dean (1965), considers the patterns of eye contact within the framework of *equilibrium* theories of behavior: In any given situation participants may increase the proportion of time spent in mutual gaze; eventually, however, they reach a level of eye contact that is psychologically satisfying or comfortable. This balance, or equilibrium, is achieved as a result of striking a balance between approach and avoidance. As eye contact increases, the greater is the involvement of each party in the interaction, and consequently a point is reached where there is too much mutual looking. Excessive eye contact arouses anxiety. Since people avoid anxiety, eye contact falls below the level required to maintain mutual interest and personal regard. Though eye contact is only one determinant of personal intimacy, the equilibrium theory predicts that any marked shift in the forces working toward interpersonal attraction will correspond to an adjustment in eye contact and vice versa. As evidence for the *approach-avoidance* explanation of eye contact, Argyle and Dean (1965) reported that the amount of time spent in eye contact between two parties seated at various distances from each other increased until the persons sat too close; then each party tended to compensate by spending less time looking at the other. The pressure to avoid eye contact is apt to increase where the respective parties become highly ego-involved in the situation or where there is no opportunity to adjust the distance at which they interact. Taken together, the evidence indicates that the typical patterns of eye contact are strongly tied to factors as complex and various as those which influence the overall dynamics of communication.

Determinants of Looking Behavior

One important influence on mutual looking behavior is, as mentioned, the nature of each person's involvement in the task. We have already examined the differences in eye contact during introductory periods of talk, during changes from listening to speaking, and during the utterance of certain phases of a verbal sequence. In addition to these formal aspects of interaction, the type of

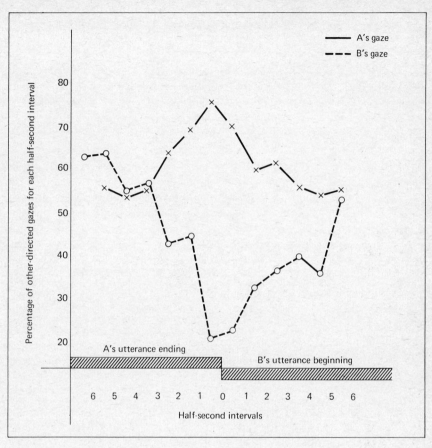

Figure 6.9 *Direction of eye gaze at the beginning and end of long sentences. (Reprinted with permission from Kendon, as cited in Argyle, 1967.)*

conversation similarly influences the pattern of eye contact. Within the limits of psychological equilibrium, mutual eye contact increases as individuals become more and more involved in their interpersonal activities and relationships. As a case in point, Exline (et al., 1965) created an informal discussion where an interviewer gazed continuously at a subject while raising very personal and embarrassing questions. For another group of subjects, the interview dealt only with innocuous topics. Results showed that proportionately greater periods of silence occurred in sessions where interviewers raised the personal topics. Moreover, regardless of sex, subjects maintained eye contact only about 39 percent of the time when they spoke of personal matters, whereas those conversing on innocuous topics looked at the interviewer almost half the time.

The influence of highly personal and ego-involving matters has also been examined in the context of varying group conditions and settings. In a study of students' behavior in a seminar, Weisbrod (1969) found that the power coalitions which emerged in the groups had a marked impact on the mutual eye gaze of group members. The study disclosed a close relationship between the proportion of time spent looking at the speaker of the group and the regard which each participant later expressed for various speakers. A larger proportion of those who spent a greater amount of time looking at the speakers were seen by themselves and other group members as being more influential than those who spent less time looking at the speakers. These findings are consistent with evidence that mutual eye contact increases when the participants expect approval or recognition from other group members (Efran, 1968; Efran and Broughton, 1966) or when the participants obtain strongly positive feedback and evaluations from interviewers (Ellsworth and Carlsmith, 1968). Closely related is the finding that frequent eye contact produces *positive* evaluations of an interviewer when he communicates with a subject in a positive manner but that the *same exact proportion of eye contact* from the same interviewer produces *negative* rankings when the verbal content is negative (Ellsworth and Carlsmith, 1968; Merrill, 1968). Finally, such factors as the *perceived sincerity of a speaker* (Argyle, 1967), the degree of *judged potency* of participants in a discussion (Argyle, 1967), the *attitudes* of each person (Mehrabian, 1967), and the *degree of attitude change* of a persuasive speech (Cobin, 1962) have all been linked to the patterns of eye contact. Clearly, as with so many findings in communication research, the significance of eye contact results in its relation to the interests of each interactant.

Some people are highly sensitive to looking behavior, others are not. Moreover, some seem to have a strong need to look constantly at those around them. This range of sensitivity is suggested earlier by the fact that proportionate time spent in looking has been observed under laboratory conditions to range from virtually no eye contact to a steady gaze. One contributing factor is sex; there is some evidence that women engage in more mutual glancing than men do. In the study where respondents answered interviewers' questions of either a personal or an innocuous nature (Exline et al., 1965), women looked at the interviewer almost half the time they spent in speaking. During their speaking intervals men looked less than 40 percent. In the course of silent periods, women looked approximately a third of the time, while men looked less than a fourth of the time. A similar study by Argyle and Dean (1965) reported confirming evidence of greater looking behavior on the part of women than men and added the finding that there is more proportionate mutual eye gaze when the parties are members of the same sex.

Eye contact is also a function of personality factors. Some people are both highly aware of their immediate surroundings and extremely dependent upon the environment for reinforcement; these persons are termed to be high in *field dependence.* Mutual glancing seems to be higher among those high in field dependence than those low in field dependence (Argyle and Kendon, 1967). In another aspect of personality, research by Exline and Winters (1965) indicated that differences in thinking patterns also seem to account for patterns of looking behavior; those who are prone to think abstractly look far more frequently than those who think in concrete ways. Looking decreases among persons with emotional problems or those who have strong feelings of guilt (Exline and Winter, 1965).

Finally, looking behavior is also correlated to psychological dominance and submissiveness. In a fascinating testing situation (Champness, 1969), two subjects entered a room separately and sat in seats on opposite sides of a table divided by an opaque screen. The subjects knew only that someone with whom they were expected to talk would be in the room. As a result of prior testing, each had been informed that one of them was judged to have a more dominant personality. When the screen was suddenly lifted, each person looked at the other before one averted his eyes. In almost all instances, the dominant subject looked away first. The person who first averted eye contact did so as a signal that he was about to take over the conversation. Recall the finding (p. 242) that people are apt to look away just before they start to talk. Apparently a parallel force is at work for those who have a strong need to dominate a conversation. Of added importance is the finding that a single glance is often all that is necessary for a person to assert his place in a social hierarchy. On nine separate occasions in the course of one testing situation, students confronted subjects who had dominant-submission ratings previously established; in each encounter the two parties knew of the prior testing. In virtually all encounters the initial reactions confirmed the expectation that the most dominant is the first to avert eye contact (Champness, 1969).

Eye Contact as Indicators

Eye contact serves important functions as indicators of personal orientation. People, we have seen, are typically quite sensitive to the looks of those around them, particularly when coming into direct face-to-face contact. During the initial stage of a social encounter, eye contact serves the dual purpose of indicating awareness and signaling an interest in further contact. Most social interaction, after all, begins with a mutual glance, not with a spoken word, and, therefore, much depends on each person's response to the initial glance. The power of a glance to signal a willingness for further communication is an illustration of visual reciprocity, what Goffman (1963) called the "initial move," and subsequent "clearance signs"—either because of fleeting recognition or because of indifference—may have equally severe consequences. So important is the establishment of the initial sequence of eye contact that an unpublished study by Argyle and Kendon (1967) reported that even the slightest drop of mutual looking frequently leads to an immediate loss of interest. When one recognizes just how slight a movement is necessary to avert eye contact, it is obvious that only minimum energy is required to establish interpersonal contact or to eliminate the chance for verbal exchange. It is difficult to think of an equally small unit of activity for any other part of the body which has such a powerful impact on the opening moments of an interpersonal encounter.

In addition to their role as an indicator of interpersonal awareness, the eyes can have the opposite effect of signaling what people commonly perceive as an *avoidance reaction* in certain social situations. People are more comfortable when looking at strangers from behind one-way mirrors than when watching them in situations where they can look back. The reason that excessive eye contact produces an avoidance tendency has much to do with the unsettling effects of being the object of a steady gaze. Argyle (1967) cited three commonplace reasons for the avoidance function of looking behavior: (1) past experience often produces the expectation that a person will receive disapproving facial expressions from others; (2) the very thought of being the object of another's gaze often leads to an avoidance reaction; and (3) many have a need to conceal emotional states or other aspects of the personality. Studies dealing with emotional disturbances have demonstrated that prolonged unwillingness to engage in eye contact is often a symptom of a deep-seated feeling of rejection (Laing, 1969) or a need to "wall oneself off" from any interpersonal contacts (Riemer, 1955). Clinical investigators recognize that schizophrenics often show almost no eye contact and glance only for extremely short periods of time, even when being stared at continuously.

Not all visual avoidance is the result of a flat refusal to engage in mutual eye contact. It is possible, for example, to indicate avoidance while still looking at a person, but in ways which, in effect, reduce the other to the status of a "nonperson." Visual patterns which are instances of "looking but not seeing" are common experiences in urban life. The very presence of an undifferentiated stream of people in day-to-day contacts instills in many a look of nonrecognition. Amidst the passivity and impersonality of large crowds, commuter lines, and other overcrowded public spaces, eyes come into contact without the faintest hint of interpersonal recognition. The nondifferentiated forms of eye contact in the glazed eyes of a crowd well illustrate a possibly harmless form of visual avoidance. But at the opposite end of the spectrum are the injurious looks of contempt, condescension, and blatant discrimination. The avoidance evidenced by the hate stare is best exemplified in the experience of the modern "invisible man" of Ralph Ellison's poignant novel by that name (1947). The classic lines of the prologue begin:

> I am an invisible man. . . . I am invisible, understand, simply because people refuse to see me. Like the bodiless head you see sometimes in circus side-

shows, it is as though I have been surrounded by mirrors of hard, distorting glass. When they approach me they see only my surroundings, themselves, or figments of their imagination—indeed, everything and anything except me. . . .

That invisibility to which I refer occurs because of a particular disposition of the eyes of those with whom I come in contact. A matter of the construction of their *inner* eyes, those eyes, with which they look, through their physical eyes upon reality.

Goffman (1963) described a related form of looking avoidance by the term "civil inattention." Civil inattention involves giving momentary visual notice of a person and then quickly withdrawing visual attention to avoid any further recognition or need for further contact. Goffman explained:

In performing this courtesy the eyes of the looker may pass over the eyes of the other, but no "recognition" is typically allowed. Where the courtesy is performed between two persons passing on the street, civil inattention may take the special form of eyeing the other up to approximately eight feet, during which time sides of the street are apportioned by gesture, and then casting the eyes down as the other passes—a kind of dimming of the lights [p. 84].

The ritual of civil inattention, Goffman concluded, is one that "constantly regulates the social intercourse of persons in our society."

In addition to the role of eye contact in facilitating interpersonal recognition or avoidance, looking behavior provides a means of seeking information from another person. While virtually any nonverbal cue may serve as an indicator of individual response to message cues, the fact is—as stipulated in the theory of primary affect—that the area of the human eye is the *most visible* and richly revealing of all sources of expressive meaning. Whether or not there is, as some hold, an instinctive basis for eye contact, one can hardly avoid focusing on the eye movements as an aid in gaining personal information from those around him.

METACOMMUNICATION

The concept of *metacommunication* literally involves communication about communication. The term is useful in talking about the *way* a person signals how he intends others to view his behavior. Metacommunication, in other words, is a subject that covers nothing less than the elaborate assumptions and largely implicit rules by which the subject matter of communication is interpreted. Just as one "cannot *not* communicate" in the sense discussed in Chapter 2, so also one cannot avoid giving others impressions of how he intends to have them decode his verbal behavior. The signals may be indicated in an explicit and verbal manner; for example, a person may preface his comments by saying, "Now I do not want my statement to be taken lightly for I am quite serious." Other examples include: "Now, don't get me wrong"; "Please don't misunderstand . . ."; "I am not suggesting that anyone here would . . ."; "Just kidding, of course"; "I am simply trying to point out . . ."; "It's really hard to put into words. . . ."

Much metacommunication occurs at an implicit, nonverbal level of interaction. The visibility and transparency of the nonverbal mode virtually ensure that it will be taken as implicit instructions or guidelines for interpreting the intended meaning of concomitant verbal content. The potential for nonverbal cues to become metacommunication cuts through all the categories and units discussed in this chapter.

Metacommunication and Affect Display. The concept of affect display is closely tied to the idea of metacommunication. Though affective cues function mainly as expressive acts, they ordinarily have a contagious quality about them. Rarely do affective expressions fail to rub off on others in ways that color their interpretation of whatever is being said and done. For instance, if an air of excitement and personal interest accompanies a given verbal statement, the metacommunication is apt to elevate the assigned import of what is said. In another instance, the fact that a person exhibits confidence when speaking is apt to heighten impressions of his credibility and the authoritative value of his assertions. On the other hand, statements that are accompanied by a manner suggesting personal uncertainty and defensiveness may imply that whatever is said cannot be taken at face value. The same interplay applies to the link between metacommunication and the primary affects of distress, fear, shame, contempt, and anger.

Metacommunication and Body Movement. Body movement also contributes to metacommunication because of its value in specifying the intensity of affect displays. One level of intensity may be inferred by a speaker who paces back and forth behind a podium, all the while shifting his body and giving evidence of uneasiness and discomfort. Clearly another level of intensity would be conveyed under circumstances identical in all respects except for differences in body movement. The domain of paralanguage—particularly speech hesitations, stammering, and other malfunctioning—also markedly influences the impressions formed of credibility, trust, power, and other personal constructs. As a rule, the greater the inconsistency between whatever is said and done, the more negative will be the metacommunication. Probably the only affect display that comes close to being devoid of metacommunicative value is one of strict emotional neutrality; yet even neutrality can be invested with significance, perhaps an air of personal detachment or aloofness which in turn colors the meaning assigned to the subject material proper. So again we see the relevance of the proactive dimension of psychological orientation as discussed in Chapter 2; for insofar as man is proactive, he is committed to assigning meaning to the subtext of communication along lines that fit his own expectations and biases. If his mood is one of excitement and intense interest, he will read into the remarks of others a metacommunicative importance that otherwise would go unnoticed.

Metacommunication and Regulators. Regulators are of strategic importance in metacommunication. Recall that regulators are composed of interactive units of behavior, as opposed to individualistic ones, as defined by rules of relationship. And it is the subtext of a relationship that determines how the back-and-forth sequence of speaking and listening is to be carried out. The proportion of time spent talking, the frequency and length of comments, and the number of interruptions all influence the interpretation of what is said. The person who monopolizes a conversation indicates, by his action, that the right of each person to contribute to the discussion is not to be shared equally. As a consequence, the others who are present are placed in a subordinate relationship. Obviously what is said in a subordinate relationship is rarely interpreted in the same light as that expressed in a coequal relationship. Consider also the person who regulates the ebb and flow of talk by persistently interrupting others. Now the very act of interrupting the flow of conversation has significance in delimiting the value as well as the right of others to express themselves. Interruptions are a way of devaluating verbal currency. It implies that what one person says is not judged to be of sufficient importance to permit its completion.

Proxemic regulators function primarily in defining the social standing and context in which metacommunication is assigned. The greater the proxemity, the farther each person will move from a detached, objective interpretation of what is said and done. When the spatial distance becomes excessively proxemic, it tends to be judged as a violation of personal space. The effect of such intrusions may be so nominal as to cause slight uneasiness or so serious as to disrupt the flow of words or even to threaten the existence of a relationship. When relationships are threatened, the respective parties are apt to read into the behavior of others selfish or cohesive intent.

Metacommunication and Indicators. Indicators are at once the most implicit and pervasive influences on the subject of metacommunication. Recall that indicators function in ways which define the larger psychological orientations maintained by the respective parties. Indicators are also the most personal and subjective of nonverbal cues; the information they signal clusters around what each person thinks of the personal attributes of others as well as how each person defines his own role in a given interchange. Recall the numerous links between eye contact and judgments of sincerity, degree of social influence, feelings of guilt, dominance, personal awareness, interest in continuing communication, information seeking, and a host of others. It is the personal relevance, the subtext of a relationship, that defines the ultimate meaning of the subject matter proper.

Three Examples of Metacommunication

The interplay of affect display, regulators, and indicators can be observed in the metacommunication of almost any sample discourse. We will examine three samples as cases in point. The first is an excerpt taken from an article entitled "How to Survive in a French Restaurant," by Ungerer (1970), who offered this advice:

> There is only one way to outfox the Frenchman at his worst. Be arrogant, contemptuous, petty, rude, and mean. . . . Just for kicks, return something. Act angry, disgusted, scandalized. . . . Without looking at the fruit or vegetables, ask if they are fresh. . . . Order only estate-bottled wines. Just check the cork for its imprint, and insist on sniffing it when it is extracted. Harass the owner with suggestions. Denounce his unpredictability. Compare his place with others. Complain about the wine-glasses. Let your name be known, and your profession, if it is a glamorous one [pp. 172, 173, 227].

For comparative purposes with the metacommunication in the advice just cited, consider the following excerpt from Albee's (1962) play *Who's Afraid of Virginia Woolf?*:

George: (Barely contained anger now): You can sit there in that chair of yours, you can sit there with gin running out of your mouth, and you can humiliate me, you can tear me apart. . . . ALL NIGHT . . . and that's perfectly all right . . . that's O.K. . . .
Martha: YOU CAN STAND IT.
George: I CANNOT STAND IT.
Martha: YOU CAN STAND IT!! YOU MARRIED ME FOR IT!! (A silence)
George: (Quietly): That is a desperately sick lie.
Martha: DON'T YOU KNOW IT, EVEN YET?
George: (Shaking his head): Oh . . . Martha.
Martha: My arm has gotten tired whipping you.
George: (Stares at her in disbelief): You're mad.
Martha: For twenty-three years!
George: You're deluded . . . Martha, you're deluded.
Martha: IT'S NOT WHAT I'VE WANTED!
George: I thought at least you were . . . on to yourself. I didn't know. I . . . didn't know [pp. 152–153].

A final excerpt appears in the novel *The Ambassadors*, where Henry James (1948) described an initial encounter between Lambert Strether, an American visiting Paris, and Gloriana, his host at a garden party:

Gloriana (the sculptor) shaved him, in such perfect confidence . . . a fine, worn, handsome face, a face that was like an open letter in a foreign tongue. With his genius in his eyes, his manners, on his lips, his long career behind him and his honours and rewards all round, the great artist, in the course of a single, sustained look and a few words of delight at receiving him, affected our friend as a dazzling prodigy of type. . . . He was to see again repeatedly, in remembrance, the medal-like Italian face, in which every line was an artist's own, in which time told only as tone and consecration; and he was to recall in especial, as the penetrating radiance, as the communication of the illustrious spirit itself, the manner in which, while they stood briefly, in welcome and response, face to face, he was held by the sculptor's eyes . . . the source of the deepest intellectual sounding to which he had ever been exposed. . . . The deep human expertness in Gloriana's charming smile—oh, the terrible life behind it!—was flashed upon him as a test of his stuff [pp. 135–136].

Despite obvious dissimilarities, the three excerpts all illustrate fundamental aspects of metacommunication. Each passage presupposes that metacommunication is implicit in all verbal statements. For example, the heavy-handed advice on surviving in a French restaurant makes little sense apart from the assumption—never made explicit—that the sequence of recommended action will be taken as having certain metacommunicative importance in a relationship where the customer wants to establish one-upsmanship in the game with the waiter. For instance, the part about the checking of the cork on the wine bottle is pointless aside from the series of related moves designed to establish superiority. Also, the act of returning the food would otherwise be taken as an unnecessary inconvenience aside from the subtext of harassment.

The clash between George and Martha points out the subtlety and nuances of metacommunication, many of which have significance only to the particulars of a relationship and cannot, therefore, be generalized to any other communicative situation. Almost every line in the bitter exchange reflects the multidimensionality of metacommunication. Each combatant reacts to the other's remarks not only on a verbal level but in retort to an evolving relationship where each views his own actions as mere responses to the other's continued willingness to go beyond the rules of the game. Amid the charges and countercharges, each views the other on grounds of his own private view of their metacommunication. So Martha rants "YOU CAN STAND IT," and George counters with "I CANNOT STAND IT," and each realizes that the significance of the exchange is far deeper than the text itself. Throughout the sequence of increasingly bitter denunciation, each gravitates to an increasingly desperate and idiosyncratic way of interpreting the subtext of their interaction.

Lastly, the excerpt from James's novel contains a variety of nonverbal and contextual cues used in establishing the delicate metacommunication of a relationship between two people. With meticulous care James drew upon a variety of elusive qualities that effectively work together to achieve a mood or psychological atmosphere for communication to take place: the aura of a famous personage, the qualities of physical appearance, the positioning of the body, the face, the eyes and eye contact, the mouth and its movement, proxemic considerations, and a host of contextual factors. As complex as the two interwoven levels of meaning are—the subject matter and the subtext— they still retain a dynamic interplay of verbal, nonverbal, and contextual cues which, taken together, define the tenor and fabric of the metacommunication of communication.

SUGGESTED READINGS

Birdwhistell, R. Kinesics and Context. Philadelphia: University of Pennsylvania Press, 1970.

Costanzo, F. S., Markel, N. N., and **Costanzo, P. R.** "Voice Quality Profile and Perceived Emotion," Journal of Counseling Psychology, 16:267–270, 1969.

Davitz, J. The Communication of Emotional Meaning. New York: McGraw-Hill, 1964.

Dittmann, A. T., and **Llewellyn, L. G.** "Body Movement and Speech Rhythm in Social Conversation," Journal of Personality and Social Psychology, 11:98–106, 1969.

Duncan, S. "Nonverbal Communication," Psychological Bulletin, 72:118–137, 1969.

Ekman, P. "Communication through Nonverbal Behavior: A Source of Information about an Interpersonal Relationship," in S. E. Tomkins and C. E. Izard (eds.), Affect, Cognition, and Personality. New York: Springer, 1965, pp. 390–442.

Ekman, P., and **Friesen, W. V.** "Nonverbal Behavior in Psychotherapy Research," Psychotherapy, 3:179–216, 1968.

Ekman, P., and **Friesen, W. V.** "The Repertoire of Nonverbal Behavior: Categories, Origins, Usage, and Coding," Semiotica, I:49–98, 1969.

Frank, L. "Tactile Communication," Genetic Psychology Monographs, 56:211–255, 1957.

Gibson, J. J., and **Pick, A. D.** "Perception of Another Person's Looking Behavior," The American Journal of Psychology, 76:386–394, 1963.

Kramer, E. "Judgment of Personal Characteristics and Emotions from Nonverbal Properties of Speech," Psychological Bulletin, 60:408–420, 1963.

Mahl, G. F., and **Schultz, G.** "Psychological Research in the Extra-linguistic Area," in T. A. Sebok, A. S. Hayes, and M. C. Bateson (eds.), Approaches to Semiotics. The Hague: Mouton, 1964.

Mehrabian, A. "A Semantic Space for Nonverbal Behavior," in C. D. Mortensen and K. K. Sereno (eds.), *Advances in Communication Research*. New York: Harper & Row, in press.

Ruesch, J., and **Kees, W.** *Nonverbal Communication*. Berkeley, Calif.: University of California Press, 1956.

Scheflen, A. E. "The Significance of Posture in Communication Systems," *Psychiatry*, 27:316–321, 1964.

Schlosberg, H. "Three Dimensions of Emotion," *Psychological Review*, 61:81–88, 1954.

Tomkins, S. S., and **McCarter, R.** "What and Where Are the Primary Affects? Some Evidence for a Theory," *Perceptual and Motor Skills*, 18:119–158, 1964.

seven

interpersonal contacts

Man lives in a world of interpersonal contacts, each offering unique risks and rewards. The entrance fee to a given encounter may be anything from the willingness to talk to a total risk of self. The prize may range from something trivial to survival itself. Some encounters require nothing more than a game of adult babble, sustained solely by the participants' need to hear themselves talk. Others place a premium on specialized skills: bartering, persuading, threatening, cajoling, informing, negotiating, or haggling over words. Still others entail a thirst for competition, recognition, dominance, catharsis, or status. Whenever the personal climate fosters sufficient sense of mutual trust and understanding, the respective parties may probe their most private thoughts, disclosing even their deepest fears and anxieties or their sense of worthlessness, superiority, or despair. The possibilities range from the painstakingly reasoned to the purest impulse, from comments lasting but an instant to conversations spanning a lifetime, from idle chatter to negotiations over the fate of mankind. The themes are endless.

Despite the forces of habit and routine, man has the capacity to anticipate and seek encounters that promise to match his uppermost drives and needs. Conduct that is judged to be appropriate in one social setting may be inconsistent with the requirements of another. The appropriateness of a given encounter is defined not only by *who* is present but by *how many*. In some cases, obviously, the *number* of people talking may be of incidental importance; in most, however, the communicative outcomes depend in some measure on how many are present at the time. Some matters can be shared most openly in the company of only one other person. Others may require two, three, or perhaps several interactants. Still others may function best when aired in a large group or before an audience. Most people have an intuitive feeling for the number present at any social situation and learn to adjust their communicative behavior accordingly. When persons sense that they are coming into direct contact with "too many people," they tend to react in characteristic fashion. The same applies when interactants sense there are not enough people present to sustain the conversation. Moreover, size is important because the inclusion or withdrawal of even one person can have a disproportionate impact on the social forces at work in any given communicative situation. Generally, the fewer people present, the more each person can influence the balance of forces needed to facilitate communication. In this chapter we will survey the forces underlying various types of interpersonal contacts, progressing from the simplest possible to those of increasing levels of complexity.

SOCIAL ISOLATION

Man reveals much about his need for communication by the way he responds to situations that deny him the opportunity. Most striking is the way in which people deprived of contact with others show the urgent need to establish communication as soon as possible (Vernon and Hoffman, 1956). Reports of prisoners in solitary confinement underscore man's need to maintain more-or-less constant interchange with others. Even the inhabitants of death row are known to shuttle messages back and forth between their cells. Some communicate simply by shouting from cell to cell. Others use more ingenious devices, including codes tapped out on the bars of the cells, kites pulled from cell to cell, and arrangements with trustees who deliver messages along with the meals.

Important changes in communication occur among people who are isolated from contact with the outside world; they experience severe stress, anxiety, and often acute trauma. When a group undergoes prolonged isolation, predictable and profound changes in interaction occur. At first spirits are high and morale is good. At the end of the first day, virtually all volunteers remain. A small number quit after a second day in isolation, and by the third day one-fourth or more of the volunteers may withdraw because the discomfort is too great (Zuckerman, 1964). During the first few days, most participants manifest what is technically called a "stimulus-action hunger," or "communication hunger." They show an eagerness to gain stimulation by the sheer act of talking (Lilly, 1956; Oyamada and Sato, 1965). Apparently, the absence of a chance to communicate with the outside world creates anxiety and frustration that can be relieved only by prolonged interaction with those who share common surroundings (Weinstein et al., 1967; Zuckerman et al., 1962). One study found that during a 4½-hour period of isolation, subjects never kept quiet even for as long as 6 consecutive minutes (Shurley, 1960).

Over time the object of communication tends to become increasingly personal in nature. The less access people have to others in the outside world, the more they resort to frequent discussion of personal and intimate topics (Altman and Haythorn, 1965). Many find themselves discussing aspects of their personal lives that are unknown even by close relatives. The testimony of Admiral Byrd (1938), a veteran of months of isolation in the Antarctic, captured the tenor of this personal type of disclosure:

> It doesn't take two men long to find each other out. And, inevitably, this is what they do, whether they will it or not, if only because once the simple tasks of the day are finished there is little else to do but take each other's measure. Not deliberately. Not maliciously. But the time comes when one has nothing left to reveal to the other; when even his unformed thoughts can be anticipated, his pet ideas become a meaningless drool, and the way he blows out a pressure lamp or drops his boots on the floor or eats his food becomes a rasping annoyance. And this could happen between the best of friends [p. 16].

Note Byrd's observation about having "nothing left to reveal to the other." This observation supports findings on the differences between short-term and prolonged isolation. For example, experiments on social deprivation find that the effectiveness of positive feedback increases markedly after a person is cut off from personal contact for even a brief time; often as short a period as twenty minutes is all that is needed to increase the need for social recognition and approval (Gewirtz and Baer, 1958a, 1958b). At some unspecified point, the interactants' eagerness to talk begins to conflict with certain disruptive forces at work in isolated social situations. Gradually, speech activity becomes impaired along with deterioration in thinking and organization (Myers et al., 1966). Some complain of difficulties in expressing themselves coherently, as manifested by slurred speech and disorganized grammar (Mendelson et al., 1961). Often, the verbal output of a group drops by more than half over a period of confinement of eight hours (Pollard et al., 1963). When they do talk, people find it increasingly difficult to interact spontaneously (Vosberg et al., 1960), as evidenced by the greater length of time they take to react to others and the longer length of their sentences and phrases (Suedfeld, 1964; Suedfeld and Vernon, 1965; Suedfeld et al., 1967).

Eventually, prolonged isolation causes severe interpersonal stress and gradual withdrawal from social interaction (Cowan and Strickland, 1965; Gunderson and Nelson, 1966; Haythorn and Altman, 1967b; Zubek, 1969). With pronounced irritation and boredom, subjects find it difficult to interact without provoking conflict and friction. Again, Byrd's (1930) comments are instructive:

> Arguments are at once the joy and affliction of the winter night. How many roared through Little America, like fire sweeping dry timber, I should hesitate to say. But offhand, well, one or two too many. Let the temperature drop to 70° below zero outside, we never lacked for burning issues inside. . . .
> Like country cousins, arguments clung to us always. They started innocently, gathered increasing strength and became so fraught with passion as to threaten to bring down the roof. They seemed to have no end. Pertinacious minds, reluctant to concede defeat, would trot them forth, like horses under raps, and start them off again. Then the air would clear, the issue be decently interred; but before its bones had ceased to rattle, a new one was in the travail of birth [p. 210].

The experience Byrd described is consistent with scientific findings. Representative is a study that required six men to be socially confined for a period lasting up to 12 weeks (Cowan and Strickland, 1965). During the first four weeks, records indicate the men spent from 44 to 48 percent of their waking hours in passive activities while in the presence of others—reading, watching TV, listening to records, and so forth—and one-third of the time they engaged in active communication. By the end of the sixth week, a dramatic change took place: The subjects were found to spend 60 percent of their time in passive activity and just 20 percent in direct interaction. By the end of eight weeks, little explicit communication occurred, and what did take place was abrupt and impersonal.

During the withdrawal stages of social isolation, people show increasing concern over their physical belongings and their territory. They become possessive over the occupancy of chairs, beds, and other aspects of the living quarters (Altman and Haythorn, 1967; Taylor et al., 1968). This heightened concern about personal territory suggests again the communicative significance that is signaled by the mere recognition of another person's presence. The problem of personal recognition is central to the underlying nature of interpersonal contacts and has far-reaching implications that should now be explored in some detail.

THE PRESENCE OF ANOTHER PERSON

All interpersonal contacts, however simple or complex, progress through a succession of stages of activity. The first is a stage of *anticipation* which comprises the impressions or expectations toward a forthcoming encounter. The next stage might be termed an awareness of the *mere presence* of others; it occurs when interactants first come into common surroundings yet have only a vague awareness of each other. Then comes the process of direct contact itself; it is governed initially by a period of *first impressions* and then by the back-and-forth sequence of interaction that follows along lines of mutual dependence, or *reciprocity*. Each of these four stages of behavior has several characteristics which we will examine in turn.

Anticipation of the Encounter

The influence of another person's presence begins with the anticipation the respective parties have about the nature of their forthcoming encounter. This process of anticipation can be extraordinarily complex. Fortunately, we have already examined many contributing influences. It results in part from the need to reduce uncertainty and the need for some consistency in psychological orientation (pp. 134–139). Other factors include the human tendency to personalize all incoming sensory data (pp. 100–106). In this regard it may be useful to recall the notion of man as proactive (pp. 16–18), the idea of selective perception (pp. 101–104), and the evidence against the notion of neutrality in psychological orientation (pp. 71–72). Also related to the topic at hand are the larger ways in which presituational factors influence the impressions gained of credibility (pp. 147–150). All of these factors indicate something of both the *intensity* and the *regularity* with which man seeks to impose his expectations on the succession of events. People, after all, can absorb only a limited amount of social contact. Hence, their early estimates of the possibilities for communication are necessary not only to affirm certain interpersonal choices but also to ignore or rule out others.

The anticipation of social contact may be likened to a dress rehearsal. Most people have at least a vague sense of what they are about to say and how they expect others to handle themselves. If the dress rehearsal is favorable and positive, the probability of subsequent communication increases; if unfavorable, a person may avoid the encounter altogether (Blumer, 1967; Mead, 1930; Turner, 1956). Again, the tendency is to personalize all information about an event, whether positive or negative. For example, consider this instance: A group of girls was told that they were about to be paired with someone to talk about acceptable sexual standards of dating. Before meeting their partners, each girl was asked to read a personality description of two people — one was to be her partner, the other's only identity was a "total stranger." After reading the descriptions, each girl was asked to make judgments about the two personality descriptions. Results showed that the very anticipation of communication colored the interpretations given in each case. In virtually all instances, the most positive evaluations were attributed to the person who was supposed to be a future contact, even though *both* of the people ranked were *total strangers* (Darley and Bersheid, 1967).

The Mere Presence of Another

Between the time when people anticipate events and when they actually engage in them, an interim period occurs—often quite brief—during which each party is only minimally aware of the other's presence. Long ago Cooley (1902) hinted at the importance of this stage in *Human Nature and the Social Order*:

> There is a vague excitement of the social self more general than any particular emotion or sentiment. Thus the mere presence of people, a "sense of other persons" and an awareness of their observation, often causes a vague discomfort, doubt and tension. One feels that there is a social image of himself lurking about, and not knowing what it is he is obscurely alarmed. Many people, perhaps most, feel more or less agitation and embarrassment under the observation of strangers, and for some even sitting in the same room with unfamiliar or uncongenial people is harassing and exhausting [p. 207].

The mere presence of another person—without any verbal interchange—can have a marked impact on the course of interpersonal relationships. Consider the following report from the Associated Press (1967):

> A mysterious student has been attending a class at Oregon State University for the past two months enveloped in a big black bag. Only his bare feet show. Each Monday, Wednesday, and Friday at 11:00 A.M. the Black Bag sits on a small table near the back of the classroom. The class is Speech 113—basic persuasion. . . . Charles Goetzinger, professor of the class, knows the identity of the person inside. None of the 20 students in the class do. Goetzinger said the students' *attitude changed from hostility toward the Black Bag to curiosity and finally to friendship* [italics added].

This incident raises an important question: Is the mere presence of a person itself sufficient to change attitudes from indifference or hostility to curiosity and even to positive attraction? If so, perhaps the mere act of recognition alters the meaning of interpersonal contacts. One possibility, suggested by the Cooley's observation above, is that the mere presence of others functions as a source of emotional arousal. Such a possibility is consistent with the assumptions associated with nonverbal communication discussed in Chapter 6 (pp. 211-217). Recall also people's tendency to become possessive over their own territory (pp. 256-258). In addition, people who work by themselves report experiencing less emotional excitement and urge to work rapidly than they do when coworkers are visibly present (Kelley and Thibaut, 1969).

Some evidence from studies of animal arousal may be relevant to the question. For example, the mere presence of other animals in cages in a room with caged mice produces increased adrenal weights in the mice (Thiessen, 1964). Significantly, the adrenal weights of mice housed in groups of twenty are higher than among those housed alone. Moreover, the density of population also contributes to overt signs of severe stress and withdrawal (Mason and

Brady, 1964). The main question, of course, is whether findings from animal studies can be taken as representative of human reactions. Though the problem can never be conclusively resolved, there is a close parallel between the pattern of emotional arousal in human hospital patients and those shown in monkeys; in each instance the emotional arousal is found to be highest during periods when others are present, either in laboratory or in hospital, and lowest during the less active periods of weekends (Mason and Brady, 1964). Clearly, in the animal studies many factors other than mere exposure are at work; yet the parallels between human arousal and that of lower animals are striking and also consistent with the larger evidence of a link between mere exposure and emotional arousal.

Additional evidence supports the notion that mere exposure influences more than emotional arousal. Most impressive is the fascinating evidence that exposure heightens the bonds of *interpersonal attraction.* For example, Zajonc (1968) noted that studies of the most frequently used words reveal patterns that imply the existence of a link between exposure and interpersonal attraction. Zajonc's reasoning began with a comparison of the meanings of the most often used words with those used infrequently. The logic behind such a comparison is indirect but straightforward: The use of a given word, after all, is a form of exposure. Now, if repeated exposure does indeed create *positive attitudes,* and if it can be demonstrated that popular words have a higher probability of having *positive evaluative meanings* than do infrequently used words, then the bond between exposure and positive attraction can be established. And, Zajonc reasoned, if the bond between words and exposure holds in a manner consistent with the link between mere presence of people and interpersonal attraction, then one may conclude that positive associations follow from the mere recognition of other people in communicative situations. Later (see pp. 262 to 263) we will discover that people indeed are more attracted to others as frequency of contact increases. The same principle is at work in the "Black Bag" incident. And Zajonc discovered that words used most frequently do have a higher probability of having positive meanings than those used infrequently. Words with positive overtones (*happiness, beauty, wealth, laugh,* and *love*) turn out to be employed far more frequently than do their counterparts (*unhappiness, ugly, poverty, cry,* and *hate*). Similarly, it is five times more likely that things will be called "good" than "bad" and almost three times more often that they will be termed "possible" than "impossible." Some of the most commonly heard words in the English language outdo their negative counterparts in frequency of usage by ratios of as much as 10 or even 15 to 1. On the strength of such consistency in meaning and usage, Zajonc concluded:

> While they are unfaithful in representing reality, word frequencies are extraordinarily accurate in representing real values: words that stand for good, desirable, and preferred aspects of reality are more frequently used [1968, p. 3].

The effect of mere exposure, whether to words or to people, is much the same. Exposure creates arousal which in turn generates tension and a need for recognition and further interaction. The simultaneous presence of two or more people produces the greatest stress in those situations that require direct body orientation and physical proximity. For example, the last two people to walk out of the opposite ends of a ballpark are under no pressure, nor are they even apt to be influenced by the presence of the other. However, were the same two individuals to meet in the close quarters of an elevator, a doctor's office, a cafeteria, or a living room, they would be under much pressure to recognize the presence of the other. When two strangers are brought into a room and seated across from each other with instructions "not to talk or communicate in any way," they are known to experience acute stress that increases in intensity as time and silence continue (Luft, 1966).

Long before the first words of a conversation are spoken, important changes take place in the perceptual field of a person who notices the presence of another. Each party begins to focus less on the larger features of his physical surroundings and more on the nonverbal cues given off by the other person. The process of focusing, or "zeroing in," on the presence of another, is like the action of a zoom lens on a television camera in moving from a long shot to a close-up. As the perceptual field becomes more focused, the interactants begin to change the direction of their own psychological orientations, as evidenced by an increase in the number of verbal requests for personal information among coworkers who can talk but not see each other (Exline, 1962). However, where members of a two-member exchange are allowed to work in the physical view of each other, communication between them becomes more active than it would be otherwise, with far more frequent talking and less personal tension than where coworkers attempt to coordinate their activities without being in the physical presence of one another (Argyle et al., 1963).

First Impressions

In an initial encounter between two strangers, first impressions are critically important in setting the tone for their subsequent interaction. First impressions function as anchorage points from which the respective parties subjectively color their interpretation of all that follows. For example, if new acquaintances have an initial impression that they will be able to get along well with another person, they later report far more liking and positive attraction than they would otherwise (Schachter et al., 1951). In fact, they are apt to like one another far more than subjects who talk under identical conditions but who have been given an initial impression that they may have been mismatched. Another example of the significance of first impressions is one that occurred in a classroom experiment (Kelley, 1950). Psychology students examined a series of personality descriptions of people who allegedly were being considered for the post of class instructor. The descriptions were identical except for one section where the candidate was depicted as either "rather warm" or "rather cold." So slight a difference in first impressions was later found to strongly influence the students' attitudes toward the instructors described in the briefings.

First impressions are also important because of their effectiveness as signals of what each interactant likes or dislikes about the other. As an illustration, take the situation where pairs of female college students were led to believe that they would either like or dislike partners assigned for a forthcoming conversation. The pairs then exchanged written messages containing what each thought the other's view was toward college fraternities. Actually, previously written notes were substituted so that each girl received a message that differed in varying degrees from her attitude on the subject. When the subjects were later asked to estimate their partners' views, results showed that regardless of how far apart their views really were, those in the high-liking condition minimized the differences between themselves and the person they were conditioned to like (Berkowitz and Goranson, 1964).

First impressions can also be a most deceptive indicator of what sort of communication is likely to follow. At a first meeting people tend to be quite conscious of themselves and how they are behaving; they are also particularly sensitive to the initial reactions of others. Consequently, each party presents a somewhat idealized version of himself for public inspection. First moments are typically the most guarded ones. Each reveals what he feels the other will be least apt to reject. Interpersonal tension is greatest during the initial moments, when people know least what to expect by way of interpersonal feedback. During the early stages of interpersonal contact, each person tends to avoid the more risky, ego-involving topics such as sex and money (Jourard, 1964). This preference for minimal self-disclosure was aptly demonstrated in a study of the behavior of college roommates (Taylor, 1965). During the first few weeks of living together, selected pairs of roommates engaged in superficial and formalized talk. There was the usual uneasiness, the groping for things to talk about, the embarrassing moments of silence, and the ritualistic conversations on matters ranging from recreational interests to tastes in books, sports, and movies. However, the amount of self-disclosure was found to increase markedly over a period of nine weeks, then level off, with certain pairs of high revealers discussing more of their views on intimate topics, personal values, and matters of confidence (Figure 7.1). Such findings parallel those cited earlier which indicated that intimate disclosure is greatest, even initially, among groups that are isolated for prolonged periods. The same principle holds for the initial contacts of people who are under the impression they will never meet again. It is far more likely that those who happen to strike up a conversation with a stranger miles away from home will reveal aspects of their personal life that are unknown to their closest neighbors and associates.

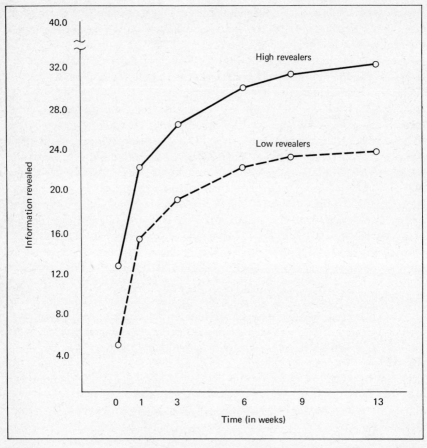

Figure 7.1 *Amount of self-disclosure over time by high revealers and low revealers. (Reprinted with permission from Argyle, 1967.)*

Reciprocity

Once interpersonal contact moves beyond the strain and self-editing of the first moments, the sequence tends to follow the general principle of reciprocity; that is, whatever A does, B is under social constraint to do much the same (Argyle, 1967; Gouldner, 1960). Without the stabilizing influence of a reciprocal reaction, communication can readily become unstable or one-sided. Hence, an act of disclosure by A automatically carries with it the assumption that B will act in kind. For B to refuse to follow A's implicit invitation would constitute a potential breach of trust. The concept of reciprocity does not require exact equity in the exchange, only an approximate dove-tailing of responses (Bauer, 1964; Feffer and Suchotliff, 1966). Typically, the greater the ambiguity in the situation, the less each party knows what to expect from the other; hence, the greater becomes the pressure to follow whatever form of behavior will approximate the initial activity of the other. It is commonly reported, for example, that two strangers who sit in a room and suddenly notice smoke curling from under the door typically react in accordance with whatever another does first, either leaving the room or continuing to sit calmly. In a related line of investigation, two-person groups were introduced for the purpose of completing a joint task. Half the pairs were lead to believe that their partners would be agreeable or understanding; the other half expected the opposite. As anticipated, the initial set produced a chain reaction in a direction consistent with the notion of reciprocity: Those anticipating congeniality reacted in kind; those who looked for evidence of antagonism became increasingly antagonistic themselves (Back, 1951).

The many studies of friendship patterns and norms governing interpersonal attraction underscore the principle that communicative behavior tends to be reciprocal. Homans (1950), for example, wrote:

> "Friendliness" unquestionably conceals a complicated process. For one reason or another, you associate with someone for a period of time; your behavior becomes adjusted to his, and his to yours; you feel at home with him and say he is a good fellow. The friendliness may be no more than the *emotional reflection of adjustment,* and it is perhaps for this reason that your liking for someone is so often independent of his personality [p. 115, italics added].

Whether first impressions are congenial or hostile, subsequent interaction tends to confirm whatever expectations and subjective interpretation are formed during the all-important early moments of the encounter

Individual Differences

So far we have examined the dynamics of the early moments of interpersonal contact in rather idealized and abstract terms. No mention has been made of the import of individual differences. Hence, the underlying assumption is that some factors are common to any one-to-one interchange, irrespective of *who* the persons are. This is not to deny the equally important influence of the particular make-up of the people themselves. Without the mediating influence of individual differences, the principle of reciprocity could easily lead to a relationship that would be utterly barren and meaningless. On one hand the response of A to B is a consequence of such formal aspects of the interaction as emotional arousal, expectations, first impressions, and the like. On the other hand it is the influence of the *person* of B and who he is in the eyes of A. A classic illustration of the import of such individual differences is discussed in a case study of relationships between different pairs of people by Block and Bennett (1966). The study concerned the personal relations of a single female subject, a thirty-four-year-old clinical psychologist, and twenty-three people who knew her in different social situations. Despite some similarities among many of the relationships, the investigators found evidence of striking differences in the way the subject interacted with each of the twenty-three persons in one-to-one situations. When characterizing her interactions with a next-door neighbor, the study found the subject "at ease with these people, she trusts and confides in them, and likes them very much. She tries to please, to win their affection, and to impress them [p. 177]. In the case of another associate, a person of the same profession, status, and background as the next-door neighbor, the subject related on a far different basis:

> With these people, S [subject] feels extremely uneasy, inhibited, awkward, and inadequate. She resents them, feels guilty, and tries to hide her feelings. She is self-abasing and enforces interpersonal distance. The ambivalence of her feelings in this role is marked—although she likes these people, she also dislikes them with equal intensity [p. 177].

The same subject reportedly interpreted some of her relationships in ways that conflicted with those held by the other persons. Particularly striking was the difference in the relationship with her divorced husband. The following descriptions appear to refer to entirely different relationships:

> S's divorced husband does not perceive that he is important to S or that she treats him differently from other people. He feels less influenced by her than she thinks. S's vigorous statement of ambivalence—she likes him somewhat but she dislikes him a great deal more—is not apparent to him. He believes that she likes him a great deal, respects him, and is willing to express disagreements frankly. She does not affirm this. He regards her as considerate, trusting, encouraging. She contends she is not. She views herself as being unkind to him, accusing, dominating, discouraging, depressing, distant. He says she is not [p. 179].

These excerpts indicate that the mere presence of a given number of people does not operate independently of other psychological and social influences on communication. In each time and place, interactants react to each other in ways that invariably reflect the nuances of their past circumstance, prior acquaintance, existing attitudes, social pressures, and countless other factors that can be interpreted only by knowing something about the individual differences of the respective personalities.

THE PRESENCE OF TWO OR MORE PEOPLE

In most face-to-face situations, the inclusion or withdrawal of one person can alter the nature of all subsequent interaction, often in dramatic ways. The difference of even one person, say three instead of two, has an effect that is more than simply $+1$ or -1; the difference must be understood, as we will soon see, in geometric terms rather than simply additive ones. Even the person who says nothing, or perhaps offers a few comments, still contributes in significant ways to the complexity of the encounter. The inclusion or departure of any one person requires that all remaining interactants make some adjustments by reorienting themselves to the physical aspects of their surroundings and, equally important, to the changed spatial arrangements, or "body jockeying," that often occurs when someone enters or leaves a room. Each person, however active or silent, represents a potential source of emotional arousal and an object of psychological orientation for all others present. Finally, the number of people present constitutes a constraining and delimiting influence, both on the amount and flow of messages and on the general climate at work in the social situation.

It is important to note that size is not a matter which can be explained solely in numerical terms; the effects associated with size ordinarily interact with other factors such as the nature of the task, the degree of interpersonal attraction, the length of time available for interaction, and the degree of ego involvement in the situation. Hence, a brief conversation among five people in an elevator may not be analogous to the dynamic forces at work should the same people begin the identical conversation in a business office. Similarly, a telephone call from a stockbroker to a client is not apt to have the same effect as one from a car salesman to a prospective customer, even though both situations involve the communication of two persons through an identical medium at the same time of day about matters of comparable financial consequence. In short, the progression of encounters between two interactants to complex social units must always be understood within the larger social context in which the communication occurs.

The Dyad

A dyadic interaction, or communication between two persons, may seem in many respects to be the least complex of all possible interpersonal contacts. Despite the fact that a meeting between two persons is the simplest of all social units, a dyad is a unique and complicated form of communicative activity. Contrary to what might be expected, the dyad tends to be a highly unstable, tension-producing form of interchange. It is unstable because everything depends on the continuous reactions of only one person—either A or B. In cases of hostility or disagreement, there is no court of appeal, no majority power, no independent form of arbitration. Either person in a dyad virtually has veto power over decision making. More importantly, either member can prevent future interaction merely by exercising the ultimate threat of withdrawal. When several people are present, the sudden withdrawal of one may damage the affairs at hand, but no one person can single-handedly prevent the future actions of other members. Hence, given the power of each member in a dyad to alter the course of the interaction, it is hardly surprising to find that *tension* is highest, particularly at the outset, in communications between two people (Slater, 1958; Thomas and Fink, 1963).

Despite the delicate balance of power, dyads are vulnerable to the emergence of marked differences in individual behavior. Given sufficient time for interaction, one person typically gravitates to a position of dominance with its powers of initiative and directive; the other must then assume a passive position. The less-dominant person is not without power, however, since he can always rely on the threat of veto. In such an unstable, asymmetrical social situation, it is often difficult to determine who has the greatest influence, particularly since the power of initiative and dominance tends to be counteracted by the controlling reactions of the more passive member (Hare, 1962).

Another characteristic of the two-member exchange is its unique communicative content. Dyads have a high rate of acts that show interpersonal tension, a low rate of overt antagonism, and relatively few instances in which one person asks another for his ideas and opinions (Bales and Borgotta, 1955). Dyadic interaction also has fewer personal expressions of either agreement or disagreement than do encounters among more people. Apparently, the reluctance to express personal agreement or disagreement occurs because the strain of a one-to-one exchange often destroys the cohesion and trust necessary for each party to feel free to express his own feelings. The evidence that instability and interpersonal tension are relatively greater problems in dyads than in larger social units may explain why dyads are reported to produce only three-fourths as much verbal interaction as that which characterizes three- or four-person interactions over a comparable length of time (O'Dell, 1968). Overall, the communication process that occurs between two persons in task-oriented situations shows signs of tension, instability, and imbalance both in role relationships and in the proportion of total verbal activity; it also is characterized by fewer questions and directives than that which occurs when more than two people are present.

The Triad

The triad, or three-member exchange, exhibits many characteristics of the dyad, with one important exception. In two-member groups, majority rule is possible only by unanimity; the two parties either agree or they do not. In a triad, however, majority rule can be reached by unanimity or by a coalition of two against one. The very possibility of a coalition complicates both the number and type of relationships that are possible among three people. A dyad can have only two relationships, whereas a triad has a potential for eight forms of coalition (Caplow, 1959). In those triads which have an *unequal* distribution of social power, the most likely outcome is for the most powerful person to dominate (the two weakest against the strongest) or for the weakest to initiate a coalition with the strongest person (Caplow, 1956; Vinacke and Arkoff, 1957). The potential for internal struggling is further complicated by the sex of participating members (Uesugi and Vinacke, 1963). The presence of three men frequently produces a struggle for dominance among any two members with the greatest power, the third being excluded from a position of authority in the process. However, where a woman is present, the two males tend to vie for the allegiance of the female. In contrast is the jockeying for position among three females; typically, the two strongest members tend to encourage participation by the weakest person.

However, the existence of a triad does not ensure that a given coalition will form. Contrary to popular belief, three do not invariably pair two against one. Much depends on the mix between conflict and coordination; for if either ingredient is missing, no one person is apt to feel a compulsion to take concerted action. Pressures mount whenever the initial distribution of resources (the power to influence others) prevents any one person from controlling group decisions (Gamson, 1964). Hence, coalitions tend to form among those who can expect the highest proportionate gain from taking joint action (Gamson, 1961; Vinacke, 1959). For example, if person A controls 40 percent of the resources, person B has 34 percent, and person C has 26 percent, B and C will probably join against A, since they have the most to gain from collaboration. However, should the combined power be less than that of A, B and C could be expected to compete with each other for the chance to align with A. (For a detailed account of the predictions of minimum resources, see Gamson, 1964.) Though other factors are undoubtedly involved (Chertkoff, 1966), we can conclude that coalitions form mainly in interactions which occur among at least three people over matters entailing mixed motives (conflict and coordination) and relatively clear and equal distribution of initial resources over decision making.

Communication in triadic situations is not without many of the tensions associated with two-member exchange. A study by Slater (1958) reported that members of triads tend to be excessively tense, passive, and tactful. They also go to great lengths to produce an atmosphere in which task-oriented work can be completed in a satisfying manner. Such deliberateness and instability seem to stem from the pressure in triads to form coalitions which produce *asymmetrical* role relations. Mills (1953) has reported that disagreement between the two most dominant members leads each into competition for the support of the weak member; as a consequence, stress remains high until a coalition is formed which excludes the less powerful of the two strongest members. In an important investigation by Schachter (1951) confederates were placed in a number of different groups with instructions to deviate as much as possible from whatever views were maintained by others at any given moment. The initial response of the group members to such deviate behavior was evidenced by the disproportionate amount of time they spent interacting with the deviate member (in comparison with confederates in control groups who did not violate group norms). Interestingly enough, as the deviate behavior continued, the other members gradually spent less and less of their time talking to the confederate, until he was virtually excluded from the discussion. Apparently, the internal struggling continues as long as participants think there is a reasonable chance of correcting or winning the support of the one who is in the minority. However, continued resistance to majority pressure soon leads to a marked decrease in the number of comments directed to the minority (Sampson and Brandon, 1964). Moreover, some of the pressures common to triads result from the existence of an odd number of participants. Odd-sized larger groups, particularly one with five members, typically exhibit coalitions that also focus on gaining support from the minority interest, though in a less extreme form of struggle than what typifies a triad.

Contact with Several People

Whenever the number of people engaged in communication increases from four to ten or more, important changes take place in the character and complexity of their interaction. For one thing, the inclusion of one additional person greatly alters the number of possible relationships. Consider first the number of potential relationships between any set of combinations of two people. A dyad has only one such relationship, AB. A triad has three relationships, AB, AC, and BC. A group of six, in contrast, has fifteen such relationships, and a group of twelve has sixty-six potential relationships between any two individuals. As the size increases, the number of relationships increases more dramatically. Because each numerical increase produces a geometric increase in the number of possible relationships, the mere inclusion of more people greatly magnifies the forces at work in a group situation.

It must also be noted that relationships develop between *subgroups* as well as between *pairs* of individuals. Therefore, a better estimate of interpersonal relationships in groups must be one that takes into account *all* potential relationships between individuals, combinations of subgroups, and all possible variations of individuals and subgroups. The dramatic effect of size on the combination of potential relationships is indicated in Table 1. The significance of size is readily apparent if we think of Table 1 as representing the number of potential persons engaged in conversation at a dinner table. If the group initially consists of a mother, father, and three children, the inclusion of a single guest at the table adds 211 potential relationships, and the addition of still another unanticipated visitor adds 655 more potential relationships. In other words, the two guests produce a total of 866 more relationships than those at work for a family of five. Such an exponential increase results largely from the number of new subgroupings which are possible whenever a single person is added to an interaction. In most situations, only a fraction of potential relationships will ever be utilized.

TABLE 1. POTENTIAL RELATIONSHIPS BETWEEN
NUMBERS OF PEOPLE ENGAGED IN
COMMUNICATION

Number of communicators	Number of relationships
2	1
3	6
4	25
5	90
6	301
7	966

Increases in size may have a spectacular influence on what Bass (1960) termed the "interaction potential" of any given number of participants. Generally speaking, the more people present, the less likely it is that any one person will interact with any other given person or that he will interact as long and as frequently as he would if fewer were present. While the total number of communicative acts increases as size increases, a higher proportion of people will say far less than they would otherwise. Hare (1952) found members of discussion groups to be aware of the pressures imposed by group size; they reported having far fewer chances to talk in groups of twelve than in groups of five. Related studies (Miller, 1951; Stephen, 1952; Stephen and Mishler, 1952) indicate that the average amount of participation per member decreases as size increases anywhere from three to ten or fifteen members or more. Part of the explanation for these findings is simply a matter of the time available for verbal interaction between each set of members. The larger the group, the less time there is for each member to speak. As a consequence, larger-sized groups require more time to complete various judgmental and problem-solving tasks than do groups of three and four (Gibb, 1951; Morrissette, 1966; South, 1927).

The number of people engaged in verbal interaction also has a bearing on the distribution of communicative acts. Here, again, the effect of increased size is to reduce the distribution of acts among the group members. However, size does not influence relative proportion of exchange in any simple way. In larger groups, in fact, the disparity between the most active and the least active members is greater than it is under circumstances where fewer people are present. Generally, research indicates that the greater relative discrepancies between persons ranked first and second in amount of overall verbal activity occurs in large-sized groups (Thomas and Fink, 1963). Similarly, the differences in amount of participation by members not ranked first or second has been found to be *smaller* with increases in group size. As size increases from three to eight, a larger and larger proportion of people talk less than their "equal share"; that is, they participate less than the mean of the group. Moreover, if the group has an assigned or delegated leader, the difference between the most active member and the other members is proportionately greater as the number of people in the group increases (Bales, 1951). Kelley and Thibaut (1954) summarized the findings on size and participation as follows:

> As size increases, the most active member becomes increasingly differentiated from the rest of the group, who become increasingly similar to one another in the participation output. In addition, over the range from about two to seven there appears to be an increase in the proportion of the group who are "undercontributors" in the sense that they account for less than their equal share of the total volume in interaction. The latter result may indicate an increase in the restraints against participation, which result in an increasingly large proportion of the group being discouraged from making overt contributions [p. 762].

Size and "Directionality" of Communication. In any social setting that becomes too large for every member to feel he can communicate freely, two changes in interaction take place, often simultaneously. First, as size increases, members direct more communications to "the group as a whole." Second, as communication becomes more group-directed, those who feel the most inhibited by the size of the group are most apt to direct more of their comments to someone sitting next to them. Therefore, factions and cliques are far more characteristic of larger groups than situations involving three or four members (Hare, 1952). One measure of such fractionalization is simply the proportion of time that two members spend talking between themselves rather than to the entire group. Using just such a measure as this, Miller (1951) reported a positive correlation between the number of cliques or factions and the number of people engaged in communication; talk between two members occurred more frequently as group size increased from three to four to twenty members. Clearly, then, size has a bearing not just upon how much is said but also upon the number of people engaged in verbal interaction at any one point and upon the proportion of members who share in the exchange.

Size and Member Satisfaction. Size, as we have just seen, acts largely as a constraining influence on social interaction. Sheer size, in effect, rules out or delimits what is said, how often it is said, and to whom it is said. Persons typically react adversely to any severe social constraint, particularly when it affects the need for free and open exchange between all participants. Size, therefore, assumes significance in understanding the conditions which govern reactions of individuals to their participation in a group situation. For those who have a genuine desire to contribute to group goals, a constraint stemming from the sheer presence of too many people produces feelings of dissatisfaction. Only when the group is the "right size" for a given task—that is, when it is neither too large for free discussion nor too small for comfortable participation —are members apt to find the experience personally fulfilling and productive. While size is obviously not the only determinant of member satisfaction, it is, nonetheless, an important one.

Small groups exhibit certain types of stress and tension. They also have greater potential for strengthening interpersonal ties among members than that attributed to larger groups (Kinney, 1953). A related measure of inter-personal attraction—degree of intimacy—has also been found to characterize exchanges among three or four people more than those of larger groups (Fisher, 1953). Membership satisfaction in studies reported by Bales (1954) and Slater (1958) were highest in five-member groups; apparently, that number avoids the strains which characterize smaller groups and the restrictions associated with larger groups. Five-member groups, as Hare observed (1962, pp. 243–244), have other characteristics. With an odd number of participants, five-member groups cannot reach a strict deadlock or stalemate. Moreover, any division tends to have a majority of three and a minority of two. Hence, no one in a minority is totally isolated or devoid of support from at least one other member. Finally, five-member groups have a high degree of flexibility; members can readily change their positions or styles of participation without calling undue attention to their behavior. Any increase in size well beyond five members reduces both individual participation and overall individual satisfaction with a group task (Hare, 1962; Slater, 1958).

The results of the effects of size in large organizations are remark-ably consistent with findings from small-group research. In the larger work units of departments and factories, increases in size lead to several highly predictable barometers of member dissatisfaction: absenteeism, job turnover, and frequency of labor disputes (Porter and Lawler, 1965). Substantial increases in work units were found by Indik (1965) to create difficulties in maintaining communication among subgroups and individuals, together with problems in coordination, regulation, and feelings of impersonality. This does not mean, of course, that increasing size always leads to decreased satisfaction. Some goals or projects seemingly require the presence and participation of large numbers of people. Satisfaction with political campaigns and philanthropic causes, for example, is highest when there is an abundant number of volun-teers. In the case of spectator sports, a larger number may be required for optimal satisfaction, both for the players and for the spectators. Hence, the influence of size is neither uniform nor simple. The optimal number of people depends on a balance between the needs for free expression and unconstrained participation on the one hand and the particular requirements of the group task on the other.

SIZE AND MAJORITY INFLUENCE

It has long been recognized that the coercive power of the will of the majority is largely a function of the number of people who publicly commit themselves to a common stand on a topic. Nevertheless, there are certain general conditions of conformity, independent of the number who assume the majority position. For one thing, if people are under no obligation to come to a definite group decision, individual opinion typically does not as readily bend to majority will. A study by Pennington (et al., 1958) reported that groups which interact without an explicitly stated goal of reaching consensus show less convergence of individual opinion than do groups instructed to discuss a topic for the expressed purpose of arriving at a group decision. Another condition which affects the power of a majority is the degree of ambiguity in the situation or task under consideration. A number of studies report evidence that majority influence lessens when the task is free of ambiguity; conversely, pressures to conform tend to increase sharply with heightened ambiguity (Blake et al., 1957; Crutchfield, 1955). Of additional impact is the degree to which the parties are attracted to the group in which they are in the minority. When individuals are not group members, or when they feel no particular attachment or loyalty to group activity, the power of the majority is substantially weakened (Deutsch and Gerard, 1955; Jackson and Saltzstein, 1958; Kidd, 1958; Steiner and Peters, 1958). Furthermore, personality factors also influence individual susceptibility to majority will. Some people seem far more resistant to majority influence from situation to situation than others. When compared with those who are consistently resistant, people who conform to majority influence are found to be less secure and more dependent on others for social reinforcement, approval, and ego support (Klein, 1967).

The general conditions governing conformity are not to be considered absolute requirements; that is, they do not automatically rule out or ensure majority influence. Indeed, there is some evidence (Festinger and Thibaut, 1951) for what Brown (1965) called an "almost ineradicable tendency for members of a group to move toward agreement [p. 669]." Probably the clearest demonstration of the power of sheer size occurs when people simply make their judgment or complete a task in the presence of others without the confounding factors of verbal exchange, obligation to reach consensus, or explicit attempts at persuasion. The early studies of coworking groups by Allport (1924) come closest to a pure test of majority influence. In making comparisons of working performance and judgments of people who worked either alone or in the presence of others, Allport found evidence of convergence in the coworking group. In experiments requiring individual judgments recorded on ranking scales, for example, it was found that extreme ranking at the end of the scales occurred most often among those working alone. Those in the coworking situation, in contrast, avoided making extreme judgments in preference for central positions which presumably would not deviate from the will of the group. So even though no explicit communication was allowed and subjects knew that no comparisons would be revealed, the workers were influenced, Allport concluded, by their guesses or estimates of what others thought. Each person showed a need to act in accordance with those who worked around him.

Probably the classic demonstration of majority will, apart from negotiation or argument, is found in the early studies of Sherif (1956, 1958) on what is called the *autokinetic effect.* Subjects were placed in a dark room and instructed to estimate the movement of a point of light on the wall in front of them. In such a totally ambiguous situation, the dot of light, with no reference points, does actually appear to move erratically, even though it is fixed in a stationary position. The initial judgments of each subject ranged widely, but after several hundred trials, each developed a stable range of estimates. After establishing individual ranges for each subject in private sessions, the same people were brought together in groups of two and three and asked to report their judgments aloud. With no request for consensus or any attempt to persuade or sanction poor estimates, individual judgments converged dramatically. Moreover, when subjects made their initial estimates in a group situation, convergence was even greater. When subjects later faced the same stimulus alone, the group range still influenced their judgments. The same results have been obtained in numerous other studies, using variations of Sherif's basic design (Blake and Brehm, 1954; Downing, 1958; Linton, 1954; Olmstead and Blake, 1955; Rohrer et al., 1954).

The *number* of people who make up a majority has much to do with the amount of influence exerted on a minority. Generally, majority influence is heightened as the individual perceives near unanimity of opinion and also as the *number* giving assent to majority view increases (Kelley and Woodruff, 1956; Luchins, 1955). Anxiety, for example, as measured by galvanic skin response, is found to increase when subjects disagree with increasing numbers of opposing majorities (Hoffman, 1957; Lawson and Stagner, 1957).

The classic illustration of the power of increasing majority size is found in the frequently cited studies of a gestalt psychologist, Solomon Asch (1951, 1952, 1955, 1956). In his original research, Asch used college students in a laboratory study of visual perception. As the group of subjects entered to take their places in a row of seats in the laboratory, one unwitting subject was maneuvered into a position next to or at the far left of the row. All other participants were, in actuality, confederates instructed beforehand to give inaccurate but unanimous responses about the comparative lengths of lines shown on a card. With each trial, subjects expressed their judgments orally, one by one, from right to left, ending up with the one naive subject seated at the left. Though it would be easy for an outside observer to distinguish among the line lengths used in the trials, the consequence of having a majority of subjects on selected trials give incorrect judgments had a powerful impact on the responses of the one uncoached participant. The judgments of subjects who worked alone were virtually free of error over repeated trials; of thirty-seven subjects, one gave one inaccurate judgment, and another made two errors. In the group situation, however, approximately three-quarters of the naive subjects yielded to the unanimous but incorrect estimates of the other group members on at least one trial, and one-third relented on half the trials. The import of facing a unanimous majority is underscored by the discovery that the error rate of subjects went down considerably when just one other person sided with his correct judgment (Gorfein, D. S.). Obviously, then, the mere expression of majority will, particularly in the form of a unanimous estimate, acts as a powerful influence on the individual's own judgment.

The importance of the number of people who make up the majority is further suggested in an interesting variation of the Asch experiment. The results of varying the size of the majority from one to fifteen, as shown in Figure 7.2, show a dramatic trend. Clearly, majority influence increases as the size of the opposition increases. In a dyadic situation, with just one person present to express a contradictory stand, individuals maintain independence and answer correctly nearly all the time. The pressures mount when two opposing members are present; in a triad, minority subjects go along with incorrect majorities 13.6 percent of the time. The inclusion of yet another person yields a marked increase to almost one-third. However, any further increases beyond a majority of three creates only slightly greater influence. When group members express their views one after another, thereby suggesting a "follow the leader" chain reaction, majority influence diminishes more rapidly than when each person seems to express his position independent of other members. Although the exact influence is open to question (Gerald et al., 1968), it seems safe to conclude that while conformity pressures may vary widely, the value of increases in majority size soon diminishes the power of their influence until a point is reached where further increases will have no added effect (Blake and Mouton, 1961; Nord, 1969; Rosenberg, 1961).

The importance of Asch's findings must be understood in their proper context. Recall that subjects merely expressed their judgments without any overt attempt to influence the view held by the minority. Furthermore, the setting was in a laboratory, among unacquainted college students, on a matter of little consequence to them or their future relationships. Cartwright and Zander (1968) suggested that even stronger pressures to conform could be expected outside the laboratory and particularly on topics of greater personal importance. Under some circumstances, perhaps so. But an important number of forces could also work against the power of majority influence. For example, if a subject in a minority position is highly ego-involved in this stand, even in natural settings, the power of the majority could be expected to be *less* rather than more. After all, it is one thing for a person to conform to majority pressure on trivial and non-ego-involving taks such as judging line lengths, the move-

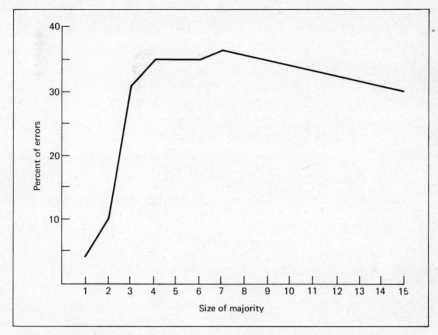

Figure 7.2 *Percentage of errors in judging line length with majorities of one to fifteen opponents. (Based on Asch, 1955.)*

ment of light, and the number of beans in a bottle. It is quite another to relent on matters of great personal import. In this regard recall the study by Sereno and Mortensen (1969, discussed on p. 165) where highly ego-involved subjects came to mutual agreement on a topic with far less frequency than did equally opposed but slightly involved persons.

Furthermore, suppose that certain social circumstances are in effect to heighten a sense of personal involvement on the part of the minority. Again, there is every reason to expect the power of majority influence to diminish. Striking cases in point are those where the people making up minority have strong convictions (Allen, 1966) or opinions on the topic of discussion (Carment, 1961; Kiesler, 1963). Closely related is the finding that minority members who have high personal status (Back and Davis, 1965; Jones et al., 1963) or high self-evaluation (Crowne and Liverant, 1963) give in less than do their counterparts. Also, when there is no reward for conformity or no negative consequences for holding out, conformity also predictably goes down (Iscoe and Williams, 1963; Nord, 1969; Wyer, 1966). Moreover, the longer the time allowed for the expression of differences, the less influence the majority is apt to have (Gerard, 1964). Majority influence is also known to diminish when the task in question is difficult (McDavid and Sistrunk, 1964) or when no ambiguity exists in the nature of the task (Graham, 1962; London and Lin, 1964; Nord,

1969). The implication from these findings is clear: The power of the majority does not operate in an automatic fashion or independent of the larger forces at work in interpersonal encounters. Conformity pressures may be counteracted at any time with a heightened sense of personal involvement or with a reward for resistance.

CONTACT WITH AN AUDIENCE

Contact with an audience differs from that of a large group in a number of important ways. Most striking is the diminished potential for interaction among members of an audience. An audience, after all, is an undifferentiated collective unit, addressed in the aggregate rather than on a one-to-one basis. The collective basis of interaction before an audience markedly alters the psychological and social atmosphere of communication. A person who speaks before an audience has less control over its behavior than he would with the same number gathered as a large discussion group. Unlike other forms of personal contact, interaction with an audience diminishes the reciprocal aspects of communication; ordinarily, the verbal messages originate with the speaker, the responses from the audience. Also, the physical surroundings — seating arrangement, podium, background — all enhance the sense of demarcation between source and receivers.

Traditionally, the study of audience-related effects has been hindered by the persistence of popular, stereotyped notions of what characterizes audiences. Ironically, the two most prevalent stereotypes are contradictory. One is the myth of the passive audience; the other equates the reactions of audiences to that of public crowds.

The concept of the passive audience regards the listeners as merely a collection of inactive respondents to a message, much like an empty container to be filled with water. As Fotheringham (1966) and March and Simon (1958) noted, early theories in business organizations did much to foster the image of audiences as mere objects or persons to be acted upon. Early theories of Taylor (1911) and Gilbreth (1912) conceived of the employees who made up the audiences for management as essentially "passive instruments, capable of performing work and accepting directions, but not initiating action or exerting influence in any significant way [March and Simon, 1958]." Much of the research on mass media during the 1930s and 1940s implied that audiences could be treated as blocks of undifferentiated targets for political campaigns and commercial advertising. More recent research into mass communications refutes the myth of the audience as inactive listeners who sit pat, merely waiting for an opportune time to applaud or exit.

Another common stereotype stems from failure to separate the distinctive characteristics of audiences from those associated with public crowds. Current conceptions of crowd behavior stem largely from the early formulations of Le Bon (1895, 1960). In direct contrast to the notions of passivity and inactivity, Le Bon based his formations of crowd behavior on the pathological and the bizarre. Le Bon regarded public crowds as intellectually inferior to isolated persons and characterized a man in a crowd as "fickle," "credulous," and "intolerant." Contemporary theories of crowd behavior give tacit assent to the view of crowds as primitive and pathological. Smelser (1963), some sixty years after Le Bon, depicted crowds as "credulous," "excessive," "marked by eccentricity," and "clumsy and primitive." After reviewing the literature on collective behavior, Couch (1968) concluded that sociologists tend to use such concepts as "suggestibility," "destructiveness," "irrationality," "emotionality," "spontaneity," and "mental disturbance" to depict crowds made up largely of the lower echelons of society. As an alternative to a preoccupation with the supposedly "abnormal" and "bizarre" aspects of collective behavior, where scientific evidence is negligible, Couch stressed the need for understanding the relationships between crowd activity and the gathering of people for varying social interests.

Although far from conclusive, there are data indicating that audiences have two distinct types of effects on speaking behavior. The first is similar to that associated with the mere presence of other persons and is known as an *energizer effect.* The energizing influence is one which leads to a quickening of the senses, a state of heightened alertness or physical readiness on the part of the source. Since it is generally known that performance of well-learned tasks can be improved by heightened physical arousal, Zajonc (1965) viewed the presence of an audience as *enhancing* the *well-learned* or *dominant* aspects of a speaker's verbal activity but interfering with those facets which are poorly learned. Zajonc reasoned:

> Audience enhances the emission of dominant responses. If the dominant responses are correct ones as in the case upon achieving mastery, the presence of an audience will be of benefit to the individual. But if they are mostly wrong, as in the case of the early stages of learning, then these wrong responses will be enhanced in the presence of an audience, and the emission of correct responses will be postponed or prevented [p. 269].

Zajonc's explanation seems to account for the fact that some individuals tend to be stimulated to do their best in the presence of an audience. For others only frustration, anxiety, and diminished self-confidence result when an audience is present. In the early stages of a play's production, for example, actors often prefer to work on an empty stage, even though they feel a need for a full house on opening night to give a successful performance. In much the same way, amateur athletes are typically unnerved by the presence of too many spectators, whereas professionals perform best before a full stadium.

Evidence for the energizing effect of audiences is found in investigations by Zajonc (1965), Zajonc and Sales (1966), and Matlin and Zajonc (1968). Using various word-recognition tasks, Zajonc and his associates reported the probability that individuals will rely on well-learned (dominant) words more when an audience is present than when they work alone. It is not clear, however, whether the energizing effect results from the presence of an audience per se or from the mere presence of people as spectators. One study (Cottrell et al., 1968) shed some light on this problem by reporting that the presence of an audience enhances the emission of dominant responses by the speaker, while the mere presence of spectators does not. One thing appears certain. The so-called energizing influence changes the emotional state of the source, which in turn leads to either improved or impaired speech performance, depending on the degree of learning and past experience associated with the task.

The presence of an audience also effects changes in the nature of, or stand taken by, a speaker. Once a speaker makes a commitment or decision on a topic in the presence of an audience, it is less likely that he will later reverse his stand. Indirect evidence of the power of public commitment is found in some of the reviewed studies on conformity. In the Asch studies (p. 275), people who committed themselves to a given judgment very early in a session tended to maintain their stands over time. In a related study by Deutsch and Gerard (1955) line lengths were judged, as in the Asch studies, but under three conditions ranging from public to private. In the private condition, subjects marked their responses on a "magic pad" before seeing others' pads; each subject then erased his own response. In a second condition, subjects were instructed to make their initial responses on a sheet of paper which, they were told, would not be collected later. In the third and most public condition, each subject made his judgment on a sheet of paper, and then, after seeing the judgments of others, signed his name on the paper and handed it to the investigator. Results showed that conformity to the inaccurate opinion of the majority was greatest where a private commitment was made; in the situation where they had made a public commitment, people were least apt to yield to group pressure. Related studies by Fisher (et al., 1956) and Gerard (1964) confirmed the finding that the more public the commitment, the more strongly the stand will be maintained in the future. To fall back on a decision or stand made before an audience is obviously quite different from relenting on a commitment made only to oneself. A reversal on a public stand risks loss of self-esteem, to say nothing of the tension and general stress associated with the abandonment of public promises.

Audiences effect changes in the behavior of their members in ways not unlike those just discussed in connection with the source. The presence of receivers in the form of an audience changes the psychological mix, the social atmosphere and context of collective behavior. An audience, in other words, is not simply the composite of its individuals. As Turner and Killian (1957) and

Brown (1965) noted, an audience produces new psychological elements, a different totality. A number of different terms have been used by social psychologists in referring to the power of audiences to produce a sense of "collective oneness" or what Brown called "mental unity." The early writing of Woolbert (1916) made reference to "polarization" as an "all-to-one" relation among members of an audience. Much the same thought is suggested in McDougall's (1920) use of "primitive sympathy," which governs audience effect. "The principle," McDougall suggested, "is that, in men and in the gregarious animals generally, each instinct with its characteristic primary emotion and specific impulse is capable of being excited in one individual by the expressions of the same emotion in another . . . [p. 25]." Allport (1924) spoke of "social facilitation" as responses generated by the mere "sight or sound of others making the same movements." More recently, Miller and Dollard (1941) and Blumer (1951) spoke of "circular reactions," and Meerloo (1967) referred to "mental contagion." All these concepts underscore the tendency for the behavior of audience members to serve as cues for the behavior of others. In popular parlance we hear reference to the same thought in phrases like "being caught up" or "swept away" by the crowd. One giggle in response to a joke followed by more of the same from two or three others is often sufficient to produce a spontaneous wave of laughter. A few hand claps, robust shouts of "Amen" or boos can generate much more of the same, often several times over what initially triggered the reaction. In large audiences individuals tend to wait for the audience to react before doing so themselves. In short, the principle underlying the concepts of social contagion or "mental unity" is one of an increase in like response.

Personal versus Impersonal Contacts

The question of audience effects raises a related problem of determining the conditions that foster the perception of *impersonal* contacts. The boundary between "personal" and "impersonal" may seem tenuous and rather difficult to establish on numerical grounds alone. Clearly, a conversation among twelve people during a coffee break may be considered by a bystander to be strained and impersonal, while a speech delivered before a small audience of fifteen or so in a warm and congenial atmosphere may well be regarded as personal and even intimate. The ingredients that contribute to feelings of personal contact entail matters of psychological orientation, social climate, and prior acquaintance, among others. And yet another look at the progression from simple to complex social units may be instructive.

We have seen that the mere presence of people creates inner arousal or tension which often can be relieved by acts of personal recognition. Whether mutual recognition leads to subsequent interpersonal contact depends, among other things, on the expectations of each party and the nature of their first impressions. It may be tempting to conclude that face-to-face encounters between two or three people are, almost by definition, superior to impersonal ones. Yet it is not necessarily easier to "be oneself" where there are few people around. On the contrary, a small gathering often only increases the sense of strain, pressure, and responsibility. The reason is simply that there are a given number of pressures in any situation, irrespective of the number of people; these inherent social forces tend to be strongest per inhabitant in undermanned situations. Consequently, an insufficient number of people places all the more pressure on the average member to assume responsibility for participation. Also, recall the instability that is inherent in dyads and the struggles over the formation of coalitions where three persons are present; these frictions greatly heighten problems in their own right, particularly the difficulties associated with maintaining a variety of stimulation and an even flow of ideas from person to person.

As the number of people increases, a single person finds that he has less and less power over the direction taken by other interactants. Moreover, the inclusion of each additional member greatly increases the number of possible relationships until the distribution of overt contribution becomes more and more out of balance. This imbalance in participation heightens feelings of impersonality, as evidenced by problems in member satisfaction and morale previously associated with large social units. As the average amount of participation diminishes, people find it increasingly difficult to interact on a one-to-one basis. Eventually, an increasingly larger proportion of those present feel coerced by the majority; those who are isolated become discouraged from making overt contributions. When interactants feel they are in contact with "too many people," they react by directing comments to the group as a whole. In short, perceptions of impersonality stem largely from the potential for spontaneous, unconstrained interaction. Size mitigates against both spontaneity and the potential for relating to others on a one-to-one basis.

Given the picture just described, it is hardly surprising to find that the greatest variation in forms of participation (Thomas, 1959), and frequency of volunteering (Le Compte and Barker, 1960) occur in social situations where only a small number of participants are present. Also, the fewer people present, the more a premium is placed on each person's familiarity with the norms at work in the immediate situation (Wright, 1968) and achieving personal acquaintance with outstanding members of the group (Coleman, 1961). Consequently, the more personal the social climate becomes, the more the interactants feel a sense of solidarity (Slater, 1958), personal importance (Barker and Barker, 1961), accomplishment, and worth to the goals of others (Anderson et al., 1954). In further contrast to large social units, the smaller encounters have a high rate of active participation per participant, more social interaction generally (Bales and Borgotta, 1955), more personal greetings, and greater focus on face-to-face contact with those who differ most strongly from prevailing norms (Barker, 1968). In an interesting comparison of social activities in small schools and large schools, Barker (1968) observed:

> The students of the small schools report more frequently that they achieve satisfactions by being competent, by accepting challenges, by doing important things, by engaging in group activities, and by engaging in valued actions, all of which can be gained only by serious performance in the programs of the settings. The students of the large schools report more frequently that they achieve satisfactions by watching others participate, by mingling with the crowd, by learning about the school, and by gaining points, none of which require serious performance in the school settings. Performance satisfactions undoubtedly elicit stronger goal actions than visitor and spectator satisfactions, and the former are available to almost all students of the small schools but only to those students of the large school who have not been vetoed or allowed to veto themselves from the performance zones of the setting [pp. 202–203].

As interaction becomes increasingly less differentiated and impersonal, the behavior of those present follows more and more along lines of mental unity or contagion effects mentioned earlier (p. 281). Since only a small proportion of people can interact in an explicit verbal manner at any one time, a person must rely on the larger, undifferentiated responses of others as clues to his own actions. Sometimes the facilitating effects of contagion fit in well with the aims of whoever is in control at the moment. In others they have the opposite effect. Examples of reinforcing and facilitating social responses include standing ovations, waves of laughter in response to an entertainer, mass rallies and demonstrations, and spontaneous testimonials at religious revivals. The opposite type of undifferentiated social behavior, one triggering disruption and confusion, occurs in a situation when a handful of people begin to act in ways that are instinctively followed by all others present. One case in point is the protest action of a group of people who deliberately walk out of an auditorium in the middle of a speech and a mass defection follows. Some of the more spectacular forms of disruption, which attest to the enormous power of audience response, are illustrated by reports of audience panic. One such chain response was given in the following account by Brown (1965):

> Eugene O'Neill's *Long Day's Journey into Night* opened in Boston several years ago with Florence Eldridge and Frederic March. The play is a harrowing one and the audience was properly filled with pity and terror the night we were there. Suddenly the first row of the audience was on its feet *and then the second and with a smooth motion each successive row went up. The wave reached us in the balcony in a few seconds and swept us to our feet in our turn.* The actors cut off their speeches; the audience strained

forward. We stood so for half a minute. I heard someone say "Fire" and I looked around to check the exits. An elderly man started to move out to the aisle and when he stumbled over my feet I remember that I felt a kind of rage at him for blocking my path.

Frederic March stepped to the footlights and calmly said, "Please be seated, ladies and gentlemen, nothing serious has happened. Just a little accident with a cigarette." Then for the first time we saw a curl of smoke, an innocuous curl it seemed, since March was saying: "The fire is out now and if you will sit down again we can resume." He walked off the stage looking like Frederic March and came immediately out again, totally in character, and speaking his entrance lines. The audience laughed and sat down [p. 714].

Sometimes the outcome is not so fortunate. Comedian Eddie Foy (1928) gave the following account of an afternoon performance at the Iroquois Theatre in Chicago in December, 1903:

As I ran around back of the rear drop, I could hear the murmur of excitement growing in the audience. Somebody had of course yelled "Fire!"— there is almost always a fool of that species in an audience; and there are always hundreds of people who go crazy the moment they hear the word. The crowd was beginning to surge toward the doors and already showing signs of a stampede. Those on the lower floor were not so badly frightened as those in the more dangerous balcony and gallery. Up there they were falling into panic.

I began shouting at the top of my voice, "Don't get excited. There's no danger. Take it easy!" And to Dillea, the orchestra leader, "Play, start an overture, anything! But play!" Some of his musicians were fleeing, but a few, and especially a fat little violinist, stuck nobly.

I stood perfectly still, hoping my apparent calm would have an equally calming effect on the crowd. Those on the lower floor heard me and seemed somewhat reassured. But up above, and especially in the gallery, they had gone mad.

As I left the stage the last of the ropes holding up the drops burned through, and with them the whole loft collapsed with a terrifying crash, bringing down tons of burning material. With that, all the lights in the house went out and another great balloon of flame leaped out into the auditorium, licking even the ceiling and killing scores who had not yet succeeded in escaping from the gallery [pp. 73–74].

The first of the two incidents described above bordered on panic; then, with the admonition of one man, it returned to near normalcy. In the second, the forces of panic were too strong to be checked by the attempted communication of any one individual. The difference, then, was largely one of the potential for behavior to be determined through communication on a one-to-group basis. So long as such explicit verbal interchange is still possible, the activity of the given social aggregate still falls within the domain of interpersonal contacts. However, once the forces of contagion reach panic proportions, the responses of those present may be properly termed collective behavior but not interpersonal in the sense used in this chapter. The boundary between the personal and the impersonal cannot be fully understood apart from the physical environment in which the interaction takes place. What man senses as personal depends in part on his response to his immediate physical situation. In the next chapter we will examine the fascinating interplay that continuously occurs between man as communicator and man as respondent to his physical surroundings.

SUGGESTED READINGS

Altman, I., and **Haythorn, W.** "The Ecology of Isolated Groups," *Behavioral Science,* 12:169–182, 1967.

Altman, I., and **Haythorn, W.** "Interpersonal Exchanges in Isolation," *Sociometry,* 28:411–426, 1965.

Back, K. W., and **Davis, K. E.** "Some Personal and Situational Factors Relevant to the Consistency and Prediction of Conforming Behavior," *Sociometry,* 28:227–240, 1965.

Couch, C. "Collective Behavior: An Examination of Some Stereotypes," *Social Problems,* 15:310–322, 1968.

Gouldner, A. "The Norm of Reciprocity: A Preliminary Statement," *American Sociological Review,* 29:161–178, 1960.

Hare, A. P. "Group Size," in *Handbook of Small Group Research.* New York: Free Press, 1962, pp. 224–245.

Iscoe, I., and **Williams, M. S.** "Experimental Variables Affecting the Conformity Behavior of Children," *Journal of Personality,* 31:234–246, 1963.

Jones, E. E., Jones, R. G., and **Gergen, K. J.** "Some Conditions Affecting the Evaluations of a Conformist," *Journal of Personality,* 31:270–288, 1963.

Nord, W. R. "Social Exchange Theory: An Integrative Approach to Social Conformity," *Psychological Bulletin,* 71:174–208, 1969.

Slater, P. "Contrasting Correlates of Group Size," *Sociometry,* 21:129–139, 1958.

Thomas, E. J., and **Fink, C. I.** "Effects of Group Size," *Psychological Bulletin,* 60:371–384, 1963.

Zajonc, R. "Attitudinal Effects of Mere Exposure," *Journal of Personality and Social Psychology: Monograph Supplement,* 9:1–27, June 1968.

Zajonc, R. "Social Facilitation," *Science,* 149:269–274, 1965.

Zubek, J. P. (ed.). *Sensory Deprivation: Fifteen Years of Research.* New York: Appleton-Century-Crofts, 1969.

four

the socio-cultural system

eight
situational
geography

One important tenet of communication asserts that human interaction must be examined in its *proper context*. Communication is not something that merely happens, devoid of background or context. It is neither a pure process nor an isolated phenomenon. Rather, an act of communication is something that is defined by a particular set of forces at work in the immediate physical environment: coffee shop or patio, station wagon or reception room, crowded ghetto or isolated ranch. Communication cannot be regarded meaningfully as a process of individuals reacting solely to messages; ordinarily there is no way to divorce the particular meaning of verbal and nonverbal cues from the significance of the larger social context in which they occur. Hence, to assert that given persons are engaged in an act of communication is to say that they are somehow interacting in ways in which the setting imposes on the significance of their behavior. One of the most well-documented findings in communication research is that human beings react to face-to-face encounters in ways that are invariably determined by environmental influences (Davitz, 1964; Manis,

1967; Mehrabian, 1968; Sherif, 1967). Situational elements define matters both of mood and atmosphere, of content and relationship. Contextual factors also help to define the exact physical orientation that people maintain toward each other. Moreover, the physical distance established by the interactants serves as a constraint on the number of people who can comfortably engage in communication at any given point. In short, the impact of man's surroundings is so pervasive that the meaning of any message is dependent upon the total influences at work in a dynamic, ever-changing setting.

The claim that communication must be placed in a particular physical, social, and cultural context creates a potential obstacle to our study. Simply stated, the question is whether one can even expect to study *context* when the characteristics of each communicative setting are themselves unique —not only unique but ever-changing. The atmosphere of a room, for example, consists of such fluctuating factors as temperature, color and lighting, time of day, amount of background noise, and so forth; what further complicates matters is the extent to which these situational factors are also in a state of change. Also important is the fact that a person's perception of even the stationary, fixed aspects of the surroundings is itself in a state of constant flux.

The problem posed by the uniqueness and changing nature of each communicative setting can be reduced to more manageable proportions only by looking at the dynamics of situations in somewhat idealized and abstract form. Like the methods of geography, where the physical environment is studied by generalizing from physical characteristics common to particular *types* of land mass, the communication scientist may make profitable use, on a limited scale, of an idealized form that may be termed the *situational geography* of communication. When viewed from a geographical standpoint, every communicative setting, no matter how unique or changeable, may be analyzed from within a geographical matrix consisting of the dimensions of *space, time,* and *physical setting.*

The concepts of space, time, and setting all have a dual aspect. One is *physical,* the other *psychological.* For example, the spatial dimension of a communicative situation includes all the purely physical matters of distance and size, whereas the personal or psychological components pertain to how people interpret and use space in maintaining their relationships with others. The temporal dimension covers both the actual physical changes that occur over time in given settings—fluctuations in light and temperature, physical atmosphere, and the like. On the psychological side is the human perception of time. It has been repeatedly found that people differ greatly in their orientations and attitudes toward time and that these differences manifest themselves in matters ranging from promptness and scheduling of interpersonal contacts to the actual rate and sequence of a communicative exchange itself. Finally, the notion of physical setting covers all the fixed physical characteristics of a communicative setting—architecture and furniture, all the physical conditions which affect the way individuals relate to each other. In subtle and pervasive ways, the features of space, time, and setting influence the dynamic interplay between the physical environment and the social-psychological aspects of human communication.

SPACE

It is natural to think of space in physical terms. Physical space is stationary and immobile. Although the physical attributes of space such as distance, boundary, location, zone, and territory are obviously fixed, this does not mean that they merely exert a massive or incidental influence on the dynamics of social interaction. On the contrary, space in the physical world *acts upon* the range of human communication in the sense of virtually prohibiting certain encounters and assuring that others will take place. Without the expanse of physical distance, the possibilities for human interaction— except for language and time limitations—would be endless. If we suppose that all people now living on earth were placed in a setting as densely populated as a theater, everyone in the world would fit into a 300-square-mile area. Under such circumstances, by eliminating all physical boundaries, a person chosen at random could transmit a fifteen-minute message to any other person; thereby, with each person requiring the same amount of time to transmit the identical information to someone else, the chain of personal contact would soon reach staggering proportions. If two people convey identical information to two others during one fifteen-minute period, and all four in turn relate the same message to four others, the rate of diffusion would—sparing any duplication or inter- ruption—expand from two to four, to eight, to sixty-four, and so on until every- one in the world could be reached in the course of a single eight-hour workday! Clearly, sheer physical distance plays a major role in determining who has an opportunity to interact with any other given person. Given the reality of a world that is defined both by enormous overcrowding and by immense physical sepa- ration among people, the chances that one person chosen at random will ever talk with any other living person is more a matter of physical proximity than it is any other single factor.

Space, then, acts in a particular way upon man's behavior. More- over, as man defines the boundaries of his physical space, he in turn also acts upon that space. Every work of human architecture, every man-made object— from walls and maps, buildings and freeways, to city limits and national bound- aries—defines the units of human space. And in the course of defining his spatial domain, man determines what communication is possible and what is not. Then, too, the matter is further complicated by all the finer gradations of space, the subboundaries and physical objects that constrain or facilitate our use of space. Boundaries of public spaces such as malls and city parks invite free access and open exchange between the citizenry, while the spatial domains of private territory—patios and backyards, homes and trailers—have the opposite effect of preserving privacy and sanctuary. And in a less dramatic way, the smaller units of physical space, say a pathway or entranceway, exert subtle, pervasive constraints upon the physical arrangement of people who share common spatial territories, public or private.

Personal Space

Although space is a physical reality, it is also highly personal and subjective. All humans have a "built-in" sense of "personal space," a highly individualized and subjective awareness of space that surrounds them. This invisible boundary is personal in the sense that one feels immediate physical space "belongs" to him. W. H. Auden (1965) captured the personal aspect of space in his prologue to *About the House*:

> Some thirty inches from my nose
> The frontier of my Person goes,
> And all the untilled air between
> Is private *pagus* or demesne.
> Stranger, unless with bedroom eyes
> I beckon you to fraternize,
> Beware of rudely crossing it:
> I have no gun, but I can spit.

Ordinarily no one-to-one correspondence exists between the dimensions of physical space and the experience of personal space. Personal space simply cannot be understood in a yardstick manner. How much space "belongs" to a person depends upon the nature and requirements of the situation and the unique frame of reference of each person. When viewed in physical terms, some individuals have very expansive spatial boundaries, while others have a sense of relatively *thin* outer spatial boundaries. Katz (1937) likened personal space to the shell of a snail, an encircling extension of self. But unlike the physical space which has no center, the "shell," or membrane, of personal space has a center in a person's physic orientation. This highly personalized core may be considered analogous to a window through which an individual orientates all aspects of the physical world to himself.

Personal space bears only slight resemblance to the concept of physical territory. Sommer (1967) characterized personal space as fluid and mobile, something carried with an individual, while physical territory remains stationary. He also observed that men "usually mark the boundaries of territory so that they are visible to others, but the boundaries of personal space are invisible. Personal space has the body as its center, while territory does not." Lyman and Scott (1967) referred to personal space as "the most private and inviolate of territories belonging to an individual." It has even been suggested by

Horowitz (et al., 1964) that personal space is a buffer zone, a protective device against threats of bodily harm and self-esteem. Also there is evidence that people strive to enlarge the area of their personal space when confronted with stress-provoking acts by others (Leipold, 1963; Dosey and Meisels, 1969).

Space and Physical Orientation

If personal space has the body as its center, then physical space may be regarded as significant in determining how people attempt to orient themselves to their physical surroundings. Thus, the problem of physical orientation is a good deal more complex than the matter of proximity or sheer physical distance as discussed in Chapter 6. In physical terms, proximity is simply the distance maintained by any number of people who engage in face-to-face interaction. In psychological terms, proximity consists of meanings that are attributes of body movement and spatially oriented nonverbal cues from another person. Physical orientation, on the other hand, includes not only distance but also the larger interplay that occurs among the interactants and the defining aspects of their immediate physical surroundings. People, after all, orient themselves not only to the distance they maintain between themselves and others but also to the movements of all others *in relation to stationary aspects of the immediate situation*. The distinction between matters of proximity and physical orientation may be further illustrated by Figure 8.1. The solid arrows between person A and person B indicate the distance separating them, their proximity per se. But the larger matter of the physical orientation maintained by A and B is influenced by their relationship to their surroundings, both physical and interpersonal. Of relevance to this larger concern are, among other things, the distance between A and B and the other circles of conversation around them, their body orientations vis-à-vis one another (indicated by the arrowheads in Figure 8.1), the location of other people in the room, and the arrangement of physical objects. Note that each person orients himself by gauging the activity around him; hence, A notices that person H is walking toward them, but B does not. Such differences do not result so much from sheer distance but rather from the larger forces at work in the immediate physical surroundings of each interactant.

Despite differences, many principles that underlie proximity factors apply equally to the larger matter of physical orientation. It is, for example, as appropriate to refer to the maintenance of a "comfortable" physical orientation toward one's surroundings as it is to the distance between him and another person. Person B in Figure 8.1 may well feel comfortable in the distance he maintains from person A; but it is doubtful that he feels the same toward his surroundings and his remoteness from other circles of conversation. Conceivably, of course, the conversation is one of those where the participants happen to be oblivious to their surroundings, at least momentarily. In matters

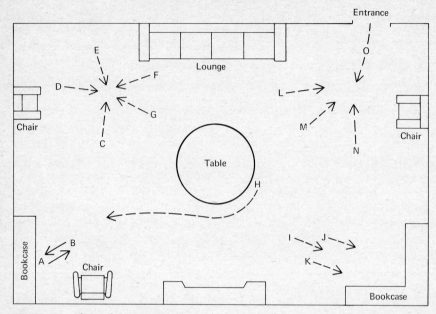

Figure 8.1 *Physical orientation between two interactants and their physical surroundings.*

of both proximity and orientation, much depends on such factors as personality make-up (see p. 233), degree of interpersonal attraction (p. 234), type and purpose of interaction (p. 233), activities of senses other than vision (p. 211), degree of prior acquaintance (p. 234), interplay between personal space and people (pp. 292–293), and, of course, the many consequences associated with intrusions of space (p. 235). When friction develops over matters of physical orientation, the reactions of each interactant are not apt to differ in *kind* from those previously associated with intrusions of personal space: changes in eye contact, gesture, posture, verbal interaction, and even involvement (see pp. 237–247).

Still, some complications are more characteristic of physical orientation than of the narrower concern with distance. One complication is the matter of how people orient themselves to a new environment. Goffman (1963) observed that people who are about to engage in social interaction tend to group in ways that make themselves and others open to maximum visual inspection. Physical orientation, then, entails the total positioning and juxtapositioning of each person present in a communicative situation. The constant body jockeying inevitably provides inferences and cues which people use, often unconsciously, in making their judgments of the approximate attitudes held by others and the nature of their respective relationships. It is not always necessary to have detailed information in order to make reasonably accurate estimates concerning the personal orientations which interactants maintain toward each other. Consider, for instance, the four movements depicted in Figure 8.2. Each diagram shows the general movement and body orientation of two men, one entering the office of the other. With nothing but the sketchy information shown, many people find they can infer something about the relationship enjoyed by the two persons. In fact, Burns (1964) showed versions of the diagrams in the form of silent films and found people able to accurately infer the type of social relationship that existed between the two parties.

Physical orientation depends in no small measure on degree of prior acquaintance. Strangers, when given the opportunity, prefer to maintain greater physical distance, remote seating arrangements, and—when proximity and personal contact is required—prefer a side-by-side orientation with another person, rather than a direct one (see pp. 296–299). The unacquainted also gravitate toward physical orientations which avoid full body orientation, seeking instead either back-to-back orientations or those which preserve the greatest degree of regularity of space from all others present. One example is the tendency of strangers to select that section of a row of telephone booths

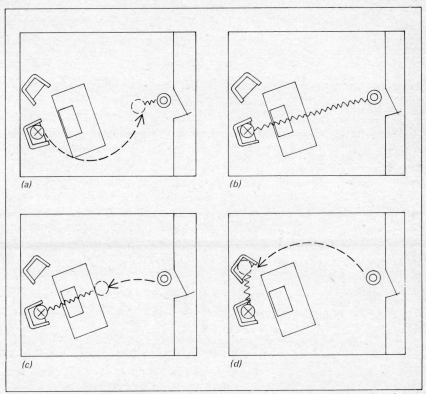

Figure 8.2 *Key movements between two men while meeting in an office. What do you think is the relationship between the men in each diagram? (Reprinted with permission from Burns, 1964.)*

where there is the greatest number of vacant booths nearby. Brown (1965) compared the physical orientation of strangers to the regular intervals maintained by "unacquainted birds on telephone wires."

Further insight into the complex matter of physical orientation can be readily obtained by creating a communicative situation in which everything is equal—or held constant—except for the body orientation of the interactants. Suppose, for example, that two people are directed into a room and seated on two chairs that have been positioned previously to face a place where another person is about to enter and sit down. The three chairs are six feet apart from each other, with the two subjects placed symmetrically toward the third person, an investigator, thus forming an equilateral triangle. While the experimenter speaks casually on ways in which people form attitudes and opinions about others, an observer who is stationed behind a one-way mirror records the body orientation maintained by the speaker toward each subject. Unknown to the two participants, the experimenter shifts his head and body slightly toward one of the subjects. After the discussion, the participants are told to fill out a scale designated as "most positive" to "most negative" in estimating what each thinks were the attitudes held by the investigator toward himself and the other person. Using the procedures just described, Mehrabian (1968*b*) found that body orientation markedly influences personal attitudes; subjects consistently designated positiveness in attitude in direct proportion to the time spent in direct body orientation. Incidentally, the results cannot be attributed to distance per se since it is held constant throughout.

Of added interest is the tie between directness of body orientation and judgments of personal recognition by others. Consider a case where people estimate whether they are being looked at by others oriented from varying directions, to the left and to the right of where they stand. Eye contact, of course, makes much of the difference in their judgments. So also does the directness of orientation maintained by various people toward each other. Even more important, however, are the expectations of each interactant. When people are lead to believe that others are about to show overt signs of recognizing their presence, they are far more apt than they would otherwise be to see the other persons—whatever their body orientation—as about to establish face-to-face contact (Nachshon and Wapner, 1967). Apparently, judgments of orientation reflect not only the "way things really are" but also personal expectations held by given interactants toward the body jockeying of others.

Investigations by Steinzor (1950) and Bass and Klubeck (1952) showed that a side-by-side orientation between two people promotes less interaction than one that places them opposite each other. In addition, Moscovici (1967)—in a study comparing the language styles of opposite, side-by-side, and back-to-back body orientations—reported that subjects speak more, use more verbs, and are more redundant when talking in a position that places them opposite each other. The conversations of those who sit side-by-side or back-to-back are found to be less spontaneous and fluid and are conducted in a style more nearly resembling formal writing than casual conversation. Such a finding is consistent with the experience of sitting side by side in a banquette in a restaurant and finding that the conversation somehow progresses with more difficulty than what commonly occurs at the small round table in the corner. For reasons that are not clear, females seem to have a stronger preference for interacting in a side-by-side orientation than do males (Argyle and Dean, 1965). In a study of the occupancy patterns at tables in a staff dining hall of a mental hospital, Sommer (1959) noted that more interaction occurred among those seated close together than those one seat apart, and still more among those seated at some angle than those sitting directly opposite or side-by-side. He found that women also tended to prefer closer physical orientations than men.

In a subsequent study of physical orientation, Sommer (1965) found that the physical orientation of communicators tends to vary with the type of interaction. Subjects were asked to complete a questionnaire which asked them to imagine how they and a friend of the same sex would seat themselves under four conditions: (1) an informal chat before class, (2) joint study for an exam, (3) study for different exams, and (4) an effort to determine who could first solve a series of puzzles. Preferences were compared also for either rectangular or round tables. The responses, shown in Figures 8.3 and 8.4, indicated a close relationship between the type of physical orientation and the nature of the interaction. In competitive two-member groups, the students clearly preferred to sit opposite each other. For the more cooperative situation, they preferred to sit at an angle, usually in corner-to-corner orientations. In unfocused interaction, subjects felt they would prefer greater distances and avoided any orientation which required facing each other.

Sommer (1961, 1962) also reported evidence for an "arc of comfortable conversation," where people were found to prefer the opposite rather than side-by-side positioning, but only so long as the available opposite seats were not moved closer than the space available side-by-side or farther apart than adjacent seating options. In the same study Sommer reported evidence that physical orientation, like so many other communication variables, is dependent upon the type of setting. In a large, furnished lounge, when chairs were set 5 feet apart (opposite or side-by-side), subjects tended to move the chairs closer together for conversation; they also mentioned how far apart the chairs seemed to have been placed. Sommer found, however, that chairs in most homes were typically positioned much farther than 5 feet apart, yet apparently did not, in the context of a living room, appear to be unnatural. This wide arc of comfortable conversation may result from the tendency of most people to regard their home as a place that minimizes secrecy, where friends and guests can interact in the most relaxed and spontaneous manner

Seating arrangement	Condition 1 (conversing)	Condition 2 (cooperating)	Condition 3 (coacting)	Condition 4 (competing)
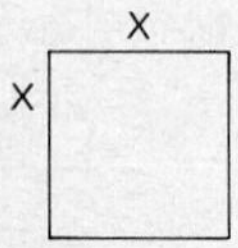 [table with X top, X left]	42	19	3	7
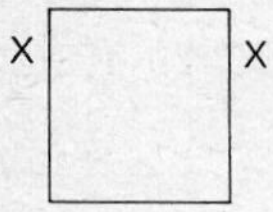 [table with X left, X right]	46	25	3	41
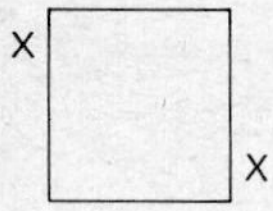 [table with X top-left, X bottom-right]	1	5	43	20
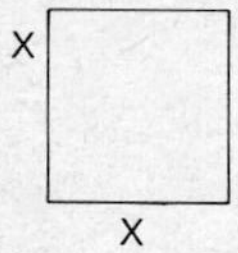 [table with X top-left, X bottom]	0	0	3	5
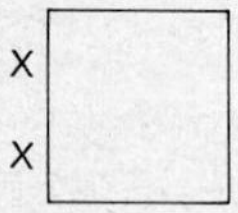 [table with X left-top, X left-bottom]	11	51	7	8
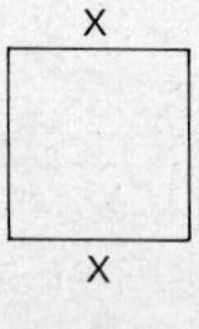 [table with X top, X bottom]	0	0	13	18

Figure 8.3 *Percentage of subjects choosing various seating arrangements at square tables. (Reprinted with permission from Sommer, 1965.)*

possible. In any case, such a finding provides additional support for the complexity of forces at work in defining the meaning of physical orientation.

The logistics of physical orientation cannot be fully understood simply by focusing on the behavior of people in isolation or even in relation to others. Individuals, to be sure, do orient their bodies in relation to the movements of others. But many of the forces which determine physical orientation are at work in the immediate physical surroundings. According to Hall (1959), Americans have characteristic ways of orientating themselves to the spatial

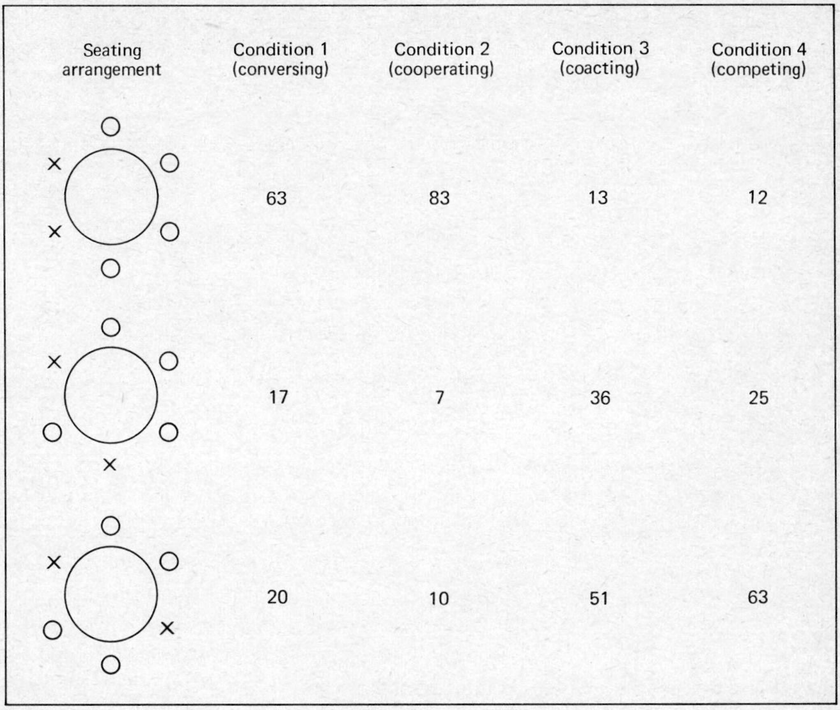

Seating arrangement	Condition 1 (conversing)	Condition 2 (cooperating)	Condition 3 (coacting)	Condition 4 (competing)
(diagram)	63	83	13	12
(diagram)	17	7	36	25
(diagram)	20	10	51	63

Figure 8.4 *Percentage of subjects choosing various seating arrangements at round tables. (Reprinted with permission from Sommer, 1965.)*

requirements of each social situation. One guiding principle ensures that whichever body positions are assumed, they will serve to divide up in roughly equal proportions whatever physical space is available. Hall cited the American business practice of dividing available office space so that a newcomer will have his "fair" share. Such adjustments are made voluntarily, often even when an office staff is accustomed to long-standing arrangements. A related custom is the familiar picture of a large room, the scene, say, of a reception or cocktail party, where people tend to gravitate toward walls and corners, preserving equal spatial intervals in such a way as to leave the center areas unoccupied for group activity.

The notion that certain social occasions require an equalizing of body orientation in available space seems to suggest a culturally defined pattern of behavior. Anthropologists have gathered considerable evidence to indicate that people in primitive cultures avoid orientations that place them in close proximity to walls and corners, regardless of how many are present. Their preference is always to be in the center of whatever space is available, even if it means coming into close proximity or even physical contact with others. Part of the explanation for the pull toward central space seems to rest in the learned orientation of particular cultures. This instinct for occupying central space, according to Eliade (1961) is all-encompassing in the organization of experience for the primitive man, whom he characterized as endeavoring to live in the center of the world. Eliade wrote:

> He knew that his country lay at the midpoint of the earth; he knew too that his city constituted the navel of the universe, and, above all, that the temple or the palace were veritable Centers of the World. But he also wanted his own house to be at the Center. . . . In other words, the man of traditional societies could only live in a space opening upward, where the break in plane was symbolically assured and hence communication with the *other world,* the transcendental world, was ritually possible. Of course the sanctuary—the Center par excellence—was there, close to him, in the city, and he could be sure of communicating with the world of the gods simply be entering the temple. But he felt the need to live at the Center *always* . . . [p. 43].

Probably the most recurrent feature of physical orientation is the way people gravitate toward the most comfortable position in establishing physical orientation toward others. By and large this takes the form of sitting in whatever position is assumed during the initial interaction. The best prediction of where students will sit in a college classroom on any given day is simply the position in which they sat—perhaps unconsciously or arbitrarily—on the first day the class met. The tendency to gravitate to favored locations, and to assume favored body orientations, is also common outside the classroom. We are all familiar with people who have "their" stool in a local tavern, or who head for a favorite seat in a restaurant, or who use a particular chair at home. Even in less frequented surroundings, people who are given a choice tend to orient themselves in predictable ways. Some head for the back of a room; others prefer the front. Some insist on aisle seats in airplanes, while others frequent window positions. Some theater-goers find themselves unable to fully enjoy a good movie if forced to sit in side sections; for others the opposite pattern holds. The urge to equalize available space in maintaining a comfortable orientation overlaps with another culturally defined pattern of behavior. For Americans, distance and orientation follow along functional lines. The key maxim in business, for example, is one of striving for the more efficient layout of physical objects in relation to the people present. Place objects in corners. Fill up odd spaces. Aim for proximity to entrances and file cabinets. At all costs avoid placing objects close together. The Japanese, in contrast, define their relation to physical surroundings in different terms, as indicated in the following commentary by Hall (1966):

> Lacking wide-open spaces, and living close together as they do, the Japanese learned to make the most of small spaces. They were particularly ingenious in stretching visual space by exaggerating kinesthetic involvement. Not only are their gardens designed to be viewed with the eyes, but more than the usual number of muscular sensations are built into the

experience of walking through a Japanese garden. The visitor is periodically forced to watch his step as he picks his way along irregularly-spaced stepstones set in a pool. At each rock he must pause and look down to see where to step next. Even the neck muscles are deliberately brought into play. Looking up, he is arrested for a moment by a view that is broken as soon as he moves his foot to take up a new perch. In the use of interior space, the Japanese keep the edges of their rooms clear because everything takes place in the middle. Europeans tend to fill up the edges by placing furniture near or against walls. As a consequence, Western rooms often look less cluttered to the Japanese than they do to us [pp. 49–50].

Some ground rules of physical orientation can be readily predicted and verified on scientific grounds. An interesting case in point is a study by Sommer (1959) that dealt with the patterns of seating occupancy during the initial minutes after the opening of a reference room in a university library. He reported that approximately 80 percent of the first ten people who entered the room alone each day sat at empty tables. In the instances where a second person sat at an occupied table, the choice was overwhelmingly the far end or middle seating positions. An added finding was that people who chose to orient themselves away from others already present drifted toward end chairs at tables closest to a wall or corner, particularly in the rear half of the room; they also showed a preference for the smallest tables and an avoidance of aisles and positions where they faced the main door. The greater the number of occupied seats, the greater was the effort to physically retreat. In a second phase of the same study, Sommer placed objects—either books or jackets—at empty tables and reported that the presence of these "territorial markers" protected individuals almost completely from occupancy of the seat next to them. The markers delayed the use of entire tables and diverted groups away from tables. Even where markers were used during peak library hours, similar results occurred. In a two-hour period, seventeen of twenty-five marked chairs remained vacant while none of the control chairs (without markers) remained unoccupied. Clearly, personal space rests on a complex interaction of forces at work in the immediate surroundings as well as in the dynamics of the interpersonal relationships and the frame of reference of each communicator present.

The importance of physical orientation does not diminish when a large number of people congregate. When an audience enters an auditorium, for example, the architectural planning virtually ensures that each member will find himself in close proximity to another. Lighting, ventilation, seating arrangement, positioning of aisles and platform all enhance feelings of uniformity. Practitioners ranging from politicians to evangelists have long presumed that it is better to turn part of an audience away from a small room than to take the chance of leaving a larger room sparsely filled. Unfortunately, what little research has been conducted has yet to confirm La Pierre's (1938) prin-

ciple that "spatial relationships of the members of an audience have a significant effect upon audience behavior." Thomas and Ralph (1959) and Furley
(1965) failed to support the import of compact seating and audience density,
though each was concerned with only gross measures of two classes of audience response, that of attitude change and retention, in the less than ideal
confines of a college classroom. The problem of measuring the effect of
audience density is compounded by the difficulties in attempting to control
individual differences.

The lack of reliable data on audience density is all the more puzzling
in light of the striking evidence that is available on the effects of overcrowding.
The problem of overcrowding stems from a certain physical orientation characterized by involuntary and often prolonged exposure to the presence of a
large number of people grouped in uncomfortable and densely populated settings. The evidence about such situations is consistent and striking. People
and lower animals alike react in aversive ways to situations that force them to
maintain unnatural physical orientation toward each other and common surroundings. In dramatic studies dealing with overcrowding among Norway rats,
a colony of rats was allowed to populate without interference in protected
dwellings complete with a food hopper, a drinking trough, nesting places, and
rooms for separate colonies to form. Trained observers recorded the behavior
of three generations of rats without intervening. At first their behavior was
normal. But as the room became overcrowded, certain disruptive effects
occurred—even though the rats' physical needs were all satisfied. Social
behavior became disorganized and unstable. The rats then ignored territorial
taboos and sexual rituals. Eventually the females neglected their offspring, and
the males exhibited "pansexuality," mounting other males and young offspring
indiscriminately, with intense aggression, biting each other's tails, and so
forth (Calhoun, 1962). In another study, overcrowding among rats led to dis-
arrangement of the females' reproductive capacities (Wynne-Edwards, 1962).
These findings are more dramatic than, yet still consistent with, the effect
previously associated with social facilitation (pp. 261–262). Recall also the stress
produced among both lower animals and human beings when in the presence
of too many others at one time (p. 261). Closely related is the finding that overcrowding among human beings is directly linked to social and physical pathology (Hall, 1966). There is, in short, no known evidence to conflict with Hall's
conclusion that "crowding disrupts important social functions and so leads to
disorganization and ultimately to population collapse or large-scale die-off
[p. 29]."

Status Implications of Space

One reason that people strive for comfortable spatial orientations is the critical
status implications of misusing space. Physical space, of course, knows no
status differences. In nature no one spatial area, zone, or territory is superior

to any other so long as other physical conditions are equal. Status is a uniquely human concept, both defined and sustained by long-standing cultural conventions which ensure that the "best people" are entitled to the "best places." An elaborate vocabulary preserves the sanctity of superior spatial domains. We commonly allude to "upper echelon," "first place," "top spot," "higher status," "upper class," "inner circle," "in crowd," and "headship." In face-to-face relations superior people find the "central positions," while less able individuals must be content to occupy the "outer," or "peripheral" spots. Superior status for most Americans, Brown (1965) noted, is largely a matter of being *above* or *in front of*. Being above is to be part of "high society," or the "upper class." The less fortunate must resign themselves to other domains in the social hierarchy—some gradation of "middle" or "lower." American protocol preserves the superior status of officers, guests, and speakers by assigning them to spatial positions "up front," or at the "head of the line." Presidents, jury foremen, and chairmen of the board assume "head positions," or "headships." Superior status is ensured by architectural designs which allot positions of higher status disproportionate amounts of space—often with spotlights, backdrops, podiums, and platforms. The priest delivers a sermon from an elevated pulpit, the politician speaks from center-front station, and the board chairman's office is on the highest floor of the company building (see Figure 8.5).

If spatial concepts are important in creating status differences, they are equally important in preserving superior-inferior relations (Russo, 1967; Sommer, 1969). The best people maintain their positions by an assortment of activities suggested by "looking down on" people who are "beneath" them. The best people are most apt to be "above it all," often because of "high motivation," "high motives," an urge to "move up." Those who strive "climb" or are "on the way to the top" or at least are "on the move." There seems to be some ethical sanction for space-status relations as reflected in terms like "above board," "on the level," and "highest of intent." For centuries the highest space has been regarded in religious thought as attributed with supernatural or transcendent qualities. The symbolism of traditional religious thought abounds with spatial reference to spiritual domains—typically evil is associated with the lower regions, good with the heavenly spheres. But how important traditional religious thought has been in the formation of ethical sanctions for superior spaces and domains is uncertain.

The close relationship between space and status can also be seen in descriptions of interpersonal relations. Some people are viewed as "close" friends, others are "distant." For those who are distant, we speak of "staying at arm's length," "being aloof," "keeping your distance," or "being withdrawn." There is an assortment of conventions associated with "staying in one's place." A study of jury deliberations by Strodtbeck and Hook (1961) reported evidence that jurors from professional classes sat at the head chairs far more frequently than did those from nonprofessional backgrounds; moreover, persons who sat in these positions also talked more and were perceived to exert greater influ-

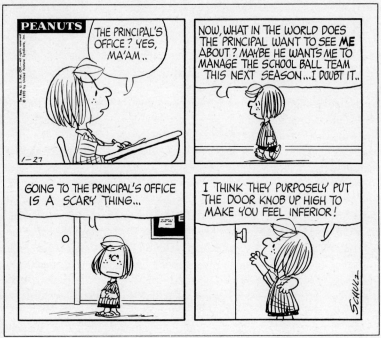

Figure 8.5 *The status implications of space.* © 1970 United Feature Syndicate, Inc.)

ence during the course of the deliberations than did those seated along the sides. The importance of the head position is suggested in studies by Bass and Klubeck (1952) and Hearn (1957): People who sit in head positions, it was found, attain higher status and talk far more than those who sit in other seats. Studies by Leavitt (1951) and Hare and Bales (1963) reported dissatisfaction with the group task and less group interaction from people who did not occupy central seating positions. In a related line of study, Howell and Becker (1962) analyzed the emergence of high-status positions in five-member groups where three persons sat on one side of a small rectangular table and two sat on the other. Results indicated that leaders tend to merge from the two-man side of the table more frequently than would be expected by chance.

The bond between status and seating position is further clarified in studies by Felipe (1966) and Lott and Sommer (1967). Felipe's investigation consisted of having subjects rank certain seating arrangements on a number of judgments including equality-inequality. Subjects considered dyads where one member sat at the head of a table as substantially less equal than dyads where both members were seated at the sides or ends of the table. Lott and Sommer pursued the related question of how subjects locate themselves in relation to positions already held by those of superior, equal, or inferior status.

The investigation used six diagrams of different-sized tables and questionnaries to determine seating preferences. Consistent with other studies, subjects identified end table positions with superior status; interestingly enough, when given a choice of seating at a square, four-position table, they indicated a preference to sit across from people they perceived as differing in status — either high or low. In addition, when subjects were instructed to sit at a table where a college professor (high status), a fellow student (equal status), or a flunking freshman (low status) were already seated, they again preferred seats located near those of equal status.

One question left unanswered is whether people actually *perceive* status positions in spatial terms. Perhaps the above evidence is explained simply by cultural custom and the ready availability of spatial terminology. In an interesting study by Dannenmaier and Thumin (1964), a class of forty-six nursing students drew pictures and estimated the height of four staff members whose authority differed — the assistant director of the school, the class instructor, the class president, and a fellow student. Results showed a significant relationship between authority and perceived size. School personnel were consistently overestimated in size, with the greatest error occurring for the one in greatest authority. The two student figures, on the other hand, were judged to be shorter than they actually were, the fellow student being reduced more than the class president was. Such findings are consistent with the classic study (Bruner and Goodman, 1947) in which two groups of children, one rich and the other poor, were asked to judge the size of coins and disks of equal size; both groups overestimated the size of the coins, the poor children by more than the affluent ones. Seemingly, then, the established connection between status and spatial relationships is grounded in language, culturally defined patterns of body orientation and movement, and even in perception.

TIME

Time—like space—can be considered either in an absolute and formal sense or in a highly personalized way. The formal or historical perspective treats time as pure and inviolate, like Newton's river of "absolute" and "true" movement. Historical time is a reminder of the irreversibility and succession of all human experience, an idea familiar to the ancient poet who wrote, "The moving finger writes, and having writ, moves on." Historic time is independent of human perception or eternal events in the physical world: A soldier must *wait for* the zero hour of an impending, irrevocable moment of battle. Yet, so long as we think of time as the movement of a pendulum or the ticking of a clock, its significance for communication remains obscured.

The awareness of personal time, like that of space, is neither constant nor precise. In fact, one of the most subjective and individualized of all human experience is man's orientation toward temporal events. An enormous amount of human energy is spent trying to repress time, distort it, even suspend it by futile attempts to live in "timeless human experience." It was Eliade's (1961) thesis that the sustaining power of primitive religion is embodied in various reenactments of sacred events from the mythical past as they were "in the beginning." The underlying meaning of religious ritual for Eliade is to be found in an experience which returns man to the spiritual purity of times past, that is by ritualistic participation in the renewal or rebirth of the beginning of time. This urge to recover the power of original sanctity may be why the passage of New Year, even in contemporary times, attains such significance in so many lives. New Year's resolutions and the promise of a "fresh slate" reflect a deeply important part of man's orientation toward time and temporal events—one prompted by a need for the purification of time and the expulsion of the imperfect. As Eliade (1961) explained, "It is not a matter merely of a certain temporal interval coming to its end and the beginning of another . . . it is also a matter of abolishing the past year and past time [p. 78]." Such an observation underscores the tremendous disparity that exists between historic time and our orientation toward it.

While no man can truly live outside time, an examination of our orientations toward time can enrich our understanding of the complex interplay between man and his environment. Each culture and each person and class within a culture develops characteristic time orientations which have far-reaching consequences on virtually all forms of social activity, particularly communication. Some anthropologists consider that a mature time sense, one consciously developed, directs the energies of people and cultures away from preoccupation with short-term activities and immediate self-gratification toward long-range tasks which require planning and an integration of interpersonal communication (Ketchum, 1951; Smith, 1952). Americans, for instance, have been found to have a highly sensitive, well-regulated sense of time. "As a rule," observed Hall (1959), "Americans think of time as a road or a ribbon stretching into the future, along which one progresses. The road has segments or compartments which are to be kept discrete ('one thing at a time'). People who cannot schedule time are looked down upon as impractical [p. 19]." This characteristic concern with time intervals, Hall concluded, places a premium on communicating at the right time, in the right time, with proper sensitivity shown to matters of planning, timing, scheduling, promptness, and, above all else, completion of the interaction within a *reasonable* length of time. Other cultures rank time as much less important than Americans do. Hall (1960) observed:

> In Latin America, you should expect to spend hours waiting in outer offices. If you bring your American interpretation of what constitutes punctuality to a Latin-American office, you will fray your temper and elevate your blood pressure. For a forty-five minute wait is not unusual—nor more unusual than a five-minute wait would be in the United States. No insult

is intended, no arbitrary pecking order is being established. . . . Further, the Latin American doesn't usually schedule individual appointments to the exclusion of other appointments. The informal clock of his upbringing ticks more slowly and he rather enjoys seeing several people on different matters at the same time. The three-ring circus atmosphere which results, if interpreted in the American's scale of time and propriety, seems to signal him to go away, to tell him that he is not being properly treated, to indicate that his dignity is under attack. Not so. The clock on the wall may look the same but it tells a different sort of time [p. 5].

The conflict over matters of punctuality reflects an underlying difference in the time perspectives of the two cultures. The set of assumptions in the United States rests on a heightened sense of time and a deep-seated need to preserve it. Americans' penchant for calendars, watches, schedules, deadlines, and appointment books all serve to preserve the discrete, digital nature of a formal clock. Wasting time or inefficient use of it, insensitivity to time, and poor timing are in themselves considered socially unacceptable. Specific time intervals are to be preserved against precisely held standards. When it's time for business, it's strictly business. Time, for most Americans, is to be treated as a commodity, to be attended to by accepted rules of measure and priority.

The formation of a mature time orientation is also central to psychological growth and social development. Many psychiatrists regard an individual's future time orientation to be a critical measure of mental health (Adler, 1925; Allport, 1950; May, 1958). Persons found to be psychologically disturbed are highly likely to have distorted time orientations, particularly with regard to future events (Federn, 1952; Fenichel, 1951). The pioneering studies of Chapple (1940a, 1940b, 1949, 1953) and subsequent research by Saslow and Matarazzo (1959) indicate that certain patterns of distorted time orientations can discriminate among types of mental illnesses. Attitudes toward future time also affect the social well-being of an individual. In a study of the time orientations of children, Leshan (1952) found that children who were socially and culturally deprived have very short time orientations. When compared with middle-class peers, children from less affluent surroundings are less able to plan ahead, show less responsiveness to promises of future reward, and are less interested in activities which involve a delay of gratification. Presumably, children who undergo prolonged deprivation in their daily surroundings develop a heightened need for satisfying immediate biological and social drives. Over time they are apt to become increasingly preoccupied with immediate needs, less with what they perceive as the indefiniteness and uncertainties of the future. As a consequence, the range of their temporal orientations shortens considerably. Only when the immediate needs of a child are fulfilled is a healthy time orientation—one which establishes a continuity of past, present, and future relationships and events—apt to be achieved.

Variations in time perspective are also found to be associated with differences in motivation, achievement, and numerous forms of social performance (Goldrich, 1967; McClelland et al., 1953). People who have a strong need for social achievement are found to be more conscious of time generally than are those with weaker achievement needs. The former are also characterized by a heightened sensitivity to the course of events. They are apt to see events in the physical world as being in a state of flux and rapid motion, and they also exercise more than average control over the management of their own time (Green and Knapp, 1959; Knapp and Garbutt, 1958; Meade, 1966). People with strong achievement needs are inclined to anticipate the proper time for engaging and continuing social interaction with others, and they tend to be highly affected by the experience of making progress (Knapp and Green, 1961). Such findings led McClelland (1961) to suggest that they are not only more sensitive to time than most but are more apt to regard time as a commodity not to be wasted. People with weak achievement needs tend to reflect opposite orientations toward time.

Influence of Time on Communication

In the interest of gaining background and general perspective, we have so far restricted our examination of the concept of time to somewhat idealized terms. However, time also has a direct bearing on the sequential aspects of communication. In fact, few of the major topics of previous chapters ignore the mediating influences of certain temporal factors. Perhaps a brief second look at some representative discussion of earlier concepts will serve as illustration. First, in Chapter 1 the emphasis on the dynamic aspects of communication rests largely on the blend of fleeting and momentary impressions gained of any given message cues. Recall, for instance, the postulate of irreversibility which insists that humans do not assign meaning or significance to messages in single, discrete points in time. Rather, as Whyte (1954) observed, "Time's strip of film runs forward, never backward, even when resurrected from the past" (see p. 16). Also the helical spiral discussed in Chapter 2 (Figure 2.4) gives visual testimony to the unfolding of communicative events along continuous temporal lines; and the notion of a communication mosaic (Figure 2.6) indicates how bits and pieces of messages, separated widely in space and time, become associated with a particular message set (pp. 45–48). Moreover, few aspects of information processing are interpretable apart from the effects of time. For example, the general problem of selectivity, and the details of the cocktail party problem (p. 83), center on the succession of times at which incoming sensory data assault the central nervous system. Were it not for the fact that more than one item reaches the receptor units simultaneously, the cocktail party problem would be no problem at all. Also, the enormous complexity of factors associated with the storage of information depends largely on the bond between a sense of the instant and those "indestructible vestiges" of memory mentioned by William James (p. 115). Furthermore, the very basic distinction between short-term and long-term memory results from differences in the temporal dimension of information processing.

In the interpersonal system, most of the effects associated with psychological orientation and attitude change stem also from the mediating influence of time. Recall the importance of those initial impressions of credibility and the sleeper effect, where the advantage of high source credibility remains for only a short time (pp. 147–150). Along related lines we discovered that most attempts at social influence produce quite transitory gains in persuasion; particularly is this the case in matters of primacy-recency (pp. 187–191) and the details of message organization (pp. 184–187). Further parallels exist both for nonverbal cues, particularly the effects associated with blends and microfacial expression (pp. 221–226), and the effects of feedback generally, as will be discussed in the section on delayed versus concurrent feedback (pp. 327–329). Also it is known that differences in the initial effects of communication networks diminish rapidly over time (p. 337). The reader can probably think of further instances where some sequential aspect of communication influences matters pertaining to social isolation, dovetailing of verbal responses, and many others. Clearly, the concept of time is necessary to account for a substantial proportion of communication effects discussed in previous chapters. We will return to the important matter of time in connection with some larger issues related to time-bound effects discussed in the next chapter.

At this point in our discussion, we can generalize and say that time influences virtually all sequential aspects of the communication process. Clearly, this generalization embraces a rather broad territory. It includes changes in psychological orientation; attitudes toward interpersonal encounters, particularly with regard to scheduling and keeping appointments; the rate and timing of a communicative sequence, together with any remark that reflects an orientation that is grounded in the immediate situation. Consider first a matter we briefly touched upon in Chapter 6, the problem associated with the rate and timing of what the respective parties to communication say and do.

Although the pattern and rhythm of interaction varies from one setting to another, there is evidence that the length, rate, and frequency of speaking, as well as the silent periods, remain for most people highly stable over time (Chapple, 1949; Saslow and Matarazzo, 1959). We are all familiar with the person who always seems to need the last word in any conversation or the one who simply cannot keep from interrupting others, regardless of the nature of the social situation. Then there is the person who always manages to measure every word. In sharp contrast is the person who dominates all phases of conversation—from the outset to the end. The very fact that these familiar patterns of interaction remain so stable results, no doubt, partly from learning and long-standing habit. A further element, however, is the regulative function of each person's time orientation. Generally, the more sensitive the communicator is to the passage of time, the more apt he is to be conscious of the timing, rhythm, and rate of his own voice, particularly in relation to the comments of others (Chapple, 1940, 1953).

The evidence for consistency in the patterns of verbal output does not mean that individuals are unaffected by the verbal behavior of others. We should think of consistency in communication rate and timing not in an absolute or static sense but rather as patterns modified by the other forces at work in the given situation. A small group, for example, may adjust to one highly verbal group member; yet if several members attempt to dominate, the consistency of each person's communication rate will be markedly affected, no matter how ingrained the speaking pattern. Borgatta and Bales (1953) compared the consistency of verbal interaction in a three-person conversation over extended periods of time. It was found that the lower the verbal rate of any two individuals, the closer the third person came to his own maximum rate of speaking.

In parallel lines of research, Kendon (1963) examined the time sequence of twenty-two people engaged in various communications with different partners. He recorded the rate and frequency of interaction, the lengths of silence, the total interaction time, and the delays in each person's replies. The results confirmed the larger evidence of consistency in the speaking patterns of each individual over extended periods, with a strong relationship existing between the length of silence of any one person and the total verbal activity of the other. Other research shows that the less the time pressure on a group, the more each person's pattern of speaking depends on the rhythm and timing of other group members over time (Matarazzo et al., 1965). In a follow-up study Kendon varied the timing of interviewers' responses to different interviewees. For those replies which were timed to follow immediately after each comment of the interviewee, there was increased consistency in the length, frequency, and timing of the interviewee's speech intervals. However, the condition in which the interviewer always paused for fifteen seconds before answering led to substantially shorter length of speaking and to increases in the number of total interruptions on the part of the person being interviewed. Closely related is the finding that the timing of responses in connection with positive nonverbal cues such as head nodding or "um-hums" leads to dramatic increases in the length of the speaking intervals of an individual (Matarazzo and Wiens, 1965).

As one explanation for the psychological import of time orientation, Aronson and Gerald (1966) reasoned that a person who thinks he has "excess" time in which to communicate some message to others is apt to "fill up" whatever he perceives as the allotted time. As a test of such a notion, a group of subjects was led to believe, "by accident," that they would have too much time to prepare a speech while others would not. Subsequently, when all participants were asked to prepare a second speech by working at their own pace, those who had been allotted "excess" time initially required far more time to write the second speech—even when given an incentive to complete the task quickly. The tendency of people to fill "excess" time underscores the impact which time orientation can have on subsequent expectations and even future social behavior.

Time orientation has been found also to play an important role in the attitudes which individuals have toward others in a social situation. A study by Frye and Stritch (1964) indicated that people who communicate under time pressure are less willing to accept group decisions and are far more apt than they would otherwise be to have feelings of resentment, rejection, and annoyance at other participants in the group. There is additional evidence that those who speak under severe time pressure are far less fluent and less able to coordinate their reactions to the verbal behavior of others than are those who interact where time is not a social constraint (Bass, 1960).

So far we have examined the effects of time orientation mainly from the psychological standpoint. It has been shown that time perspective is important in the attitudes, needs, aspirations, motivations, and efficiency which people demonstrate in face-to-face relationships. As a consequence of differences in time orientation, the very sequence of verbal exchange is often markedly altered. The effect of time on communication is a balance of stabilizing forces and those modifying influences which stem from the different verbal patterns of others. There is an equally important dimension of the relevance of time for interpersonal communication. Specifically, the other side of the coin is one pertaining to the overall changes that take place in situations where people communicate over extended periods. The effect of time on people who meet only once as strangers differs markedly from its effect on those who enter into an enduring relationship.

In essence time is on the side of increased stability, predictability, and equilibrium of the verbal exchanges that take place in face-to-face situations. There is, in other words, a leveling-out process, an evening of the patterns and rhythms of verbal interaction over extensive time sequences. In the course of the formation of a close relationship between two people or among group members, communication changes from initial halting and non-sequential forms of exchange to interaction which is characterized by symmetry and balance. In the early stages of interpersonal contact, individuals tend to be self-conscious, tense, and unsure of themselves and others. At the outset people tend naturally to guard against the risks of the awkward verbal reaction. With time the pattern of interaction becomes *in phase,* what psychologists call a steady state of *equilibrium.* With leveling and evening of communication comes common ground: People become more like those with whom they come into contact most frequently. Over time the strain toward symmetry in a relationship occurs simultaneously at many levels of behavior, including the perceptions and attitudes of the respective parties, their manner, tastes, and habits, and even the patterns of communication. Time, in short, works with the forces of stability and order in interpersonal relations.

SETTING

Time and space are always relative to the setting of communication. All three dimensions are needed to describe the situational dynamics of social interaction, for taken together they prescribe what communication is possible and what its outcome will be. So powerful is the influence of a particular communicative setting that Deutsch used the term "coercive" to describe its impact on human activity. Moreover, in an increasingly urban landscape, people find themselves being arranged and controlled by coercive locations which symbolize the times: high-rise apartments, hotel lobbies, convention halls and amphitheaters, condominiums, and freeways.

Certain settings have enormous power to separate people and, thereby, prevent interpersonal contact. Osmond (1957) referred to such "coercive" settings, and to surroundings in which people attempt to avoid communication, as "sociofugal space." In Sommer's (1967) words, sociofugal space "tends to be large, cold, impersonal, institutionalized, not owned by any individual, overconcentrated rather than overcrowded, without opportunity for shielded conversation, providing barriers without shelter, isolation without privacy, and concentration without cohesion [p. 655]." With the aged population increasing, the bleak atmosphere of enormous resident homes typifies sociofugal space in its most injurious form. It is little wonder that many who are confined to such lonely, bleak surroundings take refuge in the growing number of telephone services for the disconnected and lonely. In New York City, for example, an individual can pay $17.50 a month to receive two phone calls every day from "telephone companions." The brochure describing this service promises the alienated that "subscribers and companions . . . form warm, *lasting* relationships. Your companion is literally *someone who cares.*" In much of the forbidding public space of airports, train stations, building corridors, and lobbies, intimacy or even recognition among strangers is inappropriate and unwelcome. Furthermore, as the studies on seating arrangements readily demonstrated, it is precisely in large, institutional settings that some people deliberately remove themselves from interpersonal contact by using physical markers and even body orientation to avoid recognition.

Even minute features of many communicative settings can function to constrain interpersonal acquaintance. A number of studies show that the slightest details of architecture—the placement of entrances and doorways; the positioning of desks, phones, mailboxes, and file cabinets; the arrangement of chairs and the size and shape of tables and wall partitions—exert a silent influence on the meeting of personalities. Whyte (1956), for example, reported that suburbanites in the Midwest were far more apt to strike up conversations in two adjacent driveways than on the large areas of side lawn joining two neighbors' houses; presumably this is due to the tendency to regard the ordered quality of a driveway as somehow more comfortable than the undifferentiated expanse of the respective lawns. As a result of ecological research, Barker (1968) observed:

> Physical arrangements can enforce some patterns of behavior and prevent others. School corridors, for example, allow locomotion in certain directions only, their narrowness prevents the playing of circle games, and the absence of chairs or ledges encourages standing and walking and discourages sitting or lying. The layout of streets and sidewalks, the size and arrangement of rooms, and the distribution of furniture and equipment are often important factors in coercing certain features of standing patterns of behavior and in restricting others [pp. 29–30].

The power of the physical surroundings does not always rule out or force given patterns of behavior in a strict sense. Rather, as Barker (1968) noted:

> The physical forces impelling and hindering behavior do not have to be absolute, like a wall that cannot be breached; they can be effective by making actions of some kinds easier than others. It is physically easier to walk on the streets and sidewalks of the Midwest than to cut across lots; even dogs follow the streets and sidewalks to a considerable degree. In these cases, physical forces from the milieu mold behavior to conform to its shape [p. 30].

Clearly, the seductive power of man's surroundings is neither incidental nor accidental but is rather an active, potent constraint on interpersonal contact and subsequent interaction (Barker and Gump, 1964; Barker and Wright, 1955; Gump et al., 1957; Jordan, 1963; Raush et al., 1959).

The power of physical surroundings in delimiting human interaction is equaled by its force in fostering interpersonal contact. Research in settings as diverse as townships, neighborhoods, campus fraternities, and highrise apartments attests to the enormous influence of surroundings on such factors as frequency of interpersonal contact, communication, and subsequent patterns of acquaintance and friendship (Barnlund and Harland, 1963; Caplow and Forman, 1950; Festinger et al., 1950; Merton, 1948). Even the physical details of a building are known to play an important part in determining who comes in contact with whom and something of the friendships that emerge among residents of, say, a housing development. In the classic Westgate study conducted by Festinger (et al., 1950), the most minute factors of physical distance and building design were found to be major determinants of the formation of friendships. Sixty-five percent of all interpersonal contact occurred among people living in the same building, even though the various buildings all had ready access (see Figure 8.6a). Specifically, residents living in building C clearly had access to other buildings, for their sidewalk served as a direct link. And yet well over half of the residents formed friendships with other people in building C. Buildings M and G were within easy walking distance, yet a family in building C was apt to know few if any neighbors in those buildings. More striking was the discovery that even with distances of less than 100 feet between, say, buildings A and B, a strong relationship existed between friendship and physical distance. Neighboring units (Figure 8.6b) were 22 feet apart, and the total distance between apartments at opposite ends of a floor was only 88 feet. As would be expected, the most frequent contact occurred between next-door neighbors—more than twice as many as between people living two units apart: in other words, as little a difference as 22 feet accounted for a major difference in friendship patterns. Only in the rarest instance did contact take place between families living as close as four units apart in the same building.

Equally significant in this study was the role played by the design of the Westgate buildings. People living on the same floor had over twice as many contacts as those on different floors. And the frequency of interpersonal contact depended on minute architectural details: Some groups of families, for instance, came into contact with others that—though relatively far away—resided next to stairs and entrances. Even the number of stairways affected

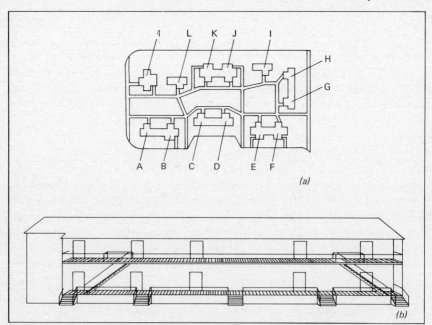

Figure 8.6 *Schematic diagram of the arrangement of (a) Westgate Court and (b) a Westgate building. (Reprinted with permission from Festinger et al., 1950.)*

the day-to-day contacts among residents; people at opposite ends of a unit rarely, if ever, met when stairways were provided at bòth ends of each floor. In short, there is much evidence that the physical details of communicative settings "determine not only specific friendships but the compositions of groups within these communities as well."

The discovery that physical geography has an important bearing on the initial contacts among neighbors does not mean that lasting relationships remain fixed by spatial requirements. Research by Priest and Sawyer (1967) indicated that residents of a university dormitory initially came in contact with those living next door but that friendship patterns over four years reflected factors other than distance, juxtaposition, and orientation of housing units. Closely related is an investigation by Barnlund and Harland (1963) which reported that the physical details of a housing development appear to be less and less important in relationships formed over *extended* periods of time. Such findings are consistent with the large body of evidence stating that virtually all communication variables operate not in *isolation* but rather in *relation* to each other.

Setting and Communicative Atmosphere

Physical settings also have a qualitative impact on what each communicator perceives to be the psychological atmosphere or mood. In part the question of atmosphere touches on matters of psychological orientation discussed in Chapter 4. Recall that simple environments, those lacking diverse, fluctuating units of sensory data, stimulate only the lowest levels of information processing. Further increases in complexity trigger higher levels of mental activity, until the point is reached where a person must reduce his intake of information (see p. 276). Also relevant is our previous discussion of the effects associated with social isolation: Lack of contact with the outside world soon created severe psychological malfunctioning (p. 256). These findings underscore man's need for optimal stimulation from physical surroundings. Some scientists hold that *variety* of stimuli is more important than *intensity* in contributing to the energizing effects of a given physical setting (Schultz, 1967). Lack of variety in physical stimuli create visual difficulties in focusing; objects appear fuzzy, depth perception diminishes, and colors soon appear more saturated than otherwise (Bexton et al., 1954). On the other hand, excessive physical stimulation can also produce adverse effects. Those living in noise-free environments, for example, have greater sensitivity to minute variations in sound than do those living in urban centers (Rosen et al., 1964). Furthermore, men whose professions expose them to great noise levels typically show greater hearing loss over time than do those not living amid constant noise. Little wonder, then, that the abrasive effects of excessive noise are so identified with urban atmospheres. Noise begins to irritate when it reaches 80 to 85 decibels. An auto-mobile horn honks at 100 decibels; a car muffler roars as high as 100 decibels; powerful motorcycles can bellow at 115 decibels, and so do pile-drivers, air hammers, and jet airplanes.

But the larger impressions of communicative setting stem from more than decibel levels, or even the variety or intensity of external stimuli. The noise that city visitors find so uncomfortable may hardly be noticed by long-time residents. Adults may consider a rock festival an ear-splitting atmosphere while younger counterparts regard it as "just right." Clearly, the complex matter of atmosphere reflects an interplay between the psychological and the physical. Yet even when allowances are made for psychological differences, the physical attributes of most social settings contribute markedly to the activities which people judge compatible or inconsistent with their immediate physical sur-roundings. For example, a cramped room with low ceilings, battered wallpaper, dim lighting, and a thick layer of dust is generally not as conducive to sponta-neous conversation among friends as a room with warm colors, cathedral ceil-ings, and a massive stone fireplace. What marks the difference is more than sheer physical space or matters of architectural and interior design. Each type of room invokes a different set of meanings. One is associated with open dis-cussion and the other is not. Similarly, a study area in a university does not invite the sort of interaction that is apt to be associated with a student lounge of equal size in the same building. So small a detail as the color scheme or the lighting conditions may markedly alter the moods of those present.

Atmosphere is not strictly a coercive influence or even a matter of psychological constraint. A school gymnasium may be ideal for boisterous activity and yet accommodate a solemn public ceremony. But this is not to say that a public ceremony, when held in a gym, would have the same ambience as one in a massive cathedral. A study by Vidulich and Wilson (1967) underscored the influence which physical settings have on the psychological atmosphere and, in turn, on the dynamics of social interaction. In rooms with distinct aesthetic characteristics—a university coffee shop and a university library—a confederate initiated a conversation with the first undergraduate she encoun-tered alone at a table. Glancing nonchalantly at two cartoons in a book she was carrying, she explained that the book was borrowed and that she was looking at it for the first time. The results of several such encounters showed that the amount of amused reactions on the part of the subjects was closely associated with the atmosphere in which the interaction took place; approximately twice as much laughter and interested verbal reaction to the cartoon occurred in the coffee shop. This finding supports the approach taken by Maslow and Mintz (1956) in a most interesting study of the short-range effects of three aesthetic conditions on social interaction. The study involved the use of three rooms: one which people had previously described as "attractive," "pretty," "comfortable," and "pleasant"; one which had earlier invoked impressions of "horrible," "disgusting," "ugly," and "repulsive"; and one which was described simply as "a nice place to work in." In each of the three conditions participants were asked to judge ten negative-print photographs with these instructions:

> We are conducting an experiment on facial stereotypy. You are familiar with Shakespeare's Cassius who had a lean and hungry look; this is an example of facial stereotypy. There cannot be any right or wrong answers as we are interested in the *impressions* faces give you.

At this point the photographs were shown to the subjects, and the rest of the instructions were given:

> In just the same way as these lines appeared to have particular concept characteristics, we think faces will have certain trait characteristics. You are going to see negative prints like this sample. By negative printing, and dressing the people in this unusual fashion, we minimized hairline, clothing, and expression and emphasized bone structure and shape. We want you to give your impressions of these faces, similar to the way you gave impressions of the lines shown previously.

As predicted, a close relationship emerged between judgments of the photographs and the atmosphere in which the task was completed. Those who completed the task in the beautiful room made significantly higher rankings than did individuals in "average" or "ugly" rooms. In the most attractive and satisfying setting, subjects perceived the photographs as being high on the dimensions of "energy" and "well-being," whereas those in the other two conditions saw the photographs in the range of "fatigued" and "displeased," according to the scales used in the study. What is so significant about these differences is that they occurred in the absence of any explicit verbal interaction with either the people in the photographs or others. The aesthetic and visual conditions in the immediate atmosphere were powerful enough to influence the subjects' perceptions.

In order to determine if the characteristics of a communicative setting have corresponding impact on the actual process of social interaction, a subsequent study undertaken by Mintz (1956) tested the long-range effects of the same "beautiful," "average," and "ugly" rooms used previously. Observational notes showed that prolonged exposure to the various settings had a profound impact on the psychological orientation and behavior of the subjects. In the ugly atmosphere, people had reactions such as monotony, fatigue, headache, drowsiness, discontent, irritability, hostility, and even avoidance of the room altogether after an extended period of exposure. In the "beautiful" room an opposite and equally powerful result occurred: Individuals reported feelings of comfort, pleasure, enjoyment, importance, energy, and a desire to continue their activity. It is apparent, then, that the effects of a particular setting are neither trivial nor illusionary. The physical attributes of a communicative situation affect the psychological orientation, perceptions, motivations, and even the overt interactions of those present.

The Interdependence of Communication and Situation

Two types of interdependence are implicit in the notion of the physical environment's coercive power on communication. One, the concept of interdependence suggests interaction or mutual influence. This occurs most strikingly within the communicative behavior itself, through the continuous influence each person has on what others say and do. The other level of interdependence, of primary interest in this chapter, is of a completely different order. It consists of the mutual interplay between behavior and the constraining influence of the environment. *This chapter may be taken as a denial of any notion which supposes that the sum total of forces at work in communication can be reduced solely to behavioral terms.* Nor can the interplay between man and environment be dismissed as less important than the process of interaction itself. Under certain circumstances, in fact, the environment may be far more important to the meaning of the event than the specifics of what the interactants say and do.

Also, we must guard against the notion that interaction between man and his surroundings is less mutual than his interchange with other people. Man *acts on* his environment, but man is also *acted upon* by the forces at work in his immediate surroundings. This concept is important, for it denies the possibility of ignoring or discounting the significance of situational and physical factors as somehow merely passive constraints. For example, schoolchildren act upon their surroundings simply by taking a short-cut across a vacant lot in an effort to get home quickly; but once the path is carved, the environment in turn acts upon their behavior by keeping them from straying off the smoothness of the path.

The question, then, is how to represent communication in all its incredible complexity, incorporating the interdependence of behavior per se with that involving the environment. One way to combine both levels of interdependence, behavioral and environmental, is to view their joint activity from a more inclusive vantage point than we have used in this and previous chapters. By using the perspective of *communication networks* in the next chapter, we will be able to better examine the accumulative impact of what Miller (1955) termed the "unthinkable magnitude of variables" manifest in social affairs.

SUGGESTED READING

Argyle, M., and **Dean, J.** "Eye-contact, Distance, and Affiliation," *Sociometry,* 28:289–304, 1965.

Aronson, E., and **Gerald, E.** "Beyond Parkinson's Law: The Effect of Excess Time on Subsequent Performance," *Journal of Personality and Social Psychology,* 3:336–339, 1966.

Dosey, M. A., and Meisels, M. "Personal Space and Self Protection," *Journal of Personality and Social Psychology*, 11:93–97, 1969.

Felipe, N. J., and Sommer, R. "Invasions of Personal Space," *Social Problems*, 14:206–214, 1966.

Festinger, L., Schachter, S., and Back, K. *Social Pressures in Informal Groups.* Stanford, Calif.: Stanford University Press, 1950.

Hall, E. *The Hidden Dimension.* Garden City, N.Y.: Doubleday, 1966.

Hall, E. *The Silent Language.* Garden City, N.Y.: Doubleday, 1959.

Hare, A. P., and Bales, R. I. "Seating Position and Small Group Interaction," *Sociometry*, 26:480–486, 1963.

Little, K. B. "Personal Space," *Journal of Experimental and Social Psychology*, 1:237–247, 1965.

Lott, D. F., and Sommer, R. "Seating Arrangement and Status," *Journal of Personality and Social Psychology*, 9:90–94, 1967.

Lyman, S., and Scott, M. "Territoriality: A Neglected Sociological Dimension," *Social Problems*, 15:236–249, 1967.

Manis, M. "Context Effects in Communication," *Journal of Personality and Social Psychology*, 5:326–334, 1967.

Maslow, A. H., and Mintz, N. L. "Effects of Esthetic Surroundings: I. Initial Effects of Three Esthetic Conditions upon Perceiving 'Energy' and 'Well-being' in Faces," *Journal of Psychology*, 41:247–254, 1956.

Mehrabian, A. "The Effect of Context on Judgments of Speaker Attitude," *Journal of Personality*, 36:21–32, 1968.

Mehrabian, A. "Relationship of Attitude to Seated Posture, Orientation, and Distance," *Journal of Personality and Social Psychology*, 10:26–30, 1968.

Mintz, N. L. "Effects of Esthetic Surroundings: II. Prolonged and Repeated Experience in a 'Beautiful' and an 'Ugly' Room," *Journal of Psychology*, 41:459–466, 1956.

Priest, R. F., and Sawyer, J. "Proximity and Peership: Bases of Balance in Interpersonal Attraction," *American Journal of Sociology*, 72:633–644, 1967.

Sommer, R. "Further Studies of Small Group Ecology," *Sociometry*, 28:337–348, 1965.

Sommer, R. "Sociofugal Space," *American Journal of Sociology*, 72:654–660, 1967.

Sommer, R. "Studies in Personal Space," *Sociometry*, 22:247–260, 1959.

Vidulich, R. H., and Wilson, D. J. "The Environmental Setting as a Factor in Social Influence," *Journal of Social Psychology*, 71:247–255, 1967.

nine

communication

networks

The study of communication networks examines the flow of messages from one person to another. A communication network resembles the operations of a telephone switchboard. Each man is a communicator, the mechanical apparatus is a channel through which information is transmitted, and each receiver is a destination. The capacity of any given network delimits the possibilities for communication, and the number of actual connections represents only a fraction of the potential arrangements. Each communicative act is itself a delimiting factor, because the decision to contact a particular party precludes other possibilities. Also, messages can be represented as a sequence of connections, or links, between two or more points in space and time. Each party thus forms one link in a vast, sprawling network that is limited only by its actual use, its efficiency, and the number of connections which define its overall organization and shape.

Note that by examining communication networks our focus shifts from the particular people and message cues involved to an interest in the larger operations of the network. In reality, of course, personal contacts are a good deal more complex than the one-to-one exchanges of a telephone; but the operations of a telephone system approximate, in principle, any complex network of social interchange. From this general vantage point, we can begin to understand the dynamics of communication networks. But first it is necessary to know something about the particular system under study: How many links and actual participants are there? What are their opportunities for contact? What type of interaction takes place? What is each person's role in processing information? How efficient is the transmission of messages? What time is needed to dispatch a message from one point to another? Finally, what restricts the use of the network—what costs, rules, regulations, protocol, status implications, and so forth limit its use?

Communication networks operate at all levels of interpersonal contact, their minimal requirement being accessibility. A simple morning greeting between new acquaintances, the verbal clamor at a lunch counter, the formalized deliberations of a state legislature, the buzz of conversation in a hotel lobby, and the shuffling of messages through a bureaucratic corporation all exhibit some characteristic pattern or structure in the way messages are transmitted. Some networks evolve naturally in a spark of conversation; others bear the stamp of long-standing traditions, institutions, or cultures. Some networks restrict the flow of messages through means as varied as loyalty oaths, customs, commandments, gentlemen's agreements, ethical sanctions, rules of protocol, parliamentary procedures, or even threats against the life or property of those who divulge information to outsiders; in sharp contrast are the countless situations ranging from international news bulletins to public forums and town meetings which permit free access to the information of a given network. The network of a rescue mission is highly mobile, whereas that of a high-rise apartment building is fixed and stationary. Indeed, although the ways to consider and categorize networks are virtually endless, this chapter focuses on one important dimension of networks: their *complexity*. Before we begin our progression from the simplest systems to the more complex, it is necessary to examine the role of a characteristic common to all networks—feedback.

FEEDBACK

The concept of feedback originated in cybernetics, where it referred to the principle of self-regulating mechanisms. An automatic, self-regulating system—or "servomechanism"—is characterized by a built-in source of energy which monitors or controls the output of energy or information. In essence what is actually *fed back* into the system is a signal which, by scanning the performance of the system, corrects indiscriminate errors and regulates output. In simplest form, the principle of feedback was used in the early devices to keep the sails of windmills facing the wind, in the mechanisms for steering steamships, and in the devices which control the flow of electrical energy through voltage regulators. In less crude form, feedback operates today in radar and sonar, in rocketry exploration, in radio circuitry, and in computers and other electronic devices.

The most familiar automatic control system in the home is thermostatic control. The thermometer in the thermostat registers the heat in a room; and the thermostat regulates the furnace, which in turn controls the amount of heat supplied to the room. Hence, the thermostat and furnace are interdependent causes and effects. A simple switching device in the thermostat triggers a signal to supply fuel whenever the temperature reading falls below one contact element in the thermometer; conversely, when the reading moves above the other contact element, fuel is no longer supplied to the furnace. This cause-and-effect relationship is not without error, however. In fact, the *existence of error* adjusts the operation of the furnace. The key to feedback is not in merely switching the furnace on or off. Many simple devices could regulate a furnace for fixed time periods, much as they do clock radios or toasters. The thermostat, however, operates on the basis of desired *actual performance* rather than expected performance. Actual performance, of course, must be *predetermined* by setting the thermostat. If the desired level cannot be maintained—perhaps because of a malfunctioning circuit or a sudden draft of cold air—the furnace will operate constantly.

The principle of self-correcting performance can be seen as readily in human affairs. In *Life on the Mississippi* Mark Twain described the depth-measurement techniques that were practiced by steamer crews navigating the dangerous channels of the mighty river. The helmsman established and adjusted his course by depth soundings taken and shouted back by the crewmen standing at the bow. He maintained a given course as long as the channels deepened, then made adjustments when a shallower channel was reported by the men below. The relationship between a steamer, its crew, and its environment is in essence the same for actions ranging in complexity from turning on a light to steering a car and using a typewriter. In each case some behavior produces or controls a mechanical signal such as the click of a light switch, the blink of a turn signal, the sound of a typewriter bell—all of which in turn regulate the human reactions throughout a given sequence of behavior.

Feedback is widely acknowledged to be "a requirement of all self-regulating, goal-seeking systems whether they be mechanical devices, living organisms, or social groups [Barnlund, 1968, p. 228]." So central is the concept of feedback to the behavioral sciences that some investigators consider feedback *the* basic element of behavior (Miller et al., 1960). Scientists also use the principle of feedback to explain the workings of the human brain (Ashby, 1954) and the production of human speech (Fairbanks, 1954; Mysak, 1966). While the self-regulating machine operates primarily on the basis of built-in feedback loops made of wire or other electrical circuitry, human behavior adjusts on the basis of physical and psychological links with the environment. The interdependence of human systems of behavior and the physical world was outlined from the perspective of feedback in the following statement by Cofer and Appley (1964):

> Reacting to disturbance (i.e., stimulation), the system (or any subsystem) responds. Its response affects the environment in some particular way, at the same time "reporting back" what has been done. The central regulatory apparatus then computes the discrepancy between performed and intended action and the succeeding response is "corrected for error." Such a sequence is repeated until the residual error is so small as to lie within the range of the target—or, in other words, until a stable equilibrium has been reached [p. 346].

Two examples of how changes in response affect the environment and vice versa were described by Wiener (1954) as follows:

> If I pick up my cigar, I do not will to move any specific muscles. Indeed in many cases, I do not know what those muscles are. What I do is to turn into action a certain feedback mechanism; namely, a reflex in which the amount by which I have yet failed to pick up the cigar is turned into a new and increased order to the lagging muscles, whichever they may be. In this way, a fairly uniform voluntary command will enable the same task to be performed from widely varying initial positions, and irrespective of the decrease of contractions due to fatigue of the muscles. Similarly, when I drive a car, I do not follow out a series of commands dependent simply on a mental image of the road and the task I am doing. If I find the car swerving too much to the right, that causes me to pull to the left. This depends on the actual performance of the car, and not simply on the road; and it allows me to drive with nearly equal efficiency a light Austin or a heavy truck, without having formed separate habits for the driving of the two [p. 26].

Although highly simplified, Wiener's description is essentially what happens in the feedback of a face-to-face encounter. At one point person A initiates a message and has expectations concerning the response from B. Once realized, B's response serves to correct expectations previously held by A. When B's response matches A's expectations, subsequent action is apt to continue along lines anticipated by both, in a manner not unlike the steering of the steamboat in deep water. Conversely, where there is a mutually perceived gap between expected and actual responses, each person adjusts his subsequent actions, bringing them more into line with the other's orientations. In the framework of Piaget (1950) effective social interaction requires a dovetailing of responses: Each person modifies his intended behavior in accordance with his anticipation of how the other will react to his message cues. In order to anticipate and adjust to another's feedback, one must have the capacity to view his intended behavior from two perspectives at once, his own and that of the other person. The description of two people who can't "get on the same wavelength" aptly applies to any situation in which the respective parties are unwilling or unable to dovetail their responses from this dual perspective.

One critical difference between the feedback activities of a thermostat and a human being is the checking level for sensitivity of each to error—the difference between anticipated and actual responses. The steering or checking levels of a thermostat are precise and unchanging. If, for example, they are set at 74° and 69° respectively, any furnace in proper working order can be expected to turn on or off whenever the discrepancy between the predetermined level (74°) and the actual performance (room temperature) is greater than 5°. In other words, the degree of error can be predetermined and held constant by the act of setting the thermostat. However, the level, or more precisely, the threshold at which information acts as a steering device in human affairs cannot be determined in so precise a way. Sensitivity to human feedback differs with the person, the situation, and the type of interaction. Equally important in determining human sensitivity to feedback is the *type* of feedback cues which influence people's adjustments to a given sequence of interaction.

Positive versus Negative Feedback

It first must be distinguished whether feedback has a positive or a negative effect on subsequent communication, and this distinction is not to be made in absolute terms. Generally, information that *enhances* behavior in progress is termed *positive*, whereas information that *inhibits* or revises behavior in progress is *negative*. Note that the definitions are based upon the way in which responses effect change in behavior and not upon judgments which imply that "positive" is necessarily "good" and "negative" is invariably "bad." They are, in other words, relative to particular types of effects. Positive feedback is not always socially desirable, and negative feedback need not always be considered undesirable. As a case in point, a person who makes a series of inaccurate statements could conceivably receive positive responses from a receiver who also happens to be misinformed; such a situation only leads to a pooling of ignorance and would not normally be regarded as socially desirable. A contrasting situation is one where a participant in a small group receives intelligent criticism from other group members, thereby learning from feedback which must be classified as negative.

As for their respective effects on communication networks, *negative feedback typically leads to the greatest modification of verbal behavior, while positive feedback produces a continuation or intensification of whatever is in progress.* This distinction is one of correcting and reinforcing influences; it is of critical importance to our general understanding of the flow of messages in communication networks. Typically, the greatest changes in communication networks occur whenever there is a sudden change from positive to negative feedback or whenever negative feedback increases in its intensity.

Striking evidence of the effect of feedback on participation can be found in the communication patterns in small groups. Bavelas (et al., 1965) seated four strangers around a table and told them to discuss a series of cases. In front of each subject, placed beyond the view of the other participants, was a reflector box containing two small lights, one red and one green, that were controlled by the experimenter. An initial session established a baseline for the amount of talk for each participant, and subjects were ranked according to their relative talkativeness. Then, before the next discussion, the experimenter announced that certain groups would be provided with feedback to promote better discussions: A flash of the green light would mean that a subject's statement was advancing group discussion, while a flash of the red light would indicate that a subject's statement was creating an obstacle to the progress of the group. Those who previously had spoken the least then received the greatest number of green signals, while the most talkative subjects were given a disproportionate number of red signals. The marked decrease in participation by talkative subjects who received more red signals provided evidence of the powerful effect of negative feedback. A corresponding increase in participation occurred among reticent subjects who suddenly received positive feedback.

The effects of mechanical feedback devices closely parallel those obtained by negative human responses. Participation has been found in a number of studies to decrease markedly when the receiver responded with negative comments such as "That's not true," "No," and "Sorry, you're wrong." Negative feedback leads to a rapid shifting from one topic to another and a marked increase in the number of defensive or hostile reactions by a speaker; positive message cues, in contrast, lead to a more systematic discussion of topics and more frequent expressions of approval and agreement on the part of the speaker (Verplanck, 1955). Similar findings occurred in studies that sought to isolate the effects of positive and negative nonverbal cues. Approving head nods, forward body posture, and steady eye gaze all signal approval, whereas nonverbal cues of disinterest or overt disapproval — even the absence of nonverbal response — have the opposite effect on the length, frequency, and tone of the speaker's comments.

In addition to effecting changes in how much a person says, feedback also influences the process of *what* is said and the *way* it is expressed. Numerous studies report that negative feedback produces problems in anxiety, personal manner, and fluency of presentation. A study by Miller (et al., 1961) examined verbal fluency under conditions of negative feedback (in the form of silence or nonresponsiveness) and positive feedback (interjections of the word *good* every twenty seconds). As expected, speech fluency was adversely affected both when negative feedback was applied to the speaker himself and when applied to the person who spoke immediately before him. Closely related is the finding that verbal nonfluencies increase dramatically and total verbal activity decreases as a consequence of negative feedback (Vlandis, 1964). Although there is evidence that negative feedback from just one person is sufficient to adversely affect verbal fluency and total verbal activity (Davis, 1967; Sereno, 1965), more severe effects on speech performance occur in audience situations (Blubaugh, 1969). Though results differ from study to study, negative feedback is known to produce twice the number of mispronunciations, word substitutions, stutterings, and other forms of nonfluency that occur normally in social conversation.

Since the effect of negative feedback rests ultimately in the eye of the beholder, some people can distort the meanings of another's responses and thereby neutralize or counteract the influence of feedback cues. Studying the reactions of normal and delinquent adolescents to situations involving praise and blame, McDavid and Schroder (1957) found that delinquent subjects tend to interpret praise (positive feedback) and criticism (negative feedback) in the exact opposite sense in which they were intended. The delinquent subjects apparently had received so much criticism in the past that they had come to expect it. They could interpret only critical reactions from others as acceptable and consistent with their expectations and frame of reference. Praise was immediately suspect, a matter to be regarded as dishonest and phony. Closely related is the finding that the predictable effects of varying feedback cues may be altered substantially when they are associated with varying degrees of accompanied silence (Buchwald, 1959; Meyer and Seidman, 1961). An approving comment uttered after prolonged silence means something quite different from the same reply made instantly. Another clue to the significance of the perception of feedback is suggested by the finding that aversion to negative feedback increases when people suddenly find themselves in positions of power or authority (Nokes, 1961).

Concurrent versus Delayed Feedback

Not all feedback occurs immediately after each sequence in a social interaction. Therefore, the concurrent-delayed dimension is necessary to account for those effects which result from the degree of delay in feedback reactions. A substantial proportion of human communication involves some delay in feedback. In the case of mass communication, virtually all reaction is of a delayed nature. But even in spontaneous, face-to-face conversation, delays of a moment or several seconds are quite common. Ordinarily, there is no way to standardize the meaning of even the briefest delay in feedback. Some people are psychologically comfortable in waiting through periods of verbal hesitations, pauses, and even extended periods of silence before others react to their comments. Other people have little tolerance for even minute delay in the responses gained from other interactants. In either case, the importance of delayed feedback depends on factors as diverse as past acquaintance, psychological orientation, type of personal relationship, and perceived importance of time and pressure to complete a particular interaction. Nevertheless, consistent delays in feedback often imply a state of uncertainty, anxiety, or misunderstanding on one hand, or a reflective weighing of each idea on the other, depending of course on the respective parties and the nature of the situation.

Delayed feedback also has a marked influence on encoding behavior. One case in point is where subjects engage in problem-solving tasks that require each to describe unique geographical designs for which no familiar names are provided to assist in the descriptions. In short, the person must somehow come up with his own set of labels. Therefore, by varying the feedback conditions and by studying each attempt to describe the designs, a reasonable inference can be drawn about the effects of delayed feedback on encoding. During the initial phases of the discussion, the participants tend to describe the unnamed figures in phrases that are long and syntactically complex; this indicates that they are having difficulty in encoding or orally describing the abstract features of the designs. Thereafter, the subjects describe other figures under various feedback conditions. What happens is that concurrent feedback produces a trend toward shorter sentences and phrases. Apparently, the very presence of concurrent feedback increases the rate and efficiency at which people translate their thoughts into speech. Also, the very shortening of phrases and sentences under concurrent feedback suggests that the communicators become increasingly confident of their ability to describe abstract figures, at least so long as they perceive their listeners as reacting immediately to their verbal comments (Krauss and Weinheimer, 1964, 1966).

The finding that concurrent feedback is necessary for encoding efficiently is consistent with evidence that only a fraction of a second's delay in hearing one's voice seriously impairs speech production. Most research on delayed speech feedback is conducted by having subjects speak while hearing their voices played back through earphones. A pioneering study by Fairbanks (1954) reported that subjects who read prose selections under the slightest delay of speech feedback produced a number of articulatory errors, increases in volume, longer average pronunciation time, and heightened emotional stress. Subsequent research noted that delays of as little as 0.03 to 0.3 second produce a range of adverse effects in speaking: repetition of syllables (Lee, 1950); mispronunciations (Atkinson, 1953); omissions (Tiffany and Hanley, 1956); substitutions (Fairbanks and Guttman, 1958); increased sentence and syllable duration time (Black, 1955); and increases in heart rate and numerous other physiological measures of emotional stress (Yates, 1963). Although these findings pertain solely to speech production, they are consistent with evidence that delays in feedback greatly impair encoding performance and psychological well-being of people engaged in social conversation (Argyle and Kendon, 1967).

Free versus Zero Feedback

In addition to variations in the type and timing of response, feedback also differs in the *amount* or *degree* of response available at any given time. *Free feedback* refers to maximum possible reaction, and *zero feedback* indicates the total absence of overt response to communication. Just as people vary in the degree of their sensitivity to the reactions of others, so also do they differ in the degree of their responsiveness to others. The stoic, poker-faced person exemplifies something approximating zero feedback, while an animated, physically active receiver approaches free feedback. A study by Scheidel and Crowell (1966) of feedback in small groups shed important light on the nature of individual differences in responsiveness. Recordings were made of the total number of "initiating comments" and "feedback comments" of each participant. Feedback ratios were then devised by dividing each person's reactions by the total number of his overt contributions. Such a ratio provided a single measure of approximately how much time a subject spent reacting or giving explicit verbal feedback to others in contrast to how much time he spent initiating or introducing his own views and opinions. The investigators then compared the ten subjects who had the highest feedback ratios with those who had the lowest ratios. Those who spent the greatest proportion of time providing maximum or free feedback scored highest on a measure of achievement motivation, dominance, and power, but low on tests of sociability and affiliation. Neither the high nor the low test scores characterized those subjects who ranked low on the feedback ratios. Such consistent differences between those who tend to give maximum feedback and those who do not suggest that responsiveness to communication is a function of the personality of an individual.

Differences between free and zero feedback have a direct bearing on the flow of messages in dyadic networks. An important investigation by Leavitt and Mueller (1951) required a class instructor to describe one of a series of abstract geometric patterns to another person, who then had to reproduce the unseen pattern by relying solely on the oral description (see Figure 9.1). Using two instructors and four groups of subjects, the task was completed under four degrees of feedback: (1) zero feedback, in which the source was not visible to the receiver and no questions or discussion were permitted; (2) a visible-audience condition, in which participants could see each other but could not talk; (3) a "yes-no" condition, in which communication was permitted only in the form of questions to be answered by "yes" or "no"; and (4) a free-feedback condition, in which full verbal exchange was allowed. Findings

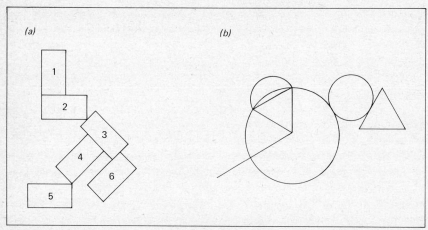

Figure 9.1 *Two designs used in feedback experiments. Under varying conditions of feedback, and relying solely on verbal descriptions, subjects are asked to reproduce the designs. (Reprinted with permission from Leavitt and Mueller, 1951.)*

showed that mean accuracy scores increased markedly as conditions changed from zero to free feedback.

Leavitt and Mueller also discovered that a strong positive correlation existed between the actual degree of accuracy in duplicating the designs and individual judgments of accuracy. Those who accurately reproduced the design estimated that they had done so, while those who drew inaccurate drawings consistently sensed their inaccuracy—even without having an opportunity to inspect the designs. Moreover, accuracy of understanding by the receivers increased as the degree of feedback shifted increasingly from zero to maximum. Although the free-feedback condition was the most accurate, it was also the most time-consuming. Over repeated trials accuracy increased under all conditions, even those in which no feedback was permitted. Also significant is the authors' observation that a higher proportion of hostile reactions and aggressive feedback occurred with those working under maximum feedback conditions. Those getting no feedback tended to follow passively the instructions without giving the nonverbal cues that people in ambiguous situations typically use to indicate their uncertainty and puzzlement. The opportunity for feedback does not remove the source of uncertainty, but it does engender a greater range of responses, both verbal and nonverbal, which are designed to seek the information necessary to complete the task accurately. In a study of task performance in dyads, Rosenberg and Hall (1958) reported that learning rate is greatest when people receive complete feedback about their performance and lowest when they obtain information only about the responses of their coworker.

An important qualification must be added to our generalizations about the need for feedback in interpersonal situations. Prolonged exposure to maximum feedback under certain social situations may bring about a condition of overstimulation and excessive feedback. Everyday conversation does not ordinarily bring about excessive stimulation, but it is possible to experience it when a person is highly involved in the discussion at hand, where high levels of cohesiveness develop in a setting, or where the reinforcement from group members is striking in its consistency and saliency. Familiar instances of over-stimulation occur at large gatherings, important social events, political rallies, and the like. From a psychological standpoint, excessive feedback upsets the balance that must exist between expectation or desired performance and actual response. The risk, as the psychiatrist Ashby (1954) noted, stems from the fact that "the conditions under which instability appears are often sharply bounded and critical. . . ." Moreover, Ashby continued, "*every dynamic system is potentially explosive*—that is, likely to develop a runaway [p. 116]." The danger in communicative situations is that an unstable psychological orientation can suddenly become totally out of proportion to the relatively minor changes which triggered the original conditions. So significant are the dangers of excessive feedback that physiologists now believe the human nervous system to have built-in mechanisms which thwart overreactions to maximal stimulus conditions.

It should now be apparent why feedback is so central to the formation and maintenance of all communication networks. Feedback alters the direction, distribution, and flow of messages in all social situations. It also assumes importance in the speech process. Unrestricted feedback is necessary to maintain reasonably accurate expectations and for adjustments made over time in speech performance. Feedback also influences factors such as length, rate, and fluency of each verbal exchange; time of responses and amount of participation; learning of tasks; feelings of interpersonal attraction; confidence in the accuracy of one's judgments; and motivation for success, power, recognition, and social status.

GROUP NETWORKS

Technically, the most simple communication network is that which connects two people, the dyad. Having only two links in its network, nearly everything works to make the exchange of information the most linear of all social units. And further unlike other social units, the dyad lacks the possibility for coalitions and competition from others; therefore, its interaction operates on an all-or-nothing principle with each person either attending to message cues or ignoring them. Only in a one-to-one exchange can the behavior of a given person assume such critical importance to the organization and flow of messages. A dyad is unique in that each person has only one source of feedback whereby to gauge reactions to his behavior. Technically, a dyad does not meet all the requirements of a group, particularly since it lacks the power of a coalition, a condition that is central to most concepts of group interaction. Nonetheless, the dyad provides a base point from which to understand the dynamics of larger social units.

Shifting from a dyadic setting to a group situation naturally complicates the influence of networks on the process of communication, for the inclusion of additional people compounds the direction and flow of information. People in groups seldom have equal access to each other, as they would in a dyadic setting. Time limitations, status differences, task requirements, size, physical distance, physical orientation, interpersonal attraction, and many other forces at work in groups all but eliminate the chance for a fully symmetrical, unrestricted network to emerge. This is not to say that relatively unrestricted networks never occur in group settings; they often do. The formation of a communication network, after all, is a spontaneous by-product of interaction itself. Groups, almost inevitably, develop characteristic patterns of communication flow among their members. But the important point is that the number of linkages actually utilized by groups is rarely more than a fraction of those possible, at least for groups having five or more members.

Suppose that groups of three, four, and five members discuss a topic of shared importance for a forty-minute period. While each group interacts an observer concealed behind a one-way glass records the number and direction of each communicative act. By comparing the number of actual linkages that are formed against the potential number available, the disparity between the two can be readily calculated. Using the procedure just described, one study (Bostrum, 1970) found that interactants generally directed their remarks either to one person (1:1 linkage) or to the group as a whole (1:group linkage). Also, as group size increased, the members deviated less from the accepted 1:1 or 1:group patterns. In groups of four, for example, only 7.6 percent of the remarks were found to be directed to something other than a 1:1 or 1:group linkage. In the case of a five-person group, only 5.3 percent of the communicative acts fell outside the two most common patterns. Another way of stating that individuals seldom use all available linkages is to say that small groups are characterized by somewhat restricted patterns of communication flow. The problem, then, is to determine the consequences that various restrictions can have on other aspects of group activity. Fortunately, restrictions in the flow of information from person to person can be readily manipulated and studied in laboratory situations.

Prescribed Networks

The logic of experimenting with prescribed group networks is to create situations in which group members can communicate only through certain formally manipulated channels; by experimentally arranging the number of available linkages, the investigator can determine how differences in the flow of communication affect other important aspects of group activity. Typically, group members sit at circular tables that are equipped with vertical partitions and slots through which they send messages back and forth (Figure 9.2). By permitting only certain slots to be used, one can create any number of restrictions in the flow of messages; the most common restrictions are reproduced in Figure 9.3.

Note particularly the differences among networks labeled "wheel," "circle," and "chain" in Figure 9.3. The essential characteristic of the *wheel* network is that only one person communicates with all others, regardless of group size. The *circle* pattern, however, permits each person to communicate with two other group members. And the *chain* pattern allows two-way exchange between all but members on the extreme outside. The essential differences in these three commonly used networks—as with group situations in everyday life—is in their respective degrees of centrality, that is, in the amount of direct contact that each person has with others. The parallel with everyday situations is roughly that of a spontaneous conversation among people at, say, a dinner table or on a street corner and the highly formalized proceedings of a group using rules of parliamentary procedure. The wheel network is the most highly centralized, the chain is relatively centralized, and the circle is decentralized. A centralized network depends on a "central" person to link communication among all other members. For example, in the wheel pattern for a five-person group, person C is in a strategic position; anyone who wants to communicate with anyone else must transmit indirectly through C. The same applies to sub-

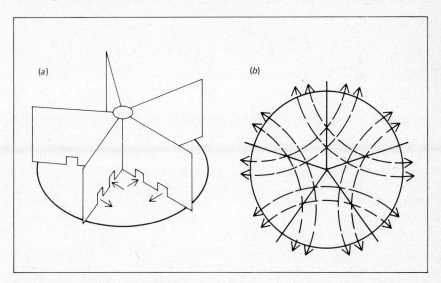

Figure 9.2 *Side view (a) and top view (b) of table used in studies of prescribed group networks. The flow of communication is controlled by opening and closing slots in the partitions that separate subjects. When all slots are open, messages flow as shown in (b).*

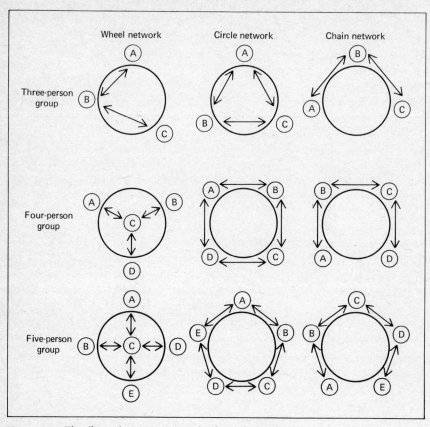

Figure 9.3 *The flow of messages in wheel, circle, and chain networks with groups ranging from three to five persons. Note that in the chain network two-way exchanges can occur between all except the outside members.*

jects C and B in the four-member and three-member groups, respectively. In the decentralized circle network, no single person controls the continuous flow of messages; each member has more than one channel to get a message to another indirectly. In the five-person group, for example, A is *not* totally dependent on B to transmit a message to C. He has the alternative of passing the message to E to D and then to C. The wheel, chain, and circle networks all have a characteristic impact on the flow of information from person to person, the efficiency of social performance, and the degree of membership satisfaction with social interaction.

Communication Flow. The relatively different message flows in various communication networks stem mainly from the degree of mechanical restriction placed on communication and from the fundamental tendency of people to respond to those who do the most talking. Mechanical restrictions preclude direct verbal exchange between members and have the added impact of concentrating the flow of ideas around those in positions of greatest centralization. The overall flow of messages generally has been found to be most restricted in the wheel network; in the circle pattern more messages are typically sent, and a greater number of errors occur than in any other network.

Much depends, however, on the distribution of relevant information among group members. Where the participants, regardless of group size, are allowed to exchange information freely, the communication flows toward those who initially display the greatest amount of pertinent information (Gilchrist et al., 1954). One exception to the rule favoring systematic distribution of information occurs when the task can best be solved by having each member perform separate functions and tasks; in this situation Lanzetta and Roby (1957) reported that the ideal network is one which allows each individual to work independently before reaching and implementing a decision. The advantage of independent work varies with the number of participants and the nature of the task. Also relevant to the flow of communication is the relative ability of each member to use and transmit information. Using unrestricted networks Guetzkow and Dill (1957) reported that on the average 2.7 messages were received by members who had supplied correct answers in previous trials as against 1.9 message units per trial by those who had not been provided with the right answer. In sum, then, the interaction rate results from a composite of factors and mainly corresponds to the opportunity for free interchange, the degree of feedback and decentralization, the specialization needed to carry out the task, and the distribution and use of relevant information by various participants.

Performance. Communication networks have a marked effect on the initial efforts of a group to solve its problems in an efficient, error-free manner. The imaginative studies of Bavelas (1950) and Leavitt (1951) were the first to examine the influence of networks on simple problem-solving effectiveness. These important early studies employed a procedure whereby group members attempted to determine which of six possible symbols they held in common (Leavitt and Mueller, 1951). For each trial a separate card with a set of five (out of a possible set of six) symbols was issued to each subject (Figure 9.4). Each member was allowed to communicate only by sending written messages through slots in the vertical partitions of the table (see Figure 9.2).

In the wheel network, the flow of messages operated in a consistent manner over fifteen successive trials. Members on the periphery passed their messages to the center from which answers went out. The most centralized network, the three-person, Y-shaped pattern, virtually gave one person complete decision-making power. The chain network was slow in forming a stable

Figure 9.4 *Set of six symbols used to study the problem-solving effectiveness of a group's communication network. Which symbol is missing from each of the cards shown? (Reprinted with permission from Leavitt and Mueller, 1951.)*

pattern of information flow, because information was funneled from both ends to the center, and then the decision was transmitted to the end positions. Performance as measured by the fastest single trial for each group was best in the wheel network. The circle pattern required more messages and resulted in more errors, with less organization, before solving the problem.

Subsequent research indicated that the superiority of centralized networks typically holds only for relatively simple tasks which require no manipulation of information. For complex tasks, the circle pattern is generally found to be the most efficient in time needed for problem solving, accuracy, and number of messages required to complete the task (Shaw, 1964). The reason is due mainly to the premium that a given network places on the mechanics of shuttling messages back and forth. Centralized networks have built-in, pre-defined means of channeling information; hence, they are well suited for simple tasks. For more complex tasks, decentralized networks permit each person to contribute to the manipulations necessary to solve the problem. Clearly, the nature of the task is a central factor in determining the effects of various communication networks (Shaw, 1971).

Membership Satisfaction. The influence of networks on individual satisfaction stems from the almost universal relationship that exists between the need for self-fulfillment and the opportunity for communication. Regardless of network characteristics, people in relatively centralized positions enjoy the group experience and their participation in it far more than do those on the periphery. The investigations of Leavitt (1951a, 1951b) found that satisfaction with each person's "job in the group" was markedly greater for those in the decentralized circle pattern, where the greatest number of messages were being sent. Closely related is the oft-repeated finding that satisfaction is highest among those who occupy the most central positions of any network (Shaw, 1945b; Shaw and Rothschild, 1956). Furthermore, whenever individuals change their network of communication, there is a tendency for morale to change in accordance with the new opportunity to participate which the shift in position gives. It is not important that a new position provide a "greater than equal" chance for interaction, but only that it offer equality with others (Cohen et al., 1962). Only when people perceive themselves to have an equal opportunity for interaction is the group experience apt to be personally rewarding. Once having participated in a network which equalizes chances for interaction, however limited, for all group members, any subsequent change to a more restrictive pattern has a marked impact on individual morale and satisfaction with group experience (Lawson, 1965).

Time Considerations. The effects of networks on communication flow, performance, and membership satisfaction are far from uniform over time. Generally, this influence is greatest at the outset of communication, when individual members must concentrate on how to organize their activities. Then, as members gradually learn to respond to the forces and pressures at work in the situation, they also learn to operate within whatever restrictions the networks impose on their activities. Research by Guetzkow and Simon (1955) indicated that the differences in performance diminish when group members in wheel, circle, and chain networks are given a pretrial period in which to organize their activities. Even more clear-cut results occur when performance is allowed to continue for several hours at a time. In a comparison of performances of wheel and circle networks Burgess (1968) permitted each group to use a training period in which to familiarize themselves with the network and the task. Also, the length of interaction was extended beyond the 25 to 69 trials used previously in such investigations to a range of from 900 to 1,000 problems, with the added provision that successful problem solving in early trials would lessen the time necessary to spend in the task. It was found that the wheel network has significantly higher solution rates than does the circle, but that the differences diminished over time, particularly when reinforcement for successful problem solving was provided. The findings of Guetzkow and Burgess do not imply that the influence of networks on communications is trivial or unimportant. After all, daily life presents a series of new network situations to which people must learn to adjust. The finding that differences in networks diminish over time is fully consistent with the larger evidence that the communication process is dynamic and not static; any single communication variable—including network restrictions—initially has the greatest impact, but this diminishes as the mediating effects of learning and experience come increasingly into play.

Emergent Networks

The laboratory findings about communication networks have relevance to virtually any everyday group situation which imposes some restriction on the flow of messages. While ordinary conversation may lack the absolute restrictions imposed by mechanical apparatus, the most spontaneous of conversations are influenced by the linkages that the parties utilize and by the differences in centralization that accrue from variations in status, influence, roles, interpersonal attraction, and the like. Yet, despite the parallels between laboratory and natural settings, there are important reasons for examining in closer detail the typical development of networks formed in more-or-less spontaneous natural settings.

At the outset of discussion among strangers who are relatively equal in status and competence, the flow of communication most closely resembles the all-channel network in the laboratory. Despite some normal gradient of activity, communication tends to be equally distributed during initial phases of the interaction. Roughly half the communications are directed to the group as a whole, and half are directed to individual members (Bales and Strodtbeck, 1951). However, small differences in status or authority are sufficient to alter the flow of messages in the direction of those in status positions. In a study of emergent and assigned leadership, Mortensen (1966) found that communication was equally divided in leaderless groups but was concentrated heavily from the very outset around members who were randomly assigned positions of leadership. This focus of initial communication around delegated leadership occurred even in groups where the assigned leaders were later found to be unable to maintain their positions in group hierarchy.

Communication networks in natural settings undergo typical changes that are far more striking than those which occur in the laboratory. As groups move from one phase of activity to another, the changes that take place are in the direction of increasing the restrictions of the communication network. If one were to keep a careful record of the flow of messages over, say, three separate sessions, the results would resemble the patterns that are shown in Figure 9.5.

There are numerous, perhaps countless, forces at work in bringing about a centralized network in everyday group situations. Of primary importance is the ability of each member to act in accordance with the prevailing group expectations or norms in such a way as to advance group tasks and goals. Problem-solving groups typically require communication that contains suggestions regarding goals, tasks, procedures, and pertinent information which serves to organize and integrate group decisions (Mortensen, 1966). Of equal importance is the avoidance of behavior that distracts or otherwise disrupts efforts at task performance. It is commonly thought that communication networks increasingly focus on those who are most successful in influencing the behavior of others. But there is also evidence that the flow of messages is as much a function of shifts away from those perceived as engaging in negative behavior. Initially, groups seem to direct a disproportionate amount of attention to those who fail to act in accordance with group expectations. When it becomes apparent that deviate behavior cannot be changed, interaction then focuses on those who contribute in constructive ways to group activity (Festinger and Thibaut, 1951; Schachter, 1951).

In a case study of leadership emergence in problem-solving groups, Geier (1967) found a two-stage pattern of communication flow. The first stage was devoted to a negative process; those who were uninformed or "extremely rigid" or who failed to participate eliminated themselves from further consideration for leadership. In the second stage the flow of communication was directed away from those who had been eliminated from high status positions to the few remaining as contenders who engaged in an intense struggle for leadership. Finally, after having established a hierarchy of positions, group networks then tend to stabilize into a pattern wherein low-status members send more messages to central figures; this happens even when persons in strategic positions do not initiate most of the communication (Kelley, 1951). As a corollary, once working lines of communication have been established, low-ranking members talk less altogether; and when they do talk, its direction is one way, that is to members in ranking positions, who, incidentally, often ignore their comments.

Further insight into the *evolving* nature of communication networks is provided by the influential studies of small-group interaction by Bales (1950). The technique devised by Bales, known as *interaction process analysis*, consists of a set of twelve general categories for coding all units of verbal

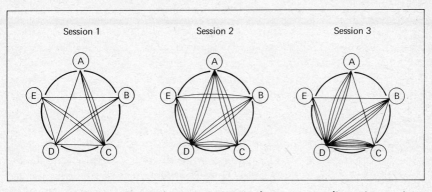

Figure 9.5   *Changing patterns of communication in three separate discussion sessions.*

behavior which are sufficient to elicit a response from other persons. Here are the twelve general categories and the percentage of response that occurred with laboratory groups:

Social-Emotional Area: Positive

1. Shows solidarity: jokes, raises other's status, gives help, reward   3.4
2. Shows tension release: laughs, shows satisfaction   6.0
3. Shows agreement: passive acceptance, understands,
concurs, complies   16.5

Task Area: Neutral

4. Gives suggestion: direction, implying autonomy for other   8.0
5. Gives opinion: evaluation, analysis, expresses feeling, wish   30.1
6. Gives information: orientation repeats, clarifies, confirms   17.9
7. Asks for information: orientation, repetition, confirmation   3.5
8. Asks for opinion: evaluation, analysis, expression of feeling   2.4
9. Asks for suggestion: direction, possible ways of action   1.1

Social-Emotional Area: Negative

10. Shows disagreement: passive rejection, formality,
withholds help   7.8
11. Shows tension: asks for help, withdraws "out of field"   2.7
12. Shows antagonism: deflates other's status; defends
or asserts self   0.7

While it is true that Bales's groups typically discussed in a laboratory setting, their interaction occurred without mechanical restrictions. Moreover, the participants were often strangers who interacted without prescribed leaders or particular formats or guidelines to follow; members were asked simply to discuss a given public-affairs topic or a problem with the goal of arriving at a consensus on the topic or a solution to the problem.

During the initial problem-solving session, the flow of messages is balanced between work-centered, topic-directed comments and those of a social-emotional nature. The pendulumlike swings between task and social-emotional orientation correspond to the initial pattern in the flow of communication. Some people understandably tend to lose sight of the task while concentrating on comments directed at the interpersonal or social needs of the group. Others are more inclined to engage in problem-solving activity. What happens is that the more the flow of information is directed at those preoccupied with the task, the greater becomes the pressure to shift the flow of communication to those more adept at interpersonal relations. This shifting was regarded by Bales to be important to maintaining equilibrium in the group's activities.

Other factors which influence the initial flow and distribution of messages pertain to three dimensions of performance that best account for individual differences in participation. The first is *activity*, or simply the total amount of interaction of each participant. The second is *task ability*, categories 4 to 9 in Bales's schema, which relates to the problem-solving or work-centered activity. And the third is the dimension of *likeability* as determined by the frequency of positive reactions. In the initial problem-solving session, a positive relationship exists among the three dimensions of performance. Those with the highest ratings of activity are also apt to be well liked and credited with the best ideas. But with each succeeding session the dimensions become increasingly independent; one person is eventually the "best liked," another is known as the "most active," and perhaps even a third, if the group is large enough, is perceived as the "best for ideas and information" (Slater, 1955). If the group meets over an extended period of time, the behavior of each participant eventually becomes so specialized that the dimensions no longer correlate with one another (Bales, 1958). When this happens, the communication tends to flow from lower-ranking members to those regarded as either the most likeable or as the best in problem solving.

A group also goes through distinct phases of interaction over time. In the first part of a session, for example, messages tend to be initiated by, and directed back to, those who are best able to supply needed information and ideas; later the network shifts the flow to those who are the most concerned with positive social-emotional activity—showing signs of solidarity, releasing of tension through joking and laughter, and making comments of agreement (see Figure 9.6). The Bales findings are not particularly useful in actually specifying who at any given time will interact with whom. What the data show is how the flow of messages corresponds to such dynamic forces as group equilibrium, differences in individual performance, and the pattern of communication that emerges between high- and low-ranking members.

Intergroup Networks

In a day of burgeoning population, urban sprawl, and instantaneous contact of world-linked mass media, it is clear that no group can ever communicate in isolation. Groups can no more interact in a social vacuum than can any individual member. Intergroup affiliation ensures that a given group network will ultimately influence all the lasting social contacts of its various members. The forces which serve to link one group network to another may all be subsumed under the concept of the *interdependence* of emergent networks. This concept provides a useful way of describing the degree to which the flow of messages in one setting influences or links the organization of verbal activity in any other setting.

Ecological studies of social organization in small Midwestern towns demonstrated that social interactions in seemingly dissimilar situations exert subtle influences on each other. Barker (1968) identified several forces which

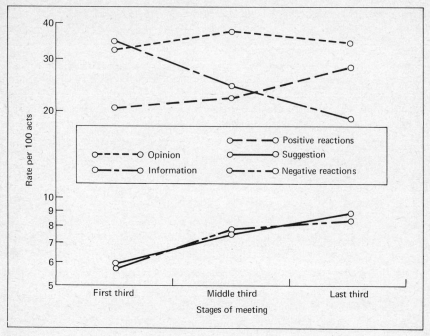

Figure 9.6 *Phases of a group's interaction over time. (Reprinted with permission from Bales, 1955.)*

affect the degree of interdependence of two particular behavior settings: (1) physical forces, such as the layout of sidewalks and corridors, which enforce certain types of interpersonal contact and prevent others; (2) the social forces, such as enforced rules and regulations, which have much to do with who comes into contact with whom and how; (3) the physiological processes, such as human reaction to temperature or humidity, which influence attention and coordination of physical activity; (4) the selectivity processes, such as age and membership requirements, which dictate who interacts with whom in settings as diverse as churches, schools, and the Masonic Lodge; (5) the influence of behavior on the ecological surroundings, arising from the tendency of people to prefer certain settings for building homes and schools, resorts and shopping centers, and to avoid settings in which past behavior, such as the creation of smog or litter, prevents desirable social interaction; (6) the temporal factors, such as store hours, schedules, and meeting dates which ensure that a small town "slowly expands in the morning and slowly closes down at night."

By knowing which combinations of forces were operating, Barker found that the degree of interdependence between two or more social situations can be reliably specified. For example, the activities of a particular gas station and nearby garage were so interdependent that the number of customers in the former could be accurately predicted by knowing the degree of activity in the other. Yet interestingly enough, the same gas station and another garage in town were completely independent of each other; even large changes in the activity of one had no bearing on the other's. Barker also found that the fountain, pharmacy, and variety departments of the local drugstore were so inter-dependent that they constituted a single, unified setting that was totally inter-dependent, rather than three independent behavior settings. As further examples, the Boy Scout soft-drink stand proved to be interdependent with the scheduling of the Old Settlers Reunion Midway. Activity at the Methodist Church Evening Guild food sale depended on the scheduling of the 4-H Club food sale. On the other hand, the activity of the Pinter Abstract and Title Com-pany was not in the slightest degree linked to the occurrence of the PTA carnival.

The interdependence of given social situations follows three key principles of interpersonal attraction. The first and most obvious is what Katz and Lazarsfeld termed the "cardinal principle" of *shared interest*: namely, that interpersonal contact from one setting to another follows a network pattern which is consistent with the beliefs, values, and attitudes of each member. The notion that people seek out those most like themselves, discussed in Chapter 7 (pp. 260–265) holds as well for the larger contact among group networks. The consistency among group affiliations can be readily demonstrated by having members of a homogenous group compare the membership cards which they carry in their wallets or purses. One group of graduate students in communica-tion research tried this demonstration only to find an unexpected degree of consistency in their association with such things as behavioral science club, library, student union, bookstore, student discount card, and cooperative mem-bership in a variety of groups oriented toward political or social activism.

The second key principle that determines the pattern of linkages among various groups is the degree of individual commitment to *common group affiliations*. People shift from one social setting to another not only for different amounts of time, but, as Barker (1968) noted, "They enter and participate in them in different capacities and with different degrees of involvement and responsibility." One measure of the degree of commitment is the depth or center to which an individual *penetrates* a given behavior setting. Barker identified several degrees of social penetration. The most peripheral form of contact is that of an *onlooker*, a person who is in the physical presence of social activity but who takes no active part in the communication. Without status or power, onlookers are unwelcome and merely tolerated. Examples include teen-agers who stand around a pinball machine in a café or people who wait for someone to get off work from a store. *Invited guests or an audience* are socially recog-nized and often welcomed but have little power or interpersonal influence. An invited guest functions like a spectator at a sporting event or a nonvoting partisan at a political meeting. Two further levels of social penetration include *members* and *active functionaries*, both of whom share in the activities but without the exercise of direct responsibility or leadership control. For the two maximum levels of penetration, Barker used the terms *joint leader* and *single leader*. Joint leaders have immediate and direct responsibility for the affairs at hand but do not have exclusive powers of decision making. Examples include a staff of city managers or the coowners of a store. A single leader represents maximum penetration, complete with absolute powers of decision making and influence over the course of affairs.

The question of penetration is of great importance in determining the extent to which the activities of one group network influence or overlap those of another. The greatest impact occurs under those who have the maximum penetration of a behavior setting. These key individuals, or the *gatekeepers* in Lewin's (1951) term, exert the strongest influence on the linkages which are formed from group to group. A gatekeeper literally refers to one who has control over some strategic point in a chain of command. Underlying the original formulation of Lewin's theory was the need to design a campaign to convince people to reduce their use of those foods that were in short supply during wartime. At issue was whether to attempt to influence the entire population or to concentrate on those who were most apt to make decisions on food purchasing. The decision to focus on married women proved a most effective way to reduce the demand on scarce items. Those principles which applied to the purchase of food, Lewin discovered, also held for the transmission of messages generally. The notion of gatekeeping was later noted in reference to the practices of journalists and editors who filter the news before it is disseminated from the mass media to the public. In one study, for example, it was found that the typical mass-media portrayal of mental illness reflected the selective gatekeeping of media decision makers who attempted to present a view of illness that was consistent with prevailing public attitude (Tannenbaum, 1963). Similar evidence of gatekeeping exists on matters ranging from editorial policy to decisions on style in the composition of news stories.

The concept of *diffusion* also helps to account for overlap in the communicative links among different groups. A diffuse network has multiple lines of personal contact that are spread among people who are widely separated in space and time. Diffusion further suggests distance and inclusiveness where information is passed from one distant point to another in a largely unrepetitive manner. In sharp contrast to a diffuse network are close, or proxemic, networks of a college fraternity or hospital. Close networks are typically smaller in number of participants than diffuse ones. The former are also more confined geographically, more stable and permanent, with greater potential for continuous face-to-face interaction (Buckner, 1965). Proxemic networks account best for information that does not get disseminated widely but rather is passed repeatedly from one person to another, often with considerable distortion and noise being added in the process. Diffused networks account for information that goes through a long succession of personal linkages until it travels through an ever-widening web of connections.

There seems to be no practical limit to the number of connections possible in a diffuse network. One spectacular example is the vast circulation given to a famous rumor known as the "Great Cabbage Hoax." One version of the false rumor appeared in the November 16, 1964, issue of the *National Observer*. The item read:

> The Ten Commandments contain 297 words. The Bill of Rights is stated in 463 words. Lincoln's Gettysburg Address contains 266 words. A recent Federal directive to regulate the price of cabbage contains 26,911 words.

In an effort to trace the false rumor to its original source, Hall (1965) described the following chain of events:

> The item was attributed to the *Messenger-Gazette*, Somerville, New Jersey. The editor of the *Messenger-Gazette* told me he did not remember where he got it. Meanwhile the *Concord* (Massachusetts) *Journal* printed exactly the same paragraph on November 12, and the editor told me it came from a magazine called *Quote: The Weekly Digest*, published in Richmond, Indiana. About this time I happened to see the item in *Sixty-Six Ninety-Nine*, a leaflet of amusing quotations issued periodically by the Rapid Service Press, a Boston printer. The compiler of the publication told me he took the story from *Quote*. I wrote to *Quote*, and the editor, Lotte Hoskins, promptly sent me a copy (September 20, 1964) containing the cabbage item. She explained that she got it from the August issue of *Ties*, a house organ of the Southern Railway System and that *Ties* got it from the *Atlanta Journal* where it had appeared as a letter to the editor [p. 563].

Hall then traced the rumor through a succession of stages going from the Johnson and Kennedy administrations back to the Office of Price Stabilization that existed briefly during the Korean War. En route various versions were relayed on a national quiz show, *Double or Nothing*, a one-page circular mimeographed on the letterhead of Glaser Crandall Company, a Chicago producer of pickles and preserves, as problem 6 of "Test your Horse Sense," a newspaper column by Dr. George W. Crane, and even on blotters printed by a businessman in Louisville. In all, more than fifty examples appeared despite wide publicity given to the true facts. Undoubtedly the entertainment value accounts for part of the astonishing longevity of the rumor, allegedly borrowed in the 1940s and persisting by print and word of mouth into the 1960s—and perhaps beyond. (Conceivably even this account will unwittingly perpetuate the existence of the loose network of interest in a cabbage order that never existed.) The incident illustrates that the outer limits of diffuse networks may at times seem limitless and that the longevity is often sustained by an incredible array of mediums available to transmit information in either accurate or distorted form.

INTERPOSED NETWORKS

Our examination of communication networks so far has been couched mainly in terms of face-to-face relationships. Yet it is apparent from everyday experience and the incident just cited that interpersonal relations are often created, maintained, or influenced by some shared interest in radio, TV, books, motion pictures, or other mass media. Book clubs, fan clubs, safety campaigns, conservation groups, and countless other formal organizations are held together by a common interest in the mass media. In a less formal way, much social interaction is the byproduct of the mass media. During the early 1950s, when television was still considered a luxury, the first family in a middle-class neighborhood to put up a TV aerial often found that its popularity suddenly increased. A similar phenomenon occurred later with the initial purchases of color televisions, particularly among professional football fans. In similar situations and in a countless variety of ways, interpersonal contacts of everyday life come about because of the increasingly pervasive impact of the mass media in urban life. The question, then, for the limited purposes of this chapter, is how one of the mass media alters the flow of communication from person to person and group to group. The concept of *interposed networks* is used deliberately. An interposed media is an intervening linkage in the communication process; all mass media, in fact, may be thought of as impersonal mechanisms which intervene between source and receiver.

Before television, mass-media specialists conceived of the processes of mass communication and interpersonal communication in distinct, mutually exclusive terms. Unlike interpersonal networks, mass communication was characterized as a one-way transmission of messages to a large, passive audience. *Mass audience* meant massive, homogenous, undifferentiated, highly suggestible aggregates of people. Moreover, the effects of the mass media were conceived solely as immediate and uncritical responses of people who operated in isolation from other influences and networks. Neither group affiliations nor individual differences among receivers was given systematic consideration in the early thinking about the role of the mass media in interpersonal encounters. The impact of the mass media was considered instantaneous—people either responded or they didn't. Moreover, little attention was given to the mediating influences of a person's frame of reference concerning his involvement in the programming. The early model of communication, in short, assumed a one-stage, stimulus-response process, as depicted in Figure 9.7. The tendency was to view the mass media as forming a direct, undiffer-

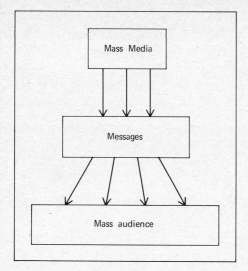

Figure 9.7 *An early model depicting mass communication as a one-stage transmission of information to an undifferentiated society.*

entiated link with a mass of disconnected individuals. Katz (1959) summarized the early view of the mass media in the following terms:

> Until very recently, the image of society in the minds of most students of communication was of atomized individuals connected with the mass media, but not with one another. Society—the "audience"—was conceived of as aggregates of age, sex, social class and the like, but little thought was given to the relationships implied thereby to more informal relationships [p. 436].

Katz further noted that students of mass media were not unaware of group relations and interpersonal networks but that they simply presumed the web of interpersonal contacts to be irrelevant to the links and effects of the mass media.

The notion of a two-step flow of communication was an initial advance in thinking about the effects of the mass media on interpersonal networks of communication. In the influential study of voting behavior in the 1940 presidential election, Lazarsfeld (et al., 1954) found that interpersonal contacts were more important than the mass media in influencing voting decisions. Instead of a single flow of messages from mass media to an atomized audience, the linkage was found to occur in two distinct stages; first from the mass media to strategic individuals—known as opinion leaders—and then from these key people through a chain to less active individuals in society. Opinion leaders were much like the people they influenced, except for three general characteristics: (1) Opinion leaders represented the values and attitudes of their groups more clearly than did other members. (2) Opinion leaders exhibited special competence; they generally were more widely read or had some special expertise on the subjects in which they led opinion. (3) Most importantly, the key individuals in the two-step flow were found to have a strategic location; they were in greater exposure to the mass media and more readily able to share their discoveries from the media with group members.

The notion of an opinion leader, much like Lewin's concept of gatekeeper, was a clearly defined sphere of influence. In other words, there were no opinion leaders on all matters disseminated by the mass media; rather there were opinion leaders in fashion, politics, medicine, and so forth. For example, some were leaders in medicine because of their willingness to read material on new practices and drugs and to adapt these new methods and products before other physicians followed. The network of the two-step flow more closely approximates what is now known about the pervasive impact of group affiliations (Figure 9.8).

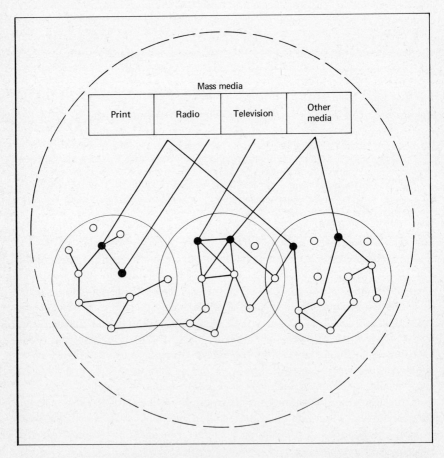

Figure 9.8 *The multistep flow of messages from mass media to opinion leaders (black circles) and their interpersonal contacts (white circles) in overlapping group networks. The cultural milieu is indicated by the broken circle encompassing the various networks and their interactants.*

Though still highly simplified, the concept of the two-step flow has been useful in clarifying the relationship between the process of mass communication and the flow of messages in interpersonal networks. More recent extensions of the two-step flow posit additional linkages which mediate the flow of messages from the mass media to society at large. Rosenau (1961) referred to a "four-step" flow (Figure 9.9) in which the mass media carry a news event (step 1) which is picked up by opinion makers, who express their views in situations which are in themselves news events (step 2); this, in turn, is learned by "opinion leaders" in the general public, who subsequently pass it on (step 3) to people with shared interests in face-to-face situations (step 4). Since each linkage in the flow of messages represents a stage in a continuous, interrelated flood of words, the pattern is probably best thought of as having *no fixed number* of "steps" or "stages." The mass media intervene in interpersonal contact in infinite ways and with any number of intervening stages. We can conclude only that the sharing of everyday experience is so woven together with the images of the mass media that it is often impossible to separate them. As Gerbner (1967) concluded, "Never have so many people in so many places

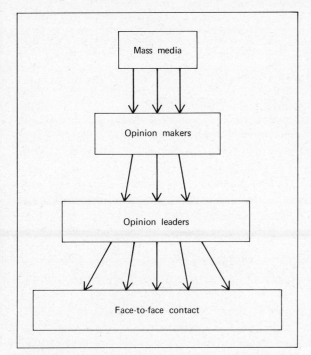

Figure 9.9 *The communication network as a four-stage flow of messages. The mass media (1) transmit events to opinion makers (2), who may themselves be "newsworthy"; opinion leaders (3) pass the information to contacts in face-to-face encounters (4).*

shared so much of a common system of messages and images and have the assumptions about life, society, and the world imbedded in them while having so little to do with their making [p. 42]."

CULTURALLY DEFINED NETWORKS

Communication networks, when viewed in the most inclusive way, are products of culturally defined patterns of behavior. The impact of culture is, in fact, implicit in the fabric of language and in socialization. Culture is an abstract concept which refers in an inclusive way to overt, patterned ways of behaving, feeling, and reacting. A culture *also* consists of built-in assumptions and rules of behavior. These *unstated* premises and categories which make up the dimension of what anthropologists term the "implicit culture" differ greatly from society to society. As an example of the implicit rules of culture, Kroeber and Kluckhohn (1952) noted:

> Thus one group unconsciously and habitually assumes that every chain of actions has a goal and that when this goal is reached tension will be reduced or disappear. To another group, thinking based upon this assumption is by no means automatic. They see life not primarily as a series of purposive sequences but more as made up of disparate experiences which may be satisfying in and of themselves, rather than means to ends [p. 643].

The overt influence of culture is apparent in the way given societies organize their internal lines of communication. The more distinct and autonomous the culture, the more its lines of communication are apt to originate and end within the society itself. We might even say that culture acts as an outer boundary, almost like the linkages permitted by technical apparatus, for the transmission of messages from person to person. Clearly, spatial factors enter in as well. Distance, density of population, communication technology, and degree of intercultural contact all conspire with the rules of the implicit culture to define emergent patterns of communication.

The constraining impact of culture is not limited solely to the number of connections and the potential range of contacts that are possible with members of one culture and another. Its influence also extends the *way* messages are transmitted and interpreted in a given cultural setting. The implicit rules of culture restrict the timing, protocol, style, and content of information exchanged by various groups and classes of people. In Chapter 6 we noted the disparity in attitudes of people from various cultures toward time and the proper time intervals for communication. Those who live in the United States place a premium on punctuality, keeping appointments with exacting fidelity, watching the time so as not to overstay their welcome, particularly in business affairs. Latin Americans, in contrast, operate on a far different cultural clock, one that is neither so exacting nor personally demanding. As for proxemic factors, the distance that "feels right" to an American is apt to seem distant and cold to a Latin American counterpart. Equally striking are the rules of physical contact. "Each cultural group," wrote Frank (1957), "has a concept of the skin and of tactile experience which may not be recognized or stated, but is implicit in its prescriptions for covering, exposing, decorating, making, and avoiding tactile communication [p. 238]." People in Mediterranean societies have a much higher tolerance for physical contact, particularly among members of the same sex, than do those living in Western Europe or the United States.

Further parallels exist in all aspects of nonverbal interaction. Tyrwhitt (1960) noted that people in Western cultures have a distinct set of rules governing eye contact. For over five-hundred years, people in the West have accepted a visual perspective based upon the single viewpoint. The result is the development of a linear perspective, or as Tyrwhitt said, "the single 'vanishing point' and the penetration of landscape by a single piercing eye— my eye, my dominating eye." The accepted pattern of vision in the West, the camera-eye viewpoint, is not universally shared by other cultures. The Chinese, according to Tyrwhitt, look from the perspective of a constantly changing relationship of man and environment. And in African cultures, children are taught very early to develop tremendous powers of concentration and fix their gaze, even in bright sunlight or blinding sandstorms, at another person or object.

Matters pertaining to gesture, voice, and posture also bear the imprint of culture. Ruesch and Kees (1956) characterized the gestures of Italians as the epitome of expressiveness and frankness directed toward maintaining warm interpersonal contact. A comparative study of the gestural pattern of Italians and Jews indicates a preference among the Eastern Jews and the Northern Italians for expression through jerky, angular, tightly knit motions of face, arms, and shoulders (Efron, 1941). In sharp contrast is the preference among the Southern Italians for more sweeping movement involving the entire body. In even greater contrast are the patterns of body movement which appear to be indigenous to the United States. These Ruesch and Kees characterized as "lacking in the ardent stylization of those of the French or the interpersonal movements conveyed through Italian gestures." The sharp differences revealed in the comparative study of body movement they summarized in this way: "Gesture among the Americans is largely oriented toward activity; among the Italians it serves the purposes of illustration and display; among the Jews it is a device of emphasis; among the Germans it specifies both attitude and commitment; and among the French it is an expression of style and containment [p. 22]."

Further evidence of the role of culture in communication stems from comparative studies of intercultural communication. A study of communication patterns in Japan and America by Bennet (et al., 1966) gave insight into how the prevailing norms of a culture influence social interaction. American rules of interpersonal communication rest in an initial implicit agreement concerning the egalitarian nature of the social situation in which two strangers find themselves. Unless proven otherwise, two persons are presumed at the outset to be on equal footing. Among Japanese an opposite norm prevails: Unless proven otherwise, inequality is expected. This assumption of social differences requires that the initial reactions of each person show deference and respect. In actual communication situations, the egalitarian principle held by Americans leads to what the Japanese regard as uncertainty and a lack of predictability in the communication. As Bennet noted:

> Thus, while in social situations the Japanese may find it difficult to communicate unless status differences are clear; the American, in view of his egalitarian preferences, may point to and actually experience status difference as a source of interpersonal tension and difficulty in communication. Thus, the Japanese may see the free flow of communication as enhanced by clear status understandings; the American may view it instead as requiring maximal intimacy and freedom of expression [p. 602].

A more direct study of cultural differences in communication pertains to a situation in which married couples from three cultural groups discussed what each thought to be the attributes of a good family (Strodtbeck, 1951). After each couple discussed the topics privately, they were brought together and asked to try to resolve their differences and come up with a single opinion. In analyzing who was responsible for giving in and whose view was the one that was announced, Strodtbeck found that cultural differences accounted for the outcomes. The highly independent wives in the Navaho couples were found to be most often responsible for the decisions that were shared by their husbands; among Mormon couples, where husbands have complete domination over their wives, the views of the husbands prevailed almost completely. But in the equalitarian situation typified by Texan couples, wives and husbands prevailed in the decision making almost an equal number of times. This finding is consistent with a conclusion drawn by Ruesch and Kees (1956):

> On the societal plane, the communication system of a nation or any of its subdivisions ostensibly serves to insure the well-being and survival of its citizens, and the organization of the communication network and the modes of communication are fitted to suit typical and recurring situations . . . variations in climate, the density of population, the prevalence of either an agricultural or an industrial economy, the availability of raw materials, the historical past, and many other facts, will all determine in part the varieties of communication. In any culture each person is prepared, therefore, through education, to assume a place in the communication network of his particular group, and the cumulative body of experience of generations reflects itself in the expressions of the individual [p. 22].

The imprint of culture on communication does not rule out the possibility that some aspect of social interaction may be common to all cultures. Though most of the evidence has accumulated only recently, many implicit rules of culture appear to be shared across cultures. They are, in other words, universal or "pan-cultural." Most interesting are the data concerning the ability of people from dissimilar cultures to recognize the primary affects discussed in Chapter 6 (pp. 220–221). Recall that the face is the primary expressor of certain basic emotive states including happiness, sadness, anger, fear, and so on. If these emotive states are truly primary to human expression, they should be amenable to verification across cultures. An unequivocal test of the notion that the primary affects can be recognized across cultures requires a comparison of responses from people in literate cultures with those from preliterate societies. To minimize problems in language, it is also necessary to create tasks that minimize problems resulting from unfamiliarity with complex research tasks. In an attempt to test the possibility of pan-cultural recognition of affective states, Ekman and Friesen (1971) created sample stories to depict given emotion states. Examples included the following:

Happy: His (her) friends have come and he (she) is happy.
Sad: His (her) child (mother) has died and he (she) is very sad.
Anger: He (she) is angry; or he (she) is angry, about to fight.
Surprise: He (she) is just now looking at something new and unexpected.
Disgust: He (she) is looking at something he (she) dislikes; or he (she) is looking at something which smells bad.
Fear: He (she) is sitting in his (her) house all alone and there is no one else in the village. There is no knife, axe, or bow and arrow in the house. A wild pig is standing in the door of the house and the man (woman) is looking at the pig and is very afraid of it. The pig has been standing in the doorway for a few minutes and the person is looking at it very afraid and the pig won't move away from the door and he (she) is afraid the pig will bite him (her) [pp. 5–6].

The stories were told to illiterate children in the highlands of New Guinea. With the exception of their inability to discriminate fear from surprise, the children were able to match the emotions depicted in the stories from accompanying groups of faces. Given the difficulties in working with children who neither understood English nor had previous contact with Caucasians, the results are impressive indeed. They are also consistent with related lines of investigation (Ekman et al., 1969; Izard, 1968), particularly with the finding that facial behavior of New Guinean's can be accurately judged in videotape form by college students in the United States. Much additional work is required to sort out the relative importance of these pan-cultural elements with those defined by particular cultures.

Networks and Selectivity in Communication

Seldom if ever are the configurations of a communication network formed and maintained in accidental or random manner. Nor is there anything capricious or arbitrary in the connections that help to define the larger web of daily social contact. Each linkage reflects a degree of selectivity both in matters of personal recognition and the willingness of interactants to dovetail their responses to keep them in line with the other. The result is a monitoring process through which feedback is judged on grounds of whether it is positive or negative, concurrent or delayed, in degrees ranging from free to zero. The continued accessibility of persons engaged in communication may be defined either in a spontaneous or a formal way, through emergent or prescribed networks, not just in a laboratory, but also indirectly through the constraining influence of social standing, formal title or credentials, protocol, rules and regulations, delegated or self-appointed positions of authority, roles in a hierarchy, and so forth.

As the number of links in a network increases the social forces at work in turn become ever more complex, thereby creating a tension between conflicting forces. One set of forces results from the need of the respective parties to validate their own self-identity and social importance by actively contributing to whatever business is at hand. Recall that people tend to judge the group product and their personal satisfaction against the degree of opportunity they have to interact with others in an unconstraining atmosphere. However, the need for free and open communication may conflict with the limits of time and procedure. Not everyone can talk at once. As size increases, the more intensely the forces of selectivity come into play. Soon the hub of activity becomes less equitable, and a gap emerges between the most active and less active persons. Another form of selectivity occurs with the tendency of communication to be more and more specialized, as evidenced by the move to independent roles, such as a task leader, "best-liked" person, and so on.

Ultimately, the powerful forces of selectivity influence the web of daily encounters formed among various groups as their members gravitate to other social encounters along lines of shared interest. The final product, from a cultural standpoint, is not a mass of disconnected, atomized individuals or even some sort of undifferentiated social aggregate, but rather a multistage flow of information that has an incalculable range of circulation.

SUGGESTED READINGS

Argyle, M., and **Kendon, A.** "The Experimental Analysis of Social Performance," in L. Berkowitz (ed.), *Advances in Experimental Social Psychology,* vol. 3. New York: Academic, 1967, pp. 55–98.

Barker, R. G. *Ecological Psychology.* Stanford, Calif.: Stanford University Press, 1968.

Bavelas, A. "Communication Patterns in Task-oriented Groups," *Journal of the Acoustical Society of America,* 22:725–730, 1950.

Buckner, H. T. "A Theory of Rumor Transmission," *Public Opinion Quarterly,* 29:54–70, 1965.

Burgess, R. L. "Communication Networks: An Experimental Reevaluation," *Journal of Experimental Social Psychology,* 4:324–337, 1968.

Ekman, P., Sorenson, P., and Friesen, W. V. "Pan-cultural Elements in Facial Displays of Emotion," *Science,* 164:86–88, 1969.

Hare, A. P. "Communication Network," in *Handbook of Small Group Research.* New York: Free Press, 1962, pp. 272–290.

Katz, E. "The Diffusion of New Ideas and Practices," in W. Schramm (ed.), *The Science of Human Communication.* New York: Basic Books, 1963, pp. 77–93.

Leavitt, H. "Some Effects of Certain Communication Patterns on Group Performance," *Journal of Abnormal and Social Psychology,* 46:38–50, 1951.

Leavitt, H., and Mueller, R. "Some Effects of Feedback on Communication," *Human Relations,* 4:401–410, 1951.

Scheidel, T., and Crowell, L. "Feedback in Small Group Communication," *Quarterly Journal of Speech,* 52:273–278, 1966.

Shaw, M. "Communication Networks," in L. Berkowitz (ed.), *Advances in Experimental Social Psychology,* vol. 1. New York: Academic, 1964, pp. 111–147.

Yates, J. A. "Delayed Auditory Feedback," *Psychological Bulletin,* 60:213–232, 1963.

ten

---

communication
and social
influence

If one theme underlies all systems of communication, it is social influence. To say that influence occurs is to insist that some necessary effects, outcomes, or consequences function as defining attributes of communication. The concept of inevitable influence has been suggested throughout much of our earlier discussion. Recall first the logic leading to the notion that you cannot not communicate. In much the same sense we may insist that you "cannot not influence", in other words, some form of influence is inevitable in any communicative act. Also, in rejecting the image of communication as breaking down (Chapter 1), we eliminate any explanation of a system of communication working in the manner of a light switch. No communicative transaction can be properly interpreted as something akin to signals that either arrive at their destination intact or break down somewhere along the line. Not even the inability of interactants to establish mutual understanding can be reduced to anything resembling a power failure. Nor can social influence be attributed to the sort of change typically associated with sheer movement. The idea of dynamic change (p. 14) suggests an evolving, elastic activity, a sequential and irreversible process that is continuously assuming new shape. Also, the related concepts of interaction and mutual dependence further underscore the inevitability of influence; both concepts imply that the very act of monitoring or decoding behavior necessarily has an accumulative impact on the meaning of *whatever* is said and done.

The idea of inevitable influence draws additional credence from other important concepts. To say that man is proactive, for example, is to view him as superimposing his own unique frame of reference on the interpretation he gives to the course of physical events; consequently, he is prone to select, amplify, rearrange—even distort and disassociate—incoming signals, making them more congruent with his view of the way things really are (p. 136). If man were truly a passive respondent to external stimuli, he might afford the luxury of remaining aloof and unaltered by the act of decoding messages. But the cycle from self to world and back again seldom allows room for passivity and neutrality. Even the decision to state one's views in the presence of others, as we discovered in Chapters 5 and 7, leads to a greater commitment to the stand being advocated; hence active verbal participation is itself a subtle form of self-influence. Moreover, the inclination to form expectations or a psychological set toward some forthcoming encounter may color all subsequent interpretations of the interaction from earliest moments of personal recognition to later feelings of threat or mutual regard (p. 259). Recall also the many influences associated with the mere presence of others and the energizing and tension-producing effects experienced by people in face-to-face encounters (pp. 260 and 261). Of added import are the urges to personalize all incoming data, to avoid undue psychological stress, and to gain feedback in forming impressions of credibility, trust, power, affect, status, interpersonal attraction, similarity, and so forth. Additional complications arise from the subtle and pervasive influences associated with situational factors—time, space, and setting—and the larger impact of culture on communication.

Our brief review underscores something of both the pervasive and dynamic aspects of communicative influence. Social influence, we have found, to be exceedingly complicated; the process consists of nothing less than an unfolding succession of fleeting and continuously interacting sources of influence that differ markedly both in *type and degree of impact*. However, the resultant picture still leaves intriguing problems unresolved. One is the issue regarding the potential or upper limit of communicative influence, that is, the maximum impact that messages have on the attitudes and conduct of receivers. The problem is most important, for in determining whether messages actually make a difference and under what conditions and why, we end up confronting one central aspect of our degree of faith in the power of language.

Until recently, the major questions dealing with the matter of potential influence have been stated and tested in simplistic and misleading terms.

For example, students of mass media have spent an enormous amount of energy designing studies that deal with the impact of mass media on public opinion. Typical issues include the following: Do comic-books cause juvenile delinquency? Does pornography lead to an increase in sex-related crimes? Do political commercials alter election results? Do advertisements of medical products lead to changes in medical practices? Do advertisements from mail-order houses have any influence on the purchases of expensive farm machinery? Notice how all these questions define the issue. Each implies the existence of a one-to-one relationship between given messages and a particular group of responses. Presumably, if receivers act in accord with the recommendations of a given message, the attempted influence is judged as successful; if they do not respond as directed, the message can be dismissed as ineffectual. This reasoning, in effect, reduces the question of potential influence to a simple correspondence between a message and the immediate responses of receivers. Hence, we are left with nothing more than a sophisticated version of the idea that either communication works or it does not. Not surprisingly, research based on such click-clack, nickel-in-the-slot notions rarely confirm the power of the mass media over public opinion. Therefore, critics claim (with somewhat deliberate overstatement) that students of the mass media spent two decades in a futile search for uniform persuasive effects only to spend an additional decade in an unsuccessful attempt to explain their earlier negative findings.

It should be noted, however, that any number of research strategies could be substituted to illustrate the charge just cited. For example, the search for the "universal effects" of verbal interaction—notably matters of fear arousal and message organization—fit nicely into the one-shot, hypodermic-type model of social influence. Moreover, much research based on stimulus-response paradigms, learning theories, and balance principles (pp. 132 and 134) lead to results that underplay the potential for communicative influence. A person who takes such findings at face value may mistakenly conclude that communication functions mainly to reinforce prior opinion and to leave the respective parties unaltered by their experience.

Ironically, the hypodermic approach can just as readily lead to an exaggerated view of the power of the spoken or written word. Recent controversy over the possible adverse effects of pornography reveals deep-seated fear among those who conceive of so-called "dirty books" as imbued with enormous power to erode the moral values of those who read them. Similar biases lead to indictments of Madison Avenue for wielding a supposedly frightening power over the purchasing decisions of an unsuspecting public. A good example of this sort of hysteria was cited in Chapter 4, where Meerloo charged the gatekeepers of the mass media as responsible for depersonalizing the critical capacities of the public. Advertising, Meerloo charged, causes continuous dissatisfaction with existing products. Likewise, TV "hypnotizes" and "warps" viewers in a "web" from which there is no "escape." Under the assault of advertising and propaganda, Meerloo fears that "barriers of criticism" break down, viewers become "passive and apathetic" and end up "a little bit slave to the great television hyponosis."

In a later section of the indictment, Meerloo invoked a string of stereotypes centering around what he called "the magic power behind the speaker," the "culturally induced submissiveness of the listener," and "the spell cast by the spoken or private token [p. 85]." He then referred to the "seductive power of a politician" who "forces" helpless audiences "to partake of their moods" by *hypomania*, a psychiatric term denoting a manipulation of human emotion for the "joy of sweeping others along, with no relation to any thought content." In the battle between man and media, Meerloo weighed the odds and found them woefully lopsided. He cast the issue as "man's suscepti-bility and vulnerability to persuasion" in a fruitless struggle against "the avalanche of noise" and "the emotional super shot of radio and television or the alluring slogan in the headlines, seeking to import dubious thought patterns on listeners and readers" by a "calculated verbocractic strategy [that] aims to invade the larger acres of man's mind and irrigate the furrows of thought with polluted water [p. 86]."

This characterization might be dismissed as crude hyperbole were it not taken so seriously within the larger tradition of social commentary that leaves man a helpless victim of collective manipulation. Interestingly enough, Meerloo built his own case by generalizing from such rare incidents as the panic in 1938 following the Orson Welles mock radio broadcast simulating an invasion from Mars and—of course—incidents from crowd reaction to Hitler. To the list might be added Vance Packard's discovery of "hidden persuaders," those forboding tools employed by technocrats who care only about manipulating people by channeling their unthinking habits and purchasing decisions.

Packard, for instance, expressed outrage and alarm in uncovering "a disquieting" and largely "successful" effort to probe "beneath our level of awareness; so that the appeals which move us are often, in a sense, 'hidden' [p. 1]." Using language that sounds strikingly like Meerloo's, Packard spoke of "awesome tools" and "ingenious techniques" of "depth probers" versed in "subterranean operations" of "mass psychoanalysis" and an effort "to work over the fabric of our minds" through the "engineering" of public consent. The culprits, according to Packard, "are systematically feeling out our hidden weaknesses and frailties" in a world of deception and manipulation controlled by men who can produce "custom-made men" and engineer a "hypnoidal trance" in housewives. After conversing with "depth probers," Packard confessed: "It is embarrassing to try to relate in cold print some of what they told me." Yet he somehow managed sufficient immodesty to announce the arrival of "the chilling world of George Orwell and his Big Brother [p. 6]." The reference to Orwell is but a variation on a theme favored by Aldous Huxley in his *Brave New World*; both Huxley and Orwell weave nightmarish visions of a society reduced to enforced slavery by "neo-Pavlovian conditioning," "hypno-paedis," and other means of standardizing the human product.

In a grim extension of the vision advanced by Huxley and Orwell, George Lucus, in his film *THX 1138* described the world of A.D. 2400 as a subterranean prison where man is held in the tyrannical grip of a nightmarish cybernetic age. In the madness of a master plan controlled solely by computers, all passion is suppressed, personal contact is minimized, and even human speech is drowned out by the ever-present loudspeakers that dispense recorded dicta and exhortation. Thus, the prophetic vision endorsed by Huxley, Orwell, Packard, Meerloo, and Lucus leaves man with little choice other than to submit as pawns to the whim of social engineers or their machinery.

The inclination to either understate or overestimate the potential impact of communication stems largely from a reactive conception of human behavior that leads to a futile search for one-to-one relationships between messages and their immediate outcomes. The attempt to find such simple causal links ignores many of the scientific findings discussed in previous chapters, particularly the mediating influence of information processing and psychological orientation and a host of social and physical forces at work in any communicative situation. Even worse is the use of post hoc reasoning and anecdotal data taken from atypical incidents like the public panic following Orson Welles's broadcast of a mock invasion from Mars. At the opposite end of the controversy, many overstate the power of the mass media by citing Kate Smith's ability to stir unprecedented sales of war bonds during a telethon after World War II. (Not surprisingly, no one yet has duplicated either the feat of Orson Welles or that of Kate Smith.)

Further parallels exist in studies on verbal interaction in face-to-face situations. Instructors in public speaking, for example, tend to exaggerate the potential impact of well-prepared, well-presented public speeches. Typically, students listen to a daily round of five-minute persuasive speeches and ten-minute panel discussions on the pretext that they thereby participate in the exalted methods of democracy and grapple with the great issues of the day. When empirical evidence is cited to support such simplistic exercises, it usually is taken from other five-minute speeches delivered under sterile laboratory conditions where a questionnaire about attitude change is administered immediately after an inert audience listens to a one-shot message. What inevitably gets ignored in such research strategy are the gamut of mediating factors such as ego involvement, selective perception, social pressure, motivational factors, psychological risks, situational factors, and the impact of long-term influences represented by the mosaic model of communication discussed in Chapter 2.

Much can be gained by examining problems associated with the hypodermic approach to social influence. Clearly, when one-shot messages are viewed as necessary and sufficient causes of socially significant changes in attitude and behavior, only confusion and contradictory results can be expected. Recall the conclusions in Chapter 4, particularly those dealing with the futility of searching for uniform or "universal" effects of verbal messages. Along related lines, the complexities associated with interpersonal contact, situational geography, and communication networks should be taken together to indicate that messages constitute only one set of factors working with numerous others to produce a *range* of responses among interactants.

Finally, the multidimensionality of communication requires that the concept of social influence—like notions of credibility, power, and many others—should be regarded not as one unitary and singular variable but as a cluster of interrelated factors. Hence, it is futile to generalize about social influence as if it consisted of a single, undifferentiated process. Hence, we need to consider some leading differences in various types of influence discussed in previous chapters. By stepping back from the details, we can see that much previous discussion dealt with *overt* influences that are available for public inspection, whereas others are based on inferences about *covert* and private modes of influence. From another perspective, some influences center on the *content* of communication while others hinge on personal *relationships.* Some verbal behavior evokes responses that are *consummatory* or complete in themselves, whereas others have mainly *instrumental* value in leading to subsequent responses that eventually fit the goals of the communicator. On another scale, some forms of influence are under *direct control* of the respective parties, whereas others remain *uncontrolled.* Finally, social influence may be either *short-term* or *persistent.* By examining each of these influences in turn, we should gain additional perspective on the interplay that goes on continually between forces that maximize or minimize the potential for socia l change.

COVERT AND OVERT INFLUENCE

The complicated relation between covert and overt influence approximates the two interacting mosaics of information discussed in Chapter 2. One is analogous to those covert influences that are internal to receivers, whereas the other is overt and within range of direct observation by others. Covert influence includes any change in perception, opinion, attitude, belief, or value or some larger shift in psychological orientation. Overt influence comprises any socially observable decision or action. The material on commitment, for instance, illustrates the distinct aspects of these two spheres of influence; commitments made only to oneself differ markedly from those made in the presence of others.

The exact relationship between covert and overt influence is a good deal more difficult to establish than the mere fact that they are distinguishable from one another. Do covert and overt influences overlap in any uniform way? Do changes in one inevitably lead to a realignment in the other? Do intentions have any bearing on the course of subsequent actions? If man truly operates on grounds of self-consistency, it seems only reasonable to expect him to align his general courses of action with his central attitudes and values. Take the case of a college student who finds himself moved by a campus speaker's convincing support of an underground newspaper. If the student's commitment is genuine, we would not expect soon thereafter to hear him announce his refusal to have anything to do with the promotion of the newspaper, even to the point of not reading it. We would probably say that the course of his conduct, if taken at face value, does not make sense; his commitment does not lead logically to his subsequent action. And yet hardly a day passes without observing inconsistency between the verbal responses of receivers and their subsequent conduct.

In a now-classic study of attitudes and subsequent behavior, La Pierre (1934) accompanied a Chinese couple during two years' travel around the country. In some 250 establishments—hotels, auto camps, tourist houses, restaurants—La Pierre kept detailed records of the overt responses of hotel clerks, waitresses, bellboys, and elevator operators to the presence of his Chinese friends; he was interested primarily in whether service was accorded or denied the couple. Six months after completing their travels, La Pierre mailed questionnaires to the establishments they had visited. His aim was to determine the degree to which covert influence (as measured by their responses to the question "Will you accept members of the Chinese race as guests in your establishment?") were related to the actual policies of the place of business. Though only one person refused to serve his Chinese friends, better than 90 percent of the hotels and restaurants indicated they would not serve members of the Chinese race. La Pierre concluded that attitudes do not serve as valid and reliable predictors of what a person actually does when confronted by the reality of the actual situation. Subsequent studies supported La Pierre's finding and led to what has since become known as the *discrepancy problem* (Ajzen, 1970; De Fluer and Westie, 1958; Lin, 1965; Wicker, 1969).

For those who suppose attitudes to be related to overt behavior, the discrepancy problem is a cause of embarrassment and heated controversy. Most attempts to resolve the problem hinge on variations of three overlapping explanations. One asserts that the problem lies not in the actual link between attitudes and behavior but in the tools and strategies used to tap the relationship (Campbell, 1963). Another spins off from the idea that talk is cheap and that there thus is little reason to expect more than a minimal positive relationship between verbal indicators of attitude and subsequent courses of action anyway (McGuire, 1969; Miller, 1967). Representative is the following reasoning by Miller (1967):

> In a number of studies, we have found that certain types of persuasive messages produce more favorable verbal attitudes toward civil defense, that individuals say they would like to be better informed about the steps to follow in case of nuclear attack or natural disaster. In several instances, we have distributed an addressed envelop and a form letter to assist

people in requesting further information about civil defense. To obtain this information, the person has only to write his name and address on the bottom of the envelop, put a stamp on the envelop, and post the letter.

A small percentage of people have expended the energy required to request further information. In addition, the data reveal no apparent relationship between the amount of attitude change resulting from the persuasive messages and subsequent information-seeking behavior. In other words, persons who reported little change in the verbal attitudinal responses toward civil defense following exposure to persuasive messages were just as likely to post letters as individuals for whom change in verbal response was marked. While our sample is small, this finding again illustrates the frequent discrepancy between verbally operationalized measures of attitude and other behaviors [p. 236].

A third approach may be best understood by returning to the instance of the college student who professed support for the underground newspaper. Assume for a moment that there is no major flaw in our measure of his change in attitude; in other words his verbal response is an accurate reflection of his intentions and commitment. Now the problem shifts to the matter of what will constitute the most appropriate measure of overt action. In other words, we want to know just what course of action to use as being *consistent* or *discrepant* with his seeming change in attitude. Consider a few of the possibilities. If we return two weeks later and find he has yet to write a single line for the newspaper, are we to conclude that we have uncovered yet more testimony for the idea that talk is cheap? If so, critics could counter by saying that he may not have had any *intention* of writing for the newspaper when he made the pledge of support, but instead was insecure about his writing skills. Or what if we find that he has yet to buy a single copy of the paper? Again, he may be flat broke—not an unlikely possibility for an undergraduate, especially after tuition falls due. Or suppose we look for any other given index of support. Clearly, no matter what the decision, we are forced to make inferences about what will be taken as consistent with something else. Hence, any one act we select may *appear discrepant* when the receiver regards it only as *irrelevant*. Said another way, the inconsistency may result from an arbitrary classification of what an outsider infers to be discrepant. The lesson is clear: The subjective and personal experience of attitude change may be expressed in any number of ways; therefore, any single course of action may or may not be a relevant barometer of the link between attitude and behavior. An exception to this generalization occurs whenever receivers know beforehand exactly what course of action will follow any commitment they may make. Examples include the expressed willingness of a college student to join a fraternity (knowing that he must be prepared for an initiation ceremony) or a person who seeks a job with the knowledge that a loyalty oath is a condition of employment.

In short, the fact that an *obvious relationship* does not exist between attitudes and behavior does not preclude the possibility that a *less obvious* one exists. The same holds true for covert and overt influence generally; in fact we chose the discrepancy problem to illustrate the larger link between covert and overt influence mainly because it is the best known and most thoroughly examined aspect of the topic at hand. Fishbein (in press), for example, argued convincingly that a link between attitudes and behavior can be established only when three conditions are met. One is availability of information pertinent to a person's *intentions*. It obviously makes quite a difference whether intent is defined on general or specific grounds. To illustrate, the fact that our student fails to buy a newspaper may seem inconsistent with his affirmative response to the question "Do you pledge every possible financial assistance to the circulation of this newspaper?" However, if he had in mind only the general intention to convince others to buy the paper, he could have well read the question as requiring only whatever form of assistance each person could offer—whether or not they could afford to buy copies for themselves. Hence, what he had in mind was to sell copies for an hour a day in front of the student union. The complex matter of intent involves further complications, for it includes not only a person's *subjective judgments* about an object of attitude but also the norms of a given situation as they influence the judgments. Two people may experience approximately the same subjective feelings yet differ in their actions because one operates under a norm of conduct dictated by a scholarship that requires him to spend some forty hours a week in a library whereas the other spends his time talking informally with people who share his judgments. Also contributing to the strength of an attitude are temporal factors (particularly the interval between measurement of attitudes and subsequent action) and the degree to which a person feels free to take a particular course of action. Hence, the link between attitude change and subsequent behavior requires information about (1) intent, (2) time factors, and (3) degree of volition. Note that Fishbein does not suggest that any one specific course of action can be predicted. It is one thing to predict that a man will honor a pledge to support his local church by attending its services; it is quite another to specify the frequency and exact pattern of his attendance. In short, our conclusion parallels the one considered in the discussion of self-consistency in Chapter 2. Interactants can be expected to align their attitudes, intentions, and other measures of covert influence on one hand, with a *general course of consistent action* on the other. However, the link between the two cannot be determined unless we know specifically what the receivers in question regard as consistent with what courses of action and unless something is known about the social forces at work in the actual communicative situation.

CONTENT AND RELATIONSHIP INFLUENCE

Few ideas underscore the inevitability of influence any more forcefully than does the interplay between messages and social relationships.

Relationships invariably impose on the meaning of social interaction. And as relationships develop over time, content fades in relative importance. Nonetheless, much hinges on the involvement of the respective parties and their manner of expressing their views. In an insightful analysis, Katz (1970) identified four functions of the attitudes as they are expressed in social situations. These functions will now be examined for their implications in understanding the type of bond that is formed by interactants in face-to-face settings.

The Adjustment Function

This function recognizes people's need to express themselves in ways that maximize personal satisfaction and minimize psychological risk. These attitudes are aroused with the activation of needs which are satisfied through association with need-related attitudes. Thus, group members who happen to be the most hungry also tend to make most frequent mention of food-related items. Likewise, students who most keenly feel the pressure of impending exams—or the effects of those just taken—are the most prone to initiate conversation questioning the merits of the grading system. Also not surprising, talk about price controls increases in times of deepest recession. In short, people try to maintain relationships in ways that maximize the satisfaction of personal needs and rewards.

   If the adjustment function helps to define the selectivity of relationships—the matter of who seeks out what persons to talk about X—it also imposes on more specific aspects of interaction. For one thing, the need for adjustment overlaps with the need for positive feedback (p. 325); Recall that, with positive feedback, people tend to talk most frequently and direct their comments toward those they perceive as reacting the most favorably to their statements; in other words, they judge the effect of their comments against the way others express their own needs for personal reward. The clearer the tie between verbal statement and need-related motives, the more people are apt to establish a positive relationship and to heighten their own satisfaction.

   Also relevant to the adjustment function is the notion of interpersonal similarity (p. 343) and the norm of reciprocity (p. 264); the first posits that relationships follow perceived similarity, and the latter suggests that what one person does initially, others tend to follow in kind. When parties permit a relationship to get out of hand (p. 61), they invariably do so in the way they show dissatisfaction with the tenor of the relationship. Recall also the idea that people are reluctant to show signs of personal trust before they have a chance to size up the other party's intentions toward their relationship. Only after both signal a willingness to extend trust—at the risk of personal loss—are the other requirements of a trusting relationship apt to be established. In all the concepts just reviewed, one common theme emerges. The tie between relationship and content is similar to the adjustment principle.

The Ego-defensive Function

Attitudes may reflect a person's need to avoid any confrontation with basic truths about himself or from threats in the physical world, particularly those harmful to the ego. Included are the devices by which the ego is shielded from inner realities—insecurity, low esteem, inadequacy—and from external pressures and constraints. Severe defense mechanisms are socially crippling—to the point of outright withdrawal or avoidance of social situations. Less severe mechanisms may cause the psychological distortions we associate with projection and rationalization.

In interpersonal affairs, ego-defensive attitudes operate mainly in a negative way. Since they are designed to shield a person from threat, they enable a person to avoid threatening relationships entirely. When a threat simply cannot be avoided, however, a defensive person will exhibit considerable hostility toward others. He will show reluctance to risk his own ego or to recognize initial acts of trust on the part of those around him. The defensive person is unduly conscious of matters of social power, authority, and credibility (pp. 142–159). Most significant, defensive mechanisms alter the psychological orientation of an interactant, particularly in reducing his willingness to share in another person's thoughts. Concomitant with ego-defense is self-preoccupation and a reluctance to engage in any act that requires maximum self-disclosure.

In the matter of social influence, ego defense is the great enemy of change. People who retreat from harsh realities to the comfort of their inner shell seldom feel responsive to the appeals initiated by others for change. The reluctance to change relates to our earlier finding that high ego involvement increases resistance to compromise and joint decision making (p. 163). Katz suggested that ego defensive attitudes can be altered only when encouragement is given to their expression in a supportive social climate, by appeals to authority, or when an individual acquires insight into psychological barriers of his own making.

The Value-expressive Function

In contrast to ego-defensive attitudes are those aiding man's effort to express his central values and to enhance his self-image. The expressive function is necessary to confirm self-identity and to find rewards associated with any attribute of the ego. Seldom do relationships develop apart from the two conditions necessary for the arousal of value-expressive attitudes: the arousal associated with any self-related thought and the need to reassert one's self-image. Once expressive attitudes come into play, they are not readily altered unless expressed in the context of a relationship that is conducive to a show of dissatisfaction with one's self-concept or a realization that certain older attitudes are inconsistent with existing values. Discomfort with old attitudes may occur anytime, of course, but ordinarily a supportive interpersonal climate is required to alter them. So again we see a close tie between the elements of what respective parties say in the context of their unique relationship and the attitudes they make verbally explicit.

The Knowledge Function

In essence this function reflects the need for order, clarity, and stability in personal frame of reference. A part of the knowledge function was described in Chapter 4 under the integrating principle of psychological orientation. Of relevance also is the connection between processing activity and one's sense of self. As cases in point, the rules of perceptual organization (p. 95), the principle of nonelementalism (p. 26), the idea of executive control (p. 110), information seeking (p. 102), hierarchies of stimulus analyzing (p. 87) and other functions contribute to the need to create a sense of order and structure out of what otherwise would be an unorganized and chaotic universe. Hence, all that is necessary to arouse knowledge-related attitudes is a relationship that leads to a sense of ambiguity or uncertainty.

Again, it is important to see how directly the knowledge function relates to the tie between message content and personal relationship. The key to the relation is the same one underlying our previous discussion of source credibility. Recall the connection between impressions of a communicator and the acceptance of what he says. In general we discovered that the credibility of information depends on the judged trustworthiness and authority of the person who expresses it (p. 145). In turn, impressions of credibility hinge on the larger influences that define a relationship: perceptions of trust, power, status, role, size, feedback, attraction, physical surroundings, nonverbal cues, and so forth. The notion of metacommunication ensures that no matter what a person says and does, he invariably signals how he intends others to interpret his behavior. So inexorably linked are the message and relationship that it is often impossible to sort their exact constituent importance.

CONSUMMATORY AND INSTRUMENTAL INFLUENCE

The concept of social influence can be probed from still another angle that cuts through both overt-covert and content-relationship aspects of our study. Suppose we order all social influence against the completeness of the goals and responses involved. At one end of the continuum are influences that are complete or finalized in the immediate responses they evoke. At the other are influences that are incomplete yet instrumental in leading to still other responses. In the former case we have instances of *consummatory* influence, and in the latter *instrumental* influence. In reality, of course, the distinction is always a matter of degree. Some influences are more or less complete with immediate responses of receivers; others are only means to further goals. Note that we are not talking about responses per se, as *instrumentality* is often used in learning research, but rather about the *link* between goals and responses of the respective communicators.

Consider first the situation in which immediate social influence is regarded as an end in itself. Artists usually define their artistic work as consummatory in emphasis. Poetry, music, drama, and literature tend to be enjoyed for their own sake; in each the intrinsic pleasure is in responding to the experience itself. The same holds for many other modes of communication. Laughter, for example, tends to be consummatory; an entertainer tells jokes to make an audience laugh, their immediate responses provide the measure of his influence. Another case in point is the knowledge function discussed earlier. The need for order and stability, the search for relevant information as a means of reducing uncertainty, tends to be pursued as an end in itself. Knowledge is the goal of many communicative situations, despite the common practice of justifying knowledge on instrumental grounds ("Stay in school: High school graduates earn more money than dropouts"). On another front, score-keepers and referees at sports events create largely consummatory messages. Both are interested in one variation of the knowledge function, relaying information, keeping spectators aware of infractions; scoring and other units of information are final at the moment they are expressed. Other examples include "No smoking" signs, highway markers, and maps.

Instrumental behavior occurs when messages function mainly to further other goals. Advertising is a key case in point. The door-to-door salesman begins his pitch to the housewife by offering her a free gift, no strings attached —just to get a foot in the door. General Motors sponsors the Soapbox Derby. American Airlines gives "promotional consideration" to those who travel with them to appear on television shows. Sears, Roebuck provides a grant to help sponsor "Mr. Rogers" on educational television. Mail-order firms send free coupons; gas companies offer double stamps or free glasses with purchases. Cereal boxes appeal to those barely old enough to read (and too young to buy cereal) with mail-order offers. In each instance the enticement is a means to some further end or goal.

Sometimes advertisers even attempt to evoke instrumental responses in the early part of a single message. Many television commercials, for example, delay mention of the sponsor for as long as possible. In the interim they try to create such instrumental responses as humor, interest, curiosity, eye-catching images, and the like. One instance shows an energetic four-year-old boy joyfully imitating the manner of his father through a sequence of actions. He imitates his father's manner of walking, throwing rocks, driving a car, using a hose, sitting under a tree and then—poking into a pack of cigarettes.

Only then does the announcer intone: "Like Father—Like Son? Think about it!" All sponsored, of course, by the American Cancer Society.

The main difference between consummatory and instrumental acts resembles the two sequences shown in Figure 10.1. Note how the consummatory sequence remains in a more or less one-to-one relationship between goals and responses. Instrumental acts, in contrast, are marked by initial responses that, yet incomplete, nonetheless lead through a chain of responses to eventual realization of communicator's goals (Fotheringham, 1966).

Figure 10.1 has relevance to much of the territory charted in previous chapters. The intrapersonal system of communication, for example, focuses on goals aimed at momentary changes in the building blocks of information processing and psychological orientation. In one sense consummatory influence is a minimal requirement of all processing activity. The idea of consummatory influence is implicit in all the momentary adjusting, filtering, selective analyzing, integrating, sorting, and reconstructing aspects of human intelligence. So also do encounters aimed at influencing the frame of reference of another person fit into the notion of consummatory goals and responses. Particularly important are those aspects of psychological orientation that arouse and alter knowledge functions, ego-defense mechanisms, and value-expressive attitudes.

The interpersonal system includes an admixture of consummatory and instrumental goals. Most of the factors in Chapter 5 ("Verbal Interaction") may be viewed as instrumental in emphasis. Decisions over primacy-recency, fear arousal, and other aspects of message content seldom assume significance in themselves. Their usefulness is simply a matter of how well they work in effecting persuasive influence. Along related lines, recall that the strategic aspects of interpersonal contact discussed in Chapter 7 function mainly in an instrumental way. For example, note the finding that people present highly

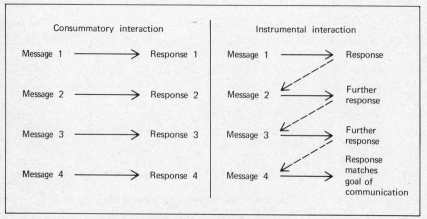

Figure 10.1   *Consummatory and instrumental interaction.*

idealized versions of themselves for public inspection; their urge to create favorable impressions may be valued somewhat for its own sake but more importantly for its instrumental value in developing a favorable climate for social interaction. Furthermore, the concepts of personal space and physical orientation show how immediate responses to the environment can have far-reaching significance for all subsequent aspects of an encounter. The person who is in charge of organizing a sensitivity group, for example, may arrange the chairs to form a close-knit, circular pattern; in so doing he is probably not conscious of any aesthetic advantage in the circular pattern, only its usefulness in maximizing the chances of facilitating spontaneous and responsive inter-action, not so much as an end in itself but as a condition necessary for the continued support of the group in subsequent meetings. Even certain com-munication networks may have instrumental value in promoting or interfering with membership satisfaction. The reader may think of implications of consum-matory and instrumental goals in other aspects of communication, particularly matters of metacommunication, risk, social power, and virtually all dimen-sions of a communicative act.

CONTROLLED AND UNCONTROLLED INFLUENCE

Implicit in any communicative act are a complex set of influences that differ markedly in the degree to which they fall under the control of the participants. The greatest degree of control occurs in such decisions as how fast to talk, what to say, when to say it and how. Other aspects of communica-tion may result from forces that are fully beyond the personal control of the respective parties. Some uncontrolled influences, for instance, may result from something fortuitous or accidental. Someone suddenly interrupts a speech; a public address system fails; the electricity goes out; or background noise prevents a speaker from being heard. Given the tremendous array of possibili-ties, it may be useful to look at the problem of controlled-versus-uncontrolled influence under three broad designations: influences that are regulated directly by the individual participants, those that are under partial individual control, and those beyond any control by the respective parties.

Direct Control

The greatest measure of control is one that interactants exercise over their own verbal conduct. Yet even though the global aspects of verbal behavior are often self-regulated, we have already discovered that control over what to say and how to say it rarely operates independent of others' conduct. Communica-tion, after all, requires some degree of mutual dependence; the conduct of any one person depends in part on the conduct of others who are present. Even in such simple matters as the right to talk or remain silent, self-regulated aspects of interaction are usually influenced by the other social and situational forces: norms, pressures for compliance, social constraint, feedback, group size, social climate, and many others. Of relevance also are those nonverbal cues, especially facial expression and body orientation, that also have regulative value, yet cannot be concealed or fully controlled (pp. 229–237). Along somewhat different lines, recall that group members rarely feel free to express themselves when they choose and on their own terms, particularly as group size increases from five to twelve or so (p. 270). The implication is clear: It may be useful to think of certain aspects of interpersonal behavior as self-regulated and therefore under direct personal control; however the degree of control falls short of what is autonomous or isolated activity operating independently of other forces.

Partial Control

At a time when the hypodermic notion of communication was much in vogue, theories of social influence tended to explain virtually any communicative outcome as a result of the power of messages per se. One person would say something to influence another. The receiver would react as directed. Presto! The message is presumed to be the causal agent. Now, however, the picture is complicated by the realization that the earlier model assumed too much for the potential of messages to control the attitudes and actions of receivers. It is now understood that control functions in the manner of social power (p. 157); the impact of both tends to be mediated by other communicative variables and, therefore, operates at far less than maximum impact.

Probably the clearest instance of social control occurs in a situation where one person enjoys some monopoly over a channel of communication (a telephone switchboard or public address system). Another instance occurs whenever interaction adheres to certain norms or rules of conduct. For example, a corporation president may control the tenor of his board meetings because his vice-presidents know the consequences of violating certain standards of conduct that apply to any formal company deliberation. However, even norms or rules of conduct may be open to question or challenge, as in the case with public protests and demonstrations. Yet even when respective parties adhere to conventional rules of behavior, they still may exercise only a certain degree of control over the actions of others, mainly because of the arsenal of psychological defenses available to anyone who seeks to resist social control.

Consider just some of the many psychological defenses that can be used to ward off the manipulative intent of other interactants in a face-to-face setting. One of the most formidable is the power of *selective exposure*; receivers may choose to limit the attempt of others to control their actions simply by *avoiding* what they say. The selectivity may assume any number of forms. The most common is *absenteeism*. Another is the sort of tactic reserved for a person who suddenly finds himself in a captive audience. He may rely on a form of *resistance* by listening to the message while actively guarding against any inclination to accept the directives or recommendations of the communicator. If the ego involvement of the listener happens to be strong, he may resort to the defense of *distortion* or *differentiation* (pp. 137 and 138). Another protective device is *selective recall*, where the person remembers only what suits his purposes. Added to the repertoire of psychological defenses is the urge to maintain self-consistency (p. 134) and the inclination to resist any attempt by others to change one's self-image (p. 139). All these defenses will function in an even stronger way when the object of interaction happens to be directed at the primitive belief system of the receiver (p. 162). Recall that primitive beliefs are those that are not dependent on what others say or do. Resistance can be maintained on grounds of credibility, where the image of the communicator works against his attempt to control the actions of his receivers (p. 142). Finally, the notion of punctuation (p. 55) suggests that a person can resist merely by defining who is in charge of whom. In short, all of these tactics are proactive in nature, thereby sharply delimiting the degree of direct control one interactant can exercise over another.

Uncontrolled Influence

Not all sources of communicative influence are under direct or even partial control of the respective parties. The determining influences may result from sheer accident. Noise is a case in point. Few situations exist free of disruptive influences; even on television talk shows one can occasionally hear the sounds of a police siren in the background. To the inadvertent sort of interruption must be added the usual minor distractions caused by such irritants as shuffling feet, coughing, dropped pens, a sudden hum from a public address system, banging doors, or clanging sounds of some late arrival. Even more disruptive is the direct intervention of a third party. Finally, the most pervasive of all uncontrolled influence may stem from physical factors in the setting: color scheme, arrangement of chairs and furniture, lighting conditions, temperature, and other aesthetic factors. Inevitably the salient features of the communicative environment impose on the meaning of the event itself, quite apart from the behavior of the respective parties. So interrelated are message and contextual elements that their relative import often cannot be specified.

SHORT–TERM AND PERSISTENT INFLUENCE

In the course of day-to-day affairs, we are constantly subject to social influence which leads to a succession of changes in thinking, habit, taste, and life style. At times the process of influence occurs so gradually that we hardly notice it. At others it may border on the spectacular. For example, in a relatively short period of time, the motorcycle has been transformed from a public stereotype of a lethal machine favored only by those in sympathy with the Hell's Angels. On more important matters of public policy, the American public has reversed itself on Vietnam, racial discrimination, birth control, capital punishment, matters of air pollution, automobile design, consumer protection, freeways, cigarette advertising on TV and so on. Even more spectacular are the recent changes in attitudes held by young people toward the use of marijuana, sexual codes, style of dress, work, military service, and related aspects of life style.

In short, it is not difficult to see evidence of persistent and significant forms of social influence all around us. Yet, compare what we experience in the course of day-to-day experience with the scientific findings available on the subject. The most transitory form of influence occurs in the nervous system in the course of making an incredible number of decisions every second of our waking hours; hence, any signal that reaches short-term memory constitutes an influence of sorts. Of added relevance is the discovery that the nervous system can reconstruct only a fraction of information from past events. If we keep these aspects of information processing in mind when discussing the question of persistent influence, it should hardly seem surprising to learn that the typical five-minute speech used in laboratory studies of social influence rarely if ever produces enduring changes in attitude. Correspondingly, we discovered that the details of messages yield quite short-term advantages. Also, the power associated with high source credibility diminishes rapidly unless reinforced along the way (p. 147). Likewise, one-shot messages seem to change attitudes initially, but within a few days the receivers are apt to regress to their original stands. If the people happen to be highly ego involved in their positions, even short-term change is not apt to occur. Of related interest is that the internal details of verbal interaction—order effects, primacy-recency, fear arousal, reasoning—can *influence* attitudes but do not ordinarily *determine* them (p. 204). For the most part, then, single communicative acts produce minimal and short-term influence. Yet our everyday experience attests to the existence of persistent influence. So the question persists as to why such a disparity exists between the mainstream of laboratory findings and our daily experience.

It may be useful to gain perspective on short-term influence by conceiving of attitude change in a manner that approximates the discussion of arousal thresholds in Chapter 2. Attitudes function at various levels of response—or *response thresholds*. If the threshold is minimal, or low, the potential for change is not apt to be great. Furthermore, even when the threshold is high—that is, when receivers are predisposed toward the possibility of change —the message will probably be sufficiently powerful to produce a momentary shift in attitude. However, if the event is an isolated one, the attitude will regress rapidly to its original position (Festinger, 1964; Miller, 1968). Since most scientific work on social influence deals exclusively with immediate responses to a particular message, it is hardly an earth-shaking discovery to learn that such events produce little evidence of persistent social influence.

Now consider the problem of persistent influence in the context of the mosaic model discussed in Chapter 2. Think of influence as functioning within a larger social context defined by a deluge of messages that occur in bits and pieces. Each experience contributes to the potential or upper limit of influence by functioning in any number of ways: reinforcing, disconfirming, repeating, underscoring, overlapping, clarifying, and so on. Some message bits first seem to be the most important, yet fade quickly. Others seem insignificant at first and later trigger associations that permit the larger pieces suddenly to fit into place. In short, our picture of influence is a good deal more complex than what can be explained in terms of a particular number of variables. In fact, the very concept of a communication variable seems to be an outmoded and inappropriate unit of measure for the sort of complex social influence that occurs over extended periods. Said another way, the search for "all the relevant variables" may only obscure our understanding of the most complex forms of communicative influence and, even worse, leave us with a fragmented picture of man as an object of social change.

We realize, then, that social influence does not occur because of the impact of a single variable's operating under its own powers or even because of a cluster of interacting variables. It becomes virtually impossible for anyone to sort all the constituent factors that lead to complex changes in attitude, much less assign responsibility and relative importance to each. For example, a person who reverses his stand on a matter as complex as Vietnam would find it difficult to account in any precise way for the events that led to the conviction that the war was morally indefensible. The process of change would come to mind in bits and pieces. Certain striking influences, of course, would be recalled first. The person could scan his memory and think of prominent headlines, conversations with friends, mounting casualty reports, a gripping picture shown in *Life* of a monk in the final agonizing moments of self-immolation. Next might come images from films of protests, heated arguments, pictures, news reports, and the more diffuse recall of personal soul-searching and deliberation in moments of growing doubt and resultant change in conviction. Soon the list of influences reaches such proportions that the person is left with only a global and incomplete sense of how the change occurred.

Our example implies that the laboratory approach to studying social influence is one of severely limited utility. What is needed is some broader framework that is more suitable for studying the larger social context in which change is experienced. It may be more useful, for example, to think of social influence as one might approach the study of some complex social movement such as civil rights activity or women's liberation. A movement does not occur in one sharply defined period of time nor does it revolve around any particular communicative event or even in the context of a specifiable number of messages. Everything connected with a movement is in a state of flux; conflicting activities of competing groups, numerous sources of resistance, changing rates of adaptation, fluctuations in social pressure, changes in persuasive strategies and tactics, varying means of gaining accent and implementation, and many other defining aspects of the setting. A social movement entails different styles of leadership, various levels of esprit de corps, varying kinds of feedback, plus an array of shifting modes of activity by agitators, propagandists, gatekeepers, know-nothings, leaders, bureaucrats, by-standers, third parties, hecklers, foot draggers, opponents, bunglers, critics, and so on. All these work to define the forces of a movement and whatever eventual form of influence it produces (for an insightful introduction to the persuasion of social movements, see Simons, 1970).

Images of Communication Revisited

Final comments are reserved for a chance to return full circle to our initial discussion of images of communication. If we step back from the details and view the scientific work on communicative behavior in its larger perspective, a certain image of man as communicator emerges. The perspective is one that differs markedly from the images discussed in Chapter 1 and also from popular conceptions held only a few decades ago. Admittedly the picture afforded by any field in its infancy is bound to be incomplete and at times embarrassingly fragmented. Many findings are enlightening but many are not. Some patterns may seem obvious or merely dull to some. Yet even when allowances are made for disclaimers and gaps in knowledge, a certain image comes into focus, one that represents a distinct and significant change in contemporary images of man. It is, for example, one that stands in striking contrast to an earlier view of communication based upon the ideal of a good man speaking well. This older image drew credence at times dominated by elegant rhetoric delivered by revered men on affairs of church and state before enthralled audiences that thought themselves to be witness to the great drama of history's making. But with the transformation from an agrarian society to the electronic age, the dramatistic image tarnished and eventually gave way to the man-machine controversy. Though mechanistic images are presently going out of fashion, they have been useful in clarifying a certain range of narrow problems of the sort discussed in Chapter 3. The image now coming into focus may be taken as phenomenistic and transactional in orientation.

The transactional image of communication differs from earlier notions in several important ways. In dealing with the total constituent forces at work in any communicative setting, it departs from the traditional interest of psychology in individual units of behavior. Instead, it conceives of "persons interacting with others" as the irreducible unit of observation. The new approach also denies previous attempts to explain the behavior of receivers as passive, neutral responses conceived largely as undifferentiated social aggregates. It also rejects a yes-no, light-switch approach to messages defined in mechanistic terms as the necessary and sufficient causal agents of change in uncritical and inert listeners. The shift in orientation also denies a view of communication as a succession of discrete events marked by fixed beginnings and endings and initiated by sources that rely almost exclusively on the power of words as agents of social change. Also refuted by the shift in orientation is the exaggerated view of messages as all-powerful tools employed by engineers of public opinion. Concomitant to the change in perspective is a clearer understanding of the strategic and proactive aspects of information processing and the inexorable link between the imprint of physical events and subjective experience, between environment and message, and between content and relationship. With the denial of the hypodermic notion has come a clearer understanding of some of the far-reaching implications of man's tendency to personalize all aspects of his surroundings. Furthermore, communication is now understood to result from a dynamic interplay of a multiplicity of interacting forces and functions—physical, psychological, social, and cultural—all so inexorably linked that the gestalt impact of communicative events can only be described as having the attributes of an open system. And perhaps what is most significant of all, the very openness of the system means that our experience of communication is also open to change and redefinition. Let us hope that further modifications in the image will be the sort that reflect man's search for more authentic and responsive interpersonal encounters.

SUGGESTED READINGS

Cohen, A. R. *Attitude Change and Social Influence.* New York: Basic Books, 1964.

Fishbein, M. "The Prediction of Behaviors from Attitudinal Variables," in C. D. Mortensen and K. K. Sereno, *Advances in Communication Research,* New York: Harper & Row, in press.

Katz, D. "The Functional Approach to the Study of Attitudes," in K. K. Sereno and C. D. Mortensen, *Foundations of Communication Theory.* New York: Harper & Row, 1970, pp. 234–259.

Miller, G. R. "Communication and Persuasion Research: Current Problems and Prospects," *The Quarterly Journal of Speech,* 54:268–276, 1967.

Miller, G. R. "A Crucial Problem in Attitude Research," *The Quarterly Journal of Speech,* 53:235–240, 1967.

Rokeach, M. *Beliefs, Attitudes and Values,* San Francisco: Jossey-Bass, 1968.

references

Aaronson, D. "Temporal Factors in Per-
(1967) ception and Short-term Memory,"
Psychological Bulletin, 67:130–
144.
Aaronson, D. "Effects of Presentation Rate
(1963) and Recall Delay in Short-term
Memory." Unpublished manu-
script, University of Pennsylvania, as cited in Aaronson, 1967.
Abbs, J., and **Sussman, H.** "Neurophysio-
(in press) logical Feature Detectors and
Speech Perception: A Discussion
of Theoretical Implications,"
*Journal of Speech and Hearing
Research.*
Abelson, R., and **Sermat, V.** "Multidimen-
(1962) sional Scaling of Facial Expressions," *Journal of Experimental
Psychology,* 63:546–554.
Adams, J. S. "Reduction of Cognitive Dis-
(1961) sonance by Seeking Consonant
Information," *Journal of Abnor-
mal and Social Psychology,* 62:
74–78.
Adler, A. *Individual Psychology.* London:
(1925) Routledge.
Ajzen, I., and **Fishbein, M.** "The Prediction
(1970) of Behavior from Attitudinal and
Normative Variables," *Journal of
Experimental Social Psychology,*
6:466–487.
Albee, E. *Who's Afraid of Virginia Woolf?*
(1962) New York: Atheneum.
Allen, V. L. "Effect of Knowledge of Decep-
(1966) tion on Conformity," *Journal of
Social Psychology,* 69:101–106.
Allport, F. H. "A Structuronomic Concep-
(1962) tion of Behavior: Individual and
Collective: I. Structural Theory
and the Master Problem of Social
Psychology," *Journal of Abnormal and Social Psychology,* 64:
3–30.
Allport, F. H. *Social Psychology.* Boston:
(1924) Houghton Mifflin.
Allport, G. W. *The Nature of Prejudice.*
(1954) Reading, Mass.: Addison-Wesley.

Allport, G. W. *The Individual and His
(1950) Religion.* New York: Macmillan.
Allport, G. W., and **Postman, L.** "The Basic
(1945) Psychology of Rumor," *Transactions of the New York Academy
of Sciences,* series II, 8:61–81.
Altman, I., and **Haythorn, W. W.** "The
(1967) Ecology of Isolated Groups,"
Behavioral Science, 12:169–182.
Altman, I., and **Haythorn, W. W.** "Inter-
(1965) personal Exchange in Isolation,"
Sociometry, 28:411–426.
Andersen, K. "An Experimental Study of
(1961) the Interaction of Artistic and
Non-artistic Ethos in Persua-
sion." Unpublished doctoral dissertation, University of Wis-
consin.
Andersen, K., and **Clevenger, Jr., T.** "A
(1963) Summary of Experimental Re-
search in Ethos," *Speech Mono-
graphs,* 30:59–78.
Andersen, K., Ladd, G., and **Smith, H.**
(1954) "A Study of 2,500 Kansas High
School Graduates," *Kansas
Studies in Education.* Lawrence,
Kans.: University of Kansas
Press, p. 4.
Anderson, D. "The Effect of Various Uses
(1958) of Authoritative Testimony in
Persuasive Speaking." Unpub-
lished masters thesis, Ohio State
University.
Anderson, N. H. "Test of a Model for
(1959) Opinion Change," *Journal of
Abnormal and Social Psychology,*
59:371–381.
Anderson, N. H., and **Barrios, A. A.** "Pri-
(1961) macy Effects in Personality Im-
pression Formation," *Journal of
Abnormal and Social Psychology,*
63:346–350.
Anderson, N. S., and **Fitts, P. M.** "Amount
(1958) of Information Gained during
Brief Exposures of Numerals and
Colors," *Journal of Experimental
Psychology,* 56:362–369.

Anderson, R. L., and **Mortensen, C. D.**
(1967)   "Logic and Marketplace Argumentation," *Quarterly Journal of Speech*, 53:143–151.

Angyal, A. "A Theoretical Model for Per-
(1951)   sonality Studies," *Journal of Personality*, 20:131–142.

Appley, M., and **Moeller, G.** "Conforming
(1963)   Behavior and Personality Variables in College Women," *Journal of Abnormal and Social Psychology*, 66:284–290.

Argyle, M. *The Psychology of Interpersonal*
(1967)   *Behavior.* Baltimore: Penguin.

Argyle, M., and **Dean, J.** "Eye Contact,
(1965)   Distance, and Affiliation," *Sociometry*, 28:289–304.

Argyle, M., and **Kendon, A.** "The Experi-
(1967)   mental Analysis of Social Performance," in L. Berkowitz (ed.), *Advances in Experimental Social Psychology*, vol. 3. New York: Academic, pp. 55–98.

Argyle, M., Lalljee, M., and **Cook, M.** "The
(1963)   Effects of Visibility on Interaction in a Dyad," *Human Relations*, 21:3–17.

Arnold, E. W., and **McCroskey, J. C.** "The
(1967)   Credibility of Reluctant Testimony," *Central States Speech Journal*, 18:97–103.

Aronson, E., and **Gerald, E.** "Beyond Park-
(1966)   inson's Law: The Effect of Excess Time on Subsequent Performance," *Journal of Personality and Social Psychology*, 3:336–339.

Aronson, E., and **Golden, B. W.** "The Effect
(1962)   of Relevant and Irrelevant Aspects of Communicator Credibility on Opinion Change," *Journal of Personality*, 30:135–146.

Asch, S. E. "Studies of Independence and
(1956)   Conformity: I. A Minority of One Against a Unanimous Majority," *Psychological Monographs*, 70 (whole no. 416).

Asch, S. E. "Opinions and Social Pressure,"
(1955)   *Scientific American*, November, 193:31–35.

Asch, S. E. *Social Psychology.* Englewood
(1952)   Cliffs, N.J.: Prentice-Hall.

Asch, S. E. "Effects of Group Pressure
(1951)   upon the Modification and Distortion of Judgments," in H. Guetzkow (ed.), *Groups, Lead-*

ership, and Men. Pittsburgh: Carnegie Press, 177–190.

Ashby, W. "The Application of Cybernetics
(1954)   to Psychiatry," *Journal of Mental Science*, 100:114–124.

Ashby, W. *Design for a Brain.* New York:
(1952)   Wiley (rev. ed., 1960).

Associated Press. Release, Corvallis, Oreg.,
(1967)   Feb. 27.

Associated Press. Release, New York,
(1970)   Oct. 12.

Atkinson, C. J. "Adaptation to Delayed
(1953)   Sidetone," *Journal of Speech and Hearing Disorders*, 18:386–391.

Atkinson, R. C., and **Shifrin, R. M.** "Human
(1968)   Memory: A Proposed System and Its Control Processes," in K. W. Spence and J. T. Spence (eds.), *The Psychology of Learning and Motivation: Advances in Research and Theory*, vol. II. New York: Academic, pp. 89–195.

Atwood, L. E. "The Effects of Incongruity
(1966)   between Source and Message Credibility," *Journalism Quarterly*, 43:90–94.

Auden, W. H. *About the House.* New York:
(1965)   Random House.

Averbach, E., and **Coriell, A.** "Short-term
(1960)   Memory in Vision," *Bell Telephone System Technical Publication*, monograph no. 3756.

Ax, A. "Physiological Differentiation of
(1953)   Emotional States," *Psychological Medicine*, 15:433–442.

Back, K. W. "Influence through Social
(1951)   Communication," *Journal of Abnormal and Social Psychology*, 46:9–23.

Back, K. W., and **Davis, K. E.** "Some Per-
(1965)   sonal and Situational Factors Relevant to the Consistency and Prediction of Conforming Behavior," *Sociometry*, 28:227–240.

Backman, C. W., and **Secord, P. F.** "Liking,
(1962)   Selective Interaction, and Misperception in Congruent Interpersonal Relations," *Sociometry*, 25:321–335.

Bales, R. F. "Task Roles and Social Roles
(1958)   in Problem-solving Groups," in E. Maccoby, T. Newcomb, and E. Hartley (eds.), *Readings in Social Psychology* (3d ed.). New York: Holt, pp. 437–447.

Bales, R. F. "In Conference," *Harvard*
(1954)   *Business Review*, 2, 32:44–50.

Bales, R. F. *Interaction Process Analysis:*
(1950)   *A Method for the Study of Small*
          Groups. Reading, Mass.: Addi-
          son-Wesley.

Bales, R. F., and Borgatta, E. F. "Size of a
(1955)   Group as a Factor in the Inter-
          action Profile," in A. Hare, E. F.
          Borgatta, and R. F. Bales (eds.),
          Small Groups: Studies in Social
          Interaction. New York: Knopf,
          pp. 396–413.

Bales, R. F., and Strodtbeck, F. L. "Phases
(1951)   in Group Problem-solving," *Jour-*
          nal of Abnormal and Social
          Psychology, 46:485–495.

Bales, R. F., Strodtbeck, F. L., Mills, F.,
(1951)   and Roseborough, M. "Channels
          of Communication in Small
          Groups," *American Sociological*
          Review, 16:461–468.

Barker, R. *Ecological Psychology.* Stan-
(1968)   ford, Calif.: Stanford University
          Press.

Barker, R., and Barker, L. "Behavior Units
(1961)   for the Comparative Study of
          Culture," in B. Kaplan (ed.),
          Studying Personality Cross-cul-
          turally. Evanston, Ill.: Row Peter-
          son, pp. 457–476.

Barker, R., and Gump, P. *Big School, Small*
(1964)   *School.* Stanford, Calif.: Stan-
          ford University Press.

Barker, R., and Wright, H. *Midwest and*
(1955)   *Its Children.* New York: Harper
          & Row.

Barnlund, D. C. "A Transactional Model
(1970)   of Communication," in K. K.
          Sereno and C. D. Mortensen
          (eds.), *Foundations of Communi-*
          cation Theory. New York: Harper
          & Row, pp. 83–102.

Barnlund, D. C. *Interpersonal Communica-*
(1968a)   *tion: Survey and Studies.* Bos-
          ton: Houghton Mifflin.

Barnlund, D. C. "Communication: The
(1968b)   Context of Change," in C. E.
          Larson and F. E. Dance (eds.),
          Perspectives on Communication.
          Milwaukee: Speech Communica-
          tion Center, pp. 24–40.

Barnlund, D. C., and Harland, C. "Pro-
(1963)   pinquity and Prestige as Deter-
          minants of Communication Net-
          works," *Sociometry*, 26:467–479.

Bartlett, F. C. *Remembering.* London: Cam-
(1932)   bridge.

Bass, B. M. *Leadership, Psychology, and*
(1960)   *Organizational Behavior.* New
          York: Harper & Row.

Bass, B. M., and Fay-Tyler, M. "Group Size
(1951)   and Leaderless Discussion,"
          Journal of Applied Psychology,
          35:397–400.

Bass, B. M., and Klubeck, S. "Effects of
(1952)   Seating Arrangements in Leader-
          less Group Discussions," *Journal*
          of Abnormal and Social Psy-
          chology, 47:724–727.

Bateson, G., and Jackson, D. "Some Varie-
(1964)   ties of Pathogenic Organization,"
          in D. McRoach (ed.), *Disorders*
          of Communication, 42, Research
          Publications, Association for
          Research in Nervous and Mental
          Disease, pp. 270–283.

Bauer, R. "The Obstinate Audience: The
(1964)   Influence Process from the
          Point of View of Social Com-
          munication," *American Psycho-*
          logical Association, 74:319–328.

Bavelas, A. "Communication Patterns in
(1950)   Task-oriented Groups," *Journal*
          of the Acoustical Society of
          America, 22:725–730.

Bavelas, A., Hastorf, A., Gross, A., and
(1965)   Kite, W. "Experiments on the
          Alteration of Group Structure,"
          Journal of Experimental Social
          Psychology, 1:55–70.

Baxter, J. C., Winter, E. P., and Hammer,
(1968)   R. E. "Gestural Behavior during
          a Brief Interview as a Function
          of Cognitive Variables," *Journal*
          of Personality and Social Psy-
          chology, 8:303–307.

Becker, S. L. "What Rhetoric (Communi-
(1968)   cation Theory) Is Relevant for
          Contemporary Speech Communi-
          cation?" presented at the Uni-
          versity of Minnesota Spring
          Symposium in Speech-Communi-
          cation, pp. 9–25.

Becker, S. L. "Research on Emotional and
(1963)   Logical Proofs," *Southern States*
          Speech Journal, 28:198–207.

Beighley, K. C. "An Experimental Study
(1954)   of the Effect of Three Speech
          Variables on Listener Compre-
          hension," *Speech Monographs*,
          21:248–253.

Beighley, K. C. "An Experimental Study of (1952) the Effect of Four Speech Variables on Listener Comprehension," *Speech Monographs*, 19: 249–258.

Beldoch, M. "Sensitivity to Expression of (1964) Emotional Meaning in Three Modes of Communication," in J. Davitz, *The Communication of Emotional Meaning*. New York: McGraw-Hill.

Bennett, J. W., Passin, H., and McKnight, (1966) R. K. "Social Norms, National Imagery and Interpersonal Relations," in A. G. Smith, *Communication and Culture*. New York: Holt, pp. 595–608.

Bennis, W. G., Schein, E. H., Belew, D. E., (1964) and Steele, F. I. *Interpersonal Dynamics: Essays and Readings on Human Interaction*. Homewood, Ill.: Dorsey.

Berelson, B., Lazarsfeld, P., and McPhee, (1954) W. *Voting: A Study of Opinion Formation during a Presidential Campaign*. Chicago: University of Chicago Press.

Berelson, B., and Steiner, G. *Human (1964) Behavior: An Inventory of Scientific Findings*. New York: Harcourt, Brace & World.

Berkowitz, L., and Cottingham, D. R. "The (1960) Interest Value and Relevance of Fear-arousing Communications," *Journal of Abnormal and Social Psychology*, 60:37–43.

Berkowitz, L., and Goranson, R. E. "Moti- (1964) vational and Judgmental Determinants of Social Perception," *Journal of Abnormal and Social Psychology*, 69:296–302.

Berlo, D. K. "An Empirical Test of a Gen- (1961) eral Construct of Credibility." Paper presented to the Speech Association of America, New York.

Berlo, D. K. *The Process of Communica- (1960) tion*. New York, Holt.

Bertalanffy, L. *General Systems Theory*. (1968) New York: George Braziller.

Bettinghaus, E. P. *Message Preparation: (1966) The Nature of Proof*. New York: Bobbs-Merrill.

Bettinghaus, E. P. As cited in *Persuasive (1966) Communication:* New York: Holt.

Bettinghaus, E. P. "The Relative Effect of (1953) the Use of Testimony in a Persuasive Speech upon the Attitudes of Listeners." Unpublished masters thesis, Bradley University.

Bettinghaus, E. P., and Preston, I. L. "Dog- (1964) matism and Performance of the Communicator under Cognitive Stress," *Journalism Quarterly*, 41:399–402.

Bexton, W. H., Heron, W., and Scott, T. H. (1954) "Effects of Decreased Variation in the Sensory Environment," *Canadian Journal of Psychology*, 8:70–76.

Birdwhistell, R. *Kinesics and Context*. (1970) Philadelphia: University of Pennsylvania Press.

Birdwhistell, R. "Some Relations between (1966) American Kinesics and Spoken American English," in A. Smith (ed.), *Communication and Culture*. New York: Holt, pp. 182–189.

Birdwhistell, R. *Introduction to Kinesics*. (1952) Louisville, Ky.: University of Louisville Press.

Black, J. W. "The Persistence of Effects (1955) of Delayed Sidetone," *Journal of Speech and Hearing Disorders*, 20:65–68.

Blackman, A. "Death of a Small-town Ad- (1970) dict," Associated Press news release, Oct. 12.

Blake, R. R., and Brehm, J. W. "The Use (1954) of Tape Recording to Simulate a Group Atmosphere," *Journal of Abnormal and Social Psychology*, 49:311–313.

Blake, R. R., and Mouton, J. S. "Conformity, (1961) Resistence, and Conversion," in I. A. Berg and B. M. Bass (eds.), *Conformity and Deviation*. New York: Harper & Row, pp. 1–28.

Blake, R. R., Helson, B. H., and Mouton, (1957) J. S. "The Generality of Conformity Behavior as a Function of Anchorage, Difficulty of Task, and Amount of Social Pressure," *Journal of Personality*, 25:294–305.

Block, J., and Bennett, L. "The Assessment (1968) of Communication: Perception and Transmission as a Function of the Social Situation," in D. C. Barnlund, *Interpersonal Communication: Survey and Studies*. Boston: Houghton Mifflin, pp. 174–182.

Blubaugh, J. A. "Effects of Positive and
(1969)   Negative Audience Feedback on
          Selected Variables of Speech
          Behavior," *Speech Monographs*,
          36:131–137.

Blumer, H. "Society as Symbolic Inter-
(1967)   action," in M. J. G. Manis and
          B. N. Meltzer (eds.), *Symbolic
          Interaction*. Boston: Allyn and
          Bacon, pp. 139–148.

Blumer, H. "Psychological Import of the
(1953)   Human Group," in M. Sherif and
          M. O. Wilson (eds.), *Group Rela-
          tions at the Crossroads*. New
          York: Harper & Row, pp. 185–
          202.

Blumer, H. "Collective Behavior," in A.
(1951)   McLee (ed.), *New Outline of the
          Principles of Sociology*. New
          York: Barnes & Noble.

Bochner, S., and **Insko, C.** "Communicator
(1966)   Discrepancy, Source Credibility,
          and Opinion Change," *Journal of
          Personality and Social Psy-
          chology*, 4:614–621.

Boomer, D. S. "Hesitation and Grammatical
(1965)   Encoding," *Language and
          Speech*, 8:148–158.

Boomer, D. S. "Speech Disturbance and
(1963)   Body Movement in Interviews,"
          *Journal of Nervous and Mental
          Disease*, 136:263–266.

Boomer, D. S., and **Dittmann, A. T.** "Speech
(1964)   Rate, Filled Pause, and Body
          Movement in Interviews," *Jour-
          nal of Nervous and Mental Dis-
          ease*, 139:324–327.

Borgatta, E. F., and **Bales, R. F.** "Inter-
(1953)   action of Individuals in Recon-
          stituted Groups," *Sociometry*,
          16:302–320.

Boring, E. *American Journal of Psychol-
(1930)   ogy*, 44:444, figure 73.

Borton, T. *Read Touch and Teach.* New
(1970)   York: McGraw-Hill.

Bossart, P., and **Di Vesta, F.** "Effect of
(1966)   Context, Frequency, and Order
          of Presentation of Evaluative As-
          sertions on Impression Forma-
          tion," *Journal of Personality and
          Social Psychology*, 4:538–544.

Bostrum, R. "Patterns of Communicative
(1970)   Interaction in Small Groups,"
          Speech Monographs, 37:257–
          263.

Boucher, J., and **Ekman, P.** "A Replication
(1965)   of Schlosberg's Evaluation of
          Woodworth's Scale of Emotion."

          Paper presented to the Western
          Psychological Association.

Boulding, K. E. *The Image.* Ann Arbor: The
(1966)   University of Michigan Press.

Bousfield, W. A. "The Occurrence of Clus-
(1953)   tering in the Recall of Randomly
          Arranged Associations," *Journal
          of General Psychology*, 49:229–
          240.

Bower, G. "A Multicomponent Theory of
(1967)   the Memory Trace," in K. W.
          Spence and J. T. Spence (eds.),
          *The Psychology of Learning and
          Motivation*, vol. I. New York:
          Academic, pp. 230–321.

Bowers, J. W. "The Influence of Delivery
(1965)   on Attitudes toward Concepts
          and Speakers," *Speech Mono-
          graphs*, 32:154–158.

Bowers, J. W., and **Osborn, M. M.** "Atti-
(1966)   tudinal Effects of Selected Types
          of Concluding Metaphors in Per-
          suasive Speeches," *Speech
          Monographs*, 33:147–155.

Brehm, J. W. "Attitudinal Consequences of
(1960)   Commitment to Unpleasant Be-
          havior," *Journal of Abnormal and
          Social Psychology*, 60:379–383.

Bridgman, P. W. *The Way Things Are.*
(1959)   Cambridge, Mass.: Harvard Uni-
          versity Press.

Broadbent, D. E. *Perception and Communi-
(1958)   cation.* New York: Pergamon.

Broadbent, D. E. "A Mechanical Model for
(1957)   Human Attention and Immediate
          Memory," *Psychological Review*,
          64:205–215.

Brock, T. C. "Communicator-Recipient
(1965)   Similarity and Decision Change,"
          *Journal of Personality and Social
          Psychology*, 1:650–654.

Brockriede, W. E. "Dimensions of the Con-
(1968)   cept of Rhetoric," *The Quarterly
          Journal of Speech*, 54:1–12.

Brockriede, W. E., and **Ehninger, D.** "Toul-
(1960)   min on Argument: An Interpre-
          tation and Application," *The
          Quarterly Journal of Speech*,
          46:44–53.

Brodbeck, M. "The Role of Small Groups
(1956)   in Mediating the Effects of
          Propaganda," *Journal of Ab-
          normal and Social Psychology*,
          52:166–170.

Brooks, R. D. "The Generality of Early
(1970)   Reversals of Attitudes toward
          Communication Sources,"
          Speech Monographs, 37:152–155.

Brooks, R. D., and **Scheidel, T. M.** "Speech (1968) as Process: A Case Study," *Speech Monographs,* 35:1–7.

Brown, R. *Social Psychology.* New York: (1965) Free Press.

Bruner, J. S., and **Goodman, C. C.** "Value (1947) and Need as Organizing Factors in Perception," *Journal of Abnormal and Social Psychology,* 42:33–44.

Bruner, J. S., Goodman, J. J., and **Austin,** (1962) **G. A.** *A Study of Thinking.* New York: Science Editions, Wiley.

Bruner, T., and **Tagiuri, R.** "The Percep- (1954) tion of People," in G. Lindzey (ed.), *Handbook of Social Psychology,* vol. II. Reading, Mass.: Addison-Wesley.

Buchwald, A. "Experimental Alterations (1959) in the Effectiveness of Verbal Reinforcement Combinations," *Journal of Experimental Psychology,* 57:351–361.

Buckner, H. T. "A Theory of Rumor Trans- (1965) mission," *Public Opinion Quarterly,* 29:54–70.

Burgess, R. L. "Communication Networks: (1968) An Experimental Reevaluation," *Journal of Experimental Social Psychology,* 4:324–337.

Burns, T. "Non-verbal Communication," (1964) *Discovery,* 25:30–37.

Burt, C. "The Concept of Consciousness," (1962) *British Journal of Psychology,* 53:229–242.

Byrd, R. E. *Alone.* New York: Putnam. (1938)

Byrd, R. E. *Little America.* New York: (1930) Putnam.

Byrne, D. "Interpersonal Attraction and (1961) Attitude Similarity," *Journal of Abnormal and Social Psychology,* 62:713–715.

Byrne, D., Clore, G. L., and **Griffitt, W. A.** (1967) "Response Discrepancy versus Attitude Similarity-Dissimilarity as Determinants of Attraction," *Psychonomic Science,* 2:397–398.

Byrne, D., and **Griffitt, W. A.** "A Develop- (1966) mental Investigation of the Law of Attraction," *Journal of Personality and Social Psychology,* 4:699–702.

Byrne, D., Griffitt, W. A., and **Golightly, C.** (1966) "Prestige as a Factor in Determining the Effect of Attitude Similarity-Dissimilarity on At-

traction," *Journal of Personality,* 34:434–444.

Byrne, D., and **London, O.** "Primacy- (1966) Recency and the Sequential Presentation of Attitudinal Stimuli," *Psychonomic Science,* 6: 193–194.

Byrne, D., and **Nelson, D.** "Attraction as a (1965a) Linear Function of Proportion of Positive Reinforcements," *Journal of Personality and Social Psychology,* 1:659–663.

Byrne, D., and **Nelson, D.** "The Effect of (1965b) Topic Importance and Attitude Similarity-Dissimilarity on Attraction in a Multistranger Design," *Psychonomic Science,* 3:449–450.

Byrne, D., and **Wong, T. J.** "Racial Preju- (1962) dice, Interpersonal Attraction, and Assumed Dissimilarity of Attitudes," *Journal of Abnormal and Social Psychology,* 65:246–253.

Calhoun, B. J., "A 'Behavioral Sink,'" in E. (1962) Bliss (ed.), *Roots of Behavior.* New York: Harper & Row, pp. 295–315.

Campbell, D. C. "Social Attitudes and (1963) Other Acquired Behavioral Dispositions," in S. Koch (ed.), *Psychology: A Study of a Science,* 11:94–172.

Campbell, D. T. "Conformity in Psychol- (1961) ogy's Theories of Acquired Behavioral Dispositions," in I. A. Berg and B. M. Bass (eds.), *Conformity and Deviation.* New York: Harper, pp. 101–142.

Cannell, C. F., and **MacDonald, J. C.** "The (1956) Impact of Health News on Attitudes and Behavior," *Journalism Quarterly,* 33:315–323.

Canon, L. K. "Self-confidence and Selec- (1964) tive Exposure to Information," in L. Festinger (ed.), *Conflict, Decision, and Dissonance.* Stanford, Calif.: Stanford University Press, pp. 83–96.

Caplow, T. "Further Developments of a (1959) Theory of Coalitions in the Triad," *American Journal of Sociology,* 64:488–493.

Caplow, T. "A Theory of Coalitions in the (1956) Triad," *American Sociological Review,* 21:489–493.

Caplow, T., and Forman, R. "Neighborhood
(1950)   Interaction in a Homogeneous
          Community," American Socio-
          logical Review, 15:357–366.
Carment, D. W. "Ascendent-Submissive
(1961)   Behavior in Pairs of Human Sub-
          jects as a Function of Their
          Emotional Responsiveness and
          Opinion Strength," Canadian
          Journal of Psychology, 15:45–51.
Carmichael, L., Roberts, S., and Wessell,
(1937)   N. "A Study of the Judgment of
          Manual Expression as Presented
          in Still and Motion Pictures,"
          Journal of Social Psychology,
          8:115–142.
Carroll, J. The Study of Language. Cam-
(1955)   bridge, Mass.: Harvard Univer-
          sity Press.
Carter, R. F. "Writing Controversial Stories
(1955)   for Comprehension," Journalism
          Quarterly, 32:319–328.
Cartwright, D. (ed.). Studies in Social
(1959)   Power. Ann Arbor: The Univer-
          sity of Michigan Press.
Cartwright, D., and Zander, A. Group
(1968)   Dynamics: Research and Theory
          (3d ed.). New York: Harper &
          Row.
Cassirer, E. The Philosophy of Symbolic
(1953–   Forms. New Haven, Conn.:
1957)   Yale University Press, 3 vols.
Cathcart, R. "An Experimental Study of
(1955)   the Relativeness of Four Meth-
          ods of Presenting Evidence,"
          Speech Monographs, 22:227–233.
Champness, B. As cited in Time, Oct. 17,
(1969)   p. 74.
Chapanis, A. "Men, Machines, and
(1961)   Models," American Psycholo-
          gist, 16:113–131.
Chapanis, N. P., and Chapanis, A. "Cog-
(1964)   nitive Dissonance: Five Years
          Later," Psychological Bulletin,
          61:1–22.
Chapple, E. D. "The Standard Experi-
(1953)   mental (Stress) Interview as
          Used in Interaction Chronograph
          Investigations," Human Organi-
          zation, 12:23–32.
Chapple, E. D. "The Interaction Chrono-
(1949)   graph: Its Evolution and Present
          Applications," Personnel, 25:
          295–307.
Chapple, E. D. "Measuring Human Rela-
(1940a)   tions," Genetic and Psychologi-
          cal Monographs, 22:3–147.

Chapple, E. D. "Personality Differences
(1940b)   as Described by Invariant Prop-
          erties of Individuals in Inter-
          action," Proceedings of the Na-
          tional and Social Academy of
          Science, 26:10–16.
Charney, E. J. "Postural Configurations in
(1966)   Psychotherapy," Psychosomatic
          Medicine, 28:305–315.
Chatterjee, A. "Time Phase Sequence in
(1965)   the Pattern of Communication
          in Small Groups," Psychological
          Studies, 10:121–127.
Cherry, E. "Some Experiments on the Rec-
(1953)   ognition of Speech with One
          and with Two Ears," Journal of
          the Acoustical Society of Amer-
          ica, 25:975–979.
Chertkoff, J. M. "The Effects of Probability
(1966)   of Future Success on Coalition
          Formation," Journal of Experi-
          mental Social Psychology, 2:
          265–277.
Chu, G. C. "Fear Arousal, Efficacy, and
(1966)   Imminency," Journal of Per-
          sonality and Social Psychology,
          4:517–524.
Clevenger, Jr., T., and Knapprath, E. "A
(1966)   Quantitative Analysis of Logical
          and Emotional Content in Se-
          lected Campaign Addresses of
          Eisenhower and Stevenson,"
          Western Speech, 30:144–150.
Cline, M. "The Influence of Social Context
(1956)   on the Perception of Faces,"
          Journal of Personality, 25:142–
          158.
Cobin, M. "Response to Eye-contact,"
(1962)   Quarterly Journal of Speech, 68:
          415–418.
Cofer, C. N., and Appley, M. H. Motiva-
(1964)   tion: Theory and Research. New
          York: Wiley.
Cohen, A. R. Attitude Change and Social
(1964)   Influence. New York: Basic
          Books.
Cohen, A. R. "Situational Structure, Self-
(1959)   esteem and Threat-oriented
          Reactions to Power," in D. Cart-
          wright (ed.), Studies in Social
          Power. Ann Arbor: University of
          Michigan Press, pp. 35–62.
Cohen, A. R. "Need for Cognition and
(1957)   Order of Communication as De-
          terminants of Opinion Change,"
          in C. Hovland et al., The Order
          of Presentation in Persuasion.

New Haven, Conn.: Yale University Press, pp. 79–97.

Cohen, A. R., Bennis, W., and Wolkon, G.
(1961)   "The Effects of Continued Practice on the Behaviors of Problem-solving Groups," *Sociometry*, 24:443–461.

Cohen, A. R., Brehm, J. W., and Latané, B.
(1959)   "Choice of Strategy and Voluntary Exposure to Information under Public and Private Conditions," *Journal of Personality*, 27:63–73.

Cole, D. "'Rational Arguments' and 'Pres-
(1954)   tige-Suggestions' as Factors Influencing Judgment," *Sociometry*, 17:350–354.

Coleman, J. S. *The Adolescent Society.*
(1961)   New York: Free Press.

Combs, A. W. *Individual Behavior: A Per-*
(1959)   *ceptual Approach to Behavior.*
New York: Harper & Row.

Condon, W. S., and Ogston, W. D. "A
(1967)   Segmentation of Behavior," *Journal of Psychiatric Research*, 5: 221–235.

Conrad, R. "Acoustic Confusions in Im-
(1964)   mediate Memory," *British Journal of Psychology*, 1, 55:75–84.

Conrad, R. "Errors of Immediate Memory,"
(1959)   *British Journal of Psychology*, 50:349–359.

Conrad, R., and Hille, B. A. "The Decay
(1958)   Theory of Immediate Memory and Paced Recall," *Canadian Journal of Psychology*, 12:1–6.

Cooley, C. H. *Human Nature and the Social*
(1902)   *Order.* New York: Scribner.

Cooper, L. (trans.) *The Rhetoric of Aris-*
(1932)   *totle.* New York: Appleton Century Crofts.

Corrozi, J. F., and Rosnow, R. L. "Con-
(1968)   sonant and Dissonant Communications as Positive and Negative Reinforcements in Opinion Change," *Journal of Personality and Social Psychology*, 8:27–30.

Corso, J. F. "A Theoretico-historical Re-
(1963)   view of the Threshold Concept," *Psychological Bulletin*, 60:356–370.

**Costanzo, F. S., Markel, N. N., and Cos-
(1969)   tanzo, P. R.** "Voice Quality Profile and Perceived Emotion," *Journal of Counseling Psychology*, 16:267–270.

Costley, D. "An Experimental Study of the
(1958)   Effectiveness of Quantitative Evidence in Speeches of Advocacy." Unpublished M.A. thesis, University of Oklahoma.

**Cottrell, N. B., Wack, D. L., Sekerak, G. J.,
(1968)   and Rittle, R. H.** "Social Facilitation of Dominant Responses by the Presence of an Audience and the Mere Presence of Others," *Journal of Personality and Social Psychology*, 9:245–250.

Couch, C. "Collective Behavior: An Exam-
(1968)   ination of Some Stereotypes," *Social Problems*, 15:310–322.

Cowan, T. A., and Strickland, D. A. "The
(1965)   Legal Structure of a Confined Micro Society (A Report on the Cases of Penthouse II and III)," *Internal Working Paper No. 34*, Space Sciences Lab., Social Sciences Project, University of California, Berkeley, August.

Cromwell, H. "Relative Effect of Audience
(1950)   Attitudes of the First versus the Second Argumentative Speech of a Series," *Speech Monographs*, 17:105–122.

Cronkhite, G. *Persuasion: Speech and Be-*
(1969)   *havioral Change.* Indianapolis: Bobbs-Merrill.

Cronkhite, G. "Autonomic Correlates of Dis-
(1966)   sonance and Attitude Change," *Speech Monographs*, 33:392–399.

Crowne, D. P., and Liverant, S. "Con-
(1963)   formity under Varying Conditions of Arsenal Commitment," *Journal of Abnormal and Social Psychology*, 66:547–555.

Crutchfield, R. E. "Conformity and Char-
(1955)   acter," *American Psychologist*, 10:191–198.

Dabbs, J. M., and Leventhal, H. "Effects
(1966)   of Varying the Recommendations in a Fear-arousing Communication," *Journal of Personality and Social Psychology*, 4:525–531.

Dance, F. E. "The 'Concept' of Communi-
(1970)   cation," *The Journal of Communication*, 20:201–210.

Dance, F. E. "Toward a Theory of Human
(1967)   Communication," in *Human Communication Theory.* New York: Holt, pp. 288–309.

Daniels, V. "Communication, Incentive,
(1967) and Structural Variables in Interpersonal Exchange and Negotiation," *Journal of Experimental
Social Psychology,* 3:47–74.

Dannenmaier, W. D., and **Thumin, F. J.**
(1964) "Authority Status as a Factor in
Perceptual Distortion of Size,"
Journal of Social Psychology,
63:361–365.

Darley, J. M. "Fear and Social Comparison
(1966) as Determinants of Conformity
Behavior," *Journal of Personality
and Social Psychology,* 4:73–78.

Darley, J. M., and **Berscheid, E.** "Increased
(1967) Liking as a Result of the Anticipation of Personal Contact,"
Human Relations, 20:29–39.

Darnell, D. K. "The Relation between
(1963) Sentence Order and Comprehension," *Speech Monographs,*
30:97–100.

Davis, J. W. "Variations in Verbal Behavior
(1967) in Dyads as a Function of Varied
Reinforcing Conditions," *Speech
Monographs,* 34:443–447.

Davitz, J. *The Communication of Emotional*
(1964) *Meaning.* New York: McGraw-
Hill.

De Fleur, M. L., and **Westie, I. R.** "Verbal
(1958) Attitudes and Overt Acts: An
Experiment on the Salience of
Attitudes," *American Sociological Review,* 23:667–673.

Delia, J. "The Logic Fallacy, Cognitive
(1970) Theory, and the Enthymeme: A
Search for the Foundations of
Reasoned Discourse," *The Quarterly Journal of Speech,* 56:140–
148.

De Soto, C. B. "The Predilection for Single
(1961) Orderings," *Journal of Abnormal
and Social Psychology,* 62:16–
23.

De Soto, C. B. "Learning a Social Struc-
(1960) ture," *Journal of Abnormal and
Social Psychology,* 60:417–421.

De Soto, C. B., London, M., and **Handel, S.**
(1965) "Social Reasoning and Spatial
Paralogic," *Journal of Personality
and Social Psychology,* 2:513–
521.

Deutsch, J., and **Deutsch, D.** "Attention:
(1963) Some Theoretical Considerations," *Psychological Review,*
70:80–90.

Deutsch, K. "On Communication Models
(1952) in the Social Sciences," *Public
Opinion Quarterly,* 16:356–380.

Deutsch, M. "Trust, Trustworthiness, and
(1960) the F Scale," *Journal of Abnormal and Social Psychology,* 61:
138–140.

Deutsch, M. "Trust and Suspicion," *Journal
(1958) of Conflict Resolution,* 2:265–
279.

Deutsch, M., and **Gerard, H.** "A Study of
(1955) Normative, Informational Social
Influences upon Individual Judgment," *Journal of Abnormal and
Social Psychology,* 51:629–636.

Diggory, J. *Self-evaluation: Concepts and
(1966) Studies.* New York: Wiley.

Dittmann, A. T. "The Relationship between
(1962) Body Movements and Moods in
Interviews," *Journal of Consulting Psychology,* 26:480.

Dittmann, A. T., and **Llewellyn, L. G.** "Body
(1969) Movement and Speech Rhythm
in Social Conversation," *Journal
of Personality and Social Psychology,* 11:98–106.

Dittmann, A. T., and **Llewellyn, L. G.** "The
(1967) Phonetic Clause as a Unit of
Speech Decoding," *Journal of
Personality and Social Psychology,* 6:341–349.

Dittmann, A. T., Parloff, M. B., and **Boomer,**
(1965) **D. S.** "Facial and Bodily Expression: A Study of Receptivity of
Emotional Cues," *Psychiatry,* 28:
239–244.

Dixon, W. "Apparent Changes in the
(1958) Visual Threshold as a Function
of Subliminal Stimulation," *Quarterly Journal of Experimental
Psychology,* 10:211.

Dosey, M. A., and **Meisels, M.** "Personal
(1969) Space and Self Protection,"
*Journal of Personality and Social
Psychology,* 11:93–97.

Downing, J. "Cohesiveness, Perception,
(1958) and Values," *Human Relations,*
11:157–166.

Dresser, W. R. "The Use of Evidence in
(1964) Ten Championship Debates,"
*Journal of American Forensic
Association,* 1:101–106.

Dresser, W. R. "Effects of 'Satisfactory'
(1963) and 'Unsatisfactory' Evidence in
a Speech of Advocacy," *Speech
Monographs,* 20:302–306.

Dresser, W. R. "Studies of the Effects of (1962) Satisfactory and Unsatisfactory Evidence in a Speech of Advocacy." Unpublished doctoral dissertation, Northwestern University.

Duffy, E. *Activation and Behavior.* New (1962) York: Wiley.

Duhem, P. *The Aim and Structure of* (1954) *Physical Theory.* Princeton, N.J.: Princeton University Press.

Duke, J. D. "Critique of the Janis and (1967) Feshbach Study," *Journal of Social Psychology,* 72:71–80.

Duncan, S. "Nonverbal Communication," (1969) *Psychological Bulletin,* 72:118–137.

Dusenbury, D., and **Knower, F.** "Experi- (1939) mental Studies of the Symbolism of Action and Voice II; A Study of the Specificity of Meaning in Facial Expression," *Quarterly Journal of Speech,* 25:67–75.

Efran, J. S. "Looking for Approval Effects (1968) on Visual Behavior of Approbation from Persons Differing in Importance," *Journal of Personality and Social Psychology,* 10:21–25.

Efran, J. S., and **Broughton, A.** "Effect of (1966) Expectancies for Social Approval on Visual Behavior," *Journal of Personality and Social Psychology,* 4:103–107.

Efron, G. *Gesture and Environment.* New (1941) York: Kings Crown.

Egeth, H. "Selective Attention," *Psycho-* (1967) *logical Bulletin,* 67:41–57.

Ehninger, D., and **Brockriede, W. E.** *De-* (1963) *cision by Debate.* New York: Dodd, Mead.

Ehrlich, D., Guttman, I., Schönbach, and (1957) **Mills, J.** "Postdecision Exposure to Relevant Information," *Journal of Abnormal and Social Psychology,* 54:98–102.

Ekman, P. "Communication through Non- (1965a) verbal Behavior: A Source of Information about an Interpersonal Relationship," in S. S. Tomkins and C. E. Izard (eds.), *Affect, Cognition, and Personality.* New York: Springer, pp. 390–442.

Ekman, P. "Differential Communication (1965b) of Affect by Head and Body Cues," *Journal of Personality and Social Psychology,* 2:726–735.

Ekman, P. "A Comparison of the Informa- (1964) tion Communicated by Head and Body Cues." Paper presented to the American Psychological Association, Los Angeles.

Ekman, P., and **Friesen, W. V.** "Constants (1971) Across Cultures in the Face and Emotion." Unpublished manuscript.

Ekman, P., and **Friesen, W. V.** "The Reper- (1969) toire of Nonverbal Behavior: Categories, Origins, Usage, and Coding," *Semiotica,* 1:49–98.

Ekman, P., and **Friesen, W. V.** "Nonverbal (1968) Behavior in Psychotherapy Research," *Psychotherapy,* 3:179–216.

Ekman, P., and **Friesen, W. V.** "Head and (1967) Body Cues in the Judgment of Emotion," *Perceptual and Motor Skills,* 24:711–724.

Ekman, P., Sorenson, E. P., and **Friesen,** (1969) **W. V.** "Pan-cultural Elements in Facial Displays of Emotion," *Science,* 164:86–88.

Elegant, R. S. "Americans Can't Communi- (1970) cate," *Seattle Times,* Los Angeles Wireservice, May 17.

Eliade, M. *The Sacred and the Profane.* (1961) New York: Harper & Row.

Ellison, R. *The Invisible Man.* New York: (1947) Random House.

Ellsworth, P. C., and **Carlsmith, J. M.** "Ef- (1968) fects of Eye Contact and Verbal Content on Affective Response to a Dyadic Interaction," *Journal of Personality and Social Psychology,* 10:15–20.

Engen, T., Levy, N., and **Schlosberg, H.** (1958) "The Dimensional Analysis of a New Series of Facial Expressions," *Journal of Experimental Psychology,* 55:545–548.

Engen, T., Levy, N., and **Schlosberg, H.** "A (1957) New Series of Facial Expressions," *American Psychologist,* 12:264–266.

Eriksen, C. W., and **Collins, J. F.** "Back- (1964) ward Masking in Vision," *Psychonomic Science,* 1:101–102.

Eriksen, C. W., and **Steffy, R. A.** "Short- (1964) term Memory and Retroactive

Interference in Visual Perception," *Journal of Experimental Psychology*, 68:423–434.

Exline, R. "Effects of Need for Affiliation,
(1962) Sex and the Sight of Others upon Initial Communications in Problem Solving Groups," *Journal of Personality*, 30:541–556.

Exline, R., Gray, D., and **Schuette, D.**
(1965) "Visual Behavior in a Dyad as Affected by Interview Content and Sex of Respondent," *Journal of Personality and Social Psychology*, 1:201–209.

Exline, R., and **Winters, L. C.** "Affective
(1965) Relations and Mutual Glances in Dyads," in S. Tomkins and C. E. Izard (eds.), *Affect, Cognition, and Personality*. New York: Springer, pp. 319–350.

Fairbanks, G. "Systematic Research in
(1954) Experimental Phonetics: I. A Theory of the Speech Mechanism as a Servosystem," *Journal of Speech and Hearing Disorders*, 19:133–139.

Fairbanks, G., and **Guttman, N.** "Effects
(1958) of Delayed Auditory Feedback upon Articulation," *Journal of Speech and Hearing Research*, 1:12–22.

Fairbanks, G., and **Kodman, F.** "Word
(1957) Intelligibility as a Function of Time Compression," *Journal of the Acoustical Society of America*, 29:636–641.

Farnsworth, P. R., and **Misumi, I.** "Further
(1931) Data on Suggestion in Pictures," *American Journal of Psychology*, 43:632.

Fearing, F. "Toward a Psychological
(1953) Theory of Human Communication," *Journal of Personality*, 22:71–88.

Feather, N. T. "Acceptance and Rejection
(1964) of Arguments in Relation to Attitude Strength, Critical Abilities and Intolerance of Inconsistency," *Journal of Abnormal and Social Psychology*, 59:127–136.

Feather, N. T. "Cognitive Dissonance, Sen-
(1963) sitivity, and Evaluation," *Journal of Abnormal and Social Psychology*, 66:157–163.

Feather, N. T. "Cigarette Smoking and
(1962) Lung Cancer: A Study of Cognitive Dissonance," *Australian Journal of Psychology*, 14:55–64.

Federn, P. *Ego Psychology and the Psy-
(1952) choses*. New York: Basic Books.

Feffer, M., and **Suchotliff, L.** "Decentering
(1966) Implications of Social Interactions," *Journal of Personality and Social Psychology*, 4:415–422.

Feldman, S. *Mannerisms of Speech and
(1959) Gestures in Everyday Life*. New York: International Universities Press.

Felipe, N. J. "Interpersonal Distance and
(1966) Small Group Interaction," *Cornell Journal of Social Relations*, 1:59–64.

Felipe, N. J., and **Sommer, R.** "Invasions
(1966) of Personal Space," *Social Problems*, 14:206–214.

Fenichel, O. "On the Psychology of Bore-
(1951) dom," in D. Rapaport (ed.), *Organization and Pathology of Thought*. New York: Columbia University Press, pp. 349–361.

Festinger, L. *Conflict, Decision, and Dis-
(1964a) sonance*. Stanford: Stanford University Press.

Festinger, L. "Behavioral Support for
(1964b) Opinion Change," *Public Opinion Quarterly*, 28:404–418.

Festinger, L. *A Theory of Cognitive Dis-
(1957) sonance*. Evanston, Ill. Row Peterson.

Festinger, L., Schachter, S., and **Back, K.**
(1950) **W.** *Social Pressures in Informal Groups*. Stanford, Calif.: Stanford University Press.

Festinger, L., and **Thibaut, J.** "Interper-
(1951) sonal Communication in Small Groups," *Journal of Abnormal and Social Psychology*, 46:92–99.

Fisher, P. H. "An Analysis of the Primary
(1953) Group," *Sociometry*, 16:272–276.

Fisher, S., Rubinstein, I., and **Freeman,**
(1956) **R. W.** "Intertrial Effects of Immediate Self-committal in a Continuous Social Influence Situation," *Journal of Abnormal and Social Psychology*, 52:200–207.

Fotheringham, W. *Perspectives on Per-
(1966) suasion*. Boston: Allyn and Bacon.

Foy, E., and **Harlow, A. F.** *Clowning through
(1928) Life*. New York: Dutton.

Frandsen, K. D. "Effect of Threat Appeals
(1963) and Media of Transmission,"
Speech Monographs, 30:101–104.

Frank, L. "Tactile Communication," *Ge-*
(1957) *netic Psychology Monographs*,
56:211–255.

Fraser, D. "Decay of Immediate Memory
(1958) with Age," *Nature*, 182:1163.

Freedman, J. L. "How Important Is Cog-
(1968) nitive Consistency?" in R. P.
Abelson et al. (eds.), *Theories of
Cognitive Consistency: A Source-
book.* Chicago: Rand McNally,
pp. 497–503.

Freedman, J. L., and **Sears, D. O.** "Selec-
(1965a) tive Exposure," in L. Berkowitz
(ed.), *Advances in Experimental
Social Psychology*, vol. 2. New
York: Academic, pp. 57–97.

Freedman, J. L., and **Sears, D. O.** "Warn-
(1965b) ing, Distraction, and Resistance
to Influence," *Journal of Personality and Social Psychology*,
1:262–266.

Freedman, N., and **Hoffman, S. P.** "Kinetic
(1967) Behavior in Altered Clinical Interviews," *Perceptual and Motor
Skills*, 24:527–539.

French, J. R., and **Raven, B.** "The Bases
(1959) of Social Power," in D. Cartwright (ed.), *Studies in Social
Power.* Ann Arbor: University of
Michigan Press, pp. 150–167.

Friedman, N. *The Social Nature of Psy-*
(1967) *chological Research.* New York:
Basic Books.

Frijda, N. H. "Facial Expression and
(1958) Situational Cues," *Journal of
Abnormal and Social Psychology*, 57:149–154.

Frijda, N. H., and **Philipszoom, E.** "Dimen-
(1963) sions of Recognition of Expression," *Journal of Abnormal and
Social Psychology*, 66:45–51.

Frishkopf, L. S., and **Goldstein, M. H.**
(1963) "Response to Acoustic Stimuli
from Single Units in the Eighth
Nerve of the Bullfrog," *Journal
of Acoustical Society of America*,
35:1219–1228.

Frois-Wittman, J. "The Judgment of Facial
(1930) Expression," *Journal of Experimental Psychology*, 13:113–151.

Fromm, E. *The Sane Society.* New York:
(1955) Rinehart.

Frye, R. L., and **Stritch, T. M.** "Effect of
(1964) Timed vs. Nontimed Discussion

upon Measures of Influence and
Change in Small Groups," *Journal of Social Psychology*, 63:
139–143.

Furbay, A. L. "The Influence of Scattered
(1965) versus Compact Seating on Audience Response." *Speech Monographs*, 32:144–148.

Gamson, W. A. "Experimental Studies of
(1964) Coalition Formation," in L.
Berkowitz (ed.), *Advances in
Experimental Social Psychology*,
vol. 1. New York: Academic,
pp. 82–110.

Gamson, W. A. "An Experimental Test of
(1961) a Theory of Coalition Formation,"
American Sociological Review,
26:565–573.

Geier, J. G. "A Trait Approach to the Study
(1967) of Leadership in Small Groups,"
Journal of Communication, 17:
316–323.

Gerard, H. B. "Conformity and Commit-
(1964) ment to the Group," *Journal of
Abnormal and Social Psychology*,
68:209–211.

Gerard, H. B. "Some Determinants of Self-
(1961) evaluation," *Journal of Abnormal and Social Psychology*, 62:
288–293.

Gerard, H. B., Wilhelmy, R. A., and **Conol-**
(1968) **ley, E. S.** "Conformity and Group
Size," *Journal of Personality and
Social Psychology*, 8:79–82.

Gerbner, G. "Mass Media and Human
(1967) Communication Theory," in E.
Dance (ed.) *Human Communication Theory.* New York: Holt,
pp. 40–60.

Gerbner, G. "Toward a General Model of
(1956) Communication," *Audio-Visual
Communication Review*, 4:171–
199.

Gergen, K. J., and **Wishnow, B.** "Others'
(1965) Self-evaluations and Interaction
Anticipation as Determinants of
Self-presentation," *Journal of
Personality and Social Psychol-
ogy*, 2:348–358.

Gewirtz, J. L., and **Baer, D. M.** "Depriva-
(1958a) tion and Satiation of Social Reinforcers as Drive Conditions,"
*Journal of Abnormal and Social
Psychology*, 57:165–172.

Gewirtz, J. L., and **Baer, D. M.** "The Effect
(1958b) of Brief Social Deprivation on

Behavior for a Social Reinforcer," *Journal of Abnormal and Social Psychology*, 56:49-56.

Gibb, J. R. "The Effects of Group Size and
(1951) of Threat Reduction upon Creativity in a Problem Solving Situation," *American Psychologist*, 6:324.

Gibson, J. J., and **Pick, A. D.** "Perception of
(1963) Another Person's Looking Behavior," *The American Journal of Psychology*, 76:386-394.

Giffen, K. "The Contribution of Studies of
(1967a) Source Credibility to a Theory of Interpersonal Trust in the Communication Process," *Psychological Bulletin*, 68:104-120.

Giffen, K. "Interpersonal Trust in Small-
(1967b) group Communication," *Quarterly Journal of Speech*, 53: 224-234.

Gilbreth, F. B. *Primer of Scientific Man-
(1912) agement.* New York: Van Nostrand.

Gilchrist, J. C., Shaw, E., and **Walker, L. C.**
(1954) "Some Effects of Unequal Distribution of Information in a Wheel Group Structure," *Journal of Abnormal and Social Psychology*, 49:554-556.

Gilkinson, H., Paulson, S., and **Sikkink, D.**
(1954) "Effects of Order and Authority in an Argumentative Speech," *Quarterly Journal of Speech*, 40:183-192.

Goffman, E. *Behavior in Public Places.*
(1963) New York: Free Press.

Goffman, E. *Asylums.* Chicago: Aldine.
(1961a)

Goffman, E. *Encounters.* Indianapolis:
(1961b) Bobbs-Merrill.

Goffman, E. *The Presentation of Self in
(1959) Everyday Life.* Garden City, N.Y.: Doubleday.

Goffman, E., *Presentation of Self in Every-
(1957) day Life.* New York: Anchor, Doubleday.

Goldring, P. "Role of Distance and Posture
(1967) in the Evaluation of Interactions," *Proceedings of the 75th Annual Convention of the American Psychological Association*, 2:243-244.

Goldstein, K. *The Organism.* New York:
(1939) American Book.

Goldstein, M. J. "The Relationship between
(1959) Coping and Avoiding Behavior and Response to Fear-arousing

Propaganda," *Journal of Abnormal and Social Psychology*, 58: 247-252.

Golightly, C., and **Byrne, D.** "Attitude
(1964) Statements as Positive and Negative Reinforcements," *Science*, 146:798-799.

Gollob, H. F., and **Dittes, J. E.** "Effects of
(1965) Manipulated Self-esteem on Persuasibility Depending on Threat and Complexity of Communication," *Journal of Personality and Social Psychology*, 2:195-201.

Gorfein, D. S. "The Effects of a Nonunani-
(1964) mous Majority on Attitude Change," *Journal of Social Psychology*, 63:333-338.

Gothril, E., Corey, J., and **Paredes, A.**
(1968) "Psychological and Physical Dimensions of Personal Space," *Journal of Psychology*, 69:7-9.

Gouldner, A. "The Norm of Reciprocity: A
(1960) Preliminary Statement," *American Sociological Review*, 29: 161-178.

Graham, D. "Experimental Studies of Social
(1962) Influence in Simple Judgment Situations," *Journal of Social Psychology*, 56:245-269.

Granit, R., and **Phillips, C.** "Excitatory and
(1956) Inhibitory Processes Acting upon Individual Purkinje Cells of the Cerebellum in Cats," *Journal of Physiology*, 133:520-547.

Green, H. B., and **Knapp, R. H.** "Time
(1959) Judgment, Aesthetic Preference, and Need for Achievement," *Journal of Abnormal and Social Psychology*, 58:140-142.

Greenburg, B. S. "Media Use and Believa-
(1966) bility: Some Multiple Correlates," *Journalism Quarterly*, 43:665-670.

Greenburg, B. S. "Voting Intentions, Elec-
(1965) tion Expectations, and Exposure to Campaign Information," *Journal of Communication*, 15:149-160.

Greenburg, B. S., and **Tannenbaum, P. H.**
(1962) "Communicat or Performance under Cognitive Stress," *Journalism Quarterly*, 39:169-178.

Greenwald, A. G. "Effects of Prior Com-
(1965) mitment on Behavior Change after a Persuasive Communication," *Public Opinion Quarterly*, 2, 29:595-601.

Grey, J. A., and **Wedderburn, A. A.** "Group-
(1960)   ing Strategies with Simultaneous
Stimuli," *Quarterly Journal of
Experimental Psychology,* 12:
180–184.

Gross, N., Mason, W. S. and **McEachern,**
(1958)   **A. W.** *Explorations in Role Analysis.* New York: Wiley.

Guetzkow, H., and **Dill, W. R.** "Factors in
(1957)   the Organizational Develop-
ment of Task-oriented Groups,"
Sociometry, 20:175–204.

Guetzkow, H., and **Simon, H. A.** "The Im-
(1955)   pact of Certain Communication
Nets upon Organization and Performance in Task-oriented
Groups," *Management Science,*
1:233–250.

Guilford, J. D. "An Experiment in Learning
(1929)   to Read Facial Expressions,"
*Journal of Abnormal and Social
Psychology,* 24:191–202.

Guilford, J. D. "'Fluctuations of Attention'
(1927)   with Weak Visual Stimuli,"
American Journal of Psychology,
38:534–583.

Gulley, H. E., and **Berlo, D. K.** "Effect of
(1956)   Intercellular and Intracellular
Speech Structure on Attitude
Change and Learning," *Speech
Monographs,* 23:288–297.

Gump, P., Schoggen, P., and **Redl, F.** "The
(1957)   Camp Milieu and Its Immediate
Effects," *Journal of Social Issues,*
13:40–46.

Gunderson, E. K., and **Nelson, P. D.** "Cri-
(1966)   terion Measures for Extremely
Isolated Groups," *Personnel
Psychology,* 19:67–80.

Guthrie, G., and **Wiener, M.** "Subliminal
(1966)   Perception or Perception of Partial Cue with Pictorial Stimuli,"
*Journal of Personality and Social
Psychology,* 3:619–628.

Guze, S. B., and **Mensh, I.** "An Analysis
(1959)   of Some Features of the Interview with the Interaction Chronograph," *Journal of Abnormal
and Social Psychology,* 58:269–
271.

Haas, H. I., and **Maehr, M. L.** "Two Experi-
(1965)   ments on the Concept of Self
and the Reaction of Others,"
*Journal of Personality and Social
Psychology,* 1:100–105.

Haber, D. "For Whom the Bell Rings . . .
(1969)   and Rings," *New York* Magazine,
Nov. 17, p. 68.

Haefner, D. "Some Effects of Guilt-arous-
(1956)   ing and Fear-arousing Persuasive Communications on Opinion
Change." Unpublished paper.

Haggard, A. E., and **Isaacs, K. S.** "Micro-
(1966)   momentary Facial Expressions
as Indicators of Ego Mechanisms
in Psychotherapy," in L. Gottschalk and A. Auerbach (eds.),
*Methods of Research in Psycho-
therapy,* New York: Appleton
Century Crofts, pp. 154–165.

Haiman, F. S. "The Effects of Ethos in
(1949)   Public Speaking," *Speech Monographs,* 16:190–202.

Hall, A., and **Fagen, R.** "Definition of Sys-
(1956)   tem," *General Systems Year-
book,* 1:18–28.

Hall, C., and **Lindzey, G.** *Theories of Per-
(1957)   sonality.* New York: Wiley.

Hall, E. T. *The Hidden Dimension.* Garden
(1966)   City, N.Y.: Doubleday.

Hall, E. T. "Adumbration as a Feature of
(1964)   Intercultural Communication,"
American Anthropologist, 66:
154–163.

Hall, E. T. *The Silent Language.* Garden
(1959)   City, N.Y.: Doubleday.

Hall, E. T., and **Whyte, W. F.** "Intercul-
(1960)   tural Communication: A Guide
to Men of Action," *Human Organization,* 19:5–12.

Hall, M. "The Great Cabbage Hoax: A Case
(1965)   Study," *Journal of Personality
and Social Psychology,* 2:563–
569.

Hanson, R. C. "The Systematic Linkage
(1962)   Hypothesis and Role Consensus
Patterns in Hospital Community
Relations," *American Sociological Review,* 27:304–313.

Hare, A. P. "Communication Network,"
(1962)   in *Handbook of Small Group Research.* New York: Free Press,
pp. 272–290.

Hare, A. P. "A Study of Interaction and
(1952)   Consensus in Different Sized
Groups," *American Sociological
Review,* 17:261–267.

Hare, A. P., and **Bales, R. F.** "Seating Posi-
(1963)   tion and Small Group Interac-
tion," *Sociometry,* 26:480–486.

Harley, Jr., W. F. "The Effect of Monetary
(1965a)   Incentive in Paired-associate

Learning Using a Differential Method," *Psychonomic Science*, 2:377–378.

Harley, Jr., W. F. "The Effect of Monetary
(1965b)   Incentive in Paired-associate Learning Using an Absolute Method," *Psychonomic Science*, 3:141–142.

Harms, S. "Social Judgment of Status Cues
(1959)   in Language." Unpublished doctoral dissertation, Ohio State University, 1959; *Speech Monographs*, 1959, 27; 1960, 87.

Harrison, R. "Defenses and the Need to
(1965)   Know," in P. Lawrence and G. A. Seiler (eds.), *Organizational Behavior and Administration*. Homewood, Ill.: Irwin, pp. 266–272.

Hartman, G. W. "A Field Experiment on
(1936)   the Comparative Effectiveness of 'Emotional' and 'Rational' Political Leaflets in Determining Election Results," *Journal of Abnormal and Social Psychology*, 31:99–114.

Harvey, O. J., and **Beverly, G. D.** "Some
(1961)   Personality Correlates of Concept Change through Role Playing," *Journal of Abnormal and Social Psychology*, 63:125–130.

Harvey, O. J., Kelley, H. H., and **Shapiro,**
(1957)   **M. M.** "Reactions to Unfavorable Evaluations of the Self Made by Other Persons," *Journal of Personality*, 25:395–411.

Hastorf, A., and **Cantril, H.** "They Saw a
(1954)   Game: A Case Study," *Journal of Abnormal and Social Psychology*, 49:129–134.

Haythorn, W. W., and **Altman, I.** "Per-
(1967a)   sonality Factors in Isolated Environments," in M. H. Appley and R. Trumbell (eds.), *Psychological Stress*. New York: Appleton Century Crofts, pp. 363–386.

Haythorn, W. W., and **Altman, I.** "Together
(1967b)   in Isolation," *Trans-action*, 4:18–23.

Haythorn, W. W., Altman, I., and **Myers,**
(1966)   **T.** "Emotional Symptomatology and Subjective Stress in Isolated Pairs of Men," *Journal of Experimental Research in Personality*, 1:290–305.

Hazard, J. "Furniture Arrangement and
(1962)   Judicial Roles," *E.T.C.*, 19:181–188.

Hearn, G. "Leadership and the Spatial
(1957)   Factor in Small Groups," *Journal of Abnormal and Social Psychology*, 54:269–272.

Hebb, D. O. *The Organization of Behavior*.
(1949)   New York: Wiley.

Heider, F. *The Psychology of Interpersonal*
(1958)   *Relations*. New York: Wiley.

Heider, F. "Attitudes and Cognitive Or-
(1946)   ganization," *Journal of Psychology*, 21:107–112.

Higbee, K. L. "Fifteen Years of Fear
(1969)   Arousal: Research on Threat Appeals, 1953–1968," *Psychological Bulletin*, 72:426–444.

Hilgard, E. R. *Introduction to Psychology*
(1962)   (3d ed.). New York: Harcourt, Brace & World.

Hintzman, D. L. "Articulatory Coding in
(1967)   Short-term Memory," *Journal of Verbal Learning and Verbal Behavior*, 6:312–316.

Hintzman, D. L. "Classification and Aural
(1965)   Coding in Short-term Memory," *Psychonomic Science*, 3:161–162.

Hirsh, I. "The Relation between Localiza-
(1950)   tion and Intelligibility," *Journal of the Acoustical Society of America*, 22:196–200.

Hoffman, M. L. "Conformity as a Defense
(1957)   Mechanism and a Form of Resistance to Genuine Group Influence," *Journal of Personality*, 25:412–424.

Holtzman, P. D. "Confirmation of Ethos as
(1966)   a Confounding Element in Communication Research," *Speech Monographs*, 33:464–466.

Homans, G. *The Human Group*. New York:
(1950)   Harcourt, Brace & World.

Horowitz, M. J., Duff, D. F., and **Stratton,**
(1964)   **L. O.** "Body Buffer Zone," *Archives of General Psychiatry*, 11:651–656.

Hovland, C. "Social Communication," *Pro-
(1948)   ceedings of the American Philosophical Society*, 92:371–375.

Hovland, C., Campbell, E., and **Brock, T.**
(1957)   "The Effects of 'Commitment' on Opinion Change Following Communication," in Hovland et al., *The Order of Presentation in Persuasion*. New Haven, Conn.: Yale University Press, pp. 23–32.

Hovland, C., Janis, I., and **Kelley, H.** *Com-
(1953)   munication and Persuasion*. New

Haven, Conn.: Yale University Press.

Hovland, C., Lumsdaine, A., and Sheffield, F. (1949) *Experiments on Mass Communication: Studies on Social Psychology in World War II,* vol. 3. Princeton, N.J.: Princeton University Press.

Hovland, C., and Mandell, W. (1957) "Is There a Law of Primacy in Persuasion?" in Hovland et al., *The Order of Presentation in Persuasion.* New Haven, Conn.: Yale University Press, pp. 13–22.

Hovland, C., Mandell, W., Campbell, E., Brock, T., Luchins, A., Cohen, A., McGuire, W., Janis, I., Reierabeid, R., and Anderson, N. (1957) *The Order of Presentation in Persuasion.* New Haven, Conn.: Yale University Press.

Hovland, C., and Weiss, W. (1951) "The Influence of Source Credibility on Communication Effectiveness," *Public Opinion Quarterly,* 15:635–650.

Howard, R. C., and Berkowitz, L. (1958) "Reactions to the Evaluations of One's Performance," *Journal of Personality,* 26:494–507.

Howell, L. J., and Becker, S. W. (1962) "Seating Arrangement and Leadership Emergence," *Journal of Abnormal and Social Psychology,* 64:148–150.

Hubel, D. H., and Wiesel, T. N. (1962) "Receptive Fields, Binocular Interaction and Functional Architecture in the Cat's Visual Cortex," *Journal of Physiology,* 160:106–154.

Hubel, D. H., and Wiesel, T. N. (1959) "Receptive Fields of Single Neurones in the Cat's Striate Cortex," *Journal of Physiology,* 148:574–591.

Huenergardt, D., and Finando, S. (1969) "Micromomentary Facial Expressions as Perceivable Signs of Deception." Paper presented to Speech Association of America, New York.

Hunt, J. (1963) "Motivation Inherent in Information Processing and Action," in O. Harvey (ed.), *Motivation and Social Interaction: Cognitive Determinants.* New York: Ronald, pp. 35–74.

Hurwitz, J., Zander, A., and Hymovitch, B. (1968) "Some Effects of Power on the Relations among Group Members," in D. Cartwright and A. Zander (eds.), *Group Dynamics.* New York: Harper & Row, pp. 291–297.

Indik, B. P. (1965) "Organization Size and Member Participation: Some Empirical Tests of Alternative Explanations," *Human Relations,* 18:339–350.

Insko, C. A. (1964) "Primacy versus Recency in Persuasion as a Function of the Timing of Arguments and Measurement," *Journal of Abnormal and Social Psychology,* 69:381–391.

Iscoe, I., and Williams, M. S. (1963) "Experimental Variables Affecting the Conformity Behavior of Children," *Journal of Personality,* 31:234–246.

Izard, C. E. (1968) "Cross-cultural Research Findings on Development in Recognition of Facial Behavior," *Proceedings, American Psychological Association Convention,* 3:727.

Izard, C. E. (in press) "The Emotions and Emotion Constructs in Personality and Cultural Research," in R. B. Cattell (ed.), *Handbook of Modern Personality Theory.* Chicago: Aldine.

Jackson, D., and Messick, S. (1963) "Individual Differences in Social Perception," *British Journal of Social and Clinical Psychology,* 2:1–9.

Jackson, J. M., and Saltzstein, H. D. (1958) "The Effect of Person-Group Relationships on Conformity Processes," *Journal of Abnormal and Social Psychology,* 57:17–24.

James, H. (1948) *The Ambassadors.* New York: Harpers Modern Classics.

James, W. (1890) *The Principles of Psychology.* New York: Holt.

Janicki, W. P. (1964) "Effect of Disposition on Resolution of Incongruity," *Journal of Abnormal and Social Psychology,* 69:579–584.

Janis, I. L. (1968) *The Contours of Fear.* New York: Wiley.

Janis, I. L. "Effects of Fear Arousal on
(1967) Attitude Change: Recent Developments in Theory and Experimental Research," in L.
Berkowitz (ed.) *Advances in
Experimental Social Psychology,*
vol. 3. New York: Academic,
pp. 166–224.

Janis, I. L., and **Feierabend, R. L.** "Effects
(1957) of Alternative Ways of Ordering
Pro and Con Arguments in Per-
suasive Communications," in
C. Hovland et al., *The Order of
Presentation in Persuasion.* New
Haven, Conn.: Yale University
Press, pp. 115–128.

Janis, I. L., and **Feshbach, S.** "Effects of
(1953) Fear-arousing Communications,"
*Journal of Abnormal and Social
Psychology,* 48:78–92.

Janis, I. L., and **Leventhal, H.** "Psycho-
(1965) logical Aspects of Physical Ill-
ness and Hospital Care," in B.
Wollman (ed.), *Handbook of
Clinical Psychology.* New York:
McGraw-Hill, pp. 1360–1377.

Janis, I. L., and **Leventhal, H.** "Human
(1968) Reaction to Stress," in E. Ber-
gotta and W. Lambert (eds.),
*Handbook of Personality Theory
and Research.* Chicago: Rand
McNally.

Janis, I. L., and **Terwilliger, R. F.** "An Ex-
(1962) perimental Study of Psycho-
logical Resistance to Fear-arousing Communications," *Journal of
Abnormal and Social Psychology,*
65:403–410.

Johannsen, D. E. "Perception," *Annual
(1967) Review of Psychology,* 18:1–40.

Johnson, H. H., and **Scileppi, J. A.** "Effects
(1969) of Ego-involvement Conditions
on Attitude Change to High and
Low Credibility Communicators," *Journal of Personality
and Social Psychology,* 13:31–36.

Johnson, H. H., and **Steiner, I. D.** "Some
(1967) Effects of Discrepancy Level on
Relationships Between Authoritarianism and Conformity," *Journal of Social Psychology,* 73:
199–204.

Johnson, K. G. "Dimensions of Judgment
(1963) of Science News Stories," *Journalism Quarterly,* 40:315–322.

Johnson, W. "The Fateful Process of Mr.

(1953) A Talking to Mr. B," *Harvard
Business Review,* 31:49–56.

Jones, E. E., and **Davis, K. E.** "From Acts
(1965) to Dispositions: The Attribution
Process in Person Perception,"
in L. Berkowitz (ed.), *Advances
in Experimental Social Psychology,* vol. 2. New York: Academic,
pp. 219–266.

Jones, E. E., Jones, R. G., and **Gergen, K. J.**
(1963) "Some Conditions Affecting the
Evaluations of a Conformist,"
Journal of Personality, 31:270–
288.

Jones, E. E., and **Kohler, R.** "The Effects
(1958) of Plausibility on the Learning of
Controversial Statements," *Journal of Abnormal and Social Psychology,* 57:315–320.

Jordan, N. "Some Formal Characteristics
(1963) of the Behavior of Two Disturbed Boys," in R. G. Barker
(ed.), *The Stream of Behavior.*
New York: Appleton Century
Crofts, pp. 203–218.

Jourard, S. M. *Disclosing Man to Himself.*
(1968) Princeton, N.J.: Van Nostrand.

Jourard, S. M. *The Transparent Self.*
(1964) Princeton, N.J.:Van Nostrand.

Jourard, S. M., and **Laskow, P.** "Some
(1958) Factors in Self-disclosure,"
*Journal of Abnormal and Social
Psychology,* 56:91–98.

Jourard, S. M., and **Rubin, J.** "Self-dis-
(1968) closure and Touching: A Study
of Two Modes of Interpersonal
Encounter and Their Inter-rela-
tion," *Journal of Humanistic
Psychology,* 8:39–48.

Jung, J. *Verbal Learning.* New York: Holt.
(1968)

Kaplan, A. *The Conduct of Inquiry: Meth-
(1964) odology for Behavioral Science.*
San Francisco: Chandler.

Katz, D. "The Functional Approach to the
(1970) Study of Attitudes," in K. K.
Sereno and C. D. Mortensen,
*Foundations of Communication
Theory,* New York: Harper &
Row, pp. 234–259.

Katz, D. *Animals and Men.* New York:
(1937) Longmans, Green.

Katz, E. "The Diffusion of New Ideas and
(1963) Practices," in W. Schramm (ed.),
The Science of Human Com-

munication. New York: Basic Books, pp. 77–93.

Katz, E. "Communication Research and the
(1960)   Image of Society: Convergence of Two Traditions," *American Journal of Sociology,* 65:435–440.

Katz, E. "The Two-step Flow of Com-
(1957)   munication: An Up-to-date Report on an Hypothesis," *Public Opinion Quarterly,* 21:61–78.

Kelley, G. A. *A Theory of Personality.* New
(1963)   York: Norton.

Kelley, H. H. "Communication in Experi-
(1951)   mentally Created Hierarchies," *Human Relations,* 4:39–56.

Kelley, H. H. "The Warm-Cold Variable
(1950)   in First Impressions of Persons," *Journal of Personality,* 18:431–439.

Kelley, H. H., and **Thibaut, J. W.** "Group
(1969a)   Problem Solving," in G. Lindzey and E. Aronson (eds.), *The Handbook of Social Psychology* (2d ed.), vol. 4. Reading, Mass.: Addison-Wesley, pp. 1–101.

Kelley, H. H., and **Thibaut, J. W.** "Experi-
(1969b)   mental Studies of Group Problem Solving and Process," in G. Lindzey and E. Aronson (eds.), *The Handbook of Social Psychology* (2d ed.), vol. 2. Reading, Mass.: Addison-Wesley, pp. 735–785.

Kelley, H. H., and **Woodruff, C. L.** "Mem-
(1956)   bers' Reactions to Apparent Group Approval of a Counternorm Communication," *Journal of Abnormal and Social Psychology,* 52:67–74.

Kelman, H. C. "Human Use of Human Sub-
(1967)   jects: The Problem of Deception in Social Psychological Experiments," *Psychological Bulletin,* 67:1–11.

Kendall, P., and **Wolfe, K. M.** "The Analy-
(1949)   sis of Deviant Cases in Communications Research," in P. F. Lazarsfeld and F. N. Stanton (eds.), *Communications Research, 1948–1949.* New York: Harper, pp. 152–170.

Kendon, A. "Some Functions of Gaze Direc-
(1967)   tion in Social Interaction," *Acta Psychologicia,* 26:22–63.

Kendon, A. "Temporal Aspects of the
(1963)   Social Performance in Two-person Encounters." Unpublished

doctoral dissertation, Oxford University.

Kersten, B. "An Experimental Study to
(1958)   Determine the Effect of a Speech of Introduction upon the Persuasive Speech That Followed." Unpublished thesis, South Dakota State College.

Ketchum, J. D. "Times, Values, and Social
(1951)   Organization," *Canadian Journal of Psychology,* 5:97–109.

Kibler, R. J., and **Barker, L. L.** (eds.).
(1969)   *Conceptual Frontiers in Speech Communication.* New York: Speech Association of America.

Kidd, J. "Social Influence Phenomena in a
(1958)   Task-oriented Group Situation," *Journal of Abnormal and Social Psychology,* 56:13–17.

Kiesler, C. A. "Attraction to the Group and
(1963)   Conformity to Group Norms," *Journal of Personality,* 31:559–569.

Kilpatrick, P. F. (ed.). *Explorations in
(1961)   Transactional Psychology.* New York: New York University Press.

Kinch, J. W. "A Formalized Theory of the
(1967)   Self-concept," in J. G. Manis and B. N. Meltzer (eds.), *Symbolic Interaction.* Boston: Allyn and Bacon, pp. 232–240.

King, T. R. "An Experimental Study of the
(1966)   Effect of Ethos upon the Immediate and Delayed Recall of Information," *Central States Speech Journal,* 17:22–28.

Kinney, E. E. "A Study of Peer Group Social
(1953)   Acceptability at the Fifth Grade Level in a Public School," *Journal of Educational Research,* 47:57–64.

Klapper, J. T. *The Effects of Mass Com-
(1960)   munication.* New York: Free Press.

Klein, M. H. "Compliance, Consistent Con-
(1967)   formity, and Personality," *Journal of Personality and Social Psychology,* 5:239–249.

Klumpp, R. G., and **Webster, J. C.** "Intelli-
(1961)   gibility of Time-compressed Speech," *Journal of the Acoustical Society of America,* 33:265–267.

Knapp, R. H. "Attitudes Toward Time and
(1962)   Aesthetic Choice," *Journal of Social Psychology,* 56:79–87.

Knapp, R. H., and Garbutt, J. T. "Time
(1958)   Imagery and the Achievement
Motive," *Journal of Personality*,
26:426–434.

Knapp, R. H., and Green, H. D. "The Judg-
(1961)   ment of Music-filled Intervals
and *n* Achievement," *Journal of
Social Psychology*, 54:263–267.

Knower, F. H. "The Present State of
(1966)   Speech-Communication Research," in P. Ried (ed.), *The
Frontiers in Experimental
Speech Communication Re-
search*. Syracuse, N.Y.: Syracuse
University Press, pp. 15–24.

Knower, F. H. "Experimental Studies of
(1936)   Changes in Attitudes. II. A
Study of the Effect of Printed
Arguments on Changes in Atti-
tude," *Journal of Abnormal and
Social Psychology*, 30:522–532.

Knower, F. H. "Experimental Studies of
(1935)   Changes in Attitude: I. A Study
of the Effect of Oral Argument on
Changes of Attitude," *Journal of
Social Psychology*, 6:315–347.

Kornzweig, N. D. "Behavior Change as a
(1968)   Function of Fear-arousal and
Personality." Unpublished doctoral dissertation, Yale University.

Kramer, E. "Judgment of Personal Char-
(1963)   acteristics and Emotions from
Nonverbal Properties of Speech,"
Psychological Bulletin, 60:408–
420.

Kraus, S. "An Experimental Study of the
(1959)   Relativeness of Negroes and
Whites in Achieving Racial Attitude Change via Kinescope Recordings." Unpublished doctoral
dissertation, State University
of Iowa; *Speech Monographs*,
27:87–88, 1960.

Kraus, S., El-Assal, E., and Defluer, M. L.
(1966)   "Fear Threat Appeals in Mass
Communication: An Apparent
Contradiction," *Speech Monographs*, 33:23–29.

Krauss, R. M., and Weinheimer, S. "Con-
(1966)   current Feedback: Confirmation
and the Encoding of Referents in
Verbal Communication," *Journal
of Personality and Social Psychology*, 4:343–346.

Krauss, R. M., and Weinheimer, S.
(1964)   "Changes in the Length of Ref-
erence Phrases as a Function of
Usage in Social Interaction: A
Preliminary Study," *Psychonomic
Science*, 1:113–114.

Krech, D., and Crutchfield, R. *Elements
(1958)   of Psychology*. New York: Knopf.

Krech, D., Crutchfield, R., and Ballachey,
(1962)   E. *Individual in Society*. New
York: McGraw-Hill.

Krippendorff, K. "Values, Modes and
(1969)   Domains of Inquiry into Communication," *The Journal of
Communication*, 19:105–133.

Kroeber, A., and Kluckhohn, C. "Culture:
(1952)   A Critical Review of Concepts
and Definitions," *Papers of the
Peabody Museum*, 47:643–644.

Kuethe, J. L. "Pervasive Influence of
(1964)   Social Schemata," *Journal of
Abnormal and Social Psychology*,
68:248–254.

Kuethe, J. L. "Social Schemas," *Journal of
(1962)   Abnormal and Social Psychology*, 64:31–38.

Kuhn, M. H., and McPartland, T. S. "An
(1954)   Empirical Investigation of Self
Attitudes," *American Sociological Review*, 19:68–76.

Lachman, R. "The Model in Theory Con-
(1960)   struction," *Psychological Review*, 67:113–129.

Ladefoged, P., and Broadbent, D. "Percep-
(1960)   tion of Sequence in Auditory
Events," *Quarterly Journal of
Experimental Psychology*, 12:
162–170.

Laing, R. *The Divided Self*. New York:
(1969)   Pantheon.

Lana, R. "Three Theoretical Interpreta-
(1964)   tions of Order Effects in Persuasive Communications," *Psychological Bulletin*, 61:314–320.

Lana, R. "Controversy of the Topic and
(1963a)   the Order of Presentation in Persuasive Communications," *Psychological Reports*, 12:163–170.

Lana, R. "Interest, Media, and Order
(1963b)   Effects in Persuasive Communications," *Journal of Psychology*,
56:9–13.

Lana, R. "Familiarity and the Order of
(1961)   Presentation of Persuasive Communication," *Journal of Abnormal and Social Psychology*, 62:
573–577.

Lana, R., and **Rosnow, R.** "Subject Aware-
(1963)   ness and Order Effects in Persuasive Communications," *Psychological Reports,* 12:523–529.

Langer, S. *Philosophy in a New Key.* New
(1942)   York: New American Library,
Mentor.

Langfeld, H. "The Judgment of Emotions
(1918)   from Facial Expression," *Journal
of Abnormal and Social Psy-
chology,* 13:173–184.

Lanzetta, J. T., and **Roby T. B.** "Group
(1957)   Learning and Communication as
a Function of Task and Structure 'Demands'," *Journal of Abnormal and Social Psychology,*
55:121–131.

La Pierre, R. T. *Collective Behavior.* New
(1938)   York: McGraw-Hill.

La Pierre, R. T. "Attitudes versus Actions,"
(1934)   *Social Forces,* 13:230–237.

Lasagna, L., and **McCann, W. P.** "Effect
(1957)   of Tranquilizing Drugs on Am-
phetamine Toxicity in Aggre-
gated Mice," *Science,* 125:1241–
1242.

Lashley, K. "In Search of the Engram," in
(1960)   F. A. Beach, D. D. Hebb, C. T.
Morgan, and H. W. Nissen (eds.),
*The Neuropsychology of Lash-
ley.* New York: McGraw-Hill,
pp. 478–503.

Lashley, K. As cited in W. R. Ashby, "The
(1954)   Application of Cybernetics to
Psychiatry," *Journal of Mental
Science,* 100:114–124.

Lasswell, H. D. "The Role of Communica-
(1965)   tion Arts and Sciences in University Life," *Audio-Visual Communication Review,* 13:361–373.

Lasswell, H. D. "The Structure and Func-
(1948)   tion of Communications in Society," in L. Bryson (ed.), *The
Communication of Ideas.* Harper
& Row, pp. 37–51.

Lawson, E. D. "Change in Communication
(1965)   Nets, Performance, and Morale,"
Human Relations, 18:139–148.

Lawson, E. D., and **Stagner, R.** "Group
(1957)   Pressure, Attitude Change, and
Autonomic Involvement," *Journal of Social Psychology,* 45:
299–312.

Lazarsfeld, P. E., Berelson, B., and **Gaudet,**
(1948)   **H.** *The Peoples' Choice.* New
York: Columbia University Press.

Lazarus, R., Yousem, H., and **Arenberg, D.**

(1953)   "Hunger and Perception," *Journal of Personality,* 21:312.

Leathers, D. G. "The Process Effects of
(1970)   Trust-destroying Behavior in the
Small Group," *Speech Mono-
graphs,* 37:180–187.

Leavitt, H. J. "Some Effects of Certain
(1951)   Communication Patterns on
Group Performance," *Journal of
Abnormal and Social Psychology,* 46:38–50.

Leavitt, H. J., and **Mueller, R.** "Some Ef-
(1951)   fects of Feedback on Communication," *Human Relations,* 4:
401–410.

Le Bon, G. *The Crowd.* New York: Viking
(1960)   (1st ed., 1895).

Lecky, P. *Self-consistency.* New York:
(1945)   Island Press.

Le Compte, W., and **Barker, R.** "The Eco-
(1960)   logical Framework of Cooperative Behavior." Paper presented
to the American Psychological
Association, Chicago.

Lee, B. "Effects of Delayed Speech Feed-
(1950)   back," *Journal of the Acoustical
Society of America,* 22:824–826.

Lefford, A. "The Influence of Emotional
(1946)   Subject Matter on Logical Reasoning," *Journal of General Psychology,* 34:127–151.

Leipold, W. "Psychological Distance in a
(1963)   Dyadic Interview." Unpublished
doctoral dissertation, University of North Dakota.

Lemert, J. B. "Dimensions of Source Credi-
(1963)   bility." Paper presented to the
Association for Education in
Journalism, August.

Leshan, L. "Time Orientation and Social
(1952)   Class," *Journal of Abnormal and
Social Psychology,* 47:589–592.

Lettvin, J., Maturana, H., McCulloch, W.
(1959)   and **Pitts, W.** "What the Frog's
Eye Tells the Frog's Brain," *Proceedings of the Institute of Radio
Engineers,* 49:1940–1951.

Leventhal, H. "Fear Communications in
(1965)   the Acceptance of Health Practices," *Bulletin of the New York
Academy of Medicine,* 41:1144–
1168.

Leventhal, H., and **Niles, P.** "A Field Ex-
(1964)   periment on Fear Arousal with
Data on the Validity of Questionnaire Measures," *Journal of
Personality,* 32:459–479.

Leventhal, H., Singer, R., and Jones, S. (1965) "The Effects of Fear and Specificity of Recommendation upon Attitudes and Behavior," *Journal of Personality and Social Psychology*, 2:20–29.

Leventhal, H., and Trembly, G. (1968) "Negative Emotions and Persuasion," *Journal of Personality*, 36:154–168.

Leventhal, H., and Watts, J. (1966) "Sources of Resistence to Fear-arousing Communications on Smoking and Lung Cancer," *Journal of Personality*, 34:155–175.

Levine, R., Chein, I., and Murphy, G. (1942) "The Relation of the Intensity of a Need to the Amount of Perceptual Distortion: A Preliminary Report," *Journal of Psychology*, 13:283–293.

Levitt, A. (1964) "The Relationship between Abilities to Express Emotional Meanings Vocally and Facially," in J. Davitz (ed.), *The Communication of Emotional Meaning*. New York: McGraw-Hill, pp. 43–56.

Levonian, E. (1968) "Self-esteem and Opinion Change," *Journal of Personality and Social Psychology*, 9:257–259.

Levy, P. (1964) "The Ability to Express and Perceive Vocal Communication of Feeling," in J. Davitz (ed.), *The Communication of Emotional Meaning*. New York: McGraw-Hill, pp. 43–56.

Lewin, K. (1951) "Psychological Ecology," in Dorwin Cartwright (ed.), *Field Theory in Social Science*. New York: Harper & Row, pp. 170–187.

Linn, L. S. (1965) "Verbal Attitudes and Overt Behavior: A Study of Racial Discrimination," *Social Forces*, 44:353–364.

Linton, H. B. (1954) "Autokinetic Judgment as a Measure of Influence," *Journal of Abnormal and Social Psychology*, 49:464–466.

Little, K. B. (1965) "Personal Space," *Journal of Experimental and Social Psychology*, 1:237–247.

London, P., and Lin, H. (1964) "Yielding Reason to Social Pressure: Task Complexity and Expectation in Conformity," *Journal of Personality*, 32:75–89.

Loomis, J. L. (1959) "Communication, the Development of Trust, and Cooperative Behavior," *Human Relations*, 12:305–315.

Lorenz, K. Z. (1952) King Solomon's Ring. London: Methuen.

Lott, D. F., and Sommer, R. (1967) "Seating Arrangement and Status," *Journal of Personality and Social Psychology*, 7:90–95.

Lowin, A. (1967) "Approach and Avoidance: Alternate Modes of Selective Exposure to Information," *Journal of Personality and Social Psychology*, 6:1–9.

Luchins, A. S. (1958) "Definitiveness of Impression and Primacy-Recency in Communications," *Journal of Social Psychology*, 48:275–290

Luchins, A. S. (1957) "Experimental Attempts to Minimize the Impact of First Impressions," in Hovland et al., *The Order of Presentation in Persuasion*. New Haven, Conn.: Yale University Press, pp. 62–75.

Luchins, A. S., and Luchins, E. H. (1955) "On Conformity with True and False Communications," *Journal of Social Psychology*, 42:283–303.

Ludlum, T. (1958) "Effects of Certain Techniques of Credibility upon Audience Attitudes," *Speech Monographs*, 25:278–284.

Luft, J. (1966) "On Nonverbal Interaction," *Journal of Psychology*, 63:261–268.

Lumsdaine, A. A., and Janis, I. L. (1953) "Resistence to 'Counter-propaganda' Produced by One-sided and Two-sided 'Propaganda' Presentations," *Public Opinion Quarterly*, 17:311–318.

Lund, F. H. (1925) "The Psychology of Belief: IV. The Law of Primacy in Persuasion," *Journal of Abnormal and Social Psychology*, 20:183–191.

Lyman, S., and Scott, M. (1967) "Territoriality: A Neglected Sociological Dimension," *Social Problems*, 15:236–249.

Mahl, G. F. (1956) "Disturbances and Silences in the Patient's Speech in Psychotherapy," *Journal of Abnormal and Social Psychology*, 53:1–15.

Mahl, G. F., and Schultz, G. (1964) "Psychological Research in the Extralinguistic

Area," in T. A. Sebeok, A. S. Hayes, and M. C. Bateson (eds.), *Approaches to Semiotics*. The Hague: Mouton, pp. 51–125.

Malmo, R. "Activation: A Neuropsycho-
(1959) logical Dimension," *Psychological Review*, 66:367–386.

Manis, M. "Context Effects in Communi-
(1967) cation," *Journal of Personality and Social Psychology*, 5:326–334.

Manis, M. "Immunization, Delay, and the
(1965) Interpretation of Persuasive Messages," *Journal of Personality and Social Psychology*, 1: 541–550.

Manis, M., and Blake, J. "Interpretation
(1963) of Persuasive Messages as a Function of Prior Immunization," *Journal of Abnormal and Social Psychology*, 66:225–230.

March, J. G., and Simon, H. A. *Organiza-
(1958) tions*. New York: Wiley.

Markel, N. N. "Relationship between
(1969) Voice-quality Profiles and MMPI Profiles in Psychiatric Patients," *Journal of Abnormal Psychology*, 74:61–66.

Markel, N. N. "The Reliability of Coding
(1965) Paralanguage: Pitch, Loudness, and Tempo," *Journal of Verbal Learning and Verbal Behavior*, 4:306–308.

Markel, N. N., Eisler R. M., and Reese, H.
(1967) W. "Judging Personality from Dialect," *Journal of Verbal Learning and Verbal Behavior*, 6:33–35.

Markel, N. N., and Roblin, G. "The Effect
(1965) of Content and Sex-of-judge on Judgments of Personality from Voice," *The International Journal of Social Psychiatry*, 11:295–300.

Markham, D. "The Dimensions of Source
(1966) Credibility of Television Newscasters," *Speech Monographs*, 33:264.

Maslow, A. H. *Motivation and Personality*.
(1954) New York: Harper & Row.

Maslow, A. H., and Mintz, N. L. "Effects
(1956) of Esthetic Surroundings: I. Initial Effects of Three Esthetic Conditions upon Perceiving 'Energy' and 'Well-being' in Faces," *Journal of Psychology*, 41:247–254.

Mason, J., and Brady, J. "The Sensitivity
(1964) of Psychendocrine Systems to Social and Physical Environment," in P. Leiderman and D. Shapiro (eds.), *Psychological Approaches to Social Behavior*. Stanford, Calif.: Stanford University Press.

Matarazzo, J. D., and Saslow, G. "Differ-
(1961) ences in Interview Interaction Behavior among Normal and Deviant Groups," in I. Berg and B. M. Bass (eds.), *Conformity and Deviation*. New York: Harper & Row, pp. 286–327.

Matarazzo, J. D., Saslow, G., Wiens, A.,
(1964) Weitman, M., and Allen, B. "Interviewer Headnodding and Interviewee Speech Durations," *Psychotherapy*, 1:54–63.

Matarazzo, J. D., and Wiens, A. N. "Studies
(1965) of Interview Speech Behavior," in L. Krasner and L. Ullman (eds.), *Research in Behavior Modification: New Developments and Implications*. New York: Holt, pp. 179–210.

Matlin, M. W., and Zajonc, R. B. "Social
(1968) Facilitation of Word Associations," *Journal of Personality and Social Psychology*, 10:455–460.

May, M., and Lumsdaine, A. A. *Learning
(1958) from Films*. New Haven, Conn.: Yale University Press.

May, R. "Contributions of Existential
(1958) Psychotherapy," in R. May, E. Angel, and H. Ellenberger (eds.), *Existence*. New York: Basic Books, pp. 37–91.

Mayo, C. W., and Crockett, W. H. "Cog-
(1964) nitive Complexity and Primacy-Recency Effects in Impression Formation," *Journal of Abnormal and Social Psychology*, 68:335–338.

McBride, G., King, M. G., and James, J. W.
(1965) "Social Proximity Effects on *GSR* in Adult Humans," *Journal of Psychology*, 61:153–157.

McClelland, D. C. *The Achieving Society*.
(1961) Princeton, N.J.: Van Nostrand.

McClelland, D. C., and Atkinson, J. W.
(1948) "The Projective Expression of Needs: I. The Effects of Different Intensities of the Hunger Drive

on Perception," *Journal of Psychology*, 25:205–222.

McClelland, D. C., Atkinson, J. W., Clark, R., and Lowell, E. *The Achievement Motive*. New York: Appleton Century Crofts.
(1953)

McCroskey, J. C. "A Summary of Experimental Research on the Effects of Evidence in Persuasive Communication," *Quarterly Journal of Speech*, 55:169–176.
(1969)

McCroskey, J. C. "Studies of the Effects of Evidence in Persuasive Communication," Speech Communication Research Laboratory Report 4-67, Dept. of Speech, Michigan State University, Lansing, Mich.
(1967)

McCroskey, J. C. "Scales for the Measurement of Ethos," *Speech Monographs*, 33:65–72.
(1966)

McCroskey, J. C., and Dunham, R. E. "Ethos: A Confounding Element in Communication Research," *Speech Monographs*, 33:456–463.
(1966)

McDavid, Jr., J. W., and Schroder, H. M. "The Interpretation of Approval and Disapproval by Delinquent and Non-delinquent Adolescents," *Journal of Personality*, 25:539–558.
(1957)

McDavid, Jr., J. W., and Sistrunk, F. "Personality Correlates of Two Kinds of Conforming Behavior," *Journal of Personality*, 32:420–435.
(1964)

McDougall, W. *The Group Mind*. London: Cambridge.
(1920)

McGinnies, E., and Rosenbaum, L. L. "A Test of the Selective Exposure Hypothesis in Persuasion," *Journal of Psychology*, 61:237–240.
(1965)

McGuire, W. J. "The Nature of Attitudes and Attitude Change," in G. Lindzey and E. Aronson (eds.), *The Handbook of Social Psychology* (2d ed.), vol. 4. Reading, Mass.: Addison-Wesley.
(1969)

McGuire, W. J. "Personality and Attitude Change: An Information Processing Theory," in A. Greenwald, T. C. Brock, and T. M. Ostrum (eds.), *Psychological Foundations of Attitudes*. New York: Academic, pp. 171–196.
(1968a)

McGuire, W. J. "Personality and Attitude

McGuire, W. J. Change: A Theoretical Housing," in A. Greenwald et al. (eds.), *Attitude Change Theory and Research*. New York: Academic.
(1968b)

McGuire, W. J. "Personality and Susceptibility to Social Influence," in E. F. Borgatta and W. W. Lambert (eds.), *Handbook of Personality Theory and Research*. Chicago: Rand McNally, · pp. 1130–1187.
(1968c)

McGuire, W. J. "Immunization against Persuasion." Unpublished report, 1962, as cited in C. A. Insko, *Theories of Attitude and Change*. New York: Appleton Century Crofts.
(1967)

McGuire, W. J. "Persistence of the Resistance to Persuasion Induced by Various Types of Prior Belief Defenses," *Journal of Abnormal and Social Psychology*, 64:241–248.
(1962)

McGuire, W. J. "The Effectiveness of Supportive and Refutational Defenses in Immunizing and Restoring Beliefs against Persuasion," *Sociometry*, 24:184–197.
(1961a)

McGuire, W. J. "Resistance to Persuasion Conferred by Active and Passive Prior Refutation of the Same and Alternative Counterarguments," *Journal of Abnormal and Social Psychology*, 63:326–332.
(1961b)

McGuire, W. J. "Order of Presentation as a Factor in 'Conditioning' Persuasiveness," in Hovland et al., *The Order of Presentation in Persuasion*. New Haven, Conn.: Yale University Press, pp. 98–114.
(1957)

McGuire, W. J., and Millman, S. "Anticipatory Belief Lowering Following Forewarning of a Persuasive Attack," *Journal of Personality and Social Psychology*, 2:471–479.
(1965)

McGuire, W. J., and Papageorgis, D. "The Relative Efficacy of Various Types of Prior Belief-Defense in Producing Immunity against Persuasion," *Journal of Abnormal and Social Psychology*, 62:327–337.
(1961)

McKee, P. "An Analysis of the Use of Evidence in Ten Intercollegiate Debates." Unpublished masters thesis, University of Kansas.
(1959)

McLuhan, M. *Understanding Media: The*
(1965)   *Extensions of Man.* New York:
McGraw-Hill.

Mead, G. H. *Mind, Self and Society.* Chi-
(1934)   cago: University of Chicago
Press.

Mead, G. H. *Mind, Self, and Society from*
(1930)   *the Standpoint of a Social Be-*
haviorist. Chicago: University
of Chicago Press.

Meade, R. D. "Achievement Motivation,
(1966)   Achievement, and Psychological
Time," *Journal of Personality*
and Social Psychology, 4:577–
580.

Meerloo, J. A. "From Persuasion to Brain-
(1968)   washing: Some Clinical Variations in Persuasion and Suggestion," in C. E. Larson and F. E.
Dance (eds.), *Perspectives on*
Communication. Milwaukee:
Speech Communication Center,
pp. 78–89.

Meerloo, J. A. "Communication and Mental
(1967)   Contagion," in L. O. Thayer (ed.),
Communication: Concepts and
Perspectives, Washington, D.C.:
Spartan, pp. 1–29.

Mehrabian, A. "A Semantic Space for
(in press) Nonverbal Behavior," in C. D.
Mortensen and K. K. Sereno,
Advances in Communication Re-
search. New York: Harper & Row.

Mehrabian, A. "Significance of Posture
(1969)   and Position in the Communication of Attitude and Status Relationships," *Psychological Bul-*
letin, 71:359–372.

Mehrabian, A. "The Effect of Context on
(1968a)   Judgments of Speaker Attitude,"
Journal of Personality, 36:21–31.

Mehrabian, A. "Relationship of Attitude to
(1968b)   Seated Posture, Orientation, and
Distance," *Journal of Personality*
and Social Psychology, 10:26–30.

Mehrabian, A. "Orientation Behavior and
(1967)   Nonverbal Attitude in Communication," *The Journal of Com-*
munication, 17:324–332.

Mehrabian, A. "Communication Length
(1965)   as an Index of Communicator
Attitude," *Psychological Reports,*
17:519–522.

Mehrabian, A., and **Ferris, S. R.** "Inference
(1967)   of Attitudes from Nonverbal
Communication in Two Channels," *Journal of Consulting Psy-*
chology, 31:248–252.

Mehrabian, A., and **Wiener, M.** "Decoding
(1967)   of Inconsistent Communication,"
Journal of Personality and Social
Psychology, 6:109–114.

Mendelson, J., Kubzansky, P. E., Leider-
(1961)   **man, P. H., Wexler, D.,** and
Solomon, P. "Physiological and
Psychological Aspects of Sensory Deprivation: A Case Analysis," in P. Solomon et al. (eds.),
Sensory Deprivation. Cambridge,
Mass.: Harvard University Press,
pp. 91–113.

Meredith, P. "Toward a Taxonomy of Edu-
(1965)   cational Media," *Audio-Visual*
Communication Review, 13:374–
384.

Merton, R. K. "The Role Set," *British Jour-*
(1957)   *nal of Sociology,* 8:106–120.

Merton, R. "The Social Psychology of
(1948)   Housing," in W. Dennis et al.
(eds.), *Current Trends in Social*
Psychology. Pittsburgh: University of Pittsburgh Press, pp. 163–
217.

Meyer, W. J., and **Seidman, S. B.** "Relative
(1961)   Effectiveness of Different Reinforcement Combinations on Concept Learning of Children at
Two Developmental Levels,"
Child Development, 32:117–124.

Michael, C. R. "Receptive Fields of Direc-
(1966)   tionally Selective Units in the
Optic Nerve of the Ground Squir-
rel," *Science,* 152:1092–1094.

Miller, G. A. "Studies on the Use of Fear
(1963)   Appeals: A Summary and Analysis," *Central States Speech Jour-*
nal, 14:117–124.

Miller, G. A. "Decision Units in the Per-
(1962)   ception of Speech," *IRE Trans-*
actions on Information Theory,
IT-8:81–83.

Miller, G. A. "The Magical Number Seven,
(1956)   Plus or Minus Two: Some Limits
on Our Capacity for Processing
Information," *Psychological Re-*
view, 63:81–97.

Miller, G. A. "Speech and Language," in
(1951)   S. S. Stevens (ed.), *Handbook*
of Experimental Psychology.
New York: Wiley, pp. 789–810.

Miller, G. A., Galanter, E., and **Pribram, K.**
(1960)   *Plans and the Structure of Be-*
havior. New York: Holt.

Miller, G. R. "Some Factors Influencing
(1969)   Judgments of the Logical Validity
of Arguments: A Research Re-

view," *Quarterly Journal of Speech*, 55:276–286.

Miller, G. R. "Communication and Persuasion Research: Current Problems and Prospects," *The Quarterly Journal of Speech*, 54:268–276.
(1968)

Miller, G. R. "A Crucial Problem in Attitude Research," *The Quarterly Journal of Speech*, 53:235–240.
(1967)

Miller, G. R., and **Hewgill, M. A.** "Some Recent Research on Fear-arousing Message Appeals," *Speech Monographs*, 33:377–391.
(1966)

Miller, G. R., and **Hewgill, M. A.** "The Effects of Variations in Nonfluency on Audience Ratings of Source Credibility," *Quarterly Journal of Speech*, 50:36–44.
(1964)

Miller, G. R., Zavos, H., Vlandis, J. W., and **Rosenbaum, M. E.** "The Effect of Differential Reward on Speech Patterns," *Speech Monographs*, 28:9–15.
(1961)

Miller, J. G. "Toward a General Theory for the Behavioral Sciences," *American Psychologist*, 10:513–531.
(1955)

Miller, N. E. "The Effect of Group Size on Decision-making Discussions." Unpublished doctoral dissertation, University of Michigan.
(1951)

Miller, N. E., and **Campbell, D. T.** "Recency and Primacy in Persuasion as a Function of the Timing of Speeches and Measurements," *Journal of Abnormal and Social Psychology*, 59:1–9.
(1959)

Miller, N. E., and **Dollard, J.** *Social Learning and Imitation.* New Haven, Conn.: Yale University Press.
(1941)

Millman, S. "Anxiety, Comprehension, and Susceptibility to Social Influence," *Journal of Personality and Social Psychology*, 9:251–256.
(1968)

Mills, J. "Avoidance of Dissonant Information," *Journal of Personality and Social Psychology*, 2:589–593.
(1965a)

Mills, J. "Effect of Certainty about a Decision upon Postdecision Exposure to Consonant and Dissonant Information," *Journal of Personality and Social Psychology*, 2:749–752.
(1965b)

Mills, J., Aronson, E., and **Robinson, H.** "Selectivity in Exposure to Information," *Journal of Abnormal and Social Psychology*, 59:250–253.
(1959)

Mills, J., and **Ellison, J. M.** "Effect on Opinion Change of Similarity between the Communicator and the Audience He Addressed," *Journal of Personality and Social Psychology*, 9:153–156.
(1968)

Mills, J., and **Ross, A.** "Effects of Commitment and Certainty upon Interest in Supporting Information," *Journal of Abnormal and Social Psychology*, 68:552–555.
(1964)

Mills, T. M. "Power Relations in Three-person Groups," *American Sociological Review*, 18:351–357.
(1953)

Minter, R. L. "A Denotative and Connotative Study in Communication," *The Journal of Communication*, 18:26–36.
(1968)

Mintz, N. "Effects of Esthetic Surroundings: II. Prolonged and Repeated Experience in a 'Beautiful' and an 'Ugly' Room," *Journal of Psychology*, 41:459–466.
(1956)

Montague, W. P. *Belief Unbound.* New Haven, Conn.: Yale University Press.
(1930)

Moray, N. "Attention in Dichotic Listening: Affective Cues and the Influence of Instructions," *Quarterly Journal of Experimental Psychology*, 11:56–60.
(1959)

Moray, N., and **Taylor, A.** "The Effect of Redundancy in Shadowing One of Two Dichotic Messages," *Language and Speech*, 1:102–109.
(1958)

Morgan, C. T., and **King, R. A.** *Introduction to Psychology* (3d ed.). New York: McGraw-Hill.
(1966)

Morgan, J. J., and **Morton, T. J.** "The Distortion of Syllogistic Reasoning Produced by Personal Convictions," *Journal of Social Psychology*, 20:39–59.
(1944)

Morrissette, J. O. "Group Performance as a Function of Task Difficulty and Size and Structure of Group: II" *Journal of Personality and Social Psychology*, 3:357–359.
(1966)

Mortensen, C. D. "The Influence of Television on Policy Discussion," *Quarterly Journal of Speech*, 54:277–281.
(1968a)

Mortensen, C. D. "The Influence of Role Structure on Message Content in Political Telecast Campaigns," *Central States Speech Journal*, 19:279–285.
(1968b)

Mortensen, C. D. "A Comparative Analysis
(1967) of Political Persuasion on Four
Telecast Program Formats in the
1960 and 1964 Presidential Campaigns." Unpublished doctoral
dissertation, University of Minnesota.

Mortensen, C. D. "Should the Group Have
(1966) an Assigned Leader?" *Speech
Teacher*, 15:34–41.

Mortensen, C. D., and **Sereno, K. K.** (eds.).
(in press) *Advances in Communication Research.* New York: Harper & Row.

Mortensen, C. D., and **Sereno, K. K.** "The
(1970) Influence of Ego-involvement
and Discrepancy on Perceptions
of Communication," *Speech
Monographs*, 37:127–134.

Moscovici, S. "Communication Processes
(1967) in the Properties of Language,"
in L. Berkowitz (ed.), *Advances
in Experimental Social Psychology*, vol. 3. New York: Academic,
pp. 225–270.

Munn, N. L. "The Effect of Knowledge of
(1940) the Situation upon Judgment of
Emotion from Facial Expressions," *Journal of Abnormal and
Social Psychology*, 35:324–338.

Myers, T. I., Murphy, D. B., Smith, S.,
(1969) and **Goffard, S. J.** "Experimental
Studies of Sensory Deprivation
and Social Isolation," HumRRO
Tech. Rept. 66-8, George Washington University, June 1966, as
cited in J. P. Zubek (ed.), *Sensory Deprivation: Fifteen Years
of Research.* New York: Appleton Century Crofts.

Mysak, E. "Speech System," in K. K.
(1970) Sereno and C. D. Mortensen
(eds.), *Foundations of Communication Theory.* New York: Harper & Row, pp. 108–119.

Mysak, E. *Speech Pathology and Feed-
(1966) back Theory.* Springfield, Ill.:
Charles C Thomas.

Nachshon, I., and **Wapner, S.** "Effect of
(1967) Eye Contact and Physiognomy
on Perceived Location of Another Person," *Journal of Personality and Social Psychology*,
7:82–89.

Neisser, U. *Cognitive Psychology.* New
(1967) York: Appleton Century Crofts.

Neisser, U. "Decision Time without Reac-
(1963) tion Time: Experiments in Visual
Scanning," *American Journal of
Psychology*, 76:376–385.

Neisser, U., Novick, R., and **Lazar, R.**
(1963) "Searching for Ten Targets
Simultaneously," *Perceptual and
Motor Skills*, 17:955–961.

Newcomb, T. M. *The Acquaintance Pro-
(1961) cess.* New York: Holt.

Newcomb, T. M. "The Prediction of Inter-
(1956) personal Attraction," *American
Psychologist*, 11:575–586.

Newcomb, T. M. "An Approach to the
(1953) Study of Communicative Acts,"
Psychological Review, 60:393–
404.

Newman, E. B. "Perception," in E. G.
(1948) Boring, H. S. Langfield, and H. P.
Weld (eds.), *Foundations of
Psychology.* New York: Wiley.

Newsweek, Sept. 29, pp. 70, 72.
(1969)

Nichols, A. C. "Apparent Factors Leading
(1964) to Errors in Audition Made by
Foreign Students," *Speech Monographs*, 31:85–91.

Niles, P. "The Relationship of Suscepti-
(1964) bility and Anxiety to Acceptance
of Fear-arousing Communica-
tions." Unpublished doctoral
dissertation, Yale University.

Nisbett, R. E., and **Gordon, A.** "Self-
(1967) esteem and Susceptibility to
Social Influence," *Journal of
Personality and Social Psychology*, 5:268–275.

Nokes, P. "Feedback as an Explanatory
(1961) Device in the Study of Certain
Interpersonal and Institutional
Processes," *Human Relations*,
14:381–387.

Nord, W. R. "Social Exchange Theory: An
(1969) Interactive Approach to Social
Conformity," *Psychological Bulletin*, 71:174–208.

Norman, D. *Memory and Attention: An
(1969a) Introduction to Human Information Processing.* New York:
Wiley.

Norman, D. "Memory While Shadowing,"
(1969b) *Quarterly Journal of Experimental Psychology*, 21:85–93.

Norman, D. "Toward a Theory of Memory
(1968) and Attention," *Psychological
Review*, 75:522–536.

Norman, D. "Acquisition and Retention in

(1966) Short-term Memory," *Journal of Experimental Psychology*, 72: 369–381.

Nunnally, J. C., and **Bobren, H. M.** "Variables Governing the Willingness **(1959)** to Receive Communications on Mental Health," *Journal of Personality*, 27:38–46.

O'Dell, J. W. "Group Size and Emotional **(1968)** Interaction," *Journal of Personality and Social Psychology*, 8:75–78.

Olmstead, J. A., and **Blake, R. R.** "The Use **(1955)** of Simulated Groups to Produce Modifications in Judgment," *Journal of Personality*, 23:335–345.

Orne, M. T. "On the Social Psychology of **(1962)** the Psychological Experiment: With Particular Reference to Demand Characteristics and Their Implications," *American Psychologist*, 17:776–783.

Osgood, C. E. "Dimensionality of the **(1966)** Semantic Space for Communication via Facial Expressions," *The Scandinavian Journal of Psychology*, 7:1–30.

Osgood, C. E. (ed.) "Psycholinguistics: A **(1954)** Survey of Theory and Research Problems," *Journal of Abnormal and Social Psychology*, 49:1–203, Morton Prince Memorial Supplement.

Osgood, C. E., and **Tannenbaum, P. H.** **(1955)** "The Principle of Congruity in the Prediction of Attitude Change," *Psychological Review*, 62:42–55.

Osmond, H. "Function as the Basis of **(1957)** Psychiatry Ward Design," *Mental Hospitals*, 8:23–29.

Ostermeier, T. H. "Effects of Type and **(1967)** Frequency of Reference and Perceived Source Credibility and Attitude Change," *Speech Monographs*, 34:137–144.

Ostermeier, T. H. "An Experimental Study **(1966)** on the Type and Frequency of Reference as Used by an Unfamiliar Source in a Message and Its Effect upon Perceived Credibility and Attitude Change." Unpublished doctoral dissertation, Michigan State University.

Oswald, I., **Taylor, A.**, and **Treisman, M.** **(1960)** "Discrimination Responses to Stimulation during Human Sleep," *Brain*, 83:440–453.

Oyster, C. W., and **Barlow, H. B.** "Direction-selective Units in Rabbit **(1967)** Retina: Distribution of Preferred Directions," *Science*, 155:841–842.

Packard, V. *The Hidden Persuaders*, New **(1957)** York: McKay.

Panek, D. M., and **Martin, B.** "The Relationship between GSR and **(1959)** Speech Disturbance in Psychotherapy," *Journal of Abnormal and Social Psychology*, 58:402–405.

Park, R., and **Burgess, E.** *Introduction to* **(1921)** *the Science of Sociology*. Chicago: University of Chicago Press.

Paul, I. H. "Impressions of Personality, **(1956)** Authoritarianism, and the Fait Accompli Effect," *Journal of Abnormal and Social Psychology*, 53:338–344.

Penfield, W., and **Roberts, L.** *Speech and* **(1959)** *Brain Mechanisms*. Princeton, N.J.: Princeton University Press.

Pennington, D., **Harary, F.**, and **Bass, B. M.** **(1958)** "Some Effects of Decision and Discussion on Coalescence, Change, and Effectiveness," *Journal of Applied Psychology*, 42:404–408.

Peterson, G. "Speech and Hearing Research," *Journal of Speech and* **(1958)** *Hearing Research*, 1:3–11.

Peterson, L. R., and **Peterson, M. J.** "Short- **(1959)** term Retention of Individual Verbal Items," *Journal of Experimental Psychology*, 58:193–198.

Phillips, E. L. "Attitudes toward Self and **(1951)** Others: A Brief Questionnaire Report," *Journal of Consulting Psychology*, 15:79–81.

Piaget, J. *The Psychology of Intelligence*. **(1950)** New York: Harcourt, Brace & World.

Platt, J. R. "The Two Faces of Perception," **(1968)** in B. Rothblatt (ed.), *Changing Perspectives on Man*. Chicago: University of Chicago Press, pp. 63–116.

Plutchik, R. *The Emotions: Facts, Theories,*
(1962) *and a New Model.* New York: Random House.

Pollack, I. "The Effect of Rate of Presen-
(1952) tation of Information," report no. 25, Human Factors Operations Research Laboratories (AD 140).

Pollack, I., Rubenstein, and **Horowitz.**
(1964) "The Communication of Emotional Meaning." as cited in J. Davitz, *The Communication of Emotional Meaning.* New York: McGraw-Hill.

Pollard, J. C., Uhr, L., and **Jackson, C. W.**
(1963) "Studies in Sensory Deprivation," *Archives of General Psychiatry,* 8:435–454.

Porter, L. W., and **Lawler, E. E.** "Properties
(1965) of Organization Structure in Relation to Job Attitudes and Job Behavior," *Psychological Bulletin,* 64:23–51.

Posner, M. I. "Rate of Presentation and
(1964) Order of Recall in Immediate Memory," *British Journal of Psychology,* 55:303–306.

Powell, F. A. "The Effect of Anxiety-arous-
(1965) ing Messages When Related to Personal, Familiar, and Impersonal Referents," *Speech Monographs,* 32:102–106.

Priest, R. F., and **Sawyer, J.** "Proximity and
(1967) Peership: Bases of Balance in Interpersonal Attraction," *American Journal of Sociology,* 72: 633–649.

Quastler, H., and **Wulff, L.** "Human Per-
(1967) formance in Information Transmission," report R. 62, Control Systems Lab., University of Illinois, 1955; as cited in H. Schroder, M. Driver, and S. Streufert, *Human Information Processing.* New York: Holt.

Raush, H. L., Dittmann, A. T., and **Taylor,**
(1959) **T. J.** "Person, Setting, and Change in Social Interaction," *Human Relations,* 12:361–378.

Renneker, R. "Kinesic Research and Thera-
(1963) peutic Process," in P. Knapp (ed.), *Expressions of the Emotions in Man.* New York: International Universities Press, pp. 147–160.

Revans, W. R. "Human Relations, Manage-
(1960) ment, and Size," in M. H. Jones (ed.), *Human Relations and Modern Management.* Chicago: Quadrangle.

Riemer, M. D. "Abnormalities of the Gaze:
(1955) A Classification," *Psychiatric Quarterly,* 29:659–672.

Roeder, K. D., and **Treat, A. E.** "The Re-
(1961) ception of Bat Cries by the Tympanic Organ of Noctuid Moths," in W. Rosenblith (ed.), *Sensory Communication.* Cambridge, Mass.: M.I.T. Press, pp. 545–560.

Rogers, C. R. *Client-centered Therapy: Its*
(1951) *Current Practice, Implications, and Theory.* Boston: Houghton Mifflin.

Rohrer, J. H., Baron, S. H., Hoffman, E. L.,
(1954) and **Swander, D. V.** "The Stability of Autokinetic Judgments," *Journal of Abnormal and Social Psychology,* 49:595–597.

Rokeach, M. *Beliefs, Attitudes, and Values.*
(1968) San Francisco: Jossey-Bass.

Rokeach, M., and **Mezei, L.** "Race and
(1966) Shared Belief as Factors in Social Choice," *Science,* 151: 167–172.

Rosen, S., Plester, D., El-Mofty, A., and
(1964) **Rosen, H. V.** "High Frequency Audiometry in Presbycusis," *Archives of Otology,* 79:18–32.

Rosenau, J. N. *Public Opinion and Foreign*
(1961) *Policy.* New York: Random House.

Rosenberg, B. G., and **Langer, J.** "A Study
(1965) of Postural-Gestural Communication," *Journal of Personality and Social Psychology,* 2:593–597.

Rosenberg, L. A. "Group Size, Prior Ex-
(1961) perience, and Conformity," *Journal of Abnormal and Social Psychology,* 63:436–437.

Rosenberg, S., and **Hall, R. L.** "The Effects
(1958) of Different Social Feedback Conditions upon Performance in Dyadic Teams," *Journal of Abnormal and Social Psychology,* 57:271–277.

Rosenfeld, H. M. "Approval-seeking and
(1966a) Approval-inducing Functions of Verbal and Nonverbal Responses in a Dyad," *Journal of Personality and Social Psychology,* 4:597–605.

Rosenfeld, H. M. "Instrumental Affiliative
(1966b) Functions of Facial and Gestural

Expressions," *Journal of Personality and Social Psychology,* 4:65-72.

Rosenkrantz, P. S., and **Crockett, W. H.**
(1965)   "Some Factors Influencing the Assimilation of Disparate Information in Impression Formation," *Journal of Personality and Social Psychology,* 2:397-402.

Rosenthal, R. *Experimental Effects in*
(1966)   *Behavioral Research.* New York: Appleton Century Crofts.

Rosenthal, R. "On the Social Psychology
(1963)   of the Psychology Experiment: The Experimenter's Hypothesis as Unintended Determinant of Experimental Results," *American Scientist,* 51:268-283.

Rosnow, R. L. " 'Conditioning' the Direction
(1966a)   of Opinion Change in Persuasive Communication," *Journal of Social Psychology,* 69:291-303.

Rosnow, R. L. "What Happened to the Law
(1966b)   of Primacy?" *Journal of Communication,* 16:10-31.

Rosnow, R. L. "A Delay-of-reinforcement
(1965)   Effect in Persuasive Communication?" *Journal of Social Psychology,* 67:39-43.

Rosnow, R. L., and **Goldstein, J.** "Famili-
(1967)   arity, Salience, and the Order of Presentation of Communications," *Journal of Social Psychology,* 73:97-110.

Rosnow, R. L., Holz, R., and **Levin, J.** "Dif-
(1966)   ferential Effects of Complementary and Competing Variables in Primacy-Recency," *Journal of Social Psychology,* 69:135-147.

Rosnow, R. L., and **Lana, R.** "Complemen-
(1965)   tary and Competing-order Effects in Opinion Change," *Journal of Social Psychology,* 66: 201-207.

Rosnow, R. L., and **Robinson, E. J.** (eds.).
(1967)   *Experiments in Persuasion.* New York: Academic.

Rosnow, R. L., and **Russell, G.** "Spread of
(1963)   Effect of Reinforcement in Persuasive Communication," *Psychological Reports,* 12:731-735.

Rubin, E. "Figure and Ground," in D.
(1958)   Beardslee and M. Wertheimer (eds.), *Readings in Perception.* Princeton, N.J.: Van Nostrand, pp. 194-203.

Rubin, R. *Political Television.* Belmont,
(1967)   Calif.: Wadsworth.

Ruesch, J., and **Bateson, G.** *Communica-*
(1951)   *tion: The Social Matrix of Psychiatry.* New York: Norton.

Ruesch, J., and **Kees, W.** *Nonverbal Com-*
(1956)   *munication.* Berkeley, Calif.: University of California Press.

Rump, E. "Facial Expression and Situa-
(1960)   tional Cues: Demonstration of a Logical Error in Frijda's Report," *Acta Psychologicia,* 17:31-38.

Russo, W. F. "Connotations of Seating
(1967)   Arrangements," *Cornell Journal of Social Relations,* 2:37-44.

Sainsbury, R. "Gestural Movement during
(1955)   Psychiatric Interviews," *Psychosomatic Medicine,* 17:458-469.

Sampson, E. E., and **Brandon, A. C.** "The
(1964)   Effects of Role and Opinion Deviation on Small Group Behavior," *Sociometry,* 27:261-281.

Saslow, G., and **Matarazzo, J.** "A Tech-
(1959)   nique for Studying Changes in Interview Behavior," in E. Rubinstein and M. Parloff (eds.), *Research in Psychotherapy.* Washington, D.C.: American Psychological Association.

Schachter, J. "Pain, Fear, and Anger in
(1957)   Hypertensiveness and Normotensives: A Psychophysiologic Study," *Psychosomatic Medicine,* 19:17-29.

Schachter, S. "Deviation, Rejection, and
(1951)   Communication," *Journal of Abnormal and Social Psychology,* 46:190-207.

Schachter, S., Ellerton, N., McBride, D.,
(1951)   and **Greggory, D.** "An Experimental Study of Cohesiveness and Productivity," *Human Relations,* 4:229-238.

Schachter, S., and **Singer, J.** "Cognitive,
(1962)   Social, and Physiological Determinants of Emotional State," *Psychological Review,* 69:379-399.

Schachter, S., and **Wheeler, L.** "Epi-
(1962)   nephrine, Chlorpromazine, and Amusement," *Journal of Abnormal and Social Psychology,* 65: 121-128.

Scheflen, A. E. "Natural History Method
(1965)   in Psychotherapy: Communica-

tion Research," in L. Gottschalk and A. Auerbach (eds.), *Methods of Research in Psychotherapy*. New York: Appleton Century Crofts, pp. 263–289.

Scheflen, A. E. "The Significance of Pos-
(1964)   ture in Communication Systems," *Psychiatry*, 27:316–331.

Scheidel, T., and **Crowell, L.** "Feedback
(1966)   in Small Group Communication," *Quarterly Journal of Speech*, 52: 273–278.

Schlosberg, H. "Three Dimensions of
(1954)   Emotion," *Psychological Review*, 61:81–88.

Schlosberg, H. "The Description of Facial
(1952)   Expressions in Terms of Two Dimensions," *Journal of Experimental Psychology*, 44:229–237.

Schlosberg, H. A. "A Scale for the Judg-
(1941)   ment of Facial Expressions," *Journal of Experimental Psychology*, 29:497–510.

Schmidt, M. W., and **Kristofferson, A.** "Dis-
(1963)   crimination of Successiveness: A Test of a Model of Attention," *Science*, 139:112–113.

Schramm, W. L. "Communication Research
(1963)   in the United States," in *The Science of Human Communication*. New York: Basic Books, pp. 1–16.

Schramm, W. L. "How Communication
(1954)   Works," in *The Processes and Effects of Communication*. Urbana: University of Illinois Press, pp. 3–26.

Schroder, H. M., Driver, M. J., and **Streu-
(1967)   fert, S.** *Human Information Processing*. New York: Holt.

Schultz, D. P. "The Human Subject in
(1969)   Psychological Research," *Psychological Bulletin*, 73:214–228.

Schultz, D. P. "Evidence Suggesting a Sen-
(1967)   sory Variation Drive in Humans," *Journal of General Psychology*, 77:87–99.

Schultz, D. P. *Sensory Restriction*. New
(1965)   York: Academic.

Schwartz, C. G. "Problems for Psychiatric
(1957)   Nurses in Playing a New Role in a Mental Hospital Ward," in M. Greenblatt, D. J. Levinson, and R. H. Williams (eds.), *The Patient and the Mental Hospital*. New York: Free Press, pp. 402–426.

Schweitzer, D., and **Ginsburg, G. P.** "Fac-
(1966)   tors of Communicator Credibility," in C. W. Backman and P. F. Secord (eds.), *Problems in Social Psychology*. New York: McGraw-Hill, pp. 94–102.

Scott, R. L. "A Fresh Approach toward
(1968)   Rationalism," *The Speech Teacher*, 17:134–139.

Seattle Times, Apr. 28, p. A7.
(1970)

Secord, P., and **Backman, C.** *Social Psy-
(1964)   chology*. New York: McGraw-Hill.

Sereno, K. K. "Ego-involvement, High
(1968)   Source Credibility and Response to a Belief-discrepant Communication," *Speech Monographs*, 35:476–481.

Sereno, K. K. "Changes in Verbal Behavior
(1965)   of a Speaker during Two Successive Speech Performances as a Function of the Sequence of Listener Responses," *Speech Monographs*, 32:261.

Sereno, K. K., and **Hawkins, G. J.** "The
(1967)   Effects of Variations in Speakers' Nonfluency upon Audience Ratings of Attitude toward the Speech Topic and Speakers' Credibility," *Speech Monographs*, 34:58–64.

Sereno, K. K., and **Mortensen, C. D.** (eds.)
(1970)   *Foundations of Communication Research*. New York: Harper & Row.

Sereno, K. K., and **Mortensen, C. D.** "The
(1969)   Effects of Ego-involved Attitudes on Conflict Negotiation in Dyads," *Speech Monographs*, 36:8–12.

Shannon, C., and **Weaver, W.** *The Mathe-
(1949)   matical Theory of Communication*. Urbana, Ill.: University of Illinois Press.

Shapiro, J. G. "Responsitivity to Facial and
(1968)   Linguistic Cues," *The Journal of Communication*, 18:11–17.

Sharp, Jr., H., and **McClung, T.** "Effects of
(1966)   Organization on the Speaker's Ethos," *Speech Monographs*, 33:182–183.

Shaw, M. E. *Group Dynamics: The Psy-
(1971)   chology of Small Group Behavior*. New York: McGraw-Hill.

Shaw, M. E. "Communication Networks,"
(1964)   in L. Berkowitz (ed.), *Advances*

in Experimental Social Psychology, vol. 1. New York: Academic, pp. 111–147.

Shaw, M. E., and **Rothschild, G. H.** "Some
(1956) Effects of Prolonged Experience in Communication Nets," *Journal of Applied Psychology*, 40:281–286.

Sheffield, J., and **Byrne, D.** "Attitude Simi-
(1967) larity-Dissimilarity, Authoritarianism and Interpersonal Attraction," *Journal of Social Psychology*, 11:117–123.

Shepard, D. W. "Rhetoric and Formal
(1966) Argument," *Western Speech*, 30:241–247.

Sherif, C. W., and **Sherif, M.** *Attitude, Ego-*
(1967) *Involvement, and Change*. New York: Wiley.

Sherif, C. W., **Sherif, M.,** and **Nebergall,**
(1965) R. E. *Attitude and Attitude Change*. Philadelphia: Saunders.

Sherif, M. "Theoretical Analysis of the
(1966) Individual-Group Relationship in a Social Situation," in G. Direnzo (ed.), *Concepts, Theory, and Explanation in the Behavioral Sciences*. New York: Random House, pp. 47–72.

Sherif, M. "Group Influences upon the
(1958) Formation of Norms and Attitudes," in E. E. Maccoby, T. Newcomb, and E. Y. Hartley (eds.), *Readings in Social Psychology* (3d ed.). New York: Holt, pp. 219–232.

Sherif, M. "Experiments in Group Con-
(1956) flict," *Scientific American*, 195: 54–58.

Sherif, M., and **Hovland, C. I.** *Social Judg-*
(1961) *ment: Assimilation and Contrast Effects and Attitude Change*. New Haven, Conn.: Yale University Press.

Siegel, E. R., **Miller, G. R.,** and **Wotring,**
(1969) C. E. "Source Credibility and Credibility Proneness: A New Relationship," *Speech Monographs*, 36:118–125.

Simmel, G. "Secrecy and Group Commu-
(1961) nication," reprinted in T. Parsons et al., *Theories of Society*. New York: Free Press, pp. 318–330.

Simmel, G. *Soziologie*, in R. Park and E.
(1924) Burgess (eds.), *Introduction to the Science of Sociology* (2d ed.). Chicago: University of Chicago Press.

Simmel, G. "Sociology of the Senses: Visual
(1921) Interaction," in R. Parks and E. Burgess (eds.), *Introduction to the Science of Sociology* (2d ed.). Chicago: University of Chicago Press, pp. 356–361.

Simons, H. W., **Berkowitz, N.,** and **Moyer,**
(1970) R. J. "Similarity, Credibility, and Attitude Change: A Review and A Theory," *Psychological Bulletin*, 73:1–16.

Slater, P. "Contrasting Correlates of Group
(1958) Size," *Sociometry*, 21:129–139.

Slater, P. "Role Differentiation in Small
(1955) Groups," *American Sociological Review*, 20:300–310.

Smelser, N. *Theory of Collective Behavior.*
(1963) New York: Free Press.

Smith, A. "Introduction," in *Communica-*
(1966) *tion and Culture*. New York: Holt, pp. 1–10.

Smith, D. R. "The Fallacy of the Communi-
(1970) cation Breakdown," *The Quarterly Journal of Speech*, 34:343–346.

Smith, G. H. "Size-Distance Judgments of
(1970) Human Faces," as cited by H. Toch and M. S. MacLean, Jr., "Perception and Communication: A Transactional View," in K. K. Sereno and C. D. Mortensen (eds.), *Foundations of Communication Theory*. New York: Harper & Row, pp. 125–136.

Smith, G. J., and **Henriksson, M.** "The
(1955) Effect on an Established Percept of a Perceptual Process beyond Awareness," *Acta Psychologica*, 11:346–355.

Smith, G. J., **Spence, D.,** and **Klein, G. S.**
(1959) "Subliminal Effects of Verbal Stimuli," *Journal of Abnormal and Social Psychology*, 59:167–176.

Smith, K. R., **Parker, G. B.,** and **Robinson,**
(1951) Jr., G. A. "An Exploratory Investigation of Autistic Perception," *Journal of Abnormal and Social Psychology*, 46:324–326.

Smith, M. N. "Different Cultural Concepts
(1952) of Past, Present, and Future: A Study of Ego-extension, *Psychiatry*, 15:395–400.

Smith, R. G. "An Experimental Study of the
(1951) Effects of Speech Organization

upon Attitudes of College Students," *Speech Monographs*, 18: 291–301.

Smith, S., Cutchshaw, C., and **Kincaid, W.** (1967) "A Test of the Physical Quantum Theory of Vision Using Foveally-presented Rectangular Targets," cited in J. F. Corso, *The Experimental Psychology of Sensory Behavior*. New York: Holt.

Sommer, R. *Personal Space: The Behavioral Basis of Design*, Englewood Cliffs, N.J.: Prentice-Hall. (1969)

Sommer, R. "Sociofugal Space," *American Journal of Sociology*, 72:654–660. (1967)

Sommer, R. "Further Studies of Small Group Ecology," *Sociometry*, 28:337–348. (1965)

Sommer, R. "The Distance for Comfortable Conversation: a Further Study," *Sociometry*, 25:111–116. (1962)

Sommer, R. "Leadership and Group Geography," *Sociometry*, 24:99–110. (1961)

Sommer, R. "Studies in Personal Space," *Sociometry*, 22:247–260. (1959)

South, E. B. "Some Psychological Aspects of Committee Work," *Journal of Applied Psychology*, 11:348–368. (1927)

Sperling, G. "A Model for Visual Memory Tasks," *Human Factors*, 5:19–31. (1963)

Sperling, G. "The Information Available in Brief Visual Presentation," *Psychological Monographs*, 74, whole no. 498. (1960)

Sponberg, H. "The Relative Effectiveness of Climax and Anticlimax Order in an Argumentative Speech," *Speech Monographs*, 13:35–44. (1946)

Star, S. A., and **Hughes, H. M.** "Report on an Educational Campaign: The Cincinnati Plan for the United Nations," *American Journal of Sociology*, 55:389–400. (1950)

Steiner, I. D., and **Peters, S. C.** "Conformity and the A-B-X Model," *Journal of Personality*, 26:229–242. (1958)

Steinzor, B. "The Spatial Factor in Face-to-face Discussion Groups," *Journal of Abnormal and Social Psychology*, 45:552–555. (1950)

Stephen, F. "The Relative Rate of Communication between Members of Small Groups," *American Sociological Review*, 17:482–486. (1952)

Stephen, F., and **Mishler, E.** "The Distribution of Participation in Small (1952)

Groups: An Exponential Approximation," *American Sociological Review*, 17:598–608.

Stephenson, W. "Foundations of Communication Theory," *Psychological Record*, 19:65–82. (1969)

Stern, G. S., et al. "Fear Arousal and Order of Presentation of Persuasive Communication," *Psychological Reports*, 16:789–795. (1965)

Stevens, S. S., and **Davis, H.** *Hearing: Its Psychology and Physiology*. New York: Wiley. (1938)

Stone, G. P. "Appearance and the Self," in A. M. Rose (ed.), *Human Behavior and Social Processes*. Boston: Houghton Mifflin, pp. 86–118. (1962)

Stotland, E. "Peer Groups and Reactions to Power Figures," in D. Cartwright (ed.), *Studies in Social Power*. Ann Arbor: University of Michigan Press, pp. 53–68. (1959)

Streufert, S. "Communicator Importance and Interpersonal Attitudes toward Conforming and Deviant Group Members," *Journal of Personality and Social Psychology*, 2:242–246. (1969)

Streufert, S., Clardy, M., Driver, M., Karlins, M., Schroeder, H., and **Suedfeld, P.** "A Tactical Game for the Analysis of Complex Decision-making in Individuals and Groups," *Psychological Reports*, 17:723–729 (1965)

Streufert, S., and **Schroder, H. M.** "Conceptual Structure, Environmental Complexity, and Task Performance," *Journal of Experimental Research in Personality*, 1:132–137. (1965)

Stritch, T., and **Secord, P. F.** "Interaction Effects in the Perception of Faces," *Journal of Personality*, 24:272–284. (1956)

Strodtbeck, F. "Husband and Wife Interaction over Revealed Differences," *American Sociological Review*, 16:468–477. (1951)

Strodtbeck, F., and **Hook, L.** "The Social Dimensions of a Twelve Man Jury Table," *Sociometry*, 1, 24: 397–415. (1967)

Stroud, J. "The Fine Structure of Psychological Time," in H. Quastler (1955) (ed.), *Information Theory in Psychology.* New York: Free Press.

Suedfeld, P. "Attitude Manipulation in (1964a) Restricted Environments: 1. Conceptual Structure and Response to Propaganda," *Journal of Abnormal and Social Psychology,* 68:242–247.

Suedfeld, P. "Conceptual Structure and (1964b) Subjective Stress in Sensory Deprivation," *Perceptual and Motor Skills,* 9:896–898.

Suedfeld, P., Glucksberg, S., and **Vernon,** (1967) **J.** "Sensory Deprivation as a Drive Operation: Effects upon Problem Solving," *Journal of Experimental Psychology,* 75:166–169.

Suedfeld, P., and **Vernon, J.** "Stress and (1965) Verbal Originality in Sensory Deprivation," *Psychological Record,* 15:567–570.

Swinth, R. L. "The Establishment of the (1967) Trust Relationship," *Journal of Conflict Resolution,* 12:335–344.

Tabu, H. A. "Effects of Differential Value (1965) on Recall of Visual Symbols," *Journal of Experimental Psychology,* 69:135–143.

Tagiuri, R. "Introduction," in R. Tagiuri (1958) and L. Petrullo (eds.), *Person Perception and Interpersonal Behavior.* Stanford, Calif.: Stanford University Press, pp. ix–xvii.

Tannenbaum, P. "Communication of Sci-(1963) ence Information," *Science,* 140:579–587.

Taylor, D. A. "Some Aspects of the De-(1965) velopment of an Interpersonal Relationship: Social Penetration Process." Washington, D.C.: Naval Medical Research Institute.

Taylor, D. A., Wheeler, L., and **Altman, I.** (1968) "Stress Relations in Socially Isolated Groups," *Journal of Personality and Social Psychology,* 9:369–376.

Taylor, F. W. *The Principles of Scientific* (1911) *Management.* New York: Harper & Row.

Thibaut, J., and **Gruder, C. L.** "Formation (1969) of Contractual Agreements be-tween Parties of Unequal Power," *Journal of Personality and Social Psychology,* 11:59–65.

Thibaut, J., and **Kelley, H. H.** *The Social* (1959) *Psychology of Groups.* New York: Wiley.

Thiessen, D. D. "Population Density, (1964) Mouse Genotype, and Endocrine Function in Behavior," *Journal of Comparative and Physiological Psychology,* 57:412–416.

Thistlethwaite, D. L. "Attitude and Struc-(1950) ture as Factors in the Distortion of Reasoning," *Journal of Abnormal and Social Psychology,* 45:442–458.

Thistlethwaite, D. L., Hann, G. H., and (1955) **Kamenetzky, J.** "The Effect of 'Directive' and 'Non-directive' Communication Procedures on Attitudes," *Journal of Abnormal and Social Psychology,* 51:107–118.

Thistlethwaite, D. L., and **Kamenetzky, J.** (1955) "Attitude Change through Refutation and Elaboration of Audience Counterarguments," *Journal of Abnormal and Social Psychology,* 51:3–12.

Thistlethwaite, D. L., Kamenetzky, J., and (1956) **Schmidt, H.** "Factors Influencing Attitude Change through Refutative Communications," *Speech Monographs,* 23:13–25.

Thomas, E. J., and **Fink, C. I.** "Effects of (1963) Group Size," *Psychological Bulletin,* 60:371–384.

Thomas, E. J. "Role Conceptions and Or-(1959) ganizational Size," *American Sociological Review,* 24:30–37.

Thomas, G. L., and **Ralph, D. C.** "A Study (1959) of the Effect of Audience Proximity on Persuasion," *Speech Monographs,* 26:300–307.

Thompson, D. F., and **Meltzer, L.** "Com-(1964) munications of Emotional Intent by Facial Expression," *Journal of Abnormal and Social Psychology,* 68:129–135.

Thompson, E. "Some Effects of Message (1967) Structure on Listener Comprehension," *Speech Monographs,* 34:51–57.

Thompson, E. "An Experimental Investi-(1960) gation of the Relative Effectiveness of Organizational Structure in Oral Communication," *Southern Speech Journal*, 26:59–69.

Tiffany, W. R., and **Hanley, C.** "Adaptation
(1956)   to Delayed Sidetone," *Journal of Speech and Hearing Disorders*, 21:167–172.

Time, Dec. 22, p. 7.
(1967)

Tomkins, S. S., and **McCarter, R.** "What
(1964)   and Where Are the Primary Affects? Some Evidence for a Theory," *Perceptual and Motor Skills*, 18:119–158.

Tompkins, P. K. "The McCroskey-Dunham
(1967)   and Holtzman Reports on Ethos: Confounding Element in Communication Research," *Speech Monographs*, 34:176–179.

Toole, K. R. *Seattle Times*, March 29,
(1970)   p. 16.

Toulmin, S. *The Uses of Argument*. Lon-
(1958)   don: Cambridge.

Treisman, A. "Monitoring and Storage of
(1964)   Irrelevant Messages in Selective Attention," *Journal of Verbal Learning and Verbal Behavior*, 3:449–459.

Treisman, A. "Attention and Speech." Un-
(1960)   published doctoral dissertation, University of Oxford.

Triandis, H. C. "Cultural Influences upon
(1964)   Cognitive Processes," in L. Berkowitz (ed.), *Advances in Experimental Social Psychology*, vol. 1. New York: Academic, pp. 1–48.

Triandis, H. C., and **Lambert, W. W.** "A
(1958)   Restatement and Test of Schlosberg's Theory of Emotions with Two Kinds of Subjects from Greece," *Journal of Abnormal and Social Psychology*, 56:321–328.

Tuason, V., Guze, S., McClure, J., and
(1961)   **Begnelin, J.** "A Further Study of Some Features of the Interview with the Interaction Chronograph," *American Journal of Psychiatry*, 118:438–446.

Tubbs, S. "Explicit versus Implicit Con-
(1968)   clusions and Audience Commitment," *Speech Monographs*, 35: 14–19.

Tulving, S. "Subjective Organization in
(1962)   Free Recall of 'Unrelated' Words," *Psychological Review*, 69:344–354.

Turner, R. "Role Taking, Role Standpoint,
(1956)   and Reference Group Behavior," *American Journal of Sociology*, 21:316–328.

Turner, R., and **Killian, L.** *Collective Be-
(1957)   havior*. Englewood Cliffs, N.J.: Prentice-Hall.

Tyrwhitt, J. "The Moving Eye," in E. Car-
(1960)   penter and M. McLuhan (eds.), *Explorations in Communication*. Boston: Allyn and Bacon, pp. 90–95.

Uesugi, T. T., and **Vinacke, W. E.** "Strategy
(1963)   in a Feminine Game," *Sociometry*, 26:75–88.

Uhr, L. "Pattern Recognition," in L. Uhr
(1966)   (ed.), *Pattern Recognition*. New York: Wiley, pp. 365–387.

Ungerer, T. "How to Survive in a French
(1970)   Restaurant," *Playboy*, 17:171–173, 227.

Vernon, J., and **Hoffman, J.** "Effect of Sen-
(1956)   sory Deprivation on Learning Rate in Human Beings," *Science*, 123:1074–1075.

Vernon, N. "The Nature of Perception and
(1966)   the Fundamental Stages in the Process of Perceiving," in L. Uhr (ed.), *Pattern Recognition*. New York: Wiley, pp. 61–73.

Verplanck, W. S. "The Control of the Con-
(1955)   tent of Conversation: Reinforcement of Statements of Opinion," *Journal of Abnormal and Social Psychology*, 51:668–676.

Videbeck, R. "Self Conception and the
(1960)   Reaction of Others," *Sociometry*, 23:351–359.

Vidulich, R. H., and **Wilson, D. J.** "The
(1967)   Environmental Setting as a Factor in Social Influence," *Journal of Social Psychology*, 71:247–255.

Vinacke, W. E. "Sex Roles in a Three-person
(1959)   Game," *Sociometry*, 22:343–360.

Vinacke, W. E. "The Judgment of Facial Ex-
(1949)   pression by Three National-Racial Groups in Hawaii," *Journal of Personality*, 17:407–429.

Vinacke, W. E., and **Arkoff, A.** "An Experi-
(1957)   mental Study of Coalitions in the Triads," *American Sociological Review*, 22:406–414.

Vlandis, J. "Variation in the Verbal Be-
(1964)   havior of a Speaker as the Func-

tion of Varied Reinforcing Conditions," *Speech Monographs,* 31:116–119.

Vosberg, R., Fraser, N., and Guehl, J. (1960) "Imagery Sequence in Sensory Deprivation, *Archives of General Psychiatry,* 2:356–357.

Wada, J. A. (1961) "Modification of Cortically Induced Responses in Brain Stem by Shift of Attention in Monkey," *Science,* 133:40–42.

Wagner, G. (1958) "An Experimental Study of the Relative Effectiveness of Varying Amounts of Evidence in a Persuasive Communication." Unpublished masters thesis, Mississippi Southern University.

Waly, P., and Cook, S. W. (1965) "Effect of Attitude on Judgments of Plausibility," *Journal of Personality and Social Psychology,* 2:745–749.

Watzlawick, P., Beavin, J., and Jackson, D. (1967) *Pragmatics of Human Communication.* New York: Norton.

Weiner, N. (1954) *The Human Use of Human Beings: Cybernetics and Society.* Garden City, N.Y.: Doubleday.

Weintraub, D., and Walker, E. (1966) *Perception.* Belmont, Calif.: Brooks Cole.

Weisbrod, R. (1964) "Looking Behavior in a Discussion Group." Unpublished report cited by Argyle and M. Kendon, "The Experimental Analysis of Social Performance, in L. Berkowitz (ed.), *Advances in Experimental Social Psychology,* vol. 3, 1967, pp. 55–98.

Weisstein, N. (1969) "What the Frog's Eye Tells the Human Brain: Single Cell Analyzers in the Human Visual System," *Psychological Bulletin,* 69:157–176.

Wenburg, J. R. (1969) "The Relationships among Audience Adaptation, Source Credibility and Types of Message Cues." Paper presented to the Speech Association of America, New York.

Wertheimer, M. (1958) "Principles of Perceptual Organization," in D. C. Beardslee and M. Wertheimer (eds.), *Readings in Perception.* New York: Van Nostrand, pp. 115–135.

Westley, B. H., and MacLean, Jr., M. (1957) "A Conceptual Model for Communication Research," *Journalism Quarterly,* 34:31–38.

Westley, B. H., and Severin, W. (1964) "Some Correlates of Media Credibility," *Journalism Quarterly,* 41:325–335.

White, T. (1961) *The Making of the President 1960.* New York: Atheneum.

Whitehead, J. L. (1968) "Factors of Source Credibility," *Quarterly Journal of Speech,* 54:59–63.

Whyte, L. L. (1954) *Accent on Form.* New York: Harper & Row.

Whyte, W. (1956) *The Organization Man.* New York: Simon & Schuster.

Wicker, A. W. (1969) "Attitudes versus Action: The Relationship of Verbal and Overt Behavioral Responses to Attitude Objects," *Journal of Social Issues,* 25:41–78.

Williams, J. (1963) "Personal Space and Its Relation to Extroversion-Introversion." Unpublished masters thesis, University of Alberta.

Wilson, W., and Insko, C. (1968) "Recency Effects in Face-to-face Interaction," *Journal of Personality and Social Psychology,* 9:21–23.

Wilson, W., and Miller, H. (1968) "Repetition, Order of Presentation, and Timing of Arguments and Measures as Determinants of Opinion Change," *Journal of Personality and Social Psychology,* 9:184–188.

Wisper, L. G., and Drambarean, N. C. (1953) "Physiological Need, Word Frequency, and Visual Duration Thresholds," *Journal of Experimental Psychology,* 46:25–31.

Wittich, W. A., and Fowlkes, J. G. (1946) *Audio-Visual Paths to Learning.* New York: Harper & Row.

Wolfinger, R. E., Wolfinger, B., Prewitt, K., and Rosenhack, S. (1964) "America's Radical Right: Politics and Ideology," in D. Apter (ed.), *Ideology and Discontent.* New York: Free Press, pp. 262–293.

Woodrow, H. (1927) "The Effect of Type of Training upon Transference," *Journal of Educational Psychology,* 18:159–172.

Woodworth, R. S. (1938) *Experimental Psychology.* New York: Holt.

Woodworth, R. S., and Schlosberg, H. *Ex-*

(1954) *perimental Psychology* (2d ed.). New York: Holt.

Woolbert, C. "The Audience," in M.
(1916) Bentley (ed.), "Studies in Social and General Psychology from the University of Illinois," *Psychological Monographs*, 21:37–54.

Woolridge, D. *The Machinery of the Brain.*
(1963) New York: McGraw-Hill.

Wright, H. "The City-Town Project: A
(1968) Study of Children in Communities Differing in Size," Intern Research Report, University of Kansas; as cited in Barker, *Ecological Psychology.* Stanford, Calif.: Stanford University Press.

Wyer, Jr., R. S. "Effects of Incentive to
(1966) Perform Well, Group Attraction, and Group Acceptance on Conformity in a Judgmental Task," *Journal of Personality and Social Psychology*, 4:21–26.

Wyer, Jr. R. S., and **Schwartz, S.** "Some
(1969) Contingencies in the Effects of the Source of a Communication on the Evaluation of That Communication," *Journal of Personality and Social Psychology*, 11: 1–9.

Wynne-Edwards, V. *Animal Dispersion in*
(1962) *Relation to Social Behavior.* New York: Hafner.

Yates, J. A. "Delayed Auditory Feedback,"
(1963) *Psychological Bulletin*, 60:213–232.

Zajonc, R. B. "The Concepts of Balance,
(1970) Congruity, and Dissonance," in K. K. Sereno and C. D. Mortensen (eds.), *Foundations of Communication Theory.* New York: Harper & Row, pp. 181–196.

Zajonc, R. B. "Attitudinal Effects of Mere
(1968a) Exposure," *Journal of Social Psychology, Monograph Supplement*, June, 9:1–27.

Zajonc, R. B. "Cognitive Theories in Social
(1968b) Psychology," in G. Lindzey and E. Aronson (eds.), *The Handbook of Social Psychology* (2d ed.). Reading, Mass.: Publisher pp. 320–411.

Zajonc, R. B. "Social Facilitation," *Science*,
(1965) 149:269–274.

Zajonc, R. B., and **Nieuwenhuyse, B.** "Re-
(1964) lationship between Word Frequency and Recognition: Perceptual Process or Response Bias?" *Journal of Experimental Psychology*, 67:276–285.

Zajonc, R. B., and **Sales, S. M.** "Social
(1966) Facilitation of Dominant and Subordinate Responses," *Journal of Experimental Social Psychology*, 2:160–168.

Zander, A., Gohen, A. R., and **Stotland, E.**
(1957) *Role Relations in the Mental Health Professions.* Ann Arbor: Institute for Social Research.

Zemach, M. "The Effects of Guilt-arousing
(1966) Communications on Acceptance of Recommendations." Unpublished doctoral dissertation, Yale University.

Zimbaro, P. G., Weisenberg, M., Firestone,
(1965) **I.,** and **Levy, B.** "Communicator Effectiveness in Producing Public Conformity and Private Attitude Change," *Journal of Personality*, 33:233–255.

Zubek, J. P. (ed.). *Sensory Deprivation:*
(1969) *Fifteen Years of Research.* New York: Appleton Century Crofts.

Zubek, J. P. "Behavioral Changes after
(1964) Prolonged Perceptual Deprivation (No Intrusions)," *Perceptual and Motor Skills*, 18:413–420.

Zuckerman, M. "Perceptual Isolation as a
(1964) Stress Situation," *Archives of General Psychiatry*, 11:255–276.

indexes

name index

subject index